PARIS

Buildings and Monuments

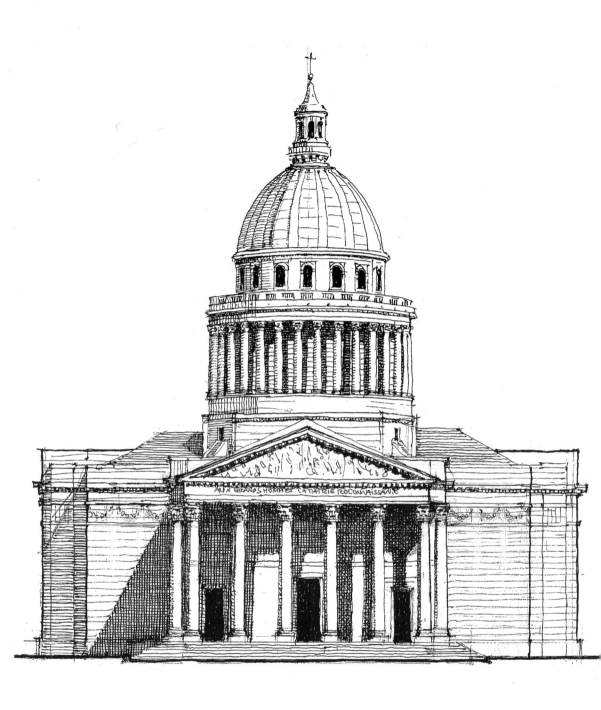

PARIS

BUILDINGS
AND
MONUMENTS

An Illustrated Guide with Over
850 Illustrations and Neighborhood Maps

Michel Poisson

Harry N. Abrams, Inc., Publishers

Editors, English-language edition: James Leggio, Lory Frankel, Barbara Burn
Designer, English-language edition: Dirk Luykx

Library of Congress Cataloging-in-Publication Data
Poisson, Michel.
  [Paris monuments. English]
  Paris: buildings and monuments : an illustrated guide with over 850
drawings and neighborhood maps / Michel Poisson : translated by John
Goodman.
    p.   cm.
  Includes index.
  ISBN 0-8109-4355-7
  1. Paris (France)—Guidebooks. 2. Paris (France)—Buildings, structures,
etc.—Pictorial works. 3. Paris (France)—Maps, Tourist.   I. Title.
DC708.P7413   1999
914.4'3604'839—dc21   98-42780

Printed and bound in Italy by Vincenzo Bona - Torino

Harry N. Abrams, Inc.
100 Fifth Avenue
New York, N.Y. 10011
www.abramsbooks.com

Contents

Hôtel Scipion · Fontaine du Pot-de-Fer · Saint-Médard · Place du Marché-des-Patriarches · Congrégation du Saint-Esprit · Saint-Jacques-du-Haut-Pas · Schola Cantorum · Val-de-Grâce

6th Arrondissement   192

Fontaine de l'Observatoire · Institut d'Art et d'Archéologie · Rue Vavin, no. 26 · Musée Hébert · Embassy of Mali · Hôtel de Choiseul-Praslin · Rue du Regard, nos. 1, 5, 7, 13, 15 · Centre André-Malraux · Maison des Sciences de l'Homme · Lutetia Hotel · Hôtel de Marsilly · Saint-Joseph-des-Carmes · Saint-Sulpice · Fontaine de la Paix · Fontaine des Quatre-Évêques · Former Seminary of Saint-Sulpice · Marché Saint-Germain · Hôtel de Brancas · Hôtel du Maréchal-d'Ancre · Hôtel de Sourdéac · Luxembourg Gardens · Fontaine Médicis · Fontaine du Regard · Palais du Luxembourg · Petit Luxembourg · Convent of the Filles du Calvaire · Théâtre de l'Odéon · Académie de Chirurgie · Refectory of the Franciscans · Faculté de Médecine · Hôtel Darlons · Rue Hautefeuille, no. 21 · Hôtel des Abbés de Fécamp · Fontaine Saint-Michel · Rue Saint-André-des-Arts · So-called Hôtel de la Vieuville · Maison Cotelle · Maison Simonnet · Rue Saint-André-des-Arts, no. 49 · Hôtel de Montholon · So-called Hôtel d'Hercule · Rue de Nevers · Cour de Rohan · Hôtel des Comédiens du Roy · Rue de Seine, no. 57 · Saint-Germain-des-Prés · Palais Abbatial · Place de Fürstenberg · Hôtel des Monnaies · Institut de France · École des Beaux-Arts

7th Arrondissement   232

Hôtel de Tessé · Hôtel de Villette · Pont Royal · Caisse des Dépôts et Consignations · Musée d'Orsay · Hôtel de Salm · Hôtel de Beauharnais · Hôtel de Seignelay · Pont de la Concorde · Palais Bourbon · Hôtel de Lassay · Ministry of Foreign Affairs · Hôtel de Brienne · Sainte-Clotilde · Hôtel de Roquelaure · Hôtel Amelot de Gournay · Saint-Thomas-d'Aquin · Hôtel de Sénectère · Hôtel de Fleury · Maison de Verre · Fontaine des Quatre-Saisons · Protestant Church of Pentemont · Abbaye de Pentemont · Hôtel de Gallifet · Hôtel de Noirmoutiers · Hôtel du Châtelet · Musée Rodin · Hôtel de Matignon · Institut d'Études Politiques · Rue du Bac, nos. 118 and 120 · Chapel of the Seminary of Foreign Missions · Le Bon Marché · Chapel of the Laënnec Hospital · Fontaine du Fellah · Hôtel des Invalides · Dome Church of the Invalides · Headquarters of UNESCO · École Militaire · Eiffel Tower · Saint-Pierre-du-Gros-Caillou · Fontaine de Mars · Lycée Italien Léonard-de-Vinci · Square Rapp, no. 3 · Avenue Rapp, no. 29

8th Arrondissement   266

Théâtre des Champs-Élysées · Place François-Iᵉʳ · Notre-Dame-de-la-Consolation · Armenian Church · Grand Palais · Petit Palais · Pont Alexandre-III · Place de la Concorde · Church of the Madeleine · Hôtel de Pourtalès · Hôtel Alexandre · Cercle de l'Union Interalliée · British Chancellory · British Embassy · Hôtel Edmond de Rothschild · Palais de l'Élysée · So-called Hôtel de Marigny · Hôtel d'Argenson · Hôtel de La Vaupalière · Gardens of the Champs-Élysées · Champs-Élysées · Arc de Triomphe · Céramic Hôtel · Saint-Alexandre-Nevski · Hospice Beaujon · Hôtel Salomon de Rothschild · Chamber of Commerce and Industry · Saint-Philippe-du-Roule · Musée Jacquemart-André · C. T. Loo Building · Parc Monceau · Rotonde de Chartres · Musée Nissim-de-Camondo · Musée Cernuschi · Expiatory Chapel · Saint-Augustin

9th Arrondissement   298

Lycée Condorcet · Théâtre National de l'Opéra · Church of the Trinity · The Grands Magasins · Galeries Lafayette · Au Printemps · La Nouvelle Athènes · Rue de la Tour-des-Dames · Rue Saint-Lazare, no. 58 · Musée Gustave-Moreau · Square d'Orléans · Place Saint-Georges Apartment Building · Notre-Dame-de-Lorette · Synagogue on the rue de la Victoire · Lutheran Church of the Redemption · Mairie of the 9th Arrondissement · Restaurant Chartier · Banque Nationale de Paris · Saint-Eugène-et-Sainte-Cécile · Hôtel Bony · Cité de Trévise

10th Arrondissement   314

Porte Saint-Denis · Porte Saint-Martin · The Faubourg Poissonnière · Hôtel Benoist de Sainte-Paulle · Hôtel de Botterel-Quintin · Hôtel Titon · Hôtel de Bourrienne · Saint-Vincent-de-Paul · Gare du Nord · Hôpital Lariboisière · Gare de l'Est · Canal Saint-Martin · Former Convent of Recollects · Saint-Laurent · Mairie of the 10th Arrondissement · Hôtel Gouthière · Hôpital Saint-Louis

11th Arrondissement   330

Cirque d'Hiver · Saint-Ambroise · Boulevard Richard-Lenoir, nos. 57–59 · Fontaine de la Roquette · Fontaine Trogneux · Hôtel de Mortagne · Sainte-Marguerite

12th Arrondissement   336

Place de la Bastille and July Column · Opéra Bastille · Entrance of the Hôpital des Quinze-Vingts · Place d'Aligre · Hôpital Saint-Antoine · Fondation Eugène-Napoléon · Place de la Nation · Musée National des Arts d'Afrique et d'Océanie · Saint-Esprit · Fontaine aux Lions · Parc de Bercy · Notre-Dame-de-Bercy · American Center · Palais Omnisports de Paris-Bercy · Ministry of Finance · Gare de Lyon–Bercy Quarter · Gare de Lyon · Administrative Building · Château de Vincennes

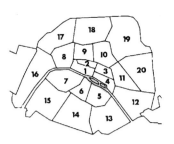

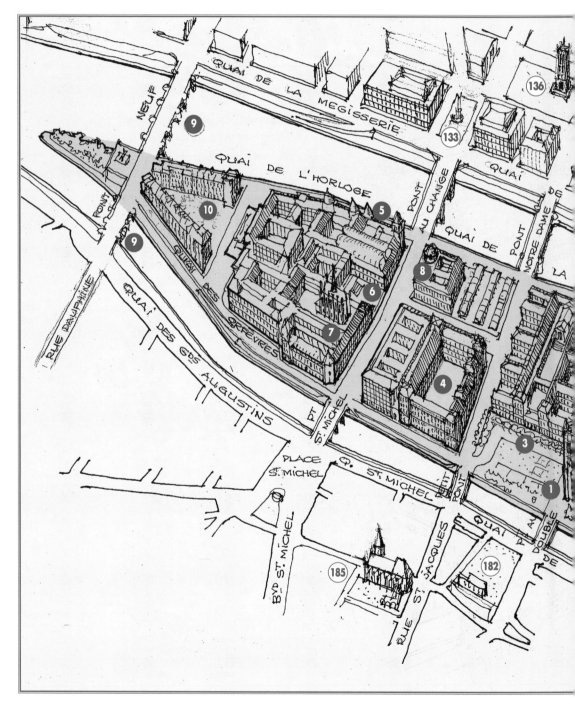

Île de la Cité

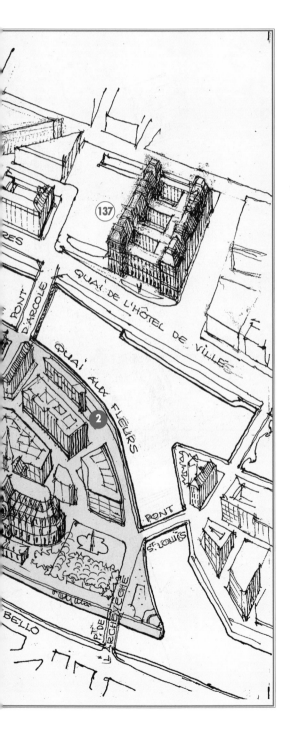

It was on the Île de la Cité that, about 200 BCE, the first important settlement was established. Its founders were a Gallic tribe known as the Parisii, who named it Lutetia (Lutèce).

This village, having become a small market town, was conquered by Roman legions in 52 BCE. It was soon replaced by a city conceived along Roman lines, taking the form of a rectangular area oriented north-south. It encompassed considerably more than the island, most of its additional territory being on the Left Bank.

During the barbarian invasions of 275–76 CE, the population sought refuge on the island, which had been hastily fortified, but this did not prevent the city from being sacked.

In their turn, the Normans pillaged Paris several times after sailing up the Seine. In 885 they laid siege to the island but were finally repulsed thanks to the action of Eudes, comte de Paris, subsequently named king of France.

Thereafter, development of the island proceeded with the construction of two large buildings at either end: the cathedral of Notre-Dame to the east and the Palais de la Cité to the west, a royal residence that, beginning in 1360, was gradually ceded to the Parlement and became the Palais de Justice (law courts).

The first significant urban development was the building of the Pont-Neuf (new bridge), dedicated in 1607, which led to the construction of the Place Dauphine at the initiative of Henri IV. Other buildings, religious as well as civil, rose haphazardly, and most could be reached only through narrow streets.

Napoléon I effected a preliminary clearing in front of Notre-Dame, but the resulting parvis, or cathedral square, was much smaller than the present one; much more extensive demolitions were to follow.

Louis-Philippe and his prefect comte de Rambuteau began to transform the island, but it was Napoléon III and his prefect Georges-Eugène Haussmann who radically altered its character by constructing several public buildings: a new Hôtel-Dieu (charity hospital), the Tribunal de Commerce (commercial law courts), the Préfecture de Police (originally a barracks), the Palais de Justice (additions), and the Marché aux Fleurs (flower market), as well as a network of new streets servicing these structures. Most of the land in question had already been developed, which made extensive demolition necessary; some 25,000 inhabitants were displaced as a result.

About twenty churches disappeared, along with countless residences of historical and artistic interest.

❶ Notre-Dame de Paris

LOCATION: Place du Parvis-Notre-Dame
MÉTRO STATION: Cité
PATRON: Maurice de Sully, bishop of Paris (1163)
ARCHITECTS: The original designer as well as the three architects who succeeded him
are unknown. Subsequent names worth citing are: Jean de Chelles (c. 1250–58);
Pierre de Montreuil (second half of the 13th century); Pierre de Chelles and Jean Ravy
(late 13th–early 14th century); Jean-Baptiste Lassus and Eugène Viollet-le-Duc
(in charge of 1841–63 restoration)

Excavations below the parvis (cathedral square) have uncovered remains of the basilica that preceded the present cathedral. This basilica was flanked to the north by a baptistery and perhaps a second basilica. It was Maurice de Sully who decided, in 1160, to replace this complex with a new cathedral.

The history of Notre-Dame encompasses several centuries and is very complicated, but a few benchmark dates follow.

1163: Work begins.
1163–82: Construction of the choir and the transept.
1180–1200: Completion of the nave.
1190–1220: Construction of the towers and the façade to the level of the rose window, above the Galerie des Rois (gallery of kings).
1225–50: Completion of the two towers; modification of the flying buttresses and enlargement of the clerestory windows.
c. 1260: Construction of the transept terminals.

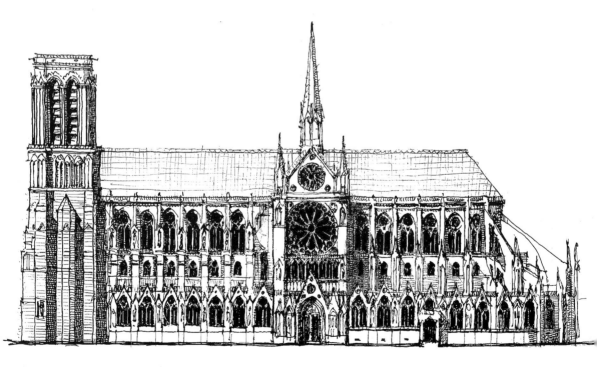

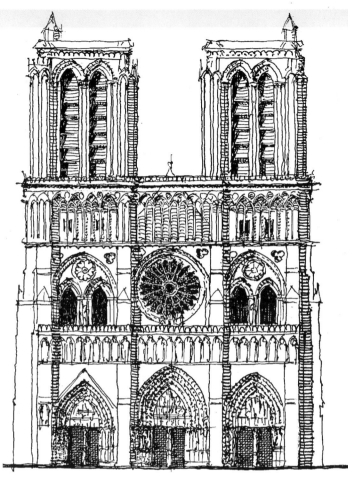

Late 13th—early 14th century: Replacement of the flying buttresses of the choir and addition of the radial chapels.

Revolutionary period: The cathedral is seriously damaged—its statues are mutilated, its spire is torn down, and all but one of its bells are melted down.

1802: Notre-Dame again becomes a Catholic sanctuary.

1804: Napoléon Bonaparte is crowned emperor in Notre-Dame.

1841—63: Restoration campaign overseen by the architects Lassus and Viollet-le-Duc.

1965—72: Important excavations carried out below the parvis, subsequently made readily accessible in an underground museum.

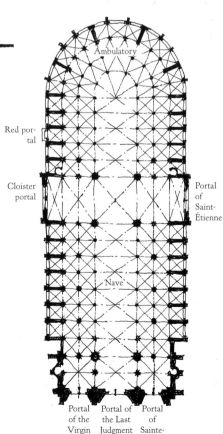

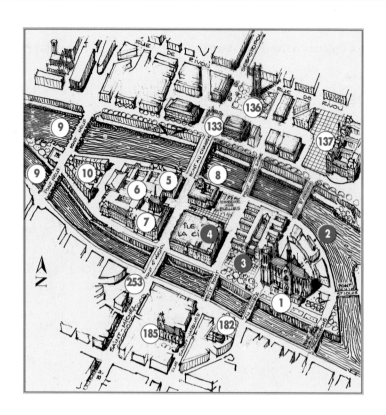

❷ Quai aux Fleurs

LOCATION: Northeastern part of
Île de la Cité
MÉTRO STATION: Cité

The quarter situated between
the quai aux Fleurs and Notre-
Dame cathedral is the only one
on the island spared by Haussmann. It still features a few
buildings of historical interest,
although they have been disfigured by their successive owners.

Hôtel-Dieu ③

LOCATION: 1, Place du Parvis-Notre-Dame
MÉTRO STATION: Cité
PATRON: L'Assistance Publique
ARCHITECTS: Jacques Gilbert (1864–74),
Stanislas Diet (1874–77)

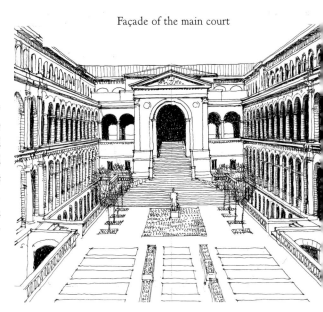

Façade of the main court

The old Hôtel-Dieu (charity hospital) was situated along and over the arm of the Seine to the south of Notre-Dame. It was demolished and rebuilt on its present site between 1864 and 1877, after the destruction, at Haussmann's orders, of the quarters in the center of the island. Jacques Gilbert, the architect, designed it in an Italianate classical style. The main court, represented at right, is not without character.

Préfecture de Police ④

LOCATION: 7, boulevard du Palais
MÉTRO STATION: Cité
PATRONS: Office of the Paris Military
Firemen and the Garde Républicaine (1862);
then the Préfecture de Police (1879)
ARCHITECT: Victor Calliat (1862–65)

This building, erected as part of Baron Haussmann's extensive reconstruction of the Île de la Cité, housed two barracks until 1879. It consists of four wings enclosing the large Court of August 19, whose name commemorates the role of the Paris police force during the liberation of Paris in 1944.

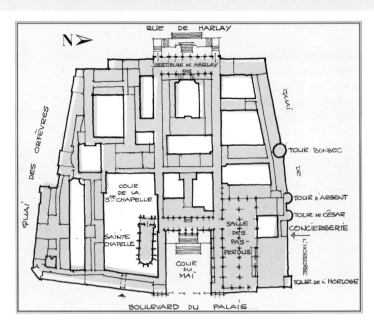

⑤ Conciergerie

(Former royal palace)

LOCATION (remains of the royal palace): Corner of the quai de l'Horloge
and the boulevard du Palais
MÉTRO STATION: Cité
PATRONS: Kings Louis IX (Saint Louis; mid-13th century), Philippe le Bel (late 13th–early 14th century), and Jean Le Bon (mid-14th century)

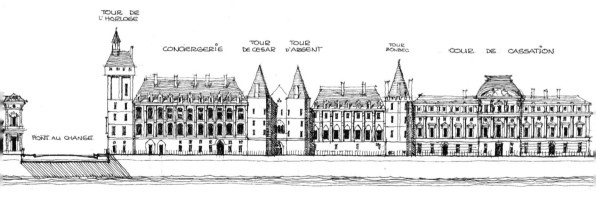

In 1360, the future Charles V abandoned the palace for the Hôtel Saint-Pol, later settling in the Louvre. No longer a royal residence, the former palace became the seat of the Parlement, the highest law court in the realm.

    The following portions of the former palace survive: Sainte-Chapelle, built by Louis IX (Saint Louis) between 1242 and 1248 (see entry 7); Tour Bonbec, likewise built by Louis IX (mid-13th century) but altered in the 16th century and partly rebuilt in the 19th century; Conciergerie, built by King Philippe le Bel (late 13th–early 14th century), whose most remarkable surviving features are three magnificent Gothic rooms: the Salle des Gardes (guardroom), the Salle des Gens d'Armes (hall of the men-at-arms), and the kitchens; Tour de l'Horloge (clock tower), built by Jean le Bon (mid-14th century).

    During the Revolution, the Conciergerie served as a prison where suspects were held before being tried and executed.

Palais de Justice ⑥

LOCATION: Western part of Île de la Cité

MÉTRO STATION: Cité

PATRONS: The Parlement of Paris (which had moved into the palace after it was abandoned by King Charles V in 1360). During the Revolution, the Parlement was abolished, and the facilities housing it were rechristened the Palais de Justice.

ARCHITECTS: Guillaume-Martin Couture, Pierre Desmaisons, and Jacques-Denis Antoine (Cour du Mai, forecourt, 1776–86). Joseph-Louis Duc and Honoré Daumet (buildings along the quai de l'Horloge between the towers, 1851–63; Cour de Cassation, 1868; Vestibule de Harlay, 1869). Albert Tournaire (façade fronting the quai des Orfèvres, 1911–13)

Cour du Mai. The "Mai" was a tree that the barristers planted in this courtyard every May 1.

Vestibule de Harlay

The Vestibule de Harlay forms the west façade of the Palais de Justice.

This vestibule is the principal feature of the building facing the Place Dauphine. Its architect, Joseph-Louis Duc, saw fit to demolish, in 1874, one of the three sides of the triangular plaza so that viewers could better admire "his" building.

17

❼ Sainte-Chapelle

LOCATION: 4, boulevard du Palais
MÉTRO STATION: Cité
PATRON: Louis IX (Saint Louis)
ARCHITECT: Pierre de Montreuil
(attributed, 1242–48)

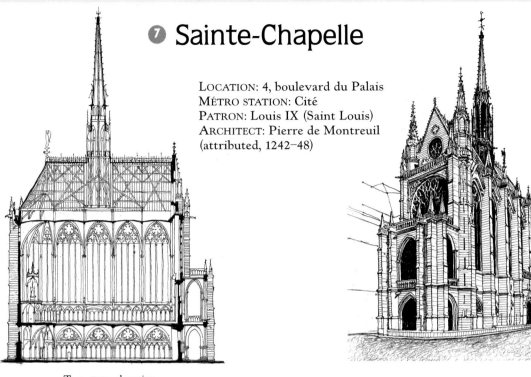

Two-story elevation

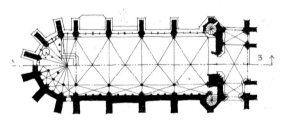

Cross section A–B

Detail of a bay

Saint Louis built the Sainte-Chapelle to house precious relics of the Passion. The building was directly accessible from the royal apartments and consisted of two superimposed chapels: a lower chapel, for use by those attached to the king's household; and an upper chapel for the king and his court that was separated from the lower one. Originally, the building was freestanding (except for a gallery linking it to the royal apartments). Construction of the Cour du Mai changed this.

The Sainte-Chapelle is one of the most beautiful achievements of French Gothic architecture. It is notable for its lightness of structure and for the extraordinary luminosity produced by its ample stained-glass windows; the oldest in Paris, they are of exceptional interest.

The attribution of the Sainte-Chapelle to Pierre de Montreuil is now disputed. The architect of the nave of the basilica of Saint-Denis, he also worked at Notre-Dame and, perhaps, at the refectory of the abbey of Notre-Dame-des-Champs.

The structural audacity of the Sainte-Chapelle was much admired, and it served as a model for many churches and chapels, notably the chapel at the Château de Vincennes (see page 353).

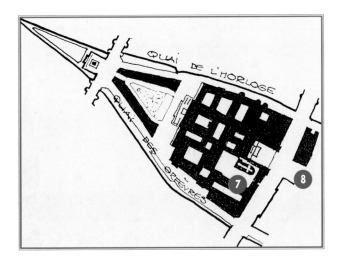

LOCATION: 1, boulevard du Palais and
quai de la Corse
MÉTRO STATION: Cité
ARCHITECT: Antoine-Nicolas Bailly
(1860–65)

Tribunal de Commerce 8

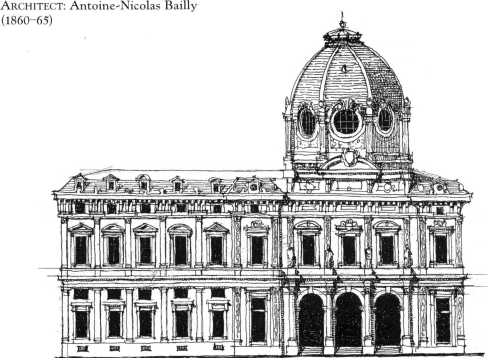

The Tribunal de Commerce (trade courts) was one of the many new administrative buildings erected during Haussmann's reconstruction of the Île de la Cité. As originally envisioned, its dome would have been aligned with the boulevard Sébastopol, which had just been pierced (opened up). But the orientation of the plot made it necessary to shift the dome off axis, as well as the entrances from the quai de Corse. The architect exploited the space below the dome to realize a monumental staircase.

⑨ Pont-Neuf

LOCATION: Links the western tip of the Île de la Cité to
the Right and Left Banks
MÉTRO STATION: Pont-Neuf
PATRONS: Henri III and Henri IV
ARCHITECT: Baptiste Androuet Du Cerceau (1578–1607)

Long span

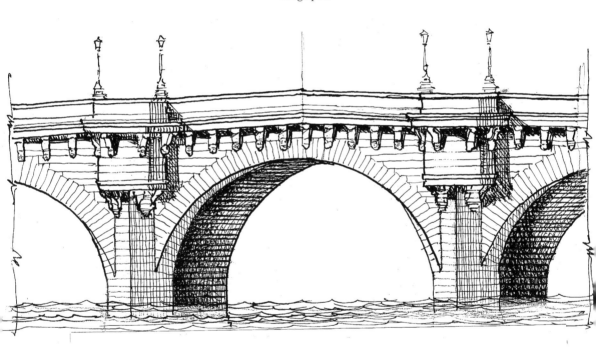

Arch of the short span

The Pont-Neuf is the oldest and most famous of
the bridges in Paris. Its first stone was laid by King
Henri III on May 31, 1578, but work continued for
almost thirty years, and Henri IV did not dedicate
it until 1607. Baptiste Androuet Du Cerceau was
the principal architect. The Pont-Neuf, unlike most
urban bridges in the period, was not lined with
houses. Small shops were built on the semicircular
platforms above its supports in 1775, but these
were demolished in the 1850s.

The statue of Henri IV now on its central platform dates only from 1818; it replaced the original
statue, destroyed in 1792.

Place Dauphine [10]

LOCATION: Western end of the Île de la Cité
MÉTRO STATIONS: Cité; Pont-Neuf
PATRONS: Henri IV and Achille de Harlay,
president of the Parlement
ARCHITECT: Louis Métezeau (attributed, 1607–19)

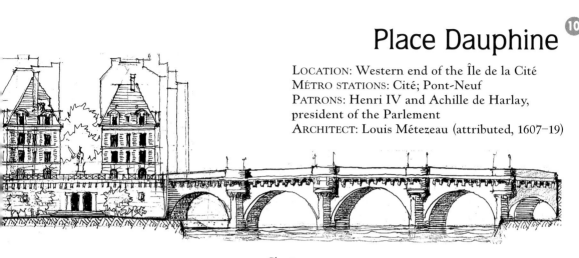

Short span

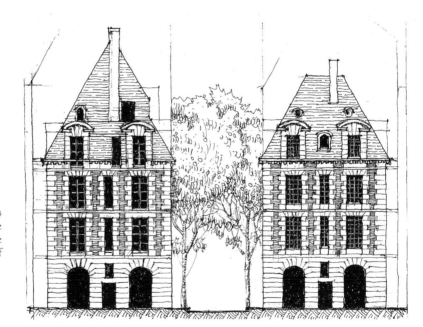

View of the pavilions
flanking the entrance
to the Place Dauphine
from the Pont-Neuf

In 1607, Henri IV decided to build a triangular place at the tip of the island and named it the Place Dauphine in honor of his eldest son. He entrusted its development to the president of the Parlement, Achille de Harlay, and asked an architect, probably Louis Métezeau, to design uniform structures made of stone and brick.

Thirty-two identical houses were built in accor-

dance with this plan. Unfortunately, there was nothing to prevent subsequent modification of the ensemble; its residences were remodeled and expanded upward in various ways over the centuries, compromising the design. One of the three sides of the original triangle, opposite the Palais de Justice, was even demolished in 1874.

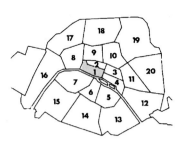

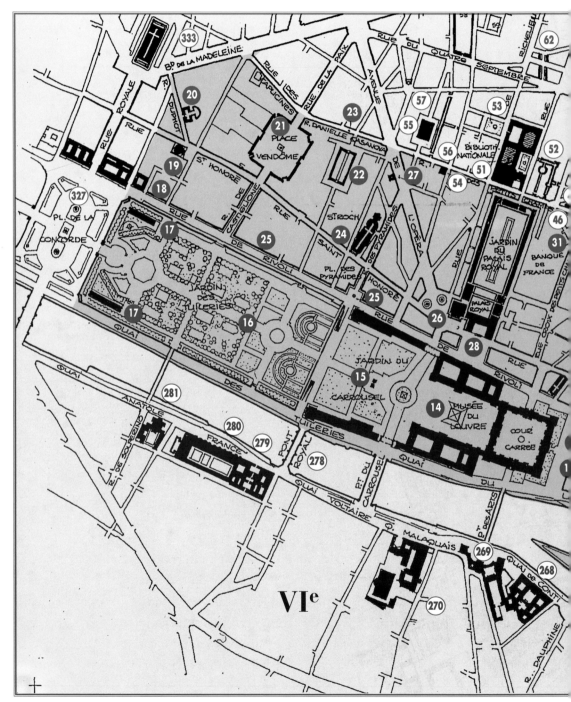

1st Arrondissement

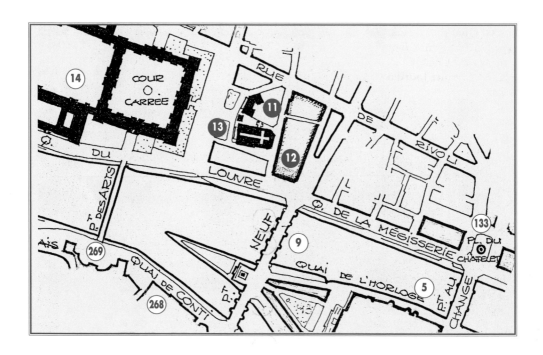

⑪ Mairie of the 1st Arrondissement

LOCATION: 4, Place du Louvre
MÉTRO STATION: Louvre
ARCHITECTS: Jacques-Ignace Hittorff
(main building, 1858–60), Théodore
Ballu (tower, 1858–62)

The mairie (town hall) of the 1st arrondissement was designed as a symmetrical complement to the church of Saint-Germain-l'Auxerrois. The result is a surprising architectural composition whose central tower, in neo-Gothic style, is often mistaken for the bell tower of the church. The architect Hittorff was responsible for the overall design.

Mairie of the 1st arrondissement

Tower
(19th century)

LOCATION: Quai du Louvre, opposite the Pont-Neuf
MÉTRO STATION: Pont-Neuf
PATRON: Ernest Cognac
ARCHITECTS: Frantz Jourdain and Henri Sauvage
(1926–28)

Samaritaine ⑫ Department Store

Southern façade (facing the Seine)

The store was named after a water pump—decorated with a relief of Christ and the Samaritan woman—adjacent to the Pont-Neuf until 1813.

The first store was built in 1905 by the architect Frantz Jourdain, who later, in 1926, asked his colleague Henri Sauvage to design the extension pictured here. The top floor of the store has a public balcony overlooking the Seine that offers spectacular views of the city.

LOCATION: 2, Place du Louvre
MÉTRO STATION: Louvre
DATES: The present church was begun in the 13th century, but part of it was rebuilt in the 15th century. The porch dates from 1431–39 and the choir was remodeled in the 16th century.

Saint-Germain- ⑬ l'Auxerrois

Saint-Germain-l'Auxerrois

Due to its proximity to the Louvre, Saint-Germain-l'Auxerrois was the parish church of the kings of France. The present structure was preceded in the 7th century by an oratory, destroyed by the Normans in 886. Another church rose on the site in the 12th century, but only the base of its bell tower survives.

The magnificent choir screen by Pierre Lescot and Jean Goujon (early 16th century) was destroyed in 1754. The bells of Saint-Germain-l'Auxerrois are notorious for having sounded the Saint Bartholomew's Day Massacre on the night of August 24, 1572.

⑭ Louvre

LOCATION: Between the rue de Rivoli and the Seine
MÉTRO STATIONS: Louvre; Palais-Royal

This text can do no more than summarize the successive phases of the Louvre's complex construction history, indicated in the plan opposite.

In 1190, King Philippe Auguste ordered construction of the initial château as well as the defensive walls, circling the city, that bear his name. The château was adjacent to the walls and defended the western side of the city.

In 1528, François I had the keep of the château demolished and commissioned the team of Pierre Lescot and Jean Goujon to build a palace on the site. His successor, Henri II, continued the work. The widow of Henri II built the Tuileries nearby but nonetheless pursued construction at the Louvre.

In 1594, after his entry into Paris, Henri IV resumed work on Catherine de Médicis's project to link the Louvre to the Tuileries (Grande Galerie). He also proceeded with construction of the south wing of the Cour Carrée (square court).

In 1624, Louis XIII commissioned Jacques Lemercier to build the Pavillon de l'Horloge, as well as a northern wing identical and symmetrical to that of Pierre Lescot.

Beginning in 1654, Louis XIV entrusted work at the Louvre to Louis Le Vau, but it was Claude Perrault who built the famous Colonnade (1668), which finally enclosed the Cour Carrée.

After a long period of neglect that began in 1678, Napoléon I resumed construction by asking the architects Charles Percier and Pierre Fontaine to build a wing alongside the rue de Rivoli.

Napoléon III placed Louis Visconti in charge of construction at the site. He was succeeded in 1853 by Hector Lefuel, who retained the post until 1880.

In 1981, President François Mitterrand launched the Grand Louvre project, which entailed refurbishing the entire complex after reassigning to the museum portions long occupied by the Ministry of Finance. Mitterrand entrusted this complex operation to the architect I. M. Pei, who designed the famous glass pyramid that now shelters the main entrance to the museum.

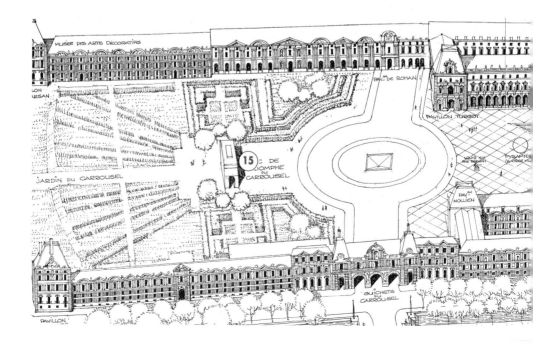

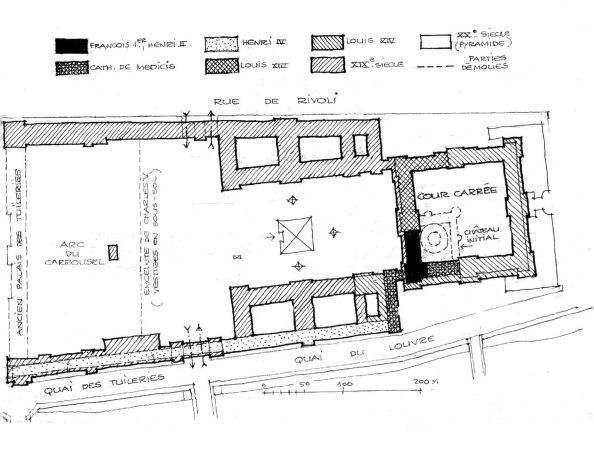

FRANCOIS 1er, HENRI II   HENRI IV   LOUIS XIV   XX.e SIECLE (PYRAMIDE)

CATH. DE MEDICIS   LOUIS XIII   XIX.e SIECLE   PARTIES DEMOLIES

RUE DE RIVOLI

ANCIEN PALAIS DES TUILERIES

ARC DU CARROUSEL

ENCEINTE DE CHARLES V (VESTIGES EN SOUS-SOL)

COUR CARRÉE

CHÂTEAU INITIAL

QUAI DU LOUVRE

QUAI DES TUILERIES

0   50   100   200 M

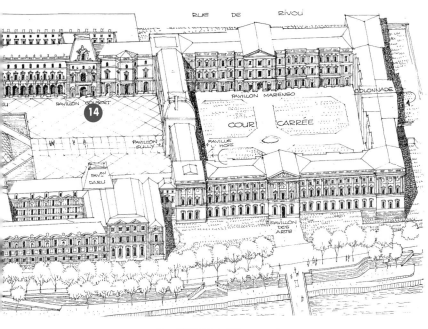

RUE DE RIVOLI

PAVILLON COLBERT

PAVILLON MARENGO

COLONNADE

(14)

COUR CARRÉE

PAVILLON SULLY

PAVILLON L'HORLOGE

PAVAN DARU

PAVILLON DES ARTS

Old Louvre

Before leaving on the Third Crusade, in 1190 Philippe Auguste ordered the construction of fortified walls around the city. What is now known as the Old Louvre was the western bastion of this defensive complex.

It featured ramparts enclosing a quadrangle roughly 256 by 236 feet and defended by ten towers and a moat. At the center of this ensemble was an enormous cylindrical keep surrounded by another moat.

Recent excavations occasioned by the Grand Louvre project uncovered the basement of the keep and a portion of the outer wall.

Louvre of Charles V

Étienne Marcel in 1358, then Charles V beginning in 1365, oversaw construction to the west of Paris of a new fortified wall beyond that of Philippe Auguste.

Subsequently, the Château du Louvre was situated within the walls and no longer served any defensive purpose. Charles V profited from this development to make it a more comfortable residence. His palace has disappeared, but work on the Grand Louvre has uncovered the foundations of the Wall of Charles V, which are now visible in new underground galleries.

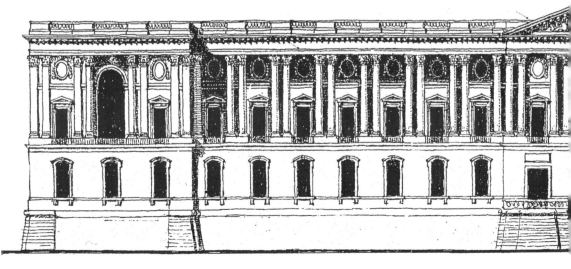

Louvre of François I

This is the oldest portion of the Louvre to survive, at least above ground. It was built after demolition of the keep of Philippe Auguste by the architect Pierre Lescot.

It was one of the first buildings in Paris to make use of superimposed classical orders. Construction began in 1546, a year before the death of François I. Fortunately, Henri II, his successor, continued work on the project with the same architect and in the same style.

In 1624, Jacques Lemercier, the architect placed in charge of the work by Louis XIII, introduced additions in the style of Pierre Lescot, in the interest of architectural consistency.

Colonnade

For this façade, intended to be the Louvre's principal entry, Louis XIV had projects drawn up by several architects, among them the Italian Gianlorenzo Bernini, whom he had brought to Paris at great expense.

In the end, the commission went to Claude Perrault, who rose to the occasion with his famous Colonnade, regarded ever since as the defining example of classical French architecture.

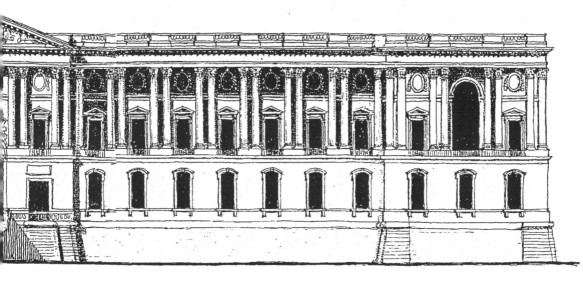

Grand Louvre

One of the first initiatives undertaken by François Mitterrand after his election as president of France in 1981 was the Grand Louvre project, which involved reclaiming for the museum areas long occupied by the Ministry of Finance as well as remodeling the entire complex.

The project was entrusted to I. M. Pei. His first concern was to rethink the problem of access, hitherto very unsatisfactory. To this end, he envisioned a large underground space—illuminated by natural light through a large glass pyramid—to serve as the main entrance to the museum.

The result is magnificent, both above ground, thanks to the pools surrounding the pyramid, and below, where the architectural spaces are carefully considered and the chosen materials apt.

The glass pyramid serves as the main entrance to the Louvre.
Beyond is the Pavillon Sully, which leads to the Cour Carrée.

Arc de Triomphe du Carrousel

LOCATION: Place du
Carrousel, situated
between the Louvre
and the Tuileries gardens
MÉTRO STATION: Palais-Royal
PATRON: Napoléon I
ARCHITECTS: Pierre Fontaine and Charles Percier (1806–8)

*The Arc du Carrousel was commissioned
by Napoléon I to commemorate his victories
in the campaigns of 1805. Closely modeled
after the triumphal arch of Septimus
Severus in Rome, it provided a ceremonial
entry to the Tuileries palace before the latter's destruction.*

*The bronze quadriga that now sur-
mounts the arch replaces a chariot drawn by
the four famous Horses of San Marco,
which Napoléon had confiscated from the
Venetians but which were returned to them
by the Austrians in 1815, when the Austrians occupied Paris.*

31

⑯ Tuileries Gardens

LOCATION: Between the Louvre and the Place de la Concorde
MÉTRO STATION: Tuileries
PATRONS: Originally Catherine de Médicis (1564); then Colbert (1664)
DESIGNER: André Le Nôtre (redesign of extant gardens, 1664)

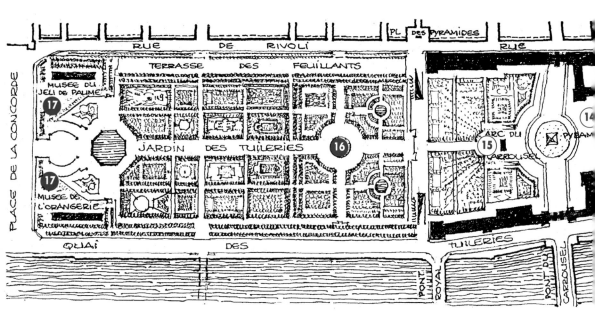

The Tuileries gardens were originally designed for the palace of the same name, now destroyed, built beginning in 1564 not far from the Louvre, perpendicular to the Seine, on the orders of Catherine de Médicis.

Subsequently, Henri IV linked the Tuileries palace to the Louvre by means of the "Galerie au Bord de l'Eau" (gallery bordering the water), so named because it fronted the Seine. But the symmetrical gallery to the north, bordering the rue de Rivoli, was erected only in the 19th century, finally integrating the complex by giving it a completely enclosed perimeter.

The gardens situated between the Tuileries palace and the present Place de la Concorde were redesigned by André Le Nôtre in 1664 on the orders of Jean-Baptiste Colbert, minister of Louis XIV. Le Nôtre decided to level it between two symmetrical terraces: the Grande Terrasse to the south,

along the river, and the Terrasse des Feuillants to the north.

The basic layout of the gardens remains largely unchanged, but such is not the case for the Tuileries palace, which was burned in 1871, during the Paris Commune. The ruins were left standing for more than ten years, until 1882, when the Parlement ordered their demolition. All that survives are the two pavilions originally at either end, which marked its junction with the Louvre: the Pavillon de Flore, on the Seine side, and the Pavillon de Marsan, on the rue de Rivoli side. The Tuileries gardens are now continuous with the Carrousel gardens, especially since the recent construction of a tunnel for the busy roadway that once severed them.

In 1991, a competition was held for refurbishing the Tuileries and Carrousel gardens. The winners were Pascal Cribier and Louis Bénech (Tuileries)

LOCATION: Tuileries gardens
near the Place de la Concorde
MÉTRO STATION: Concorde

Musée du Jeu de Paume and Musée de l'Orangerie

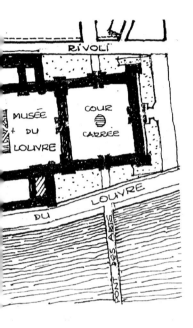

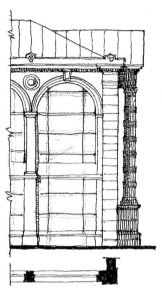

Entrance to the Jeu de Paume

These two buildings are situated on the high terraces overlooking the Place de la Concorde. As suggested by their names, their original uses (tennis court and greenhouse for raising oranges) were quite different from their present ones.

The Orangerie (Seine side) was built first, in 1853, followed in 1861 by the Jeu de Paume (rue de Rivoli side), Napoléon III having stipulated that its architecture resemble that of the Orangerie.

At the beginning of the 20th century, the French state reclaimed both buildings and turned them over to the Administration des Beaux-Arts, which was succeeded by the Musées Nationaux.

After negotiations with Claude Monet, the Orangerie was chosen as the site for his mural-size paintings Water Lilies, *for which the building was remodeled. These were the only works in its permanent collection until 1984, when, after fur-*

ther remodeling, it became home to the painting collections assembled by Paul Guillaume and Jean Walter.

The Jeu de Paume, after having served in turn as a temporary exhibition gallery and a museum of contemporary French art, became, between 1947 and 1986, an annex of the Musée du Louvre devoted to works by the Impressionists.

In 1986, with the opening of the Musée d'Orsay, to which works by the Impressionists were moved, the building was designated the Musée du Jeu de Paume, devoted to changing exhibitions of contemporary art. After a competition held in 1987, its renovation was entrusted to the architect Antoine Stinco, who deftly combined skylit exhibition rooms with transitional spaces offering superb views of the Tuileries gardens.

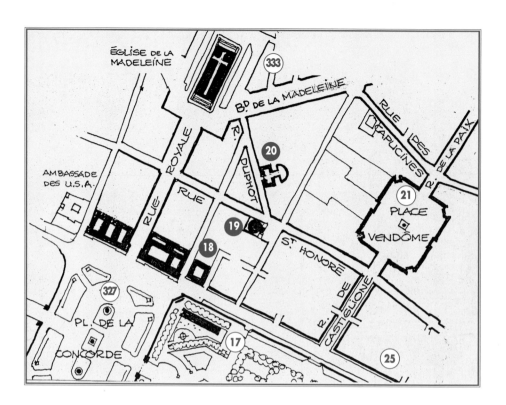

18 Hôtel de Saint-Florentin

(Hôtel de La Vrillière,

Hôtel de Talleyrand)

LOCATION: 2, rue Saint-Florentin
(corner of the rue de Rivoli)
MÉTRO STATION: Concorde
PATRON: The comte de Saint-Florentin
ARCHITECT: Jean-François Chalgrin
(1767–69)

Place de la Concorde

Rue de Rivoli

The Hôtel de Saint-Florentin was built before the rue de Rivoli was pierced; it is the work of Chalgrin, who designed its façades to harmonize with those by Jacques-Ange Gabriel fronting the Place de la Concorde.

The comte de Saint-Florentin, the patron, later became duc de La Vrillière, a name also used on occasion to designate the building.

The house's third name reflects the fact that the great statesman Talleyrand lived there between 1813 and 1838.

Notre-Dame-de-l'Assomption ⑲

LOCATION: 263 bis, rue Saint-Honoré
MÉTRO STATIONS: Concorde; Madeleine
PATRONS: The nuns of the Assumption
ARCHITECT: Charles Errard (1670–76)

This church is famous for its dome, which is disproportionately large by comparison with the rest of the building. Nonetheless, its architect was not unseasoned. He was Charles Errard, director of the French Academy in Rome, whose design is clearly inspired, if ineptly, by the ancient and Baroque architecture of that city.

Since 1850, the church has served the community of Polish Catholics in Paris.

Rue Duphot, nos. 10–14 ⑳

MÉTRO STATIONS: Madeleine; Concorde
ARCHITECT: Emmanuel-Aismé Dumesme (1806–10)

Beyond its street façade, this U-shaped building opens onto a small semicircular court, now closed off by an apartment building of more recent date. The entry is through a large, almost jambless arch of a kind favored by the architect Claude-Nicolas Ledoux, with whom Dumesme studied. The name Manège Duphot, sometimes given to the ensemble, refers to a riding school that occupied the premises between 1860 and 1914.

㉑ Place Vendôme

LOCATION: Between rue de Castiglione
and rue de la Paix
MÉTRO STATION: Concorde

As the Place Vendôme is the first of the four Parisian places royales, or royal squares, to be discussed, it is perhaps worth noting here that all of them share two characteristics: they are all dedicated to a king, hence the name places royales; they all received in their center a statue of the king to which they were dedicated.

The places royales are as follows (beginning with the oldest): Place Royale, now the Place des Vosges, commissioned by Henri IV (1605) but furnished, in 1639, with an equestrian statue of Louis XIII; Place des Victoires, dedicated to Louis XIV (1685–86); Place Vendôme, also dedicated to Louis XIV (1699–1720); Place Louis XV, now the Place de la Concorde (1755–72).

The Place Vendôme, a splendid ensemble, was

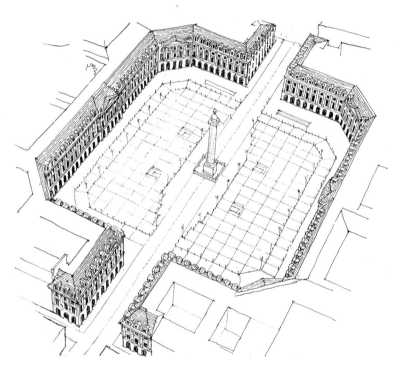

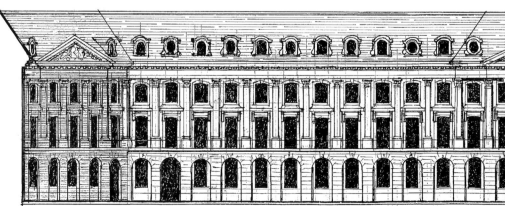

built at the instigation of Louis XIV, who originally envisioned it as a monumental square bordered by buildings housing cultural institutions. He
entrusted its design to Jules Hardouin-Mansart,
but financial difficulties necessitated a change of
plan. The site was sold to the City of Paris for
resale as individual residential plots, on the under-
standing that all prospective owners would be
obliged to adhere to the architect's design for the
façades. While essentially rectangular in plan, the
square is distinctive for its chamfered corners with
pedimented façades. The intervening façades are
articulated by colossal Corinthian pilasters.

Originally, the center of the square was occupied
by a statue of Louis XIV by François Girardon,
but it was destroyed during the Revolution. At the
initiative of Napoléon I, in 1810 it was replaced by
a column modeled after the Column of Trajan in
Rome and decorated with a spiral of bronze reliefs
evoking the emperor's martial exploits, cast from
enemy cannons seized at the Battle of Austerlitz.

The column was originally surmounted by a
statue of Napoléon I as Caesar, but in 1814 this
was replaced by a fleur-de-lys, emblem of the
restored Bourbon line. This in turn was replaced in
1833 by a Napoléon in a frock coat, which in turn
gave way, in 1863, to another Napoléon as Caesar, inspired by the original statue.

The column was toppled during the Commune
of 1871, but three years later it was rebuilt, and the
smashed statue was replaced by a replica.

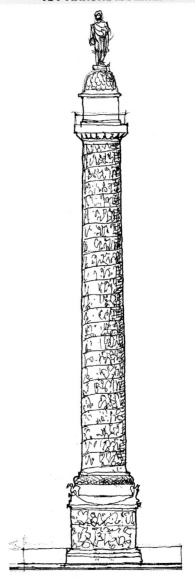

The Vendôme Column

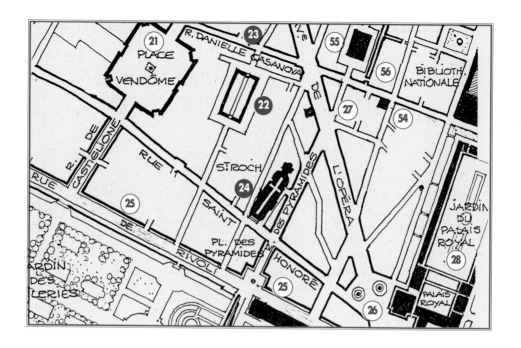

㉒ Place du Marché-Saint-Honoré

LOCATION: The square divides rue du Marché-Saint-Honoré into two segments.
MÉTRO STATION: Pyramides
PATRON: SIMSH-Paribas (central building)
ARCHITECT: Ricardo Bofill / Taller de Arquitectura (1994-96)

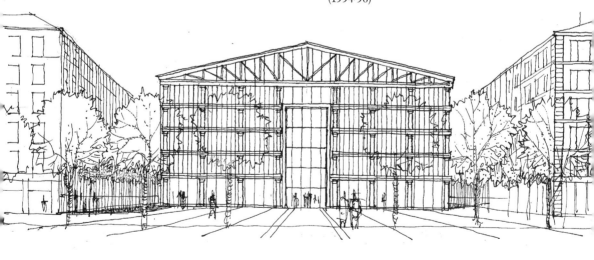

All that survives of the Saint-Honoré market is its name, for the square is now occupied by the Paribas office building. There are no shops on the complex's ground floor, and, despite the inclusion of an exhibition space, the central pedestrian passage remains essentially deserted. The final impression produced by the building, encased entirely in glass, is chilly.

LOCATION: Links the avenue de l'Opéra to the rue de la Paix
MÉTRO STATION: Pyramides

Rue Danielle-Casanova ㉓

This street, formerly part of the rue des Petits-Champs, was renamed in 1944 in honor of a member of the Resistance who died after being captured.

Its odd-numbered side boasts some interesting *early-18th-century residences, most notably: no. 15, corner of the rue du Marché-Saint-Honoré (1711); no. 21 (1703); nos. 23–27–29 (1707).*

LOCATION: 298, rue Saint-Honoré
MÉTRO STATION: Pyramides
ARCHITECTS: Jacques Lemercier (original design, 1653), who died before construction began in 1670. Jules Hardouin-Mansart (Lady Chapel, 1705). Robert de Cotte (façade, built 1738–39). Étienne-Louis Boullée (Calvary Chapel, completely recast 19th century)

Saint-Roch ㉔

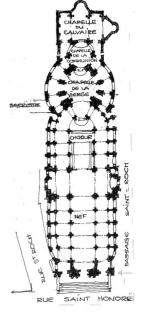

Plans were commissioned from Jacques Lemercier shortly before his death in 1654. Construction proceeded quite slowly and was interrupted by financial difficulties. Work resumed in 1705, when the axial Lady Chapel by Jules Hardouin-Mansart

was built. The vault of the church, completed only in 1719, was underwritten by the Scottish banker John Law. In 1738, Robert de Cotte commenced work on the façade, which is in a restrained Baroque style.

About 1760, Étienne-Louis Boullée extended the church even farther by building the Calvary Chapel (transformed into a Catechism Chapel in 1850), which made the church an impressive 394 feet long (in comparison with Notre-Dame's 426 feet).

The church of Saint-Roch houses many notable works of art.

㉕ Rue de Rivoli and Place des Pyramides

LOCATION: The rue de Rivoli links the Place de la Concorde to the rue Saint-Antoine.
MÉTRO STATIONS: Pyramides; Tuileries
PATRON: Napoléon I (1802)
ARCHITECTS: Charles Percier and Pierre Fontaine (façades)
SCULPTOR: Emmanuel Frémiet (statue of Joan of Arc, Place des Pyramides, 1874)

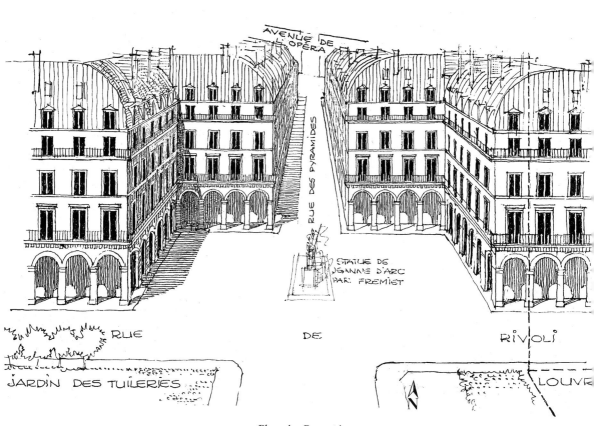

Place des Pyramides

The portion of the street between the Place de la Concorde and the Place du Palais-Royal was pierced in 1802, but construction of the apartment buildings continued until 1835. The extension from the Place du Palais-Royal to the rue Saint-Antoine was opened up in 1848–50, but the use of identical façades was discontinued west of the rue de l'Oratoire. The first apartment buildings to rise along the street featured low double-sloped roofs, but thereafter, to create more profitable rentable space, the now-familiar curving roofs were introduced. Such roof treatments became a Parisian trademark.

Place André-Malraux 26

LOCATION: At the southern end of the avenue de l'Opéra
MÉTRO STATION: Palais-Royal
ARCHITECTS: Victor Louis (Théâtre-Français, 1786–90). Gabriel Davioud (fountains, 1870–74)

The building beyond the fountain in the drawing is the Théâtre-Français (see entry 28, Palais-Royal).

27 Avenue de l'Opéra

LOCATION: Runs between the Théâtre National de l'Opéra and the Louvre
MÉTRO STATIONS: Palais-Royal; Pyramides; Opéra
PATRONS: Napoléon III and Baron Haussmann

The piercing of this avenue, which took twelve years, entailed the destruction of a great many buildings. The first portion (north) opened in 1864; the second in 1876.

The uniform design of the façades, the result of strict regulations regarding urbanism imposed by Baron Haussmann, makes the avenue rather monotonous. Noteworthy, however, is the picturesque façade of the old Au Gagne-Petit store, situated at no. 23, which dates from 1878.

㉘ Palais-Royal

LOCATION: Place du Palais-Royal
MÉTRO STATION: Palais-Royal

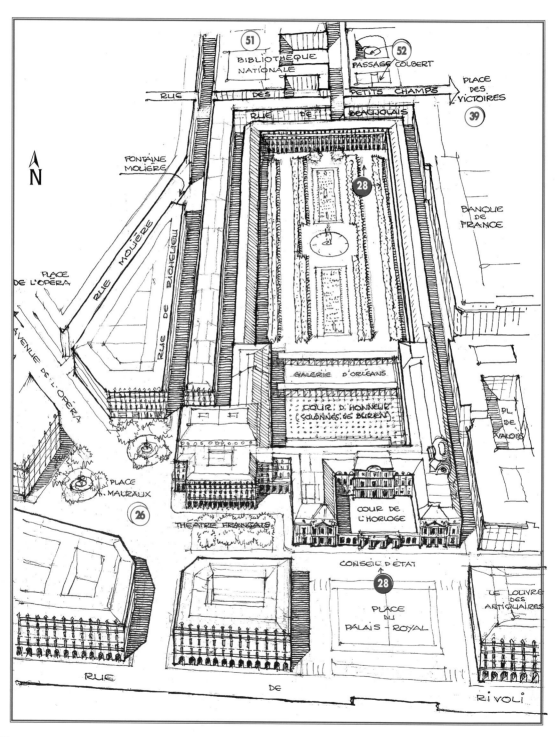

Here is a brief chronology of the palace's history.

1629–42: *Cardinal Richelieu asks the architect Jacques Lemercier to build him a palace (the Palais-Cardinal), which he then bequeaths to Louis XIII (hence its new name, Palais-Royal). All that survives from this period is the Galerie des Proues (gallery of prows) on the eastern side of the main courtyard.*

1692: *The palace becomes the property of Philippe d'Orléans.*

1763: *A fire destroys the theater in the right wing and damages the rest of the palace. The façades overlooking the Cour de l'Horloge, the southern entry court, are rebuilt by the architect of the city, Pierre-Louis Moreau-Desproux. The rest of the work is entrusted to the architect Contant d'Ivry.*

1781–84: *Continuous buildings designed by Victor Louis and containing sixty identical residential units are built around the perimeter of the gardens.*

1781: *Another fire destroys the theater in the west wing. It is not rebuilt on this site.*

1786–90: *Victor Louis builds the Théâtre-Français adjacent to the west wing, but a gap is left to accommodate a passage leading to the main courtyard.*

1789–93: *The gardens of the Palais-Royal become a center of political agitation during the revolutionary period. In 1793, the palace is appropriated for the nation.*

1814: *The palace is returned to the Orléans family. Beginning in 1815, the architect Pierre Fontaine lays out the wings on either side of the main courtyard.*

1828: *Construction of the Galerie d'Orléans. All but its columns were demolished in 1933.*

1871: *The Palais-Royal is burned during the Commune.*

1873: *The palace is restored and remodeled to accommodate the Conseil d'État (council of state), which still meets there.*

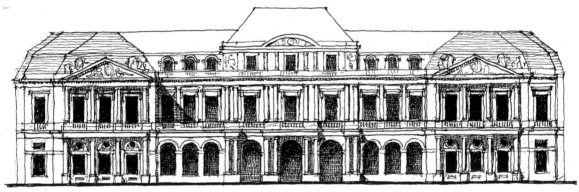

Façade facing the Place du Palais-Royal, Pierre-Louis Moreau-Desproux, architect (1766–70)

Garden façade of the Palais-Royal, Victor Louis, architect (1781–84)

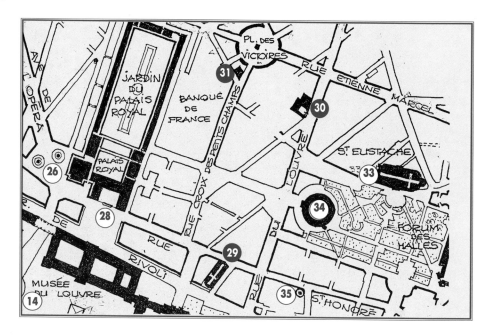

29 Oratoire du Louvre

LOCATION: 145, rue Saint-Honoré; façades on rue de l'Oratoire and rue de Rivoli
MÉTRO STATIONS: Palais-Royal; Louvre
PATRON: Cardinal de Bérulle
ARCHITECTS: Clément II Métezeau and Jacques Lemercier (1621–30).
Pierre Caqué (façade, 1745)

This church was built for the Congregation of the Oratorians, founded by Pierre de Bérulle. Its apse features curious stair turrets with culminating lanterns. The lower portion of the apse is partly obscured by the arcade of the rue de Rivoli and by a monument to Admiral Gaspard de Coligny, who was assassinated nearby during the Saint Bartholomew's Day Massacre (August 24, 1572).

Façade, rue du Faubourg-Saint-Honoré

Façade, rue de Rivoli

44

Caisse d'Épargne de Paris ③⓪

LOCATION: 19, rue du Louvre, and 9, rue du Coq-Héron
MÉTRO STATION: Châtelet–Les Halles
PATRON: The tax farmer Thoinard de Vougy (c. 1735)
ARCHITECT: François Debias-Aubry (c. 1735); some authors have proposed Germain Boffrand

The Caisse d'Épargne (savings bank) took possession of the building in 1865. When the rue du Louvre was pierced in 1880, the portal was moved to accommodate the new alignment.

Façade, corner of the rue du Louvre and the rue du Coq-Héron

③① Hôtel de Jaucourt
(Hôtel de Portalis)

LOCATION: 43, rue Croix-des-Petits-Champs, and 2, rue La Vrillière
MÉTRO STATION: Châtelet–Les Halles
ARCHITECT: Pierre Desmaisons (1733), assisted by Pierre-Jean Varin

This corner building is noteworthy for its incorporation of two overhanging half-turrets culminating in idiosyncratic curving pediments.

Façade, corner of the rue Croix-des-Petits-Champs and the rue La Vrillière

㉜ Forum des Halles

LOCATION: Rue Pierre-Lescot
MÉTRO STATION: Châtelet–Les Halles
PATRON: The City of Paris
ARCHITECTS: C. Vasconi and G. Penchréac'h (Forum).
J. Willerval (Espace Pierre Lescot). P. Chemetov
(Place Carrée). C. and F.-X. Lalanne (gardens)
DATES: Built 1979–88

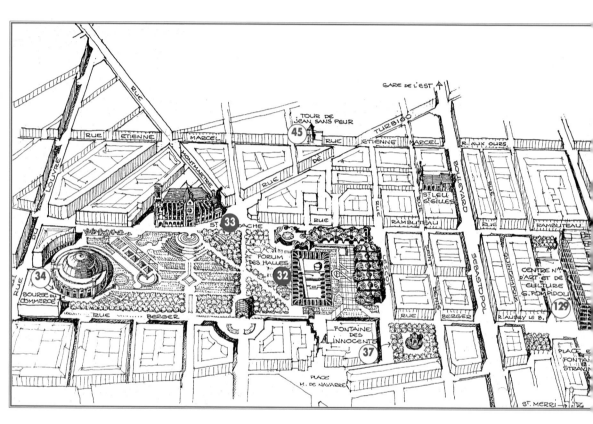

The Halles quarter was the site of the central market of Paris between the medieval period and 1962, when a decision was taken to move the facility to Rungis. The large area liberated as a result was transformed into a shopping and entertainment center complemented by extensive gardens.

The complex includes: the forum proper, a large commercial center with underground links to the métro and the RER (train network serving the out-lying suburbs); the Espace Pierre Lescot, corner of rue Pierre-Lescot and rue Rambuteau, a multipurpose cultural center; the Place Carrée, an underground extension of the commercial center that also houses cultural and sporting facilities, including a public swimming pool; extensive gardens on an elevated platform decorated with fountains, sculptures, and arched trellises.

LOCATION: 1, rue du Jour
MÉTRO STATION: Châtelet–Les Halles
ARCHITECTS: Jean Delamarre or Pierre Lemercier
(beginning in 1532). Mansart de Jouy
(new western façade, 1754)

Saint-Eustache

Although begun in 1532, at the beginning of the Renaissance in France, and although classicizing Renaissance motifs were applied to its supports, the structure of this vast church remains essentially Gothic.

Construction was protracted, and the church was consecrated only in 1637, at which time it was still not complete. In 1688, when some of the foundations shifted, the original façade was demolished along with the first bay of the nave and the side aisles. Due to a lack of funds, a new façade was not begun until May 22, 1754, when the duc de Chartres laid its foundation stone. This façade, completely different from the first one, was built to plans by Jean-Hardouin-Mansart de Jouy, grandson of the famous Jules Hardouin-Mansart. Nei-

ther it nor the square envisioned in front of it was completed.

By contrast, the piercing of the rue Rambuteau early in the 19th century and, especially, the recent construction of the Forum des Halles disengaged its southern flank, making its large size readily apparent (it is roughly 348 feet long).

In 1844, a serious fire damaged the church, which was restored between 1846 and 1854 by Victor Baltard.

The composer Jean-Philippe Rameau and Louis XIV's minister Jean Colbert are buried in the church; Colbert's tomb includes figures by the sculptors Antoine Coysevox and Jean-Baptiste Tuby.

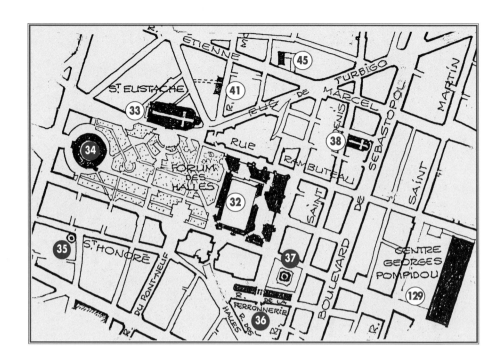

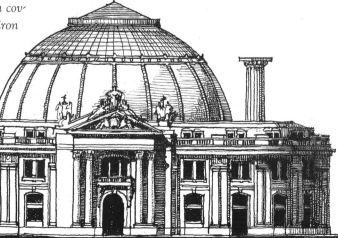

③④ Bourse de Commerce

The Bourse de Commerce (commercial exchange) occupies the remodeled structure of the old Halle au Blé (grain market), built on the site of the Hôtel de Soissons, whose only surviving remnant is the huge Doric column, originally an astronomical observatory designed by Philibert de l'Orme, now incorporated into the building. The circular central court, originally unroofed, was soon covered, first by a wooden dome, then by an iron one covered with copper plates. When it became the Bourse de Commerce, the building was remodeled by Henri Blondel, who reconstructed its peripheral ring.

LOCATION: 2, rue de Viarmes
MÉTRO STATION: Châtelet–Les Halles
PATRON: The City of Paris for the original grain market
ARCHITECTS: Nicolas Le Camus de Mézières (grain market, 1765–68). Legrand and Molinos (first dome, in wood, 1782–83). F.-J. Bélanger (second dome, in iron, 1809). Henri Blondel (transformation into the Bourse de Commerce, 1885–89)

Fontaine de la Croix-du-Trahoir ③⑤

LOCATION: 111, rue Saint-Honoré (corner of rue de l'Arbre-Sec)
MÉTRO STATION: Châtelet–Les Halles
PATRON: Louis XVI
ARCHITECT: Jacques-Germain Soufflot (1776). Restored in 1968

This fountain replaced an earlier one built in 1529 by Jean Goujon, which explains why its relief of a nymph, by the sculptor Louis Boizot, is a paraphrase of Goujon's reliefs for the Fontaine des Innocents (see entry 37).

MÉTRO STATION: Châtelet–Les Halles
PATRON: The vestry of Saint-Germain-l'Auxerrois (1670)

Rue de La Ferronnerie, ③⑥ nos. 2–14

After Henri IV was assassinated in this street, it was decided to widen it and to demolish the charnel house of the Cimetière des Innocents. The latter was replaced by a long apartment building with a gallery at ground level.

LOCATION: Place Joachim-du-Bellay
MÉTRO STATION: Châtelet–Les Halles
DESIGNER: The sculptor Jean Goujon and, perhaps, Pierre Lescot (1549). Altered and moved in 1788. Moved again in 1865

Fontaine des Innocents ③⑦

This fountain is on the site once occupied by the church of the Saints-Innocents and its cemetery.

As originally built, for the entry of Henri II into Paris, it was a corner structure consisting of three bays. In 1786, when the Saints-Innocents and its cemetery were demolished and replaced by a new square, it was recast as an independent fountain pavilion and placed in the center. Reliefs for the new fourth side were executed, in a style imitating that of Goujon, by Augustin Pajou (1788).

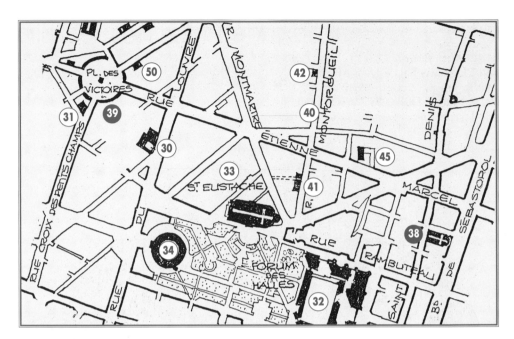

❸⑧ Saint-Leu–Saint-Gilles

LOCATION: 92, rue Saint-Denis
MÉTRO STATION: Étienne-Marcel
CONSTRUCTION: Begun (nave),
1319. Side aisles built, 16th century.
Choir built, 1611. Modified by Victor Baltard (1858–61)

The façade and its two small bell towers were modified in the 18th and 19th centuries. Furthermore, as the apse of the church projected into the course of the new boulevard Sébastopol, the architect Baltard shortened it, adding a new termination in neo-Renaissance style of dubious merit.

LOCATION: Between the 1st and 2nd arrondissements
MÉTRO STATION: Bourse
PATRON: The maréchal de La Feuillade
ARCHITECT: Jules Hardouin-Mansart (1685–86)
SCULPTOR: Martin Desjardins (first statue).
François-Joseph Bosio (present statue, 1822)

Place des Victoires ㊴

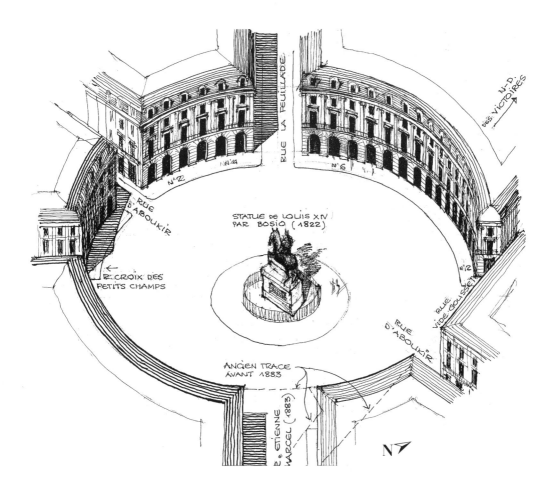

The circular Place des Victoires was designed in 1685 by the architect Jules Hardouin-Mansart to receive a statue of Louis XIV commissioned by the maréchal de La Feuillade, one of the king's courtiers.

Originally, the façades were uniform and no streets traversed the square. The subsequent opening up of new thoroughfares has disfigured the design, and some of the present buildings are not original.

The first statue of Louis XIV, by Martin Desjardins, was not equestrian; it represented the king standing on a base supported by enslaved figures personifying defeated nations. This work was destroyed during the Revolution (all that survives is the base, now in the Louvre). In 1822 it was replaced by an equestrian statue by Bosio, still in place.

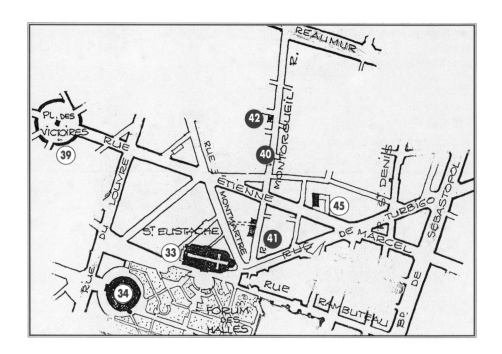

④ Rue Montorgueil

LOCATION: Links the rue de Turbigo to the rue Saint-Sauveur

MÉTRO STATION: Châtelet–Les Halles

This street, named after a hillock called Mont-Orgueil (mount pride), runs northward from the Forum des Halles to the rue Réaumur. It has recently become a pedestrian thoroughfare.

Situated right in the middle of the Halles quarter, the rue Montorgueil was a center for the sale of fish. No. 59 was the site of the restaurant Au Rocher de Cancale, famous for its oysters during the Restoration and the July Monarchy.

The following are especially noteworthy along this street: nos. 15 and 17 (see drawing opposite); no. 19, Gobin house (1776); no. 38, the restaurant L'Escargot Montorgueil, established 1875 (note sign); no. 41, 18th-century apartment building (see drawing opposite, of entrance and adjacent store-front); no. 73, early-18th-century apartment building; no. 78, former front, much damaged, of the restaurant Au Rocher de Cancale, which was moved from no. 59 to this address in 1845.

LOCATION: 15 and 17, rue Montorgueil
MÉTRO STATION: Châtelet–Les Halles
ARCHITECT: Martin Goupy (1729)

Robillard and Dumet Houses 41

Rue Montorgueil, no. 51 42

MÉTRO STATION: Châtelet–Les Halles

House dating from the 18th century. Above the entrance, to the left, is a carved trophy representing the attributes of architecture. The Pâtisserie Stohrer, to the right, boasts a remarkable interior with paintings by Paul Baudry (1864).

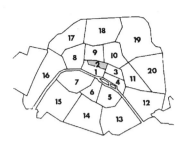

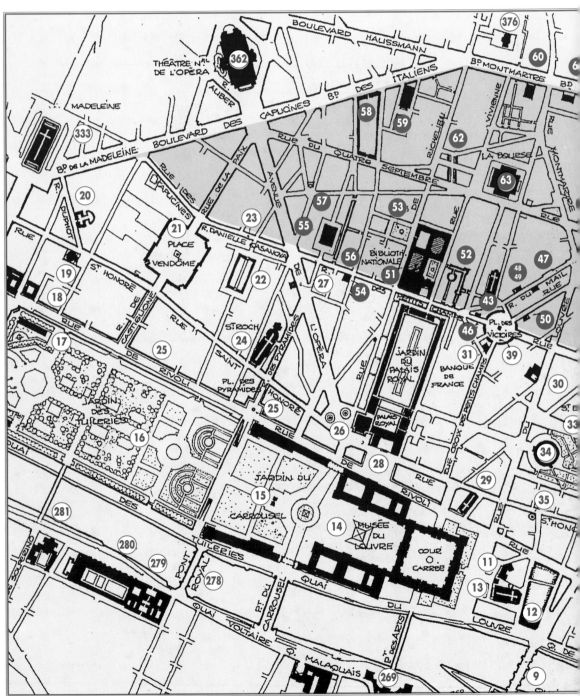

2nd Arrondissement

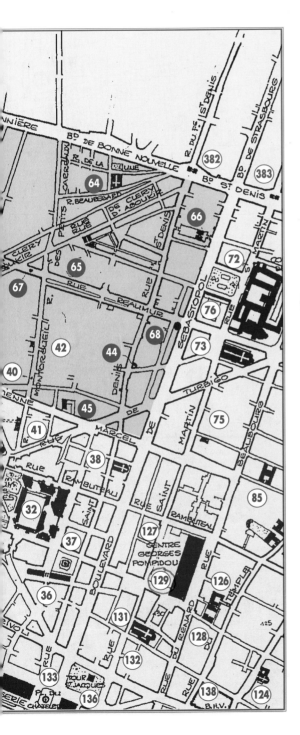

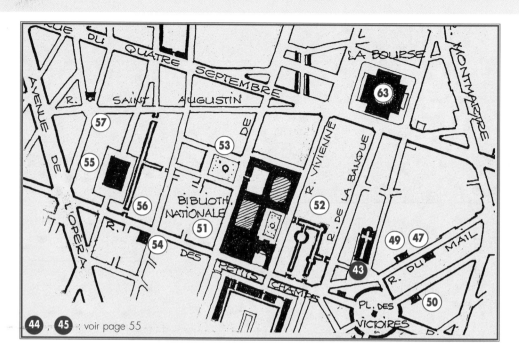

44 , 45 : voir page 55

43 Notre-Dame-des-Victoires

LOCATION: Place des Petits-Pères
MÉTRO STATION: Sentier
PATRONS: The Discalced Augustinians (nicknamed the Petits Pères), with assistance from Louis XIII
ARCHITECTS: Pierre Le Muet (design, 1628–29). Jacques Bruant (construction, 1629–66). Sylvain Cartaud (final stage, 1737–40)

The foundation stone was laid in 1629 by Louis XIII; construction continued for a century and involved at least four architects. The rest of the convent complex was demolished in 1859, leaving the church as its sole remnant. The interior houses a cycle of seven paintings by Carle Van Loo (choir); the tomb of Jean-Baptiste Lully, with a bust of the composer by Jean Collignon; and a very handsome 18th-century organ case.

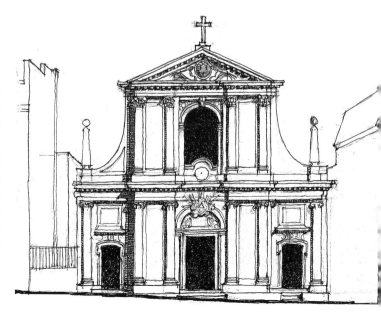

Fontaine Greneta 44

LOCATION: 142, rue Saint-Denis
(corner of rue Greneta)
MÉTRO STATION: Étienne-Marcel
PATRON (apartment building): Claude Aubry
ARCHITECT: Jacques-Richard Cochois (1732)

This fountain, sometimes called the Fontaine de la Reine, was built at the same time as the apartment building of which it is a part (1732). It replaced an older fountain dating from the 16th century.

Tour de 45
Jean-Sans-Peur

LOCATION: 20, rue Étienne-Marcel
MÉTRO STATION: Étienne-Marcel
PATRON: The duc de Bourgogne (1409–11)

This tower, which originally abutted the Wall of Philippe Auguste, was part of the Hôtel de Bourgogne. It is one of the few examples of feudal architecture to survive in Paris.

After ordering the assassination of his cousin, the duc d'Orléans, Jean sans Peur withdrew to a chamber at the top of this tower, which seemed to offer maximum security against reprisal. But he was assassinated in turn at Montereau.

South façade

East façade

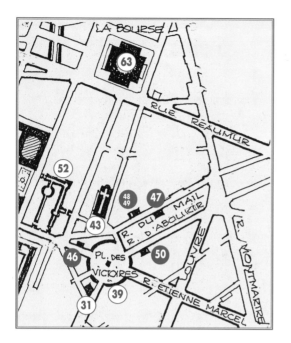

LOCATION: 4, rue La Feuillade (between Place des Victoires and rue des Petits-Champs)
MÉTRO STATIONS: Bourse; Palais-Royal
PATRON: Gabriel de La Fontaine (late 17th century)

46 Hôtel La Feuillade

This charming small town house is now known by the name of the individual who sold the land, the maréchal de La Feuillade, who was responsible for construction of the Place des Victoires (see entry 39).

47 Rue du Mail, no. 12

MÉTRO STATION: Bourse
PATRON: Berthault
ARCHITECT: Joseph-Jacques Ramée (1789)

This town house in Louis XVI style typifies the return to sobriety, even austerity, that took place about this time, a reaction prompted by the excesses of the Louis XV style.

⁴⁸ Rue du Mail, no. 5

MÉTRO STATION: Bourse
PATRON: François Le Tellier (1650)
Magnificent entrance.

⁴⁹ Rue du Mail, no. 7

MÉTRO STATION: Bourse
PATRON AND ARCHITECT: Thomas Gobert
(1669)

The façade of this handsome classical town house was disfigured under the Second Empire by the application, at considerable expense, of Renaissance elements. The pediment from that renovation has since been removed, and the elegance of the building's proportions remains striking.

Rue d'Aboukir, no. 4 ⁵⁰

MÉTRO STATION: Bourse
ARCHITECT: Jules de Joly
(early 19th century)

A very original building typical of the return to ancient models pioneered by Claude-Nicolas Ledoux some fifteen years earlier.

The use of serlianas—window units consisting of a central arched opening flanked by rectangular ones—on the first floor above street level is characteristic, as are, two floors above, the circular console niches containing busts.

Bibliothèque Nationale

LOCATION: 58, rue de Richelieu
MÉTRO STATION: Bourse
PATRONS: Charles Duret de Chevry (Hôtel Duret, then Tubeuf; 1635); Cardinal Mazarin
(Galerie Mansart and Galerie Mazarine, c. 1650); French government (19th-century additions)
ARCHITECTS: Jean Thiriot (Hôtel Duret, then Tubeuf, 1635). François Mansart (remodeling of
the Hôtel Tubeuf, 1644–45). Pierre Le Muet (continued this building campaign, 1646). Maurizio
Valperga (Galerie Mansart and Galerie Mazarin, c. 1650; their attribution to François Mansart
c. 1645 is erroneous). Robert de Cotte and son (entry court, northern and eastern wings, 1731).
Henri Labrouste (additions, especially main reading room, 1854–75). Jean-Louis Pascal (periodi-
cal reading room, 1906)

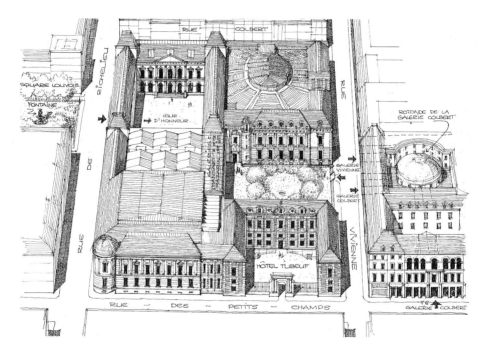

The royal library, ancestor of the Bibliothèque Nationale, was frequently shifted about until it was designated the Bibliothèque Royale and permanently located in Paris by King Charles V (reigned 1364–80). It was not moved to the Hôtel de Nevers until 1724, and only a few vestiges remain at 12, rue Colbert.

The present Bibliothèque Nationale occupies a quadrangle covering an area over 175,000 square feet, but its space has become inadequate, and it has recently been supplemented by the new Bibliothèque Nationale de France (see entry 425).

It consists of several buildings built, regrouped, and remodeled in several successive campaigns. The oldest part is the Hôtel Tubeuf (former Hôtel Duret), built in 1635 and acquired in 1641 by Cardinal Mazarin, who had it remodeled.

The principal enlargements and remodelings were overseen by the architect Henri Labrouste between 1854 and 1875, the year of his death. His most note-worthy addition is the inventive main reading room (drawing opposite), inaugurated in 1869. It is cov-ered by nine metal domes with faience revetment and supported by thin cast-iron colonnettes.

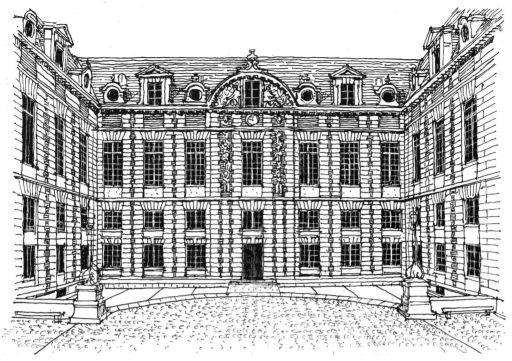

Hôtel Tubeuf

Main Reading Room

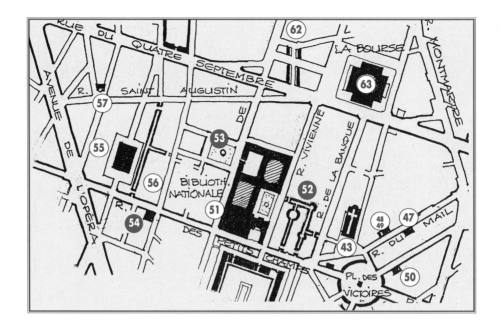

52 Passages Vivienne and Colbert

Passage Vivienne
LOCATION: 4, rue des Petits-Champs;
5, rue de la Banque; 6, rue Vivienne
MÉTRO STATION: Bourse
ARCHITECT: François-Jacques Delannoy (1823)

Passage Colbert
LOCATION: 6, rue des Petits-Champs;
2, rue Vivienne
MÉTRO STATION: Bourse
ARCHITECT: J. Billaud (1826)

These two passages (covered commercial galleries), fiercely competitive when they were new, have just been restored. The Passage Colbert (see drawing), the more lavish one, is noteworthy for its large rotunda (almost fifty feet across) and its Pompeian decoration. It is now the property of the Bibliothèque Nationale.

Passage Colbert

Square Louvois 53

LOCATION: Rue de Richelieu, opposite the entry to the Bibliothèque Nationale
MÉTRO STATION: Bourse
PATRON: Napoléon III (1859)
DESIGNER: The civil engineer Adolphe Alphand
FOUNTAIN: Louis Visconti, architect, and Jean-Baptiste Klagmann, sculptor (1844)

Beginning in 1792, the site of the Square Louvois was occupied by a theater designed by the architect Victor Louis for Mademoiselle de Montpensier; from 1794 it housed the Opéra.

After the assassination of the duc de Berry while he was leaving a performance there (February 13, 1820), the building was razed and replaced by an expiatory chapel, but this was not completed.

In 1844, Louis-Philippe erected a fountain on the site; its four female figures are personifications of French rivers.

In 1859, the site was transformed into a square by Alphand.

54 Hôtel de Lulli

LOCATION: 45, rue des Petits-Champs (corner rue Sainte-Anne)
MÉTRO STATION: Pyramides
PATRON: The composer and musician Jean-Baptiste Lully
ARCHITECT: Daniel Gittard (1671)

In this design, the architect used a very classical Corinthian order. One of the windows facing the rue Sainte-Anne has a balcony decorated with musical instruments, intended to recall the owner's identity.

⑤⑤ Salle Ventadour

LOCATION: Opposite the rue Méhul
MÉTRO STATION: Pyramides
PATRON: Maison du Roi for the troupe of the
Opéra-Comique
ARCHITECT: Jean-Jacques Huvé (1826–27)

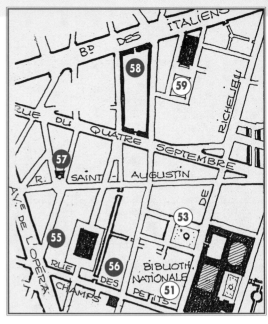

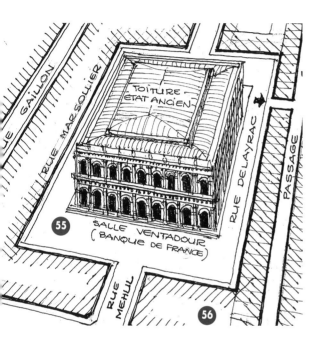

During construction of the Passage Choiseul, the Mallet Bank sold a portion of its land to accommodate this theater for the Opéra-Comique, which continued to perform there until 1832. The building then housed several troupes in succession; Victor Hugo's Ruy Blas was premiered there in 1838. The theater was closed in 1878, and the premises are now owned by the Banque de France.

⑤⑥ Passage Choiseul

LOCATION: 40, rue des Petits-Champs;
23, rue Saint-Augustin
MÉTRO STATION: Pyramides
PATRON: Mallet Bank
ARCHITECTS: François Mazois, then Antoine Tavernier (1826–27)

This passage is on a site formerly occupied by four town houses, acquired by the Mallet Bank for the same real-estate development that resulted in construction of the Salle Ventadour (see entry 55).

The writer Louis-Ferdinand Céline, who lived in this passage when he was a child, evoked it in two of his novels, Journey to the End of Night and Death on the Installment Plan.

Fontaine Gaillon 57

LOCATION: Place Gaillon
MÉTRO STATION: Opéra
ARCHITECT: Louis Visconti
SCULPTOR: Georges Jacquot
(1827)

Louis Visconti designed both the fountain and the building into which it is set. He later designed the Fontaine Molière (rue de Richelieu) and the Fontaine des Quatre-Évêques (Place Saint-Sulpice).

Crédit Lyonnais 58

LOCATION: 17–23, boulevard des Italiens
MÉTRO STATION: Richelieu-Drouot
PATRON: Crédit Lyonnais bank
ARCHITECT: William Bouwens
van der Boijen (1878)

This is a typical example of the grandiloquent style favored by banks in the late 19th century in hopes of impressing their clients (see also entry 378, formerly headquarters of the Comptoir National d'Escompte). The central pavilion was obviously inspired by the Louvre.

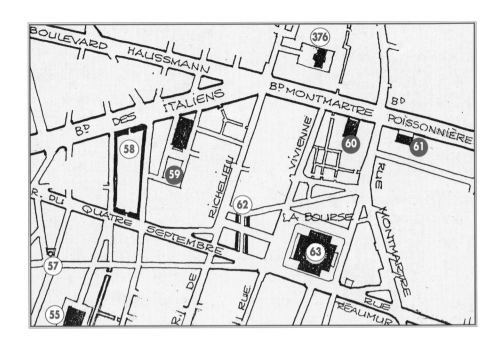

⑤⑨ Opéra-Comique

LOCATION: 1, Place Boieldieu
MÉTRO STATION: Richelieu-Drouot
ARCHITECT: Louis Bernier (1894–98)

The architect was the winner of a design competition for the theater, held in 1893. His building was the third to rise on the site; both of its predecessors were destroyed by fire (1838; 1887). It is still often called the Salle Favart, which was the name of the first of the three theaters.

Façade, place Boieldieu

Théâtre des Variétés 60

LOCATION: 7, boulevard Montmartre
MÉTRO STATION: Rue-Montmartre
PATRON: Mademoiselle Montansier, former
director of the Théâtre du Palais-Royal
ARCHITECT: Jacques Cellerier (1806–7)

This is a charming small theater whose neoclassical façade, crowned by a pediment, features superimposed orders (Doric below, Ionic above). The plane of the façade recedes beyond, creating an attractive play of light and shadow.

LOCATION: 23, boulevard Poissonnière
MÉTRO STATIONS: Rue-Montmartre;
Grands-Boulevards
PATRON: Nicolas Montholon, president
of the Parlement of Normandy
ARCHITECT: François Soufflot, known
as "le Romain" (1785)

Hôtel de Montholon 61

Original state

Façade on the boulevard Poissonnière

Many town houses were built along the boulevards to profit from their greenery, but this is the only surviving example. It has since been disfigured by *added stories (see drawings) and by a row of shops fronting the boulevard whose signs add insult to injury.*

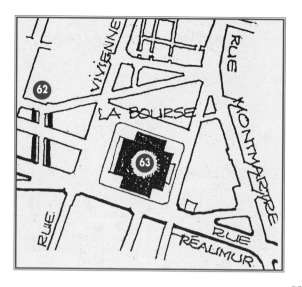

⑥₂ Rue des Colonnes

LOCATION: Begins at 4, rue du 4-Septembre
MÉTRO STATION: Bourse
ARCHITECT: Joseph Bénard (1793),
after designs by Nicolas Vestier

This street was pierced to facilitate access to the Théâtre Feydeau (destroyed 1829). It features arcaded sidewalks such as were to be used a few years later along the rue de Rivoli. The arches are supported by baseless columns inspired by the Greek Doric order. The harmony of the ensemble was damaged by the construction of the rue de la Bourse and the rue du 4-Septembre, which shortened and segmented it.

LOCATION: Place de la Bourse
MÉTRO STATION: Bourse
ARCHITECT: Alexandre-Théodore Brongniart
(original building, 1809–26). Jean-Baptiste
Clavel (expansion, 1902–7)

Palais de la Bourse ⑥③

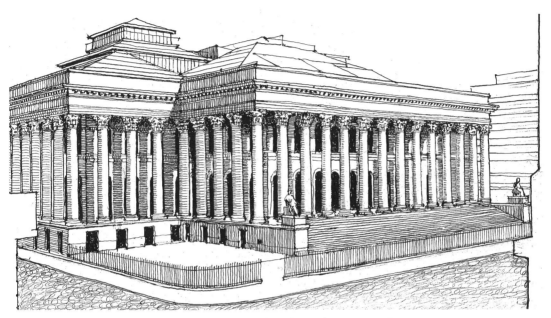

View from the north

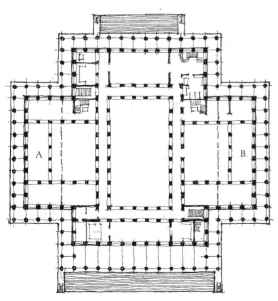

Current plan
A and B: 1905 additions

The stock market, nicknamed the Palais Brongniart in honor of its architect, was built on a site formerly occupied by the convent of the Filles Saint-Thomas. It originally housed the commercial exchange as well, subsequently moved to the former grain market (see entry 34). Even so, in 1905 it became necessary to enlarge the building, and the two new wings disfigured it, completely engulfing it in a forest of columns. The entrances are flanked by four statues, installed c. 1850, that represent Commerce and Justice (western side) and Agriculture and Industry (eastern side).

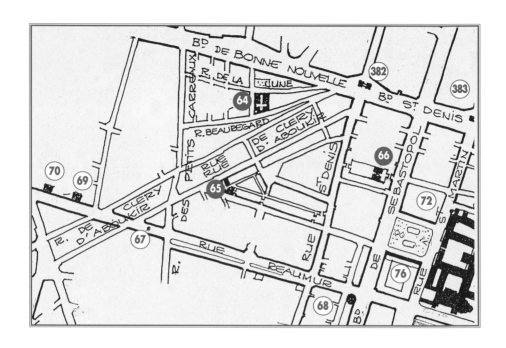

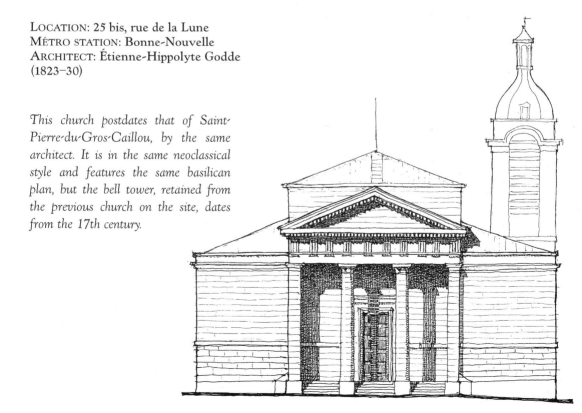 64 Notre-Dame-de-Bonne-Nouvelle

LOCATION: 25 bis, rue de la Lune
MÉTRO STATION: Bonne-Nouvelle
ARCHITECT: Étienne-Hippolyte Godde
(1823–30)

This church postdates that of Saint-Pierre-du-Gros-Caillou, by the same architect. It is in the same neoclassical style and features the same basilican plan, but the bell tower, retained from the previous church on the site, dates from the 17th century.

LOCATION: Place du Caire
MÉTRO STATION: Sentier
ARCHITECT: Philippe-Laurent
Prétrel (1798–99)

Building on the ⑥⑤ Place du Caire

This building was erected shortly after Napoléon I's Egyptian campaign had made the art of that country fashionable, which explains the name (Cairo) of the passage and the building's Egyptian decor.

The Romanesque-Gothic motifs of the building's upper stories, however, are less readily explained.

Detail of the façade

Rue Saint-Denis, no. 226 ⑥⑥

MÉTRO STATION: Réaumur-Sébastopol
PATRON: Religious community of the
Dames de Saint-Chaummond (convent of
the Filles de l'Union-Chrétienne)
ARCHITECT: Jacques Hardouin-Mansart de
Levi (grandson of Jules Hardouin-
Mansart; 1734)

Original
state   Present
                                         state

Court facing rue Saint-Denis

Nothing now remains of the 18th-century convent of the Filles de l'Union-Chrétienne. The present building is the 19th-century residential structure built to house the wealthiest of its lay pensioners.

Aside from the expansion of the two upper floors, it is essentially unaltered. To see it, enter the courtyards at 226, rue Saint-Denis or 131, boulevard de Sébastopol.

Original state   Present state
Court facing boulevard Sébastopol

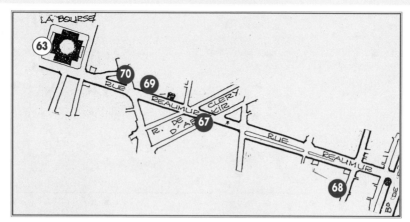

67 Rue Réaumur

Among the many interesting buildings on this street, the following are especially noteworthy.
No. 51: See below.
Nos. 61 – 63: G. Sirgery and P. Houannin, architects (c. 1900).
No. 69: Ernest Pergod, architect (1895).
No. 97: Jolivald and Devillard, architects (1900).
No. 101: Albert Walwein, architect (1895).
No. 118: See below.
No. 121: Charles Ruzé, architect (1898).
No. 124: See below.
No. 130: Charles de Montarnal, architect (1898).
No. 132: Jacques Hermant, architect (1910).

LOCATION: From the boulevard Sébastopol to the rue Notre-Dame-des-Victoires
MÉTRO STATION: Réaumur-Sébastopol

68 Rue Réaumur, no. 51

MÉTRO STATION: Réaumur-Sébastopol
PATRON: Société Félix Potin
ARCHITECT: Charles H.-C. Le Maresquier (1910)

Very successful at the time, the Félix Potin company (foodstuffs) built two prestige buildings in Paris: at 140, rue de Rennes (1904; Art Nouveau), and at 51, rue Réaumur at the corner of boulevard Sébastopol (see drawing).

This latter building is much altered at ground level, but the portion above, with its culminating lantern dome, is in its original state.

MÉTRO STATION: Réaumur-Sébastopol
ARCHITECT: Charles de Montarnal (1900)

Rue Réaumur, no. 118

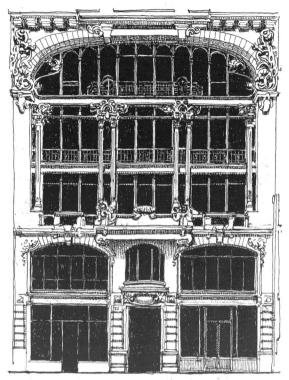

The architect skillfully combined metal and stone to give this building a surprising lightness.

See no. 130 on the same street for another building, from two years earlier, by the same architect.

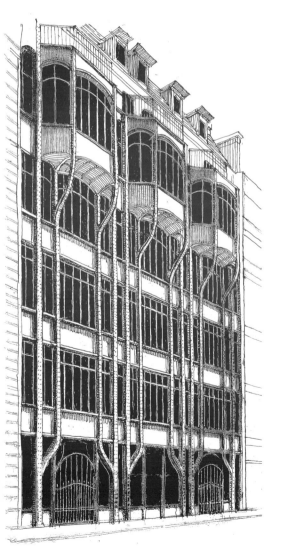

Rue Réaumur, no. 124

MÉTRO STATION: Réaumur-Sébastopol
ARCHITECT: Georges Chédanne (1903–5)

Except for its upper portion, the façade of this building consists entirely of glass and riveted metal, allowing the architect to develop a design of striking originality.

Chédanne's authorship has sometimes been contested because he also designed buildings in a more conventional classical idiom, but these doubts would seem to be unjustified.

The building has long housed the offices of the newspaper Le Parisien libéré.

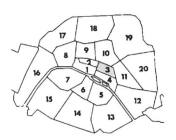

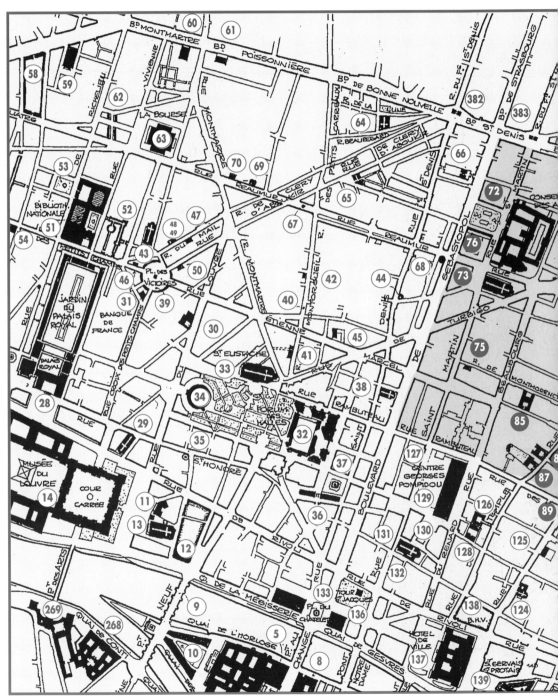

3rd Arrondissement

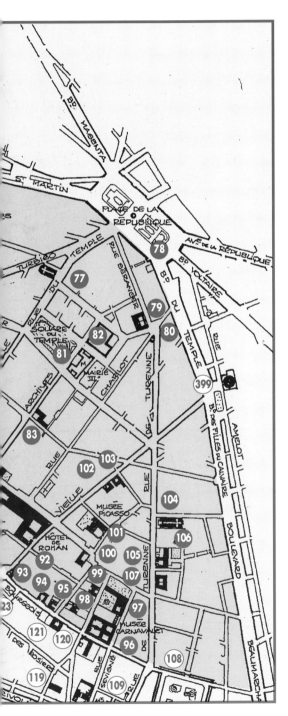

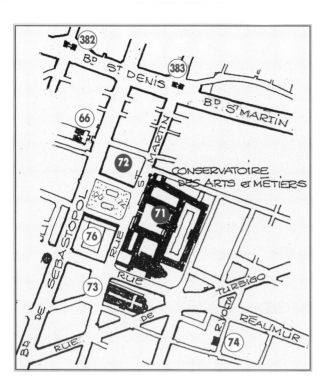

The present site of the Conservatoire National des Arts et Métiers was formerly occupied by the priory of Saint-Martin-des-Champs, of which two buildings survive: the church and the refectory.

The priory was founded in 1060, after an earlier church was destroyed by the Normans. Coming almost immediately under Benedictine jurisdiction, it grew rapidly and was surrounded by a fortified wall, of which there survives a tower, much altered, on the corner of rue Saint-Martin and the rue du Vertbois (see Fontaine Vertbois, entry 72). The priory was confiscated after the Revolution and its buildings assigned to the new Conservatoire des Arts et Métiers (1794).

Church

The church of Saint-Martin-des-Champs illustrates the stylistic transition between

⑦ Conservatoire National des Arts et Métiers

(Former priory of Saint-Martin-des-Champs)

LOCATION: 270–292, rue Saint-Martin
MÉTRO STATION: Arts-et-Métiers
KEY DATES:
1060, foundation of priory.
1060–67, construction of first church.
Early 12th century, construction of first nave and present choir.
Mid-13th century, rebuilding of nave and construction of refectory.
1794, the newly established conservatoire moves into the complex.
1845–96, construction of new buildings.
1885, construction of neo-Gothic church façade

Former refectory of the priory

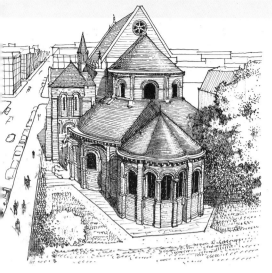

Chevet of the former church
of Notre-Dame-des-Champs

Romanesque and Gothic. The 13th-century bell tower is Romanesque, featuring round-arched bays and Romanesque capitals. It has been restored several times, however, and its second story was demolished in 1807.

The choir, with double ambulatory and radial chapels, dates from the 12th century. Its structural awkwardnesses reflect the novelty of its Gothic design. It was heavily restored in the 19th century and in the early 20th century. The nave, unvault-

ed, dates from the 13th century. The façade is a neo-Gothic construction dating from 1885. The church now houses a portion of the collections of the Musée National des Techniques.

Refectory

Built between 1230 and 1240, it is often attributed to Pierre de Montreuil, widely thought to have designed the Sainte-Chapelle. It is noteworthy for the lightness of its construction and the delicacy of the columns supporting its ribbed vault.

A pulpit remarkable for the craftsmanship of its stonework is set within the northern wall. The building now houses the library of the Conservatoire des Arts et Métiers.

19th-Century Buildings

As noted above, the buildings of the priory of Saint-Martin-des-Champs, confiscated after the Revolution, were ceded to the Conservatoire des Arts et Métiers in 1794. Between 1845 and 1896, the complex was considerably enlarged by the architects Léon Vaudoyer and Gabriel Ancelet. The entrance dates from 1850; the neo-Gothic façade, from 1885.

LOCATION: Corner of rue Saint-Martin
and rue du Vertbois
MÉTRO STATION: Arts-et-Métiers
DATES: 1712. Restored 1882

Fontaine de Vertbois 72

The fountain is inscribed as follows: "The tower from the fortified wall of the priory of Saint-Martin-des-Champs and the Fontaine de Vertbois erected in 1712 were preserved and restored by the state in 1882, in accordance with the wishes of Parisian antiquarians."

It is unfortunate that the restoration of the tower was not more scrupulous.

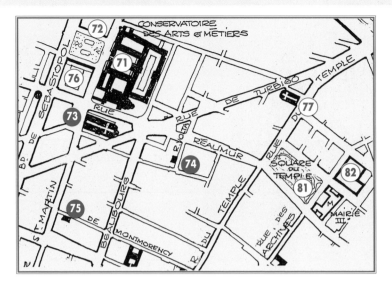

㉝ Saint-Nicolas-des-Champs

LOCATION: 254, rue Saint-Martin
MÉTRO STATION: Arts-et-Métiers
PATRONS: Monks of the priory of
Saint-Martin-des-Champs

In the 12th century, the monks of Saint-Martin-des-Champs had a chapel and then a church built outside the priory enclosure for a lay congregation. It was rebuilt in the 13th and 15th centuries, but elements of the 13th-century structure survive in the first bays of the side aisles.

Four new bays, as well as the side aisles with chapels, were added in the second half of the 16th century.

In the early 17th century, two more bays and an apse were added. The bell tower was erected in 1668. In the mid-

Renaissance portal

17th century, in accordance with prevailing fashion, the columns of the choir were fluted and given Ionic capitals.

During the Revolution, the building served as a temple of Hymen and Fidelity, but in 1802 it again became a place of Catholic worship. In 1854, the quarter was unsettled by the construction of the rue Turbigo, which liberated the southern flank of the church with its Renaissance portal (see drawing above).

Rue Volta, no. 3 ⁷⁴

[The num 74 appears in a circle]

Métro station: Arts-et-Métier

This house, long believed to be the oldest in Paris, in fact dates from the early 17th century. Nonetheless, it is one of very few surviving examples of the half-timber houses that were once ubiquitous in Paris; city regulations originally stipulated that they be plastered to prevent fire.

House of ⁷⁵ Nicolas Flamel

LOCATION: 51, rue de Montmorency
MÉTRO STATIONS: Rambuteau;
Arts-et-Métiers
PATRONS: Nicolas Flamel and his wife,
Pernelle (1407)

The fortune Nicolas Flamel amassed—through alchemy, according to legend—made it possible for him and his wife to offer food and lodging to the poor in this house, known at the time as the "house with the large gable" due to an element that has since disappeared.

The date of 1407 stipulated in the commemorative plaque refers to the carved lintel; the inscription "Auberge de Nicolas Flamel" in Gothic letters and the two shields on either side are later in date.

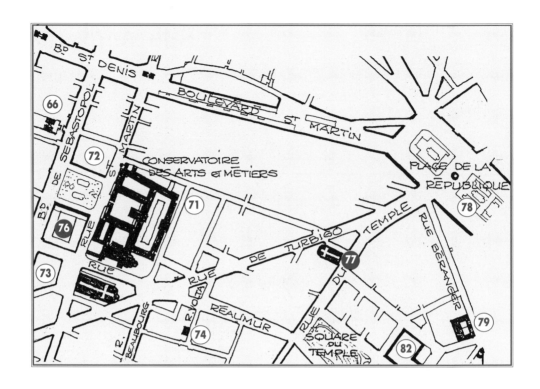

76 Théâtre de la Gaîté Lyrique

LOCATION: 3–5, rue Papin, opposite Square Émile-Chautemps
MÉTRO STATION: Réaumur-Sébastopol
ARCHITECT: Alphonse Cusin (1861–62)

This imposing ensemble consists of two flanking buildings, as well as the central theater. During its heyday, the theater was directed by Jacques Offenbach and received Sergey Diaghilev's Ballets Russes. Unfortunately, it is no longer in theatrical use. The Square Émile-Chautemps, opposite the theater, was designed by Gabriel Davioud in 1861; the sculpture of its fountains is by A. Ottin and C. Gumery.

Original state of the façade (the sculpture atop the projecting frontispiece has disappeared)

LOCATION: 195, rue du Temple
MÉTRO STATION: République
PATRON: A community of Franciscan nuns
ARCHITECT: Probably Michel Villedo (1628–45)

Sainte-Élisabeth

In 1628, Marie de Médicis, who founded this convent, laid the foundation stone of its church, which originally had only one side aisle (the right one).

The second side aisle was added in 1829 along with a Lady Chapel. The latter was destroyed in 1858 to accommodate the rue Turbigo; subsequent alterations, which included a nave extension and a new choir in the form of a hemicycle, were entrusted to Étienne-Hippolyte Godde.

The façade of the church is classical and features superimposed orders (Doric below, Ionic above). The Pietà that decorates the tympanum above the main entrance is from the 19th century, as are the statues in the niches.

Within, the ambulatory boasts handsome Flemish reliefs from the 17th century.

Place de la République

LOCATION: The intersection of the 3rd, 10th, and 11th arrondissements
MÉTRO STATION: République
PATRONS: Napoléon III and Baron Haussmann (1854)
ARCHITECTS: A. Legrom (Vérines Barracks, 1854–59). Gabriel Davioud (former Magasins Réunis, 1866)
SCULPTORS: Léopold and Charles Morice (Monument to the Republic, 1883)

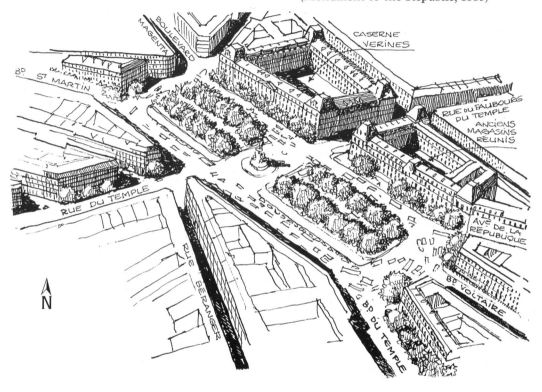

As a result of Baron Haussmann's piercing of several new streets in this quarter, the old Château-d'Eau crossroads was transformed into a vast square. To complete it, Haussmann commissioned the Vérines Barracks to the northeast and then asked Davioud to use a similar style for the Magasins Réunis, its symmetrical analogue on the other side of the rue du Faubourg-du-Temple.

The old lion fountain of the Château-d'Eau, now judged too small for the site, was moved to the slaughterhouses at La Villette, where it remains (in front of the Grande Halle, avenue Jean-Jaurès side). A new lion fountain was commissioned from Davioud. It, too, was judged ill-suited to the site and was moved to the Place Félix-Éboué, where it remains.

Finally, in 1883, an enormous statue of the Republic, the work of the Morice brothers, was installed in the center of the square atop a pedestal incorporating personifications of Liberty, Equality, and Fraternity.

Rue Béranger, 79 nos. 3–5

MÉTRO STATIONS: République; Filles-du-Calvaire
PATRONS: No. 3, Abraham Peyrenc de Moras,
financier. No. 5, Jean Pujol, conseiller du roi
and secrétaire des finances
ARCHITECT: Gabriel Dezègre (both town houses,
1719–20)

*These adjacent town houses were built on plots for-
merly within the Temple precinct (see entry 81). The
building at no. 3 was truncated by the construction of
the rue de Franche-Comté (see drawing below). The
former residences, whose magnificent entrances now face
the rue Béranger, today house an elementary school.*

Fontaine Boucherat 80

LOCATION: Corner of rue de Turenne
and rue Charlot
MÉTRO STATION: Filles-du-Calvaire
PATRON AND ARCHITECT: Jean Beausire
(1699)

*The inscription on the plaque evokes the Peace
of Ryswick, signed by Louis XIV on September
20, 1697.*

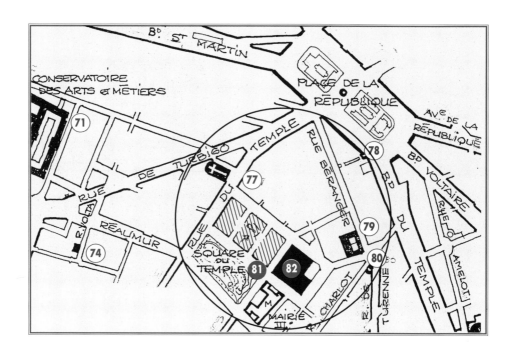

⑧¹ Square du Temple

LOCATION: Rue du Temple, rue de Bretagne, and rue Eugène-Spuller
MÉTRO STATION: Temple
PATRON: Napoléon III
DESIGNER: The engineer Adolphe Alphand (1857)

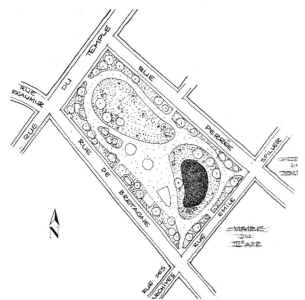

The site of the Square du Temple was formerly within a large fortified precinct that in the 12th century belonged to the Knights Templar, an order dissolved by Philippe le Bel in 1312.

During the Revolution, the Temple was transformed into a prison; Louis XVI, Marie-Antoinette, and the dauphin were detained there. The latter apparently died there on June 8, 1795, although royalists spread the rumor that he had escaped and another body had been substituted.

The medieval tower was razed in 1808, and nothing survives of the Temple complex.

The tower
before its
demolition

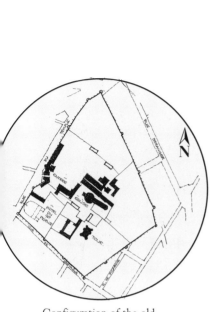

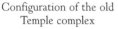

Configuration of the old
Temple complex

LOCATION: Rues Perrée, Eugène-Spuller,
de Picardie, and Dupetit-Thouars
MÉTRO STATION: Temple
PATRON: The City of Paris
ARCHITECTS: Jules de Mérindol and
Ernest Legrand (1863)
Partially demolished in 1905

Marché du Temple ⑧②
(Carreau du Temple)

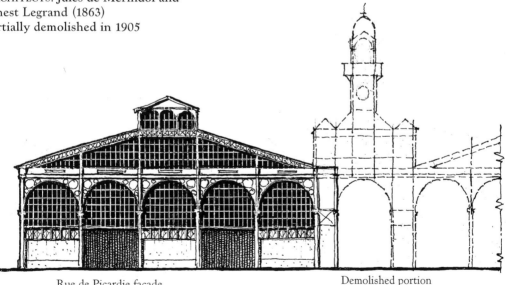

Rue de Picardie façade

Demolished portion

A clothing market was situated in a rotunda built within the Temple precinct in 1781. When the rotunda was destroyed in 1863, it was replaced by another market of which this portion survives (on the map, the surviving portion is black and the razed portion is hatched).

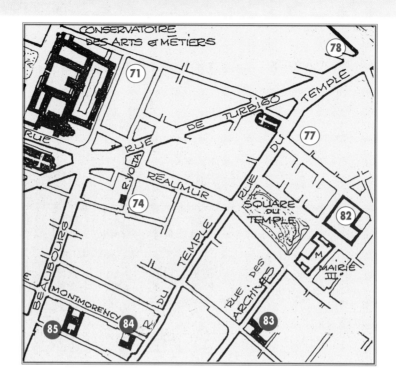

⑧③ Hôtel de Tallard

LOCATION: 78, rue des Archives; 10, rue Pastourelle; 3, rue de Beauce
MÉTRO STATIONS: Arts-et-Métiers; Rambuteau
PATRON: Jean-Denis Amelot de Chaillou. Sold to the comte de Tallard in 1722
ARCHITECT: Pierre Bullet (1702–4)

Unfortunately, the harmonious proportions of this hôtel, designed by the gifted architect Pierre Bullet, are partly obscured by a high wall enclosing two sides of the forecourt. Likewise, the garden façade can be seen only through the gate located at no. 3, rue de Beauce.

Hôtel de Montmorency

LOCATION: 5, rue de Montmorency
MÉTRO STATION: Rambuteau
PATRON: The Montmorency family;
then, in 1727, Jean Thiraux de Lailly,
who radically modified or completely rebuilt the extant structure
ARCHITECT: Michel Thévenot
(early 18th century)

*Unlike the original hôtel built by the
Montmorency family, the surviving hôtel
features a main block perpendicular to
the street. Additional floors have been
added to the projecting wing parallel
to the street. The hôtel now houses the
Direction and École des Impôts.*

Hôtel d'Hallwyll

LOCATION: 28, rue Michel-le-Comte (blind back
wall: rue de Montmorency, where no. 15 would be)
MÉTRO STATION: Rambuteau
PATRON: Franz-Joseph d'Hallwyll, colonel in the
Swiss Guard
ARCHITECT: Claude-Nicolas Ledoux (1766–67)

*This was the first of Ledoux's Parisian hôtels and
is the only one to survive. It was in large part a
transformation of the old Hôtel de Bouligneux. The
plot was too small for a conventional garden, so
Ledoux lined the rear court with colonnades and
fountains and had an illusionistic mural of columns
and treetops painted on the wall across the rue de
Montmorency.*

*The financier and statesman Jacques Necker
lived here, where his daughter, the future Madame
de Staël, was born in 1766.*

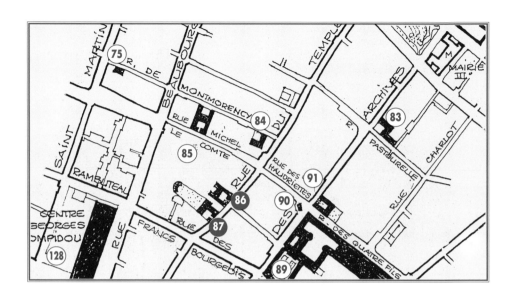

86 Hôtel de Montmort

LOCATION: 79, rue du Temple
MÉTRO STATION: Rambuteau
PATRON: Jean Habert de Montmort (c. 1623); then Laurent Charron, who had the hôtel rebuilt after acquiring it in 1751

One gains access to this magnificent Louis XV hôtel through a large portal on the rue du Temple that, on its interior side, is embellished with a mascaron (a decorative mask) said to be a portrait of Madame Charron. The passage between the first court and the second, formerly the garden, was built in 1840 on the site of the original vestibule. The buildings of this second court date from the same period.

LOCATION: 71, rue du Temple
MÉTRO STATION: Rambuteau
PATRON: Claude de Mesmes, comte d'Avaux
ARCHITECT: Pierre Le Muet (1642–47)

Hôtel d'Avaux ⑧⑦
(Hôtel de Saint-Aignan)

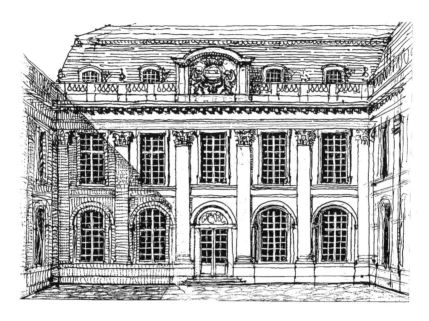

The comte d'Avaux, who died in 1650, did not long reside in the sumptuous hôtel he had just built; it has come to be known by the name of its subsequent occupant, the duc de Saint-Aignan, Colbert's son-in-law, who acquired it in 1688.

A monumental entrance leads to the forecourt, whose southern party wall has blind windows to sustain visual symmetry, a feature often found in Parisian hôtels in this period. The façades facing the court incorporate colossal Corinthian pilasters.

This magnificent building is now being restored. It will soon house the Musée d'Art et d'Histoire du Judaïsme.

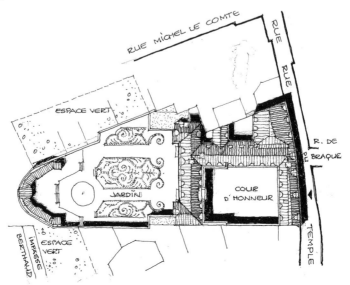

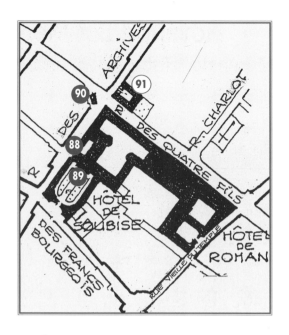

LOCATION: 58, rue des Archives, against the western gable of the Hôtel de Soubise
MÉTRO STATION: Rambuteau
PATRON: The connétable Olivier de Clisson (c. 1375)

This hôtel, built for the constable Olivier de Clisson, became the property of the Guise family in 1556. In 1700, it was acquired by François de Rohan, prince de Soubise, who radically transformed it.

All that survives of the Hôtel de Clisson is the turreted portal integrated into the Hôtel de Soubise by the architect Pierre-Alexis Delamair (see entry 89 opposite).

⁸⁸ Hôtel de Clisson

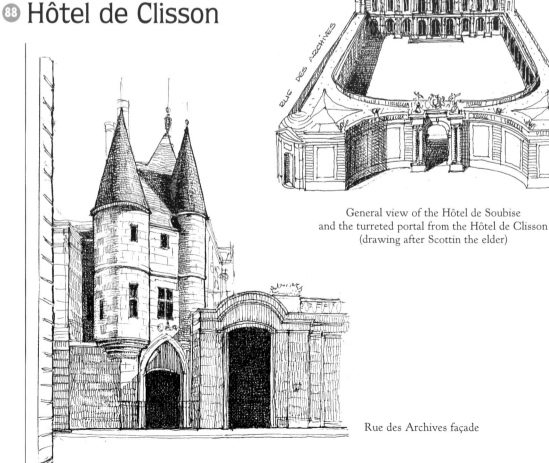

General view of the Hôtel de Soubise and the turreted portal from the Hôtel de Clisson (drawing after Scottin the elder)

Rue des Archives façade

LOCATION: 60, rue des Francs-Bourgeois
MÉTRO STATION: Rambuteau
PATRON: François de Rohan, prince de Soubise
ARCHITECT: Pierre-Alexis Delamair (1705–9)

Hôtel de Soubise 89
(Musée de l'Histoire de France)

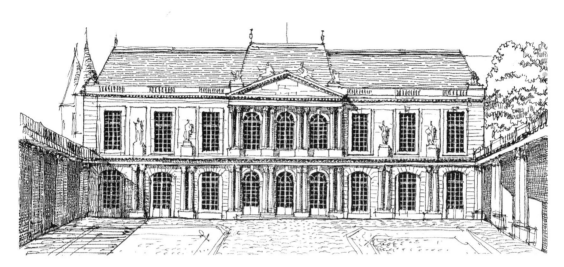

The Hôtel de Soubise was built on the site of the Hôtel de Clisson, but its architect, Pierre Delamair, retained a turreted portal from the earlier building (see entry 88). It is preceded by a large forecourt encompassed by a colonnade, and its gate was recessed from the street to facilitate carriage entry.

The paired columns of the ground floor support sculptures whose originals were by Robert Le Lor-rain, who also carved the statues surmounting the pediment of the frontispiece.

The interiors are the work of Germain Boffrand, the duc de Soubise having lost patience with the intractability of his first architect, Pierre Delamair.

Formerly occupied by the Archives Nationales, this hôtel now houses the Musée de l'Histoire de France.

Fontaine des Haudriettes
90

LOCATION: Corner of rue des Haudriettes
and rue des Archives
MÉTRO STATION: Rambuteau
ARCHITECT: Pierre-Louis Moreau-Desproux,
architect to the city (1764–65)
SCULPTOR: Mignot (naiad)

The building to which this fountain was originally attached has disappeared, and the fountain itself was moved slightly in 1933.

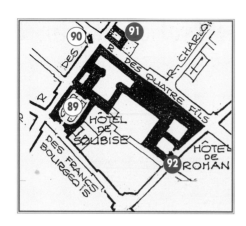

LOCATION: 60, rue des Archives
MÉTRO STATION: Rambuteau
PATRON: Jean-François Guénégaud,
conseiller d'État
ARCHITECT: François Mansart (1652–55)

91 Hôtel de Guénégaud

Garden façade (visible from the rue des Quatre-Fils)

This noble hôtel was designed by François Mansart. It was in a pitiful state when the state acquired it in 1961, leasing it for 99 years to the Société Sommer, which restored it and installed the Musée de la Chasse et de la Nature, devoted to nature and the hunt.

LOCATION: 87, rue Vieille-du-Temple
MÉTRO STATION: Rambuteau
PATRON: Armand-Gaston de Rohan Soubise,
bishop of Strasbourg, then cardinal in 1712
ARCHITECT: Pierre-Alexis Delamair (1705–8)

Hôtel de Rohan

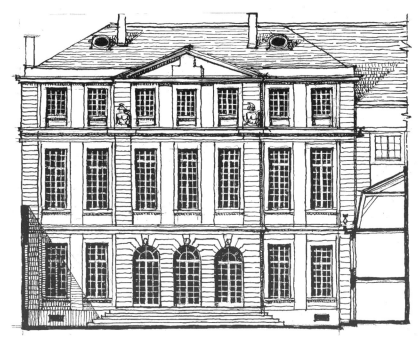

Forecourt façade

The Horses of the Sun by Robert Le Lorrain

While the prince de Soubise was building his hôtel (see entry 89), one of his sons, then bishop of Strasbourg and a future cardinal, erected one for himself nearby.

Three more cardinals from the family occupied it in succession, the last of whom was compromised by the diamond-necklace affair involving Marie-Antoinette (1785).

When he moved the Archives Nationales into the Hôtel de Soubise, Napoléon I established the imperial press in the Hôtel de Rohan. In 1927, this building, too, was ceded to the Archives Nationales.

In a courtyard to the right of the forecourt, above the entrance to the stables, there is a magnificent relief by Robert Le Lorrain representing The Horses of the Sun (see drawing).

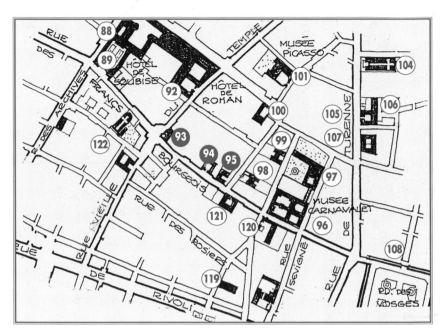

⑨ Hôtel d'Hérouet

LOCATION: 54, rue Vieille-du-Temple
MÉTRO STATION: Rambuteau
PATRONS: Jean Malingre, then Jean Hérouet
(c. 1500–1520)

The present building, heavily restored and almost completely rebuilt after World War II, doubtless has little in common with the original structure except the corner turret. Even so, restoration of this kind is preferable to the outright destruction of hôtels in the Marais, which continued until 1965, when the quarter was designated a protected historical district.

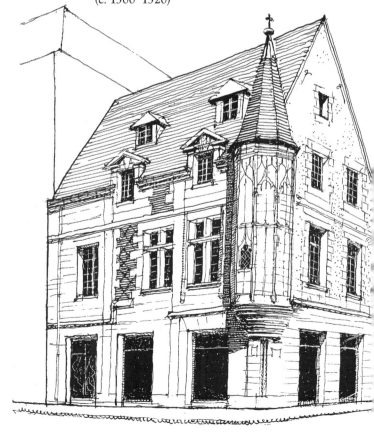

Hôtel d'Alméras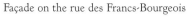

LOCATION: 30, rue des Francs-Bourgeois
MÉTRO STATION: Saint-Paul
PATRON: Pierre d'Alméras
ARCHITECT: Louis Métezeau (1611).
Some authors attribute this building
to Salomon de Brosse.

The Hôtel d'Alméras is an excellent, and rare, Parisian example of brick-and-stone construction. It is contemporary with the Place des Vosges (see entry 108).

The main block is situated between a forecourt and a garden. The street entrance boasts a magnificent Mannerist pediment whose forms, while complex, nonetheless achieve balance.

Street entrance

LOCATION: 26, rue des Francs-Bourgeois
MÉTRO STATION: Saint-Paul
PATRONS: First hôtel (c. 1585): Claude Mortier.
The name Sandreville is that of an owner of its western portion in 1635. Hôtel fronting the street rebuilt by Louis Le Mairat in 1767
ARCHITECTS: Not securely identified, but probably Baptiste Androuet Du Cerceau for the hôtel of c. 1585

Hôtel Mortier
(then Hôtel de Sandreville)

In 1604, on the death of Claude Mortier, the first owner, the hôtel was divided in half by his heirs. In the 19th century, the eastern portion was demolished and replaced by the building now on the corner of the rue des Francs-Bourgeois and the rue Elzévir. In 1767, the western portion fronting the street was replaced by a beautiful Louis XV hôtel. The garden façade of the 1585 hôtel has recently been carefully restored. It is magnificent, although it is only half of the original building.

Façade on the rue des Francs-Bourgeois

⓿ Musée Carnavalet

LOCATION: 23, rue de Sévigné
MÉTRO STATION: Saint-Paul
PATRONS: Jacques de Ligneris (1547–49); then
Madame de Kernevenoy, known as Carnavalet
(work, c. 1572); then Claude Boyslesve or Boislève
(1654–62); finally, the City of Paris (since 1866)
ARCHITECTS: The master mason Nicolas Dupuis
(1547–49), perhaps working from a design by Pierre
Lescot. François Mansart for Claude Boyslesve
(alterations, c. 1660)
SCULPTORS: Studio of Jean Goujon (*Four Seasons*,
on the court façade). Antoine Coysevox (statue of
Louis XIV in the entry court)

Façade on the rue de Sévigné

The Hôtel Carnavalet is the old Hôtel de Ligneris as transformed by François Mansart, c. 1660. The façade on the rue de Sévigné was modified but retained its Renaissance portal. The sculpture of this portal is generally attributed to Pierre Lescot, although the reliefs on the court façade are probably the work of students in his workshop. The center of the forecourt is adorned by a statue of Louis XIV by Coysevox.

When the City of Paris acquired the hôtel in 1866, it built an extension along the rue des Francs-Bourgeois. At the same time, three elements from other buildings were incorporated into the complex (see map opposite): 1) Nazarene Arch from the Palais de Justice; 2) pavilion from the headquarters of the Drapers' Guild (designed by Jacques Bruant, 1655–60; see drawing opposite); 3) pavilion from the Hôtel de Choiseul (or Desmarets), built c. 1710 on the rue Saint-Augustin.

The Hôtel Le Peletier de Saint-Fargeau (see entry 97), which houses some of the museum's collections, can now be reached through the museum.

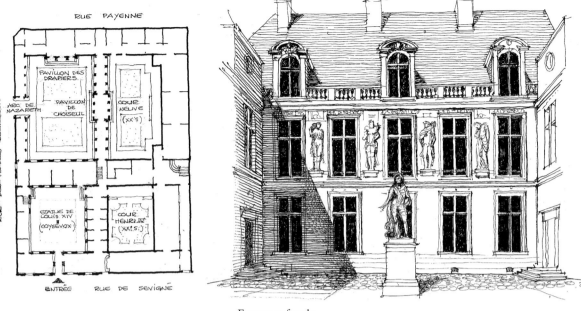

Forecourt façade

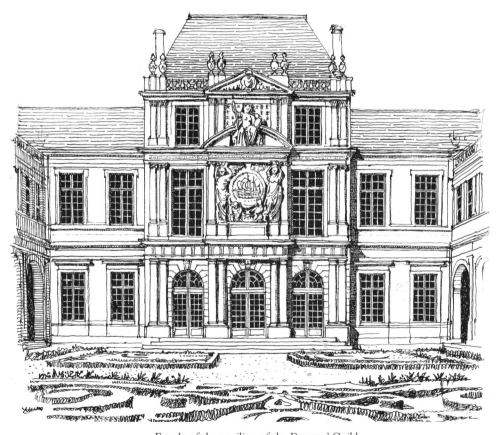

Façade of the pavilion of the Drapers' Guild

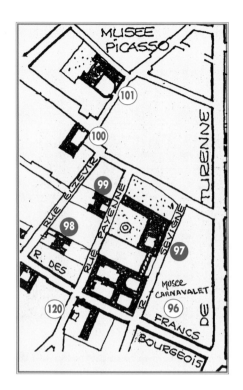

From the Square Georges-Cain, on the rue Payenne, one can see the garden façade of the Hôtel Le Peletier de Saint-Fargeau and its orangery, both designed by Pierre Bullet.

The pediment of the hôtel is decorated with an allegory of Time; that of the orangery, with a personification of Truth.

The hôtel is now an annex of the Musée Carnavalet, which owns the sculpture in the Square Georges-Cain.

Portal, rue du Sévigné

97 Hôtel Le Peletier de Saint-Fargeau

LOCATION: 29, rue de Sévigné
MÉTRO STATION: Saint-Paul
PATRON: Michel Le Peletier, intendant des Finances (1686)
ARCHITECT: Pierre Bullet (1686–90)

Façade on Square Georges-Cain

Hôtel de Donon (Musée Cognac-Jay) 98

LOCATION: 8, rue Elzévir. Garden façade visible from 9, rue Payenne
MÉTRO STATION: Saint-Paul
PATRON: Médéric de Donon, contrôleur général des bâtiments du roi
ARCHITECT: Unidentified; sometimes attributed to Jean Bullant, working in the style of Philibert de l'Orme (construction begun c. 1575)

Garden façade, facing the rue Payenne

After being remodeled, and disfigured, over the years, the hôtel was acquired in 1975 by the City of Paris, which then restored it. Vacant for a decade, in 1986 it was designated the new home of the collections assembled by Ernest Cognacq and his wife, Louise Jay, owners of the Samaritaine department store.

Both façades feature projecting pavilions at either end. On the court side, the arcaded wings and the structure along the rue Elzévir were added in the 17th century.

Hôtel de Marle 99
(Swedish Cultural Center)

LOCATION: 11, rue Payenne and 10, rue Elzévir
MÉTRO STATION: Saint-Paul
PATRON: Hector de Marle, conseiller au Parlement, who in 1572 remodeled and enlarged the extant residence. It was again remodeled c. 1640 by the son of Duret de Chevry.

Garden façade

The restoration of this hôtel by the Swedish government (1969–71) included reconstruction of the sinuous à l'impériale, or "flipped keel," roofs of the main block and lateral pavilions. Also noteworthy is the mascaron (decorative mask) on the keystone of the entry portal.

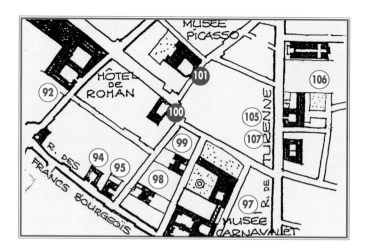

100 Hôtel Libéral-Bruant

LOCATION: 1, rue de la Perle
MÉTRO STATION: Saint-Sébastien-Froissart
PATRON AND ARCHITECT: Libéral Bruant
(1685)

Although he never lived in it, the architect Libéral Bruant, best known for the Hôtel des Invalides and the chapel of the Salpêtrière (see entries 310 and 426), built this house for himself.

Instead of the conventional projecting frontispiece, Bruant opted for a pediment encompassing the entire façade, which creates a strikingly unified design. The detailing is quite refined, with

sculpture playing a prominent role. The round niches contain busts of Roman emperors, while the pediment relief depicts winged putti sitting on cornucopias.

In 1965, the building was acquired by the Société Bricard, which installed the Musée de la Serrure (museum of metalwork and locksmithing) on the premises.

LOCATION: 5, rue Thorigny. Garden façade visible from rue Vieille-du-Temple
MÉTRO STATION: Saint-Sébastien-Froissart
PATRON: Pierre Aubert de Fontenay, fermier des gabelles (salt-tax collector)
ARCHITECT: Jean Boullier de Bourges (1656–59)

Hôtel Salé (Musée Picasso) ⑩

Detail of sphinxes (located at A and B below)

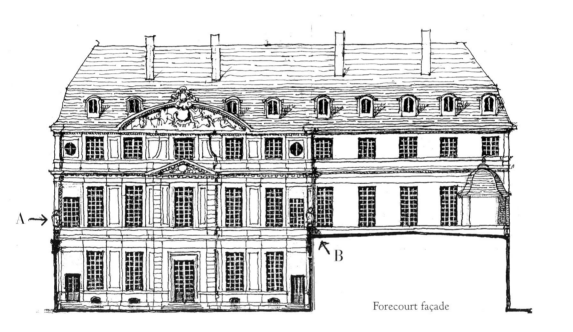

A →

↖ B

Forecourt façade

The first owner of this magnificent hôtel was a salt-tax collector. Doubtless feeling that they had paid for it out of their own pockets, Parisians soon dubbed it the Hôtel Salé ("salted" hôtel). Very likely they rejoiced in 1663, when Aubert de Fontenay's goods were seized after the disgrace of surintendant Fouquet.

Quite large, it is the only surviving Parisian work of a gifted but little-known architect, Jean Boullier de Bourges.

To maintain symmetry, the architect dressed the party wall left of the forecourt with illusionistic blind windows, a practice current at the time.

The building was occupied by the École Centrale des Arts et Manufactures (1829–84) and later by the École des Métiers d'Art (1944–62). It was in terrible condition when entrusted to Roland Simounet, who beginning in 1976 transformed it into the Musée Picasso.

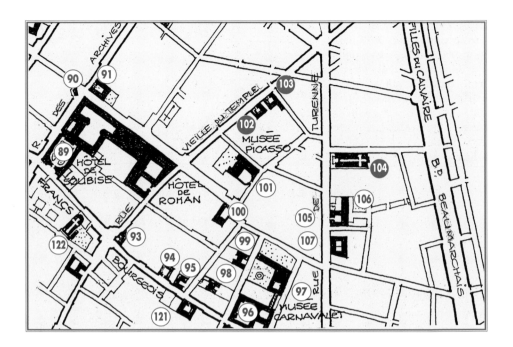

 Hôtel Mégret de Serilly

LOCATION: 106, rue Vieille-du-Temple
MÉTRO STATION: Filles-du-Calvaire
PATRON: Nicolas Malebranche (1620).
The tax farmer Antoine Mégret
de Serilly, whose name the building
bears, acquired it only in 1776.
ARCHITECT: Jean Thiriot (1620–21)

This residence is in the brick-and-stone style favored under Louis XIII. Its garden façade is visible from the court at 13, rue de Thorigny.

The street façade, altered in the late 17th century, boasts a handsome gatehouse surmounted by a pediment decorated with two lions.

Hôtel d'Hozier

LOCATION: 110, rue Vieille-du-Temple
and 9, rue Debelleyme
MÉTRO STATION: Filles-du-Calvaire
PATRON: The architect Jean Thiriot,
who upon completion sold it to
Robert Rousselin. Louis-Pierre
d'Hozier, whose name the building
bears, acquired it in 1735.
ARCHITECT: Jean Thiriot (1623).
Altered by Denis Quirot in 1731

*Though restored, the original brick-and-
stone construction of the court façades,
typical of the Louis XIII style, remains
masked. The magnificent street portal
dates from 1731; its cartouche bears the
old street number of the hôtel.*

*In the 19th century, two floors were
added to the street façade.*

Saint-Denis-du-Saint-Sacrement

LOCATION: 70, rue de Turenne
MÉTRO STATION: Saint-Sébastien-Froissart
ARCHITECT: Étienne-Hippolyte Godde
(1826–35)
SCULPTOR: J.-J. Feuchères
(tympanum)

*Before the Revolution, the site of
this neoclassical basilican church
was occupied by the convent of
the Benedictines of the Holy
Sacrament. The tympanum is
decorated with personifications
of Faith, Hope, and Charity.*

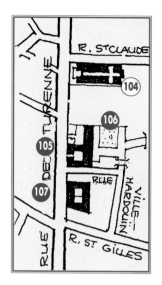

⑩⑤ Hôtel d'Ecquevilly
(Hôtel du Grand Veneur)

LOCATION: 60, rue de Turenne
MÉTRO STATION: Chemin-Vert
PATRON: Madame Martel (1637); then
Claude de Guénégaud (1646); chancelier
Boucherat (1636); and the marquis
d'Ecquevilly (1733)
ARCHITECTS: Michel Villedo (1636), then
Jean-Baptiste Beausire (1733)

Hôtel d'Ecquevilly

Garden façades, visible from

The name Grand Veneur comes from the post occupied by Augustin Hennequin, marquis d'Ecquevilly, who was capitaine général de la vénerie (hunting master) of Louis XV. Many of the hôtel's decorative motifs were inspired by the hunt. Recently restored, the hôtel now houses the offices of the Société Jacob Delafon, which accords free access to the forecourt.

A small garden square on the rue Villehardouin affords a fine view of the garden façades of this hôtel and the Hôtel de Hesse (see entry 106).

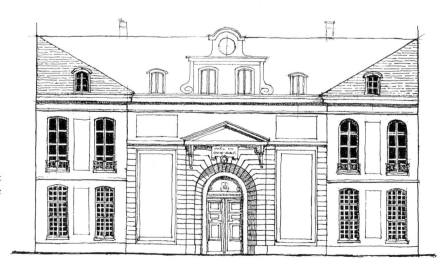

Street
façade

Hôtel de Hesse

LOCATION: 62, rue de Turenne
MÉTRO STATION: Chemin-Vert
PATRONS: Antoine Campreny (c. 1640);
then chancelier Boucherat (1660)
ARCHITECT: Michel Villedo (c. 1640)
The garden façade, the only one readily visible, can be
seen from the Square Saint-Gilles-Grand-Veneur.

*The Hôtel de Hesse and its neigh-
bor, the Hôtel d'Ecquevilly, had
common owners: first chancelier
Boucherat; then, in 1823, Franciscan nuns, who erected the structure
fronting the street that completely
masks the hôtel beyond. The garden
façade (see drawing at left) has just
been restored and forms an impressive ensemble with its neighbor.*

Hôtel de Hesse

are Saint-Gilles-Grand-Veneur

Hôtel de Montrésor

LOCATION: 52–54, rue de Turenne
MÉTRO STATION: Chemin-Vert
PATRON: Claude de Bourdeille,
comte de Montrésor
DEVELOPERS: The entrepreneurs
Villedo and Dublet (1637–54)

Street façade

*This building, probably remodeled c. 1730, was
originally two adjacent hôtels; the comte de Montrésor, who gave his name to the ensemble, occupied
only no. 54. No. 52 retains its original entry and*
*street façade, but the façade of no. 54 was remod-
eled and decorated with a pediment in 1742. The
two hôtels are now owned by the City of Paris and
house two schools.*

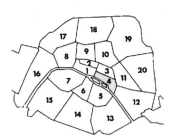

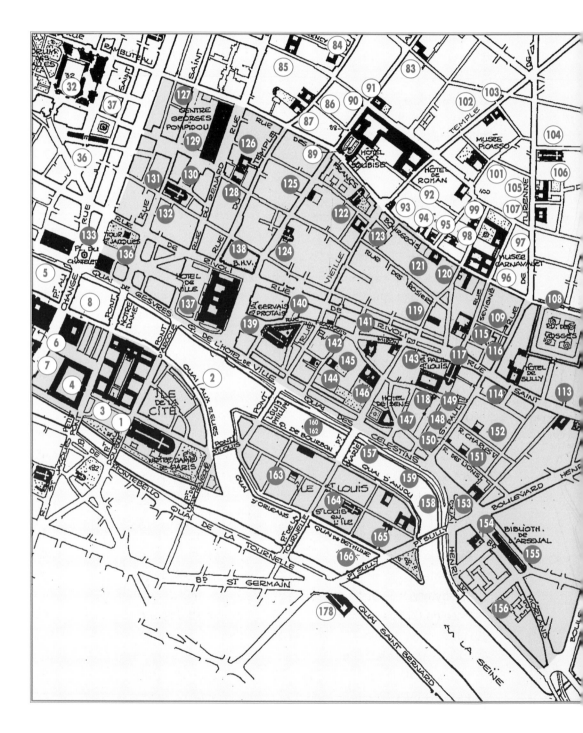

4th Arrondissement

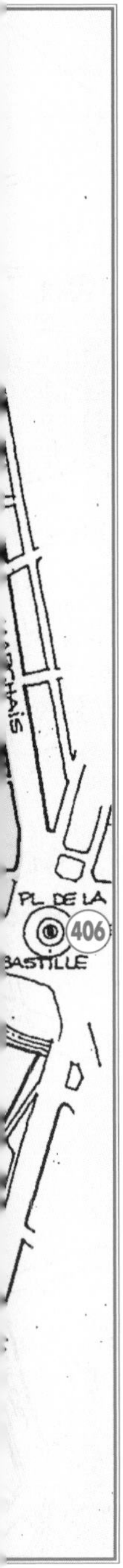

PL DE LA
406
BASTILLE

⑩⑧ Place des Vosges

LOCATION: On the boundary between the 3rd and 4th arrondissements
MÉTRO STATIONS: Saint-Paul; Chemin-Vert
PATRON: Henri IV
ARCHITECT: Probably Louis Métezeau (1605), who designed the uniform façade to be used by all owners
SCULPTORS: Jean-Pierre Cortot and Louis-Marie Dupaty (statue of Louis XIII, 1819)

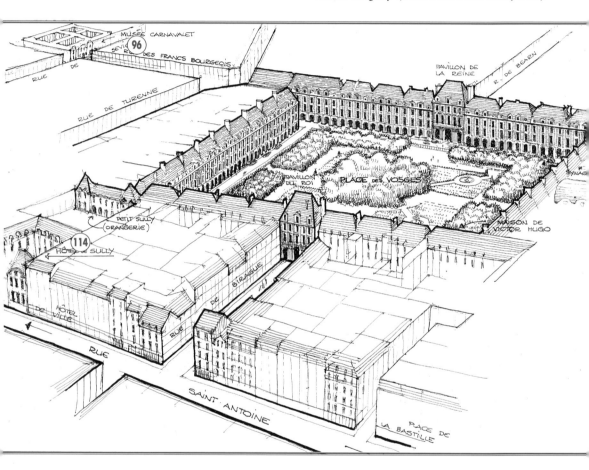

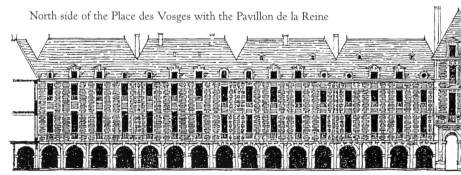

North side of the Place des Vosges with the Pavillon de la Reine

The Pavillon du Roi on the south side of the Place des Vosges

The Place des Vosges was built on the site of the Hôtel des Tournelles, which was abandoned by Catherine de Médicis after her husband, Henri II, was mortally wounded in a jousting tournament there.

It was Henri IV who decided to build a royal square on the site, ceding all the peripheral residences save those on the southern side to private individuals, all of whom had to accept the following stipulations: no parcels could be subdivided; all façades had to adhere to a uniform, brick-and-stone design (probably conceived by Louis Métezeau); and each owner had to allow for a circulation gallery on ground level in accordance with a preconceived model.

These rules were respected, even during the Revolution, when some of the residences became government property.

Note, however, that total uniformity does not reign among the various pavilions, especially regarding their dormer windows. Furthermore, some owners saved money by substituting painted masonry for the brick.

But these differences do not compromise the unified effect produced by the whole, which has miraculously survived intact.

A bronze statue of Louis XIII stood in the center between 1639 and the Revolution, when it was melted down; in 1819, it was replaced by the present stone statue.

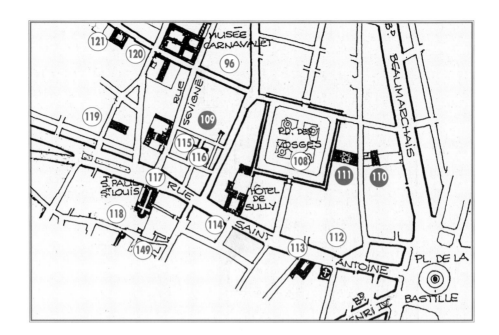

109 Fontaine de Jarente

LOCATION: Impasse (dead end) de la Poissonnerie (formerly in the Marché Sainte-Catherine)
MÉTRO STATION: Saint-Paul
ARCHITECT: Caron (1780s)

This fountain originally served the fish market situated in the present Marché Sainte-Catherine, established in 1784 after subdivision of the plot formerly occupied by the priory of Sainte-Catherine-du-Val-des-Écoliers (see entry 116).

Hôtel Mansart de Sagonne ⑪⓪

LOCATION: 28, rue des Tournelles (garden façade would correspond to 21–23, boulevard Beaumarchais)
MÉTRO STATION: Bastille
PATRON AND ARCHITECT: Jules Hardouin-Mansart (1667–70; enlarged 1687–97)

The street and court façades are quite austere. The garden façade, however, is curiously asymmetrical (with an extra bay at the right; see drawing) and is more animated, featuring a colonnade with paired columns at ground level. It can be glimpsed from 23, boulevard Beaumarchais.

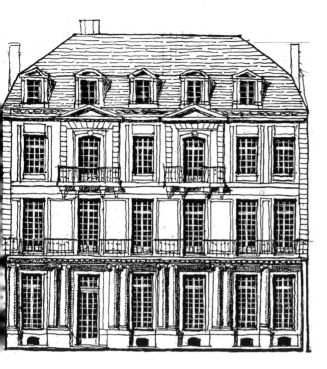

Garden façade

Synagogue on the rue des Tournelles

LOCATION: 21 bis, rue des Tournelles
MÉTRO STATION: Bastille
ARCHITECT: Marcellin Varcollier (1861–63)
METAL ARMATURE: Gustave Eiffel
Burned 1871. Rebuilt 1873

This synagogue occupies a site extending from the rue des Tournelles to the Place des Vosges. Its façade resembles that of the synagogue on the rue de la Victoire (see entry 374). Gustave Eiffel designed the metal frame. The building was certified a national monument in 1987.

⑪⑪

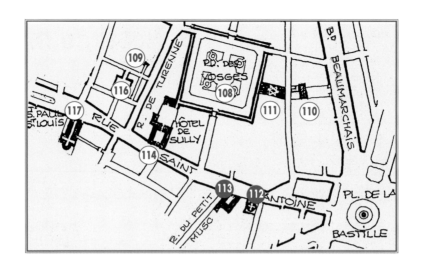

⑫ Temple des Filles-de-la-Visitation-Sainte-Marie

LOCATION: 17, rue Saint-Antoine
MÉTRO STATIONS: Bastille; Saint-Paul
PATRON: Order of the Visitation, founded 1610 and established in Paris 1619
ARCHITECT: François Mansart (1632–34)

The circular plan of this church may have been inspired by that of Santa Maria di Loreto in Rome; it also recalls the chapel of the Château d'Anet by Philibert de l'Orme. In the end, however, it is difficult to classify: an idiosyncratic masterpiece.

One of the first important buildings built by François Mansart, it in many respects anticipates the French classical style. The eight large buttresses supporting its dome originally supported decorative vases, and the annular crypt is supported by a central pillar. Until 1660, Saint Vincent de Paul was father superior at the convent, which was suppressed, with all other religious communities, during the Revolution. Since 1803, the church has been a Protestant sanctuary.

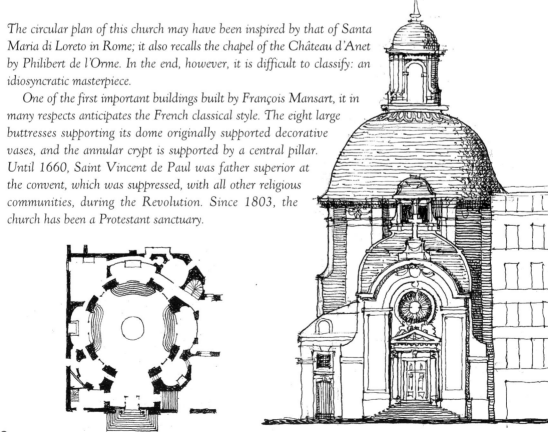

LOCATION: **21, rue Saint-Antoine**
MÉTRO STATIONS: **Bastille; Saint-Paul**
PATRON: **Charles de Lorraine, duc de Mayenne; then his son Henri**
ARCHITECT: **Initial phase of construction overseen by a master mason (1606–9), after which an architect intervened, probably Jacques II Androuet Du Cerceau**

Hôtel de Mayenne

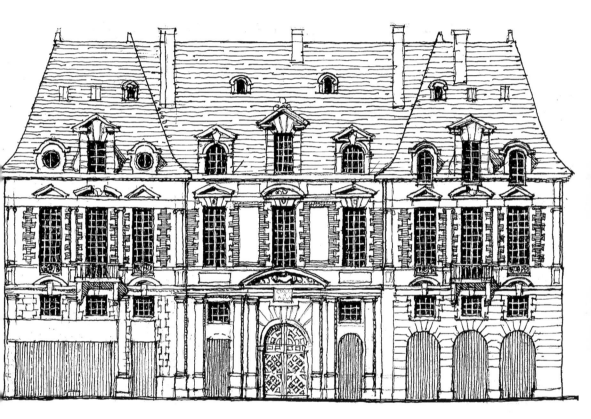

Begun by Charles de Lorraine, duc de Mayenne, the hôtel was transformed in midcourse by his son Henri, apparently in accordance with designs by Jacques II Androuet Du Cerceau.

In 1812, it was sold to the Institution Favart, which remodeled it to accommodate classrooms. It then passed to the Frères des Écoles Chrétiennes, who transformed it into the École des Francs-Bourgeois, which still occupies the building.

This hôtel was one of the first Parisian residences to adopt the between-court-and-garden

configuration that subsequently became the norm. Unfortunately, a later wing between the two entry pavilions now disfigures the original design, as was the case with the nearby Hôtel de Sully before its restoration (see entry 114).

The Hôtel de Mayenne itself is currently undergoing restoration. Perhaps, in addition to revealing its magnificent brick-and-stone construction, the process will result in removal of the offending structure between the forecourt and the street.

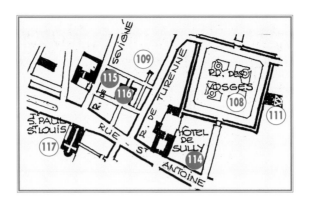

114 Hôtel de Sully

LOCATION: 62, rue Saint-Antoine
MÉTRO STATION: Saint-Paul
PATRON: Mesme Gallet, contrôleur des finances; then, in 1628, Roland de Neufbourg
ARCHITECT: Jean Androuet Du Cerceau (1624–30)

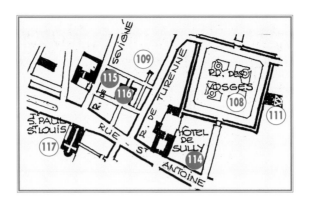

Façade on the Rue Saint-Antoine

This hôtel is named after the duc de Sully, minister of Henri IV, who acquired it in 1634, some years after its completion. He resided here only six years.

The building, U-shaped in plan, consists of a central block and two projecting wings framing an entry court. The two wings, which extend to the street, are linked by a one-story structure. The façades are decorated with allegorical sculpture: on the main block, the Four Seasons (two facing the court, two facing the garden); on the projecting wings, the Four Elements (Air, Fire, Earth, Water; two on each wing).

The building often called the Petit Hôtel Sully (1624), at the rear of the garden, is the former orangery. The building now houses the Caisse Nationale des Monuments Historiques.

LOCATION: 7–9, rue de Sévigné (northern court of the firemen's barracks)
MÉTRO STATION: Saint-Paul
PATRON: Claude Bouthillier, comte de Chavigny, who enlarged and remodeled a residence dating from c. 1580
ARCHITECT: François Mansart (1642–43)

Hôtel Bouthillier de Chavigny

This building is little known due to its location within the precinct of a firemen's barracks. The first court of the complex consists entirely of disfigured buildings, but the second, to the north, boasts admirable façades by François Mansart, built to complete the first hôtel acquired by Claude Bouthillier, of which a single bay survives to the west.

LOCATION: Between rue de Sévigné and rue de Turenne
MÉTRO STATION: Saint-Paul
PATRON: A certain Du Colombier, who acquired the land from the priory of Sainte-Catherine-du-Val-des-Écoliers
ARCHITECTS: Caron, after a plan drawn up in 1783 by Maximilien Brebion, architecte du roi. The marketplace was inaugurated in 1789. Caron also designed the surrounding apartment buildings (1790).

Place du Marché- Sainte-Catherine

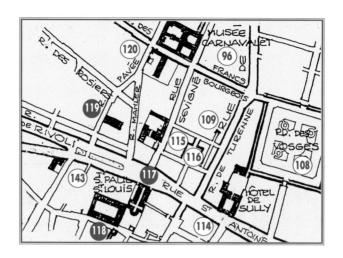

⑰ Saint-Paul–Saint-Louis

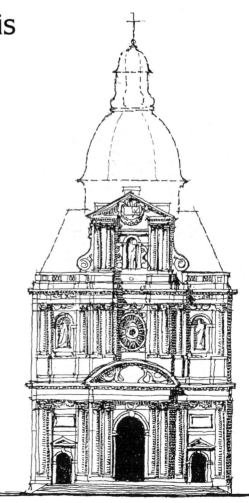

LOCATION: 99, rue Saint-Antoine
MÉTRO STATION: Saint-Paul
PATRONS: The Jesuits, who erected at the
same time the adjacent residence for their
monastery (now the Lycée Charlemagne)
ARCHITECTS: Frère Martellange (plan).
Père Durand (cupola and façade). Frère
Turmel (interior decor)
CONSTRUCTION: 1627–41

*This church, originally dedicated solely to Saint
Louis, was built for the monastery of the Jesuits,
whose Lycée Charlemagne now occupies a
portion of the complex (see entry 118).*

*Its plan was modeled after that of the Gesù
in Rome. The crossing is surmounted by a dome,
but it is less prominent than such elements would
later become in Parisian churches.*

*The façade consists of three levels, two with
the Corinthian order and the third with a
composite order close to Corinthian.*

*The elliptical window on the second level now
contains the clock from the church of Saint-Paul,
demolished in 1797. The present double
dedication, which dates from 1802, likewise
derives from this church.*

Lycée Charlemagne ⓫⓱

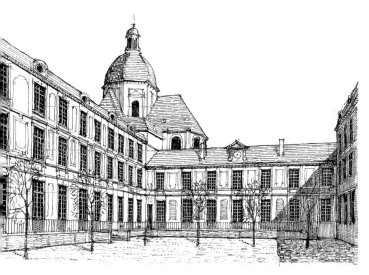

LOCATION: 14, rue Charlemagne
MÉTRO STATION: Saint-Paul
PATRONS: The Jesuits, to house
young monks who had
completed their novitiates
ARCHITECTS: Père Durand
assisted by frère Turmel
CONSTRUCTION: Simultaneous
with that of the church of Saint-
Louis (now Saint-Paul–Saint-
Louis) but completed a few years
later (c. 1647)

In the late 17th century, a monumental staircase was added to the complex, formerly a Jesuit monastery. The cupola is decorated with a fresco by Giovanni Gherardini, The Apotheosis of Saint Louis. In 1802, Napoléon I ceded the buildings to the Lycée Charlemagne.

Synagogue on the rue Pavée

⓫⓲

LOCATION: 10, rue Pavée
MÉTRO STATION: Saint-Paul
PATRONS: A group of Russian and
Polish Jewish emigrants
ARCHITECT: Hector Guimard (1913)

For this synagogue, Hector Guimard, the standard-bearer of Art Nouveau, adopted a relatively restrained idiom. The structure is reinforced concrete. The undulating façade incorporates curves and countercurves whose forms and shadows animate the surface.

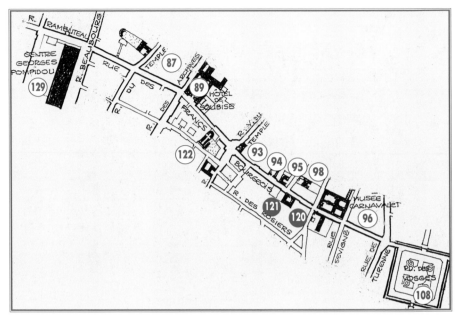

120

Hôtel de Lamoignon

LOCATION: 24, rue Pavée (corner rue des Francs-Bourgeois)
MÉTRO STATION: Saint-Paul
PATRON: Diane de France, duchesse d'Angoulême
ARCHITECT: Not securely identified; perhaps Thibault Métezeau or Baptiste Androuet Du Cerceau (c. 1610)

Turret on the corner of the rue Pavée and the rue des Francs-Bourgeois

The Hôtel de Lamoignon is the former Hôtel d'Angoulême, built by Diane de France, duchesse d'Angoulême, in 1610. It came into the Lamoignon family, whose name it now bears, only in 1688, when it was acquired by Chrétien-François de Lamoignon, president of the Parlement of Paris.

After the death of Diane de France in 1619, the residence was remodeled. About 1624, a wing was added on the left side of the court featuring a picturesque overhanging corner turret whose masonry pendentives are of admirable craftsmanship. Some years later, a right wing was added, but this was demolished in 1834. The entry portal, decorated with two putti, dates from 1718.

In 1928, the building was acquired by the City of Paris, which restored it in the 1960s as a new home for the Bibliothèque Historique de la Ville de Paris.

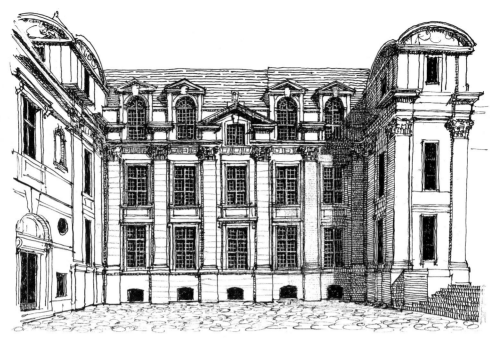

Hôtel de Lamoignon, court façade

Hôtel d'Albret

LOCATION: 31, rue des Francs-Bourgeois
MÉTRO STATION: Saint-Paul
PATRONS: The connétable Montmorency
(1563). Gabriel de Guénégaud (c. 1630),
followed by his son Henri, who left it to his
sister, wife of the maréchal d'Albret. Jean-
Baptiste du Tillet acquired it (1740) and built
the façade on the rue des Francs-Bourgeois.
ARCHITECTS: Unidentified for 16th-century
hôtel. François Mansart is known to have
worked on the building (c. 1640). The street
façade was designed by Jean-Baptiste
Vautrain, who was succeeded by Jean-Baptiste
Courtonne.

*This hôtel boasts a magnificent Louis XV street
façade animated by a discreetly undulating central
balcony. The wrought-iron railings by Hallé are also
extremely handsome, as are the carved doors. In
short, this is an exceptionally refined example of
Rococo design.*

*After repeated disfigurements, the hôtel has now
been restored. Since 1989, it has housed the cultural-
affairs office of the City of Paris.*

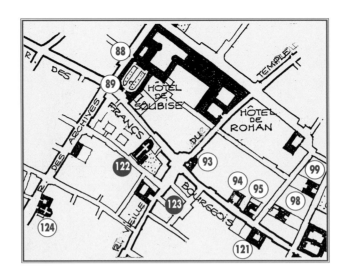

ⓘ Notre-Dame-des-Blancs-Manteaux

LOCATION: 12, rue des Blancs-Manteaux and 53, rue des Francs-Bourgeois
MÉTRO STATION: Rambuteau
PATRONS: Benedictine monks of Saint-Maur
ARCHITECT: Charles Duval (1685–90)

The façade was first erected for the Barnabite church on the Île de la Cité, but in 1863, when that building was demolished, Victor Baltard had it rebuilt here. It is the work of Sylvain Courtaud and dates from 1703. The name Blancs-Manteaux (white mantles) comes from the white robes worn by the monks in this convent before their order was suppressed. It was subsequently occupied by the brothers of Saint-Guillaume, or Guillemites, then by the Benedictines. It is the latter who built the present church at the end of the 17th century.

LOCATION: 47, rue Vieille-du-Temple
MÉTRO STATION: Rambuteau
PATRON: Jean-Baptiste Amelot de
Bisseuil
ARCHITECT: Pierre Cottard (1657–60)
SCULPTOR: Thomas Regnaudin
(portal)

Hôtel Amelot de Bisseuil (123)
(Hôtel des Ambassadeurs de Hollande)

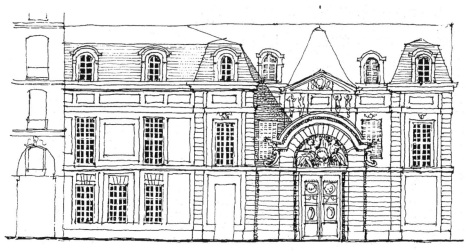

Façade on the rue Vieille-du-Temple

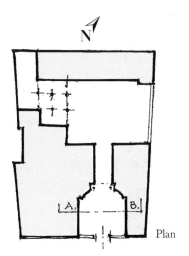

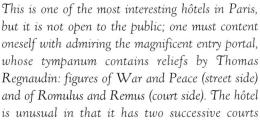

Plan

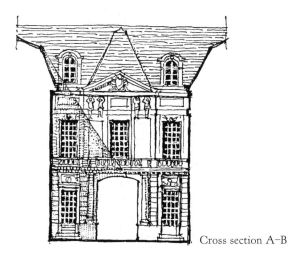

Cross section A–B

This is one of the most interesting hôtels in Paris, but it is not open to the public; one must content oneself with admiring the magnificent entry portal, whose tympanum contains reliefs by Thomas Regnaudin: figures of War and Peace (street side) and of Romulus and Remus (court side). The hôtel is unusual in that it has two successive courts (see plan). Contrary to expectation, it is the rear court that is the more richly appointed, featuring illusionistic decor and niches containing statues. Playwright Pierre-Augustin Beaumarchais resided here while he was completing The Marriage of Figaro.

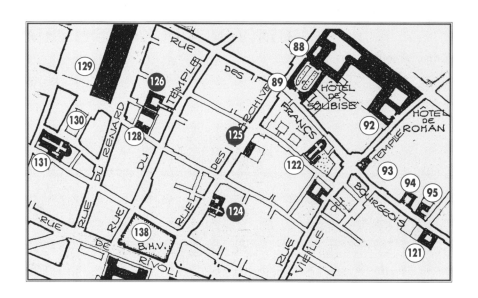

Couvent des Billettes

LOCATION: 24, rue des Archives
MÉTRO STATION: Hôtel-de-Ville
PATRONS: From 1299 to 1631, the brothers of La-Charité-Notre-Dame, nicknamed Les Billettes (the cloister is from this period, dating from 1427). Beginning in 1631, the Carmelites (who commissioned the present church, which dates from 1758)
ARCHITECT: The Dominican frère Claude ((present church, 1755–58)

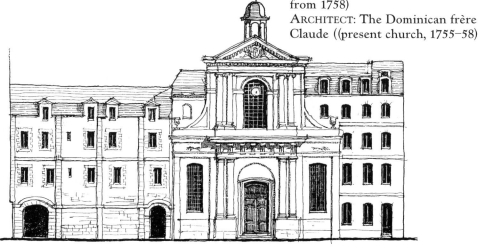

According to legend, a communion wafer profaned here in the 13th century began to bleed, an event that led to construction of an expiatory chapel. Shortly thereafter, a convent of Brothers of Charity was established on the site, where a new church *(1408; destroyed) and a cloister (1427) were built. The latter survives, although much altered and disfigured by additional stories. The present church, built by the Carmelites in 1758, became a Protestant sanctuary in 1812.*

House of Jacques-Coeur (?)

LOCATION: 38–42, rue des Archives
MÉTRO STATION: Hôtel-de-Ville
PATRON: Perhaps Jacques Coeur or his son Geoffroy (late 15th century)

This house is among the oldest brick-and-stone buildings in Paris. We know that at one time it belonged to the granddaughter of Jacques Coeur, the silversmith of Charles VII, but there is no proof that he himself ever owned it. It now houses a day-care center.

Hôtel de Berlize
(Former Auberge de l'Aigle d'Or)

LOCATION: 41, rue du Temple, at rear of courtyard
MÉTRO STATION: Rambuteau
PATRONS: Guichard Faure (early 17th century); then Nicolas Faure, sieur de Berlize, who enlarged it (1640)

The main block and left wing date from the early 17th century. The right wing, erected later, disfigures the design. The original entrance was on rue Pierre-le-Lardon; in 1640 the garden was transformed into a forecourt for a new portal opened onto the rue du Temple. Part of the hôtel is currently occupied by the Café de la Gare.

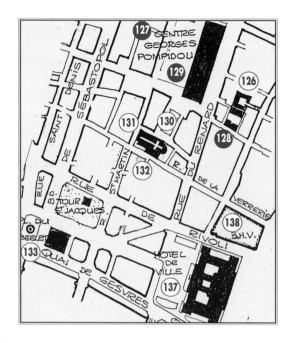

Fontaine Maubuée

LOCATION: In front of the Centre Beaubourg
MÉTRO STATION: Rambuteau

This fountain, which dates from 1734, was formerly at the corner of the rue Maubuée (no longer extant) and the rue Saint-Martin. Dismantled in 1934, it was rebuilt on its present site in the 1970s.

 Hôtel Le Rebours

Location: 12, rue Saint-Merri
MÉTRO STATION: Rambuteau
PATRONS: Jean Aubery (1624); then Thierry Le Rebours (1695), who remodeled the block fronting the street
Architect: Claude Monnard (1624)

Façade on the rue Saint-Merri

This magnificent hôtel, recently restored and now home to the Galerie Maeght, consists of a block *fronting the street with an 18th-century façade and three Louis XIII blocks around the courtyard.*

LOCATION: Place Georges-
Pompidou
MÉTRO STATION: Rambuteau
ARCHITECTS: Renzo Piano and
Richard Rogers (1971)

Centre Georges-Pompidou 129
(Centre Beaubourg)

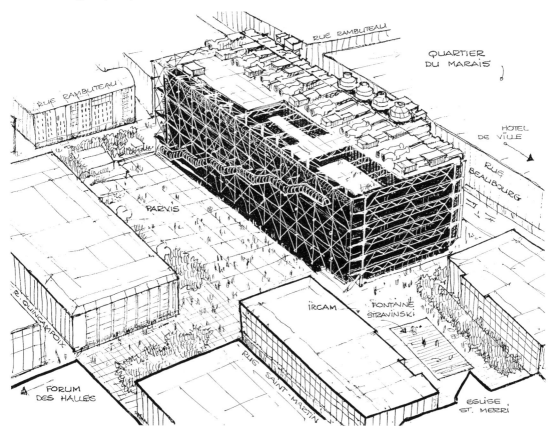

In 1971, an international competition was held for the design of the Centre National d'Art et de Culture Georges-Pompidou. It was won by a team consisting of the Italian Renzo Piano and the Englishman Richard Rogers.

Their design is notable for several reasons. First, despite the limited area of the plot, they set aside almost half of it for a square, a decision whose intelligence has become increasingly apparent with the passage of time. Second, they used a metal armature that rendered interior support unnecessary. And third, they displaced almost all mechanical systems (escalators, elevators, ductwork, and so on)

to the exterior. Thus placed, the escalators animate the western façade and afford visitors spectacular views of Paris that become more commanding as one ascends. The presence of the brightly colored pipes and ductwork on the façade, however, has occasioned criticism.

The building houses the Musée National d'Art Moderne (interiors by Gae Aulenti); a public library; and the Centre de Création Industrielle (CCI). An annex south of the square houses the Institut de Recherche et de Coordination Acoustique-Musique, known as IRCAM.

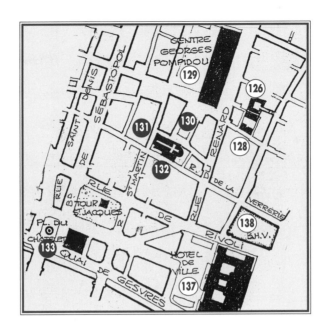

⑬⓪ Fontaine Igor-Stravinski

LOCATION: Place Igor-Stravinski (between the Centre Georges-Pompidou and the church of Saint-Merri)
MÉTRO STATION: Rambuteau
DESIGNERS: Jean Tinguely and Niki de Saint-Phalle (1983)

This project is an exemplary collaboration between two artists, with one providing movement (Jean Tinguely) and the other color (Niki de Saint-Phalle). The fountain was conceived as a playful homage to the composer Igor Stravinsky.

LOCATION: 78, rue Saint-Martin
MÉTRO STATION: Hôtel-de-Ville
ARCHITECTS: Martin Chambiges
(attributed; nave and transept, 1515–26).
Pierre Anglart (choir, completed 1552).
Germain Boffrand and Pierre-Louis
Richard (Communion Chapel, 1743)

Saint-Merri

The present church, which replaced one
dating from the 13th century, is a
restrained example of the Flamboyant
Gothic style. In the 18th century, the
choir was remodeled, its lancet arches
replaced by round ones with marble
revetment. At the same time, Germain
Boffrand drew up plans for
the Communion Chapel adjacent
to the southern side aisle; its interior
decoration was entrusted to the Slodtz
brothers. The third story of the bell
tower was demolished in 1833 after
it was damaged in a fire.

Presbytery of Saint-Merri

LOCATION: 76, rue de la Verrerie
MÉTRO STATION: Hôtel-de-Ville
ARCHITECT: Jean-François
Blondel (1732), not related
to François Blondel, designer
of the Porte Saint-Denis

The entrance to the presbytery, whose exterior is very refined,
also gives access to the transept of the church.

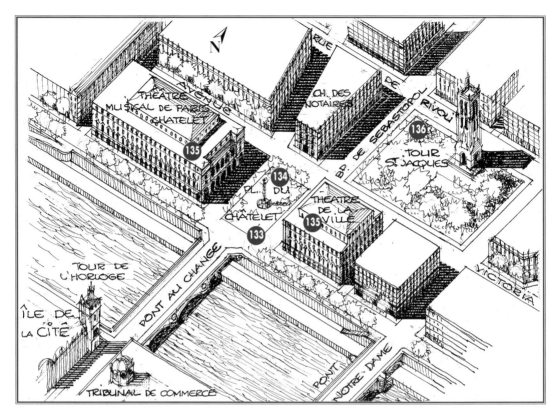

⑬ Place du Châtelet

MÉTRO STATION: Châtelet

This square is named after a small stronghold built in 1130 to defend the Grand Pont (the current Pont au Change). The stronghold was demolished in 1802; a square took its place and was enlarged between 1851 and 1856, when the rue de Rivoli was extended and the boulevard Sébastopol was pierced.

⑭ Fontaine du Palmier

LOCATION: Place du Châtelet
MÉTRO STATION: Châtelet

This fountain was commissioned in 1807 by Napoléon I to decorate the new square created by demolition of the Châtelet. After the square was enlarged, the fountain was shifted on rails and placed on a higher base decorated with sphinxes (1860–62).

Théâtre du Châtelet and Théâtre de la Ville 135

LOCATION: Place du Châtelet
MÉTRO STATION: Châtelet

After the square had been enlarged, Baron Haussmann commissioned the architect Gabriel Davioud to design two theaters situated symmetrically, one to the east and the other to the west (1860–62).

Although quite different in size, the two theaters have façades that are practically identical, unaltered despite extensive remodeling of the interiors.

The Fontaine du Palmier and the Théâtre du Châtelet

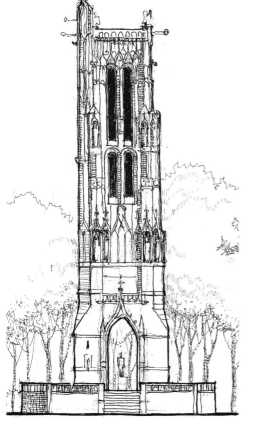

Tour Saint-Jacques 136

LOCATION: Square Saint-Jacques
MÉTRO STATION: Châtelet
PATRON: The parish of Saint-Jacques de la Boucherie (1509–23)
Church demolished in 1797

This was the bell tower of the old church of Saint-Jacques de la Boucherie, demolished in 1797. The church was built in the early 16th century in the Flamboyant Gothic style, at a time when the Renaissance was beginning to exercise its influence in France in civil architecture. In front of the tower is a statue of Blaise Pascal, which commemorates the experiments in atmospheric pressure that he carried out here in 1648.

137 Hôtel de Ville

LOCATION: Place de l'Hôtel-de-Ville
MÉTRO STATION: Hôtel-de-Ville
PATRONS: Provost of the Guilds and François I (1533)
ARCHITECTS: Domenico da Cortona, known as Le Boccador (original building, 1533). Étienne-Hippolyte Godde and J.-B. Ciceron Lesueur (additions, 1837). Théodore Ballu and Édouard Deperthes (present building, 1873)

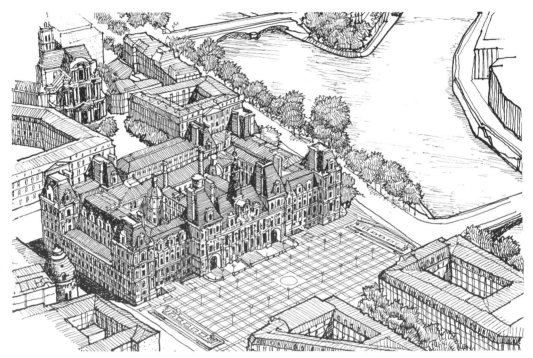

The Place de l'Hôtel-de-Ville, known as the Place de Grève until 1830, was one of the most popular gathering places of medieval Paris. It was the site of many celebrations, but condemned criminals were executed there as well. Before the Hôtel de Ville (city hall) was constructed on this site, the municipal government was installed in 1357 in the Maison aux Piliers, which had just been acquired by Étienne Marcel, then provost of the guilds.

In 1533, François I began construction of a new building, designed by Domenico da Cortona. Work on the new building was interrupted in 1551, and it was not completed until 1628.

In 1837, it was enlarged by the architects Godde and Lesueur, who added a wing and a pavilion at either end. They also enlarged the building to the east, on ground cleared by the demolition of the church of Saint-Jean-de-Grève during the First

Empire. After Louis-Philippe was overthrown in 1848, a provisional government was installed in the Hôtel de Ville, where a republic was proclaimed (February 25, 1848). Following the disastrous defeat at Sedan in 1870, Louis-Napoléon, who had had himself declared emperor in 1852, was in turn deposed, and another republic was proclaimed (September 4, 1870).

On March 18, 1871, Paris was surrendered to Germany in the Franco-Prussian War; riots followed, and the insurgents installed themselves in the Hôtel de Ville, where a commune was declared on March 28. Its supporters burned the building before abandoning it, in May. Between 1873 and 1882, the Hôtel de Ville was rebuilt, almost identically, by the architects Ballu and Deperthes, winners of a competition organized by the city government.

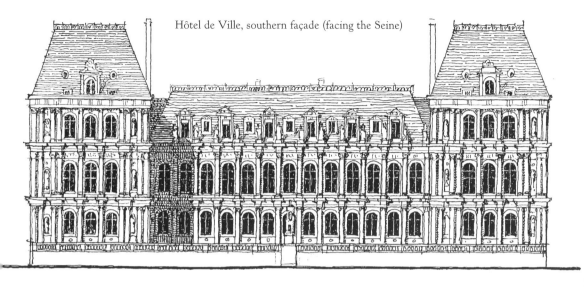

Hôtel de Ville, southern façade (facing the Seine)

Bazar de l'Hôtel de Ville (138)

LOCATION: Principal entrances
52–64, rue de Rivoli. The store
also fronts the rue du Temple,
rue de la Verrerie, and rue des
Archives
MÉTRO STATION: Hôtel-de-Ville
PATRON: Xavier Ruel, who
opened the first store on the
site in 1856
ARCHITECTS: Granon and
Roger (first phase, 1902–4).
Auguste Roy (second phase,
1912–13)

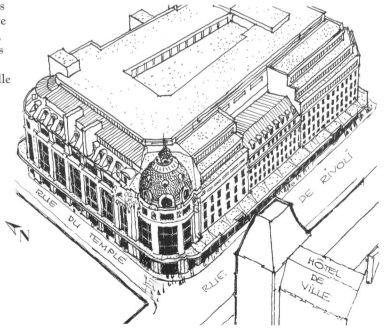

Most of the present complex postdates the death of
Xavier Ruel (1900), who initially named his store
Bazar Napoléon. The rotunda at the corner of the
rue de Rivoli and the rue du Temple has become a
kind of emblem of the store. Despite appearances, it
is made entirely of metal.

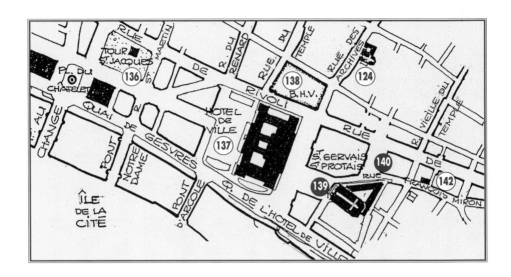

Saint-Gervais–Saint-Protais

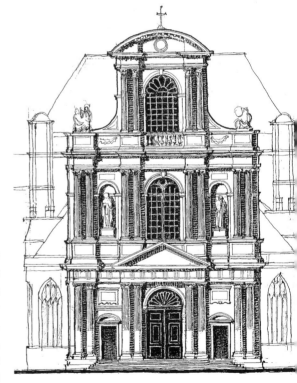

LOCATION: Place Saint-Gervais
MÉTRO STATION: Hôtel-de-Ville
ARCHITECTS: Unidentified for the first building. Façade by Salomon de Brosse (design). Clément Métezeau and Claude Monnard (construction). The base of the tower is from the earlier church of 1420. The present structure was built in stages between 1494 and 1620.

In medieval times, a solitary elm planted in a public place marked it as a site of assembly where justice could be rendered on certain occasions. An elm was planted in front of the church of Saint-Gervais–Saint-Protais as a reminder of this custom.

This church is in the Flamboyant Gothic style, but its façade, built a century after work on the church was begun, is in the classical style. Its three superimposed orders (Doric, Ionic, Corinthian), a "first" in Paris, were much imitated. The façade is modest in size, less wide than the nave, and the architect therefore designed a curving bay on each side to effect a visual transition to the side aisles.

Tragically, in modern times the church is most famous for having been hit, during mass on Good Friday in 1918, by a German shell that claimed 160 victims.

Rue François-Miron, (140) nos. 4–12

MÉTRO STATION: Saint-Paul
PATRON: Vestry of the church of
Saint-Gervais
ARCHITECT: Jacques Vinage (1733).
Saved thanks to a preservation
campaign mounted by Albert
Laprade (1943–45). Subsequent
efforts also preserved the house at
14, rue François-Miron, and 17,
rue des Barres, built by Jacques V
Gabriel (father of Jacques-Ange
Gabriel) for the lawyer Camuset
in 1735.

PLACE
SAINT-
GERVAIS

N°14   N°12   N°2

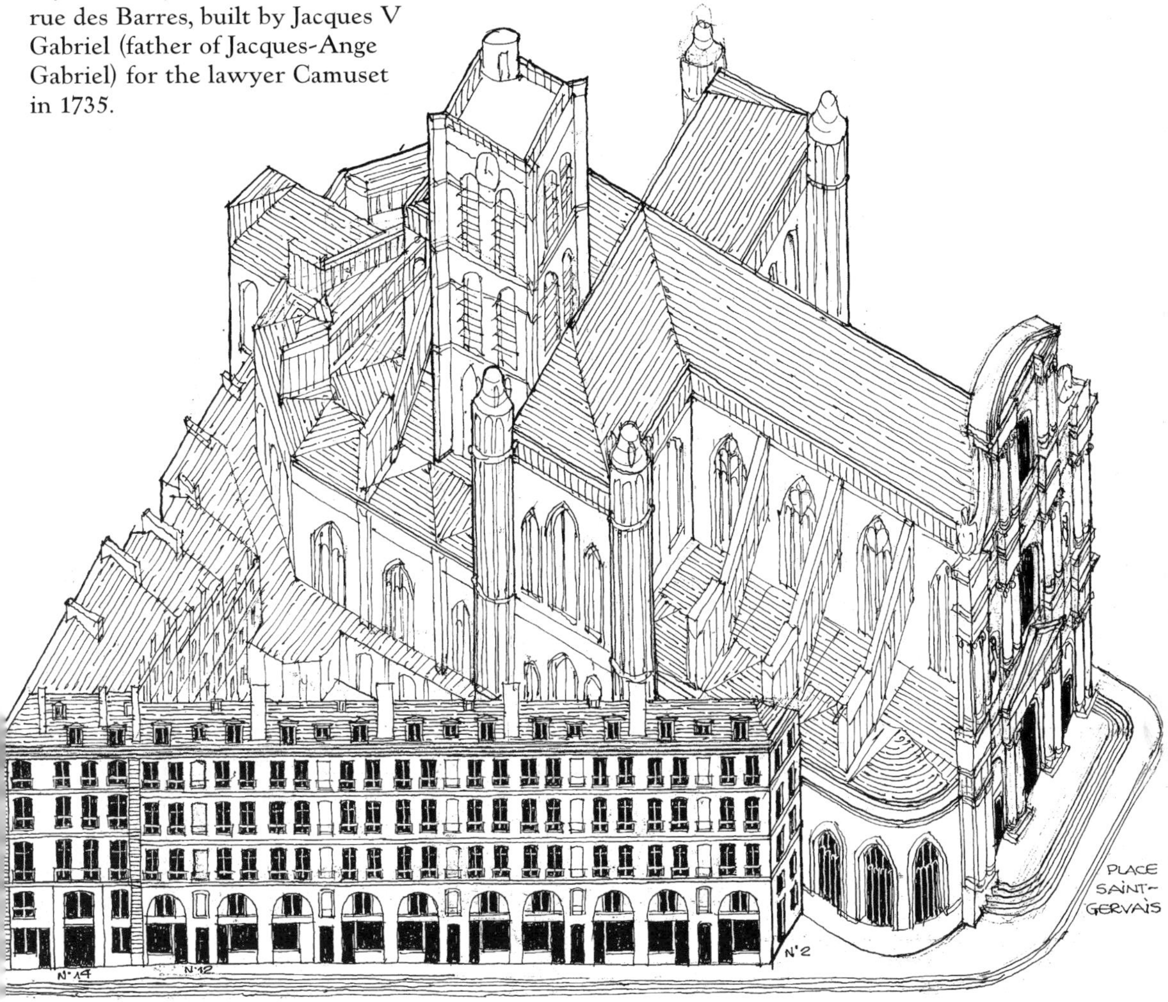

We owe the conservation and subsequent restoration of this group of apartment buildings to the architect Albert Laprade, who opposed the city's decision, taken in 1939, to demolish them. The buildings originally bordered a small cemetery adjacent to the church, the source of odors about which tenants complained.

Note the elm motif on the ironwork of the balconies.

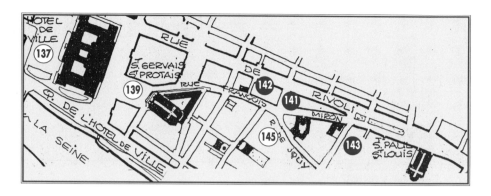

⑭ Hôtel de Beauvais

LOCATION: 68, rue François-Miron
MÉTRO STATION: Saint-Paul
PATRONS: Catherine Bellier, first
chambermaid of Anne of Austria, and
her husband, Pierre de Beauvais
ARCHITECT: Antoine Le Pautre (1655–60)

Courtyard

Present façade

This residence, long abandoned, is presently undergoing restoration.

There is consensus that the architect, Antoine Le Pautre, displayed great originality in his handling of the site, which was small and awkwardly shaped.

The residence has two more claims to fame: its balcony was the perch from which the queen mother watched the solemn entry into Paris of Louis XIV and his wife, Marie-Thérèse (August 26, 1660); and Mozart stayed here for several months when he was seven years old.

Rue François-Miron, 142 nos. 11 and 13

MÉTRO STATION: Saint-Paul
DATE: 15th century (?)
RESTORATION: 1967

In the course of restoration, the timber framing of these houses was uncovered—or perhaps added.

It must be recalled that regulations in force at the time of construction stipulated that all such framing be covered with plaster to minimize the risk of fire, to which such buildings were otherwise prone.

These two houses have gables facing the street, a disposition that was prohibited in the early 16th century.

Very few timber-frame houses with such gables survive in Paris.

LOCATION: 82, rue François-Miron, and 7, rue de Fourcy
MÉTRO STATION: Saint-Paul
PATRONS: François Hénault de Cantobre (c. 1706)
REDESIGN: Competition (1990) organized by the City of Paris for redesign of the building as the Maison Européenne de la Photographie; won by Yves Lion (construction, 1993–95)

Hôtel Hénault de 143 Cantobre
(Maison Européenne de la Photographie)

This hôtel, which boasts a magnificent balcony on the rue François-Miron, has been restored and provided with a modern addition to accommodate the Maison Européenne de la Photographie.

The architect's solution to the difficult problem of adding a contemporary extension to a certified historical monument is a complete success, notably due to his placement of the new façades on the garden and his use of simple volumes for the visible additions.

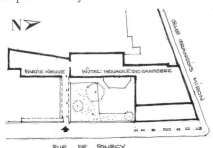

Façade on the rue
François-Miron

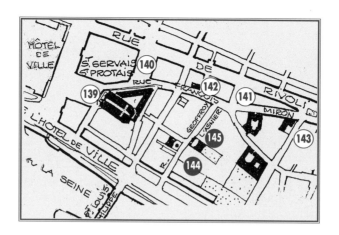

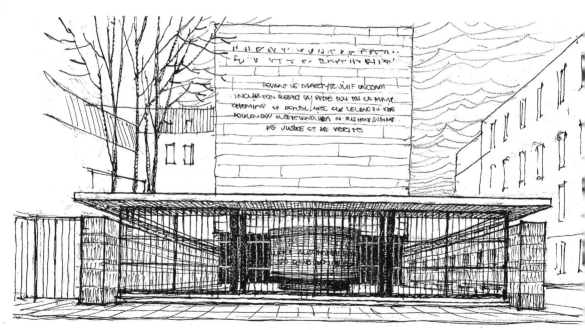

⑭ Memorial to the Unknown Jewish Martyr

LOCATION: 17, rue Geoffroy-l'Asnier
MÉTRO STATION: Pont-Marie
FINANCING: International contributions
ARCHITECTS: Georges Golberg,
Alexandre Persitz, Louis Arretche (195...

The grille separating the memorial from the street is intended to symbolize the world of the concentration camp. In the square beyond is a heavy bronze cylinder engraved with the names of the most infamous death camps set up by the Nazis during World War II.

At the rear of the square is an imposing masonry block carved with inscriptions in French and Hebrew, with the Star of David in relief on its sides. A crypt houses the tomb of the unknown Jewish martyr, marked by a black marble Star of David. The effect produced is one of great dignity.

LOCATION: 26, rue Geoffroy-l'Asnier
MÉTRO STATION: Pont-Marie
PATRON: Guillaume Perrochel, treasurer
of France (c. 1625). Sold to Marie Amelot
de Béon-Luxembourg (1659)

Hôtel de 145 Châlon-Luxembourg

This residence consists of two parallel blocks, each with a hipped roof to keep the roofs low (broken roofs made their appearance later). It was built of brick and stone, but the masonry detailing is more refined than that found in the earlier Place des Vosges. There is a magnificent portal on the rue Geoffroy-l'Asnier that bears the date 1659.

The building now houses the Institut d'Histoire de Paris.

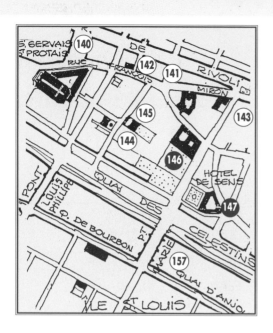

⑭⑥ Hôtel d'Aumont

LOCATION: 7, rue de Jouy. Southern façade visible from the rue des Nonnais-d'Hyères and from Square Albert-Schweitzer
MÉTRO STATION: Pont-Marie
PATRON: Michel-Antoine Scarron (c. 1630–50); then his son-in-law, the duc d'Aumont (1656)
ARCHITECTS: Michel Villedo (1649–50); then François Mansart (?) and Louis Le Vau (decoration). Georges Maurissart (extension, 1703)

Garden façade (facing the Seine)

Detail of the garden façade

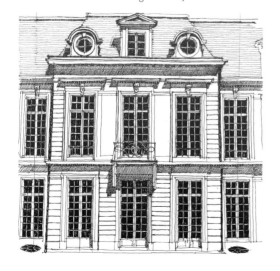

As a result of work carried out in the quarter after World War II, the garden façade of this hôtel is now open to the Seine. The present elevation bears only the slightest resemblance to the building's original appearance: in 1703, a six-bay extension with a second projecting frontispiece was added to the east; in 1957, when the City of Paris "restored" the building, another extension was added and the masonry detailing throughout was radically simplified. A better idea of the initial design is provided by the forecourt façade (entrance at 7, rue de Jouy), but the building is now occupied by the city's Tribunal Administratif and access is difficult.

LOCATION: 1, rue du Figuier
MÉTRO STATION: Pont-Marie
PATRON: Tristan de Salazar, archbishop
of Sens (beginning in 1475)
ARCHITECT: Perhaps Martin Chambiges
(construction begun 1498)

Hôtel de Sens

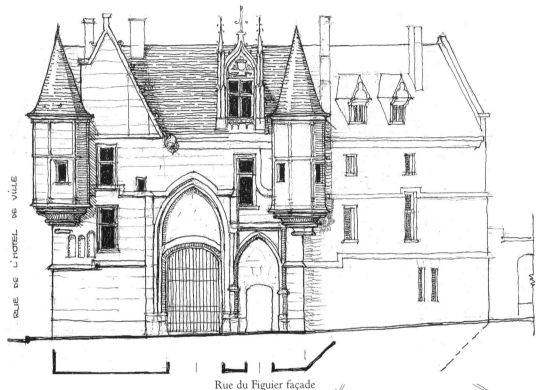

Rue du Figuier façade

The Hôtel de Sens was built for the archbishops of
Sens, to whom the bishops of Paris were
subservient until 1623. Beginning in the 17th
century, the building had various tenants and its
condition declined due to neglect.

In 1911, it was acquired by the City of Paris,
which began to restore it in 1936. By that time,
little remained of the original structure, and many
portions of it were reconstituted, some more
accurately than others.

Even so, the Hôtel de Sens is, with the Hôtel de
Cluny, one of only two important civil buildings
from medieval times to survive in Paris. It now
houses the Bibliothèque Forney, devoted to the
decorative arts and to the crafts.

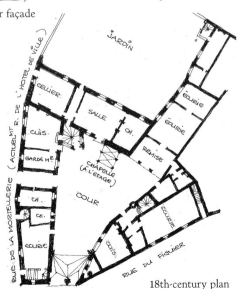

18th-century plan

148 Remains of the Wall of Philippe Auguste

LOCATION: Annex of the Lycée Charlemagne, rue des Jardins-Saint-Paul
MÉTRO STATION: Saint-Paul
PATRON: Philippe Auguste (1190)

As its name indicates, this wall was erected at the behest of King Philippe Auguste, who ordered its construction in 1190, before departing on the Crusades, to assure protection of the city during his absence.

The walls themselves are almost 33 feet high and 3 feet thick at the base. The defensive complex also included seventy towers, some of which protected gates to the city. At the Seine, defense was assured, downstream, by the fortress of the Louvre and the Tour de Nesles, and upstream, by chain barriers at the level of the Île Notre-Dame (now the Île Saint-Louis).

From the rue des Jardins-Saint-Paul one can see the remains of two towers now situated within the annex to the Lycée Charlemagne (see drawing below). With the remnants situated at 3–5, rue Clovis in the 5th arrondissement (see entry 205), this is one of the largest surviving portions of the wall.

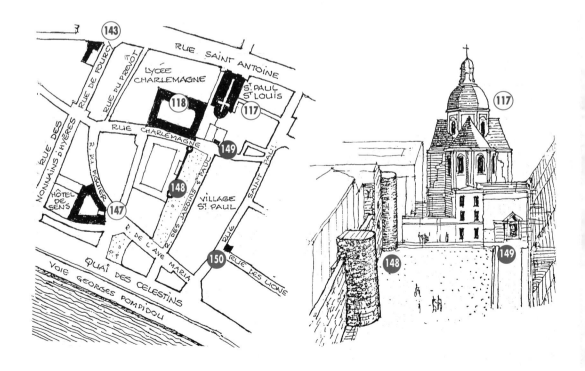

LOCATION: 8, rue Charlemagne, behind the
church of Saint-Paul–Saint-Louis
MÉTRO STATION: Saint-Paul
DATE: 1840

*This charming fountain, the work of an unknown
designer, provided the neighborhood with water
from the Ourcq Canal.*

Fontaine Charlemagne

Watchtower, 150 rue Saint-Paul

LOCATION: Corner of 8, rue Saint-Paul,
and 18, rue des Lions
MÉTRO STATION: Saint-Paul

*The watchtower situated at the corner of
these two streets dates from the late 16th or
early 17th century. By contrast, the façades
from which it projects were recast about a
century later.*

*Few such watchtowers survive in Paris. For
others in this book, see the following: Hôtel
d'Hérouet (entry 93); Hôtel de Lamoignon
(entry 120); 21, rue Hautefeuille (entry 251);
Hôtel des Abbés de Fécamp (entry 252).*

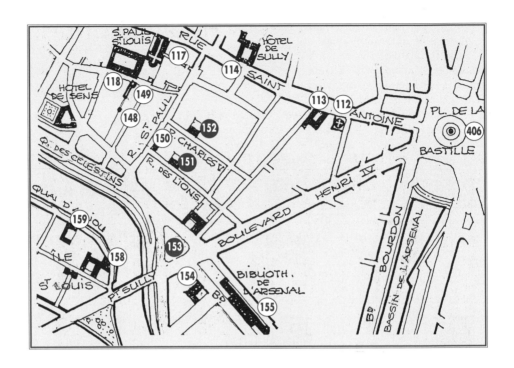

151 Rue des Lions, no. 12

MÉTRO STATION: Sully-Morland
PATRON: Daniel de Launay; then
conseiller Jacques Magdeleine
DATE: Early 17th century

This hôtel, with its broken-base pediments,
rounded on the main floor and triangular
above, is in characteristic Henri IV style. The
building has recently been restored.

Hôtel de Brinvilliers 152

LOCATION: 12, rue Charles-V
MÉTRO STATION: Saint-Paul
PATRONS: Balthazar Gobelin (c. 1629); then his
son Antoine, marquis de Brinvilliers (whose
wife was the notorious poisoner decapitated
and burned in the Place de Grève in 1676).
The portal bears the date 1709 and thus postdates the hôtel.

Hôtel Fieubet 153
(École Massillon)

LOCATION: 2, quai des Célestins
MÉTRO STATION: Sully-Morland
PATRON: Extant hôtel remodeled by Gaspard
de Fieubet (1676). Subsequent alterations
undertaken by Adrien de La Valette (1858)
ARCHITECT: Jules Hardouin-Mansart
(attributed, 1676–81). Disfigured by Jules
Gros (1858)

*In 1858, the comte de La
Valette began extravagant
alterations, including a
belvedere and Baroque-
inspired decorative elements.
They were never completed,
and the building was
acquired by the École
Massillon in 1877.*

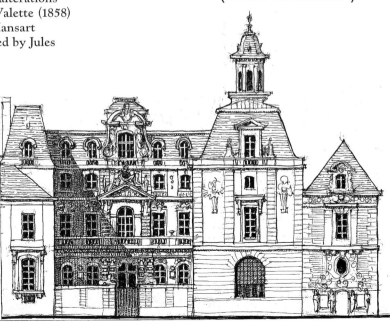

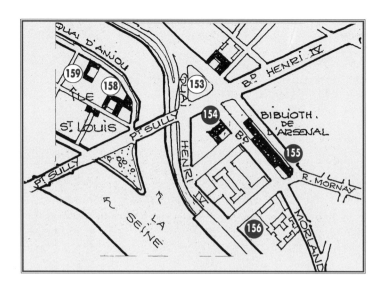

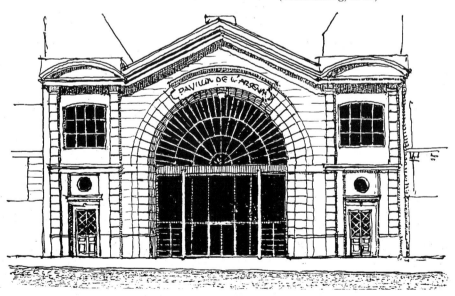

⒕ Pavillon de l'Arsenal

LOCATION: 21, boulevard Morland
MÉTRO STATION: Sully-Morland
PATRONS: The businessman Borniche
(1878). The City of Paris (1988)
ARCHITECTS: A. Clément (1878).
Bernard Reichen and Philippe Robert
(remodeling, 1988)

This building was built to house the collections of a wealthy individual. After becoming a depot, it was acquired by the City of Paris, which used it first to store archives and then as a venue for exhibitions relating to architecture. The original metal armature has proved well suited to all these different uses, and the architects of the recent remodeling used it as a framework from which to suspend mezzanines readily adaptable to various exhibition needs.

Bibliothèque de l'Arsenal

LOCATION: 1–3, rue de Sully
MÉTRO STATION: Sully-Morland
PATRON: The duc de Maine, grand
maître de l'Artillerie (1715).
The library was founded by Voyer
d'Argenson, named garde de l'Arsenal
in 1755.
ARCHITECT: Germain Boffrand
(1715–25)

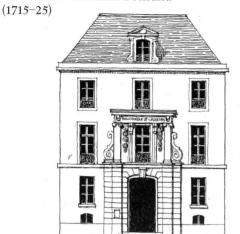

Northeast façade

Detail A

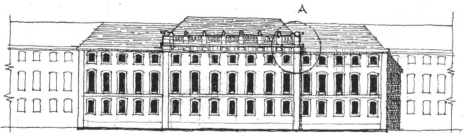

Southeast
façade, on
boulevard
Morland

The building takes its name from the royal arsenal, which in the 16th century occupied this entire quarter from the banks of the Seine to the Bastille. This structure, the only vestige of the arsenal, was originally not a library but the residence of the grand master of the artillery, a post first occupied by the duc de Sully. It was subsequently remodeled and enlarged by the architect Germain Boffrand for the duc de Maine, a later grand master. The present building was a second wing added by Boffrand to a structure that no longer exists.

LOCATION: 8, rue de Schomberg
MÉTRO STATION: Sully-Morland
ARCHITECT: Joseph-Antoine
Bouvard (1882–83)
An interesting steel-frame
structure with glazed brick walls.

Schomberg Barracks

Île Saint-Louis

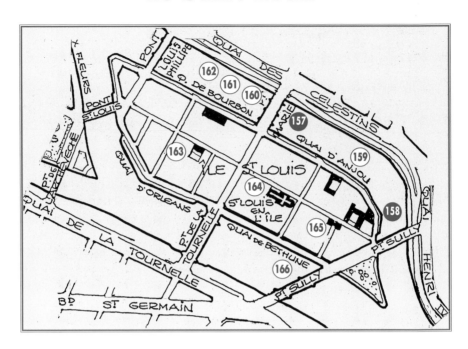

In medieval times, the Île Saint-Louis consisted of two smaller islands, the Île Notre-Dame and the Île aux Vaches, used for grazing.

At the end of the reign of Henri IV, the land was divided into lots, having been entrusted to the developer Christophe Marie and his associates Poulletier and Le Regrattier. In exchange, the developers were enjoined to build two stone bridges and quays along the Seine; to fill in the arm of the river separating the two small islands, whose placement corresponded to the present rue Poulletier; and to oversee the surveying and sale of the lots.

The Pont Marie was the first of the two bridges to be built (1614–35). It was followed by the Pont de la Tournelle (1645; rebuilt 1928). The first buildings rose in 1627, and the last ones were completed in 1664.

157 Pont Marie

LOCATION: Links the Île Saint-Louis to the Right Bank (same arrondissement)
MÉTRO STATION: Pont-Marie
PATRON AND DEVELOPER: Christophe Marie (1614–35)

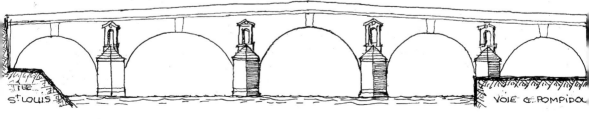

Drawing after a painting by Nicolas Raguenet (1757)

As indicated earlier, this bridge was built in conjunction with the development of the Île Saint-Louis by Marie, whose name it bears.

It was originally surmounted by two rows of houses, but in 1658 surges in the Seine led to the collapse of the two arches closest to the island. They were initially replaced by provisional wooden arches; stone ones were built beginning in 1670, but no houses were erected above them. This gave the bridge a curious appearance, as evidenced by paintings and prints from the period.

The houses above the other arches disappeared in 1788, as the result of a 1786 edict stipulating the demolition of all houses on Parisian bridges.

LOCATION: 2, rue Saint-Louis-en-l'Île, and 1, quai d'Anjou
MÉTRO STATION: Sully-Morland
PATRON: Jean-Baptiste Lambert de Thorigny; then his brother Nicolas
ARCHITECT: Louis Le Vau (1640–44)
PAINTED DECORS: Eustache Le Sueur, François Perrier, and Charles Le Brun

Hôtel Lambert 158

Upon demolition of the Hôtel de Bretonvilliers at its eastern tip, this became the most prestigious residence on the island. As indicated in the drawing above, the level of the garden terrace overlooking the Seine is higher than the entrance on the rue Saint-Louis-en-l'Île. Opening onto the garden is the great Hercules Gallery, whose ceiling is a masterpiece painted by Charles Le Brun, and, on the floor below, a library. The painted decoration is sumptuous, but the building is unfortunately closed to visitors.

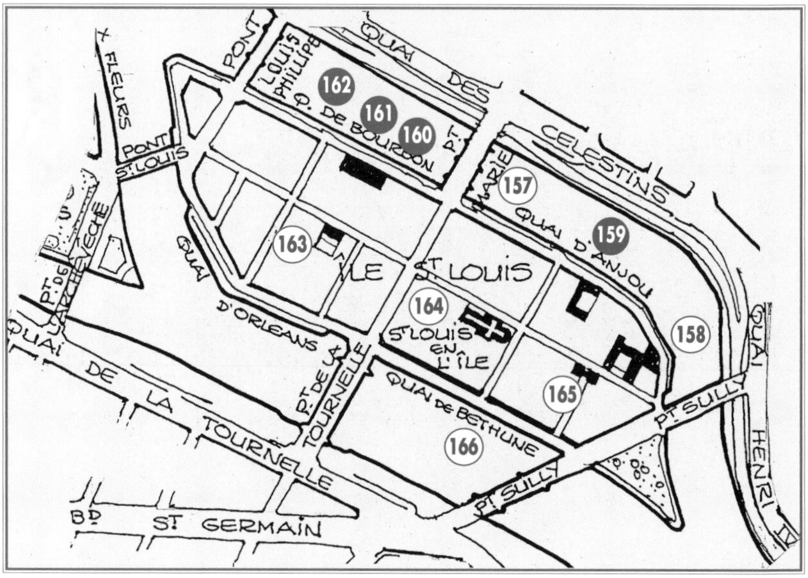

159 Hôtel de Lauzun

LOCATION: 17, quai d'Anjou
MÉTRO STATION: Pont-Marie
PATRON: Charles Gruyn, seigneur des Bordes
ARCHITECT: Louis Le Vau (attributed, 1656–57)

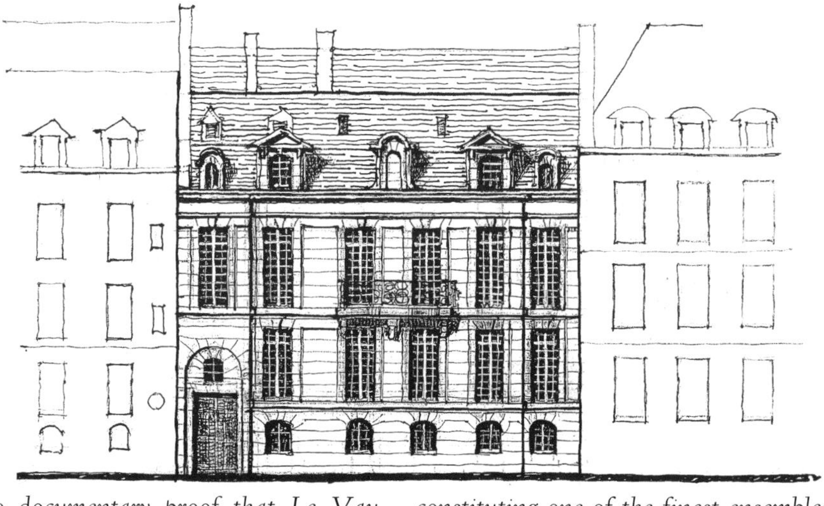

There is no documentary proof that Le Vau designed this hôtel, but his authorship is likely. Built for Charles Gruyn in 1656, it was sold in 1682 to the duc de Lauzun, who lived in it for three years with his mistress, Mademoiselle de Montpensier, known as the Grande Mademoiselle.

The restrained façade provides an ideal setting for the magnificent wrought-iron balcony in the building's center. The interior decors are splendid, constituting one of the finest ensembles of 17th-century domestic interiors in Paris. The painter Charles Le Brun was among the executants.

The hôtel has been the property of the City of Paris since 1928. Also noteworthy on the quai d'Anjou: no. 3, house designed by Louis Le Vau for himself (1640); and no. 21 (corner of rue Poulletier), house by Louis Le Vau father and son (1639).

Hôtel de Charron   No. 17, quai de   Hôtel de Jassaud
Bourbon

LOCATION: 15, quai de Bourbon
MÉTRO STATION: Pont-Marie
PATRON: Jean Charron
ARCHITECT: Sébastien Bruand (1637–40)

Hôtel de Charron

The pyramidal roof of the Hôtel de Charron recalls those of the Place des Vosges. Alignment of the entry with one of the six evenly spaced vertical rows *of windows throws it off center. The rear façade features an overhanging cabinet.*

MÉTRO STATION: Pont-Marie
MASTER MASON: Jean de la Noue (1635–40)
This house features a rounded pediment and an off-center entry.

Quai de Bourbon, no. 17

LOCATION: 19, quai de Bourbon
MÉTRO STATION: Pont-Marie
PATRON: Nicolas de Jassaud, secrétaire d'état, who owned the hôtel in 1660, probably did not commission it, for it dates from about 1635.

Hôtel de Jassaud

This hôtel is notable for the inclusion of three pediments in its façade. Camille Claudel, Rodin's friend, had her sculpture studio here at the beginning of the century.

    Also noteworthy on the quai de Bourbon: no. 1, Cabaret du Franc-Pinot, in this venue since 1616. *The grille sign dates from the 17th century; no. 29, so-called Hôtel de Boisgelin, designed by Jean Thiriot (1638); no. 45 (at the tip of the island), hôtel designed by François Le Vau, brother of the more famous Louis Le Vau, for himself.*

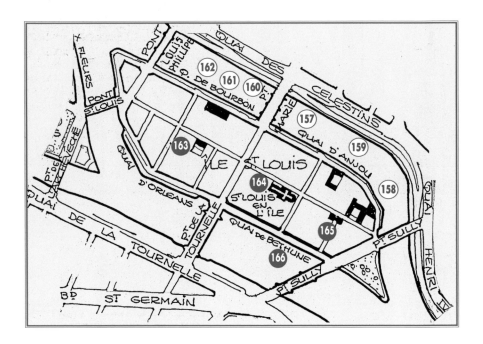

Hôtel de Chenizot

LOCATION: 51, rue Saint-Louis-en-l'Île
MÉTRO STATION: Pont-Marie
PATRONS: Pierre de Verton (c. 1620); then
Jean-François Guyot de Chenizot, who
acquired the residence in 1719 and remodeled
it in the Rococo style
ARCHITECT: Pierre Vigné de Vigny (street
block, 1726)

*The central composition of the street façade is
remarkable (see drawing). Executed in the Rococo
style in 1726, it features a portal with vermiculated
rustication and a balcony supported by dragon
consoles flanking a central mascaron (decorative
mask).*

Saint-Louis-en-l'Île

LOCATION: 19 bis, rue Saint-Louis-en-l'Île
MÉTRO STATIONS: Pont-Marie; Sully-Morland
ARCHITECTS: Louis Le Vau; after his death in 1670, Gabriel Le Duc and Jacques Doucet (choir, 1664–79; nave, 1702; tower, 1765)

The church of Saint-Louis first completed, then replaced, a chapel built at the beginning of the island's development. It was consecrated in its present form (excluding the tower, which is later) in 1726. The interior is far more spacious than the exterior suggests. The crossing is covered by a large cupola on pendentives that is not visible from the street. Some of the church's ecclesiastical furniture is remarkable.

Rue de Bretonvilliers

MÉTRO STATION: Sully-Morland
PATRON: Claude Le Ragois de Bretonvilliers, receveur des finances
ARCHITECT: Jean Androuet Du Cerceau (1637–42)

The Hôtel de Bretonvilliers, magnificently situated at the tip of the island, was demolished to make way for the boulevard Henri-IV. The pavilion, pierced by a broad arch that now marks the entrance to the rue de Bretonvilliers (see drawing), belonged to a complex of six dependent hôtels erected at the same time as the principal residence: 3–9, rue Saint-Louis-en-l'Île and 1–3, rue de Bretonvilliers.

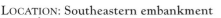

LOCATION: Southeastern embankment of the Île Saint-Louis
MÉTRO STATION: Sully-Morland

Quai de Béthune

This embankment was first called the quai des Balcons; its present name dates from 1806. The honoree is Maximilien de Béthune, the minister of Henri IV best known as Sully.

Noteworthy hôtels on the quai are: nos. 16 and 18, 17th-century hôtels, sometimes called the Hôtels de Comans; no. 18, attributed to Louis Le Vau; nos. 20 and 22, hôtels built for Antoine Lefebvre, conseiller at the Parlement; no. 24, a site formerly occupied by an hôtel built by Le Vau, demolished in 1935 to make way for the mediocre residence for Helena Rubinstein, which still stands and in which President Georges Pompidou died. All that survives of the 17th-century building is the portal, which was incorporated into the new structure.

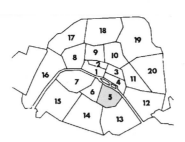

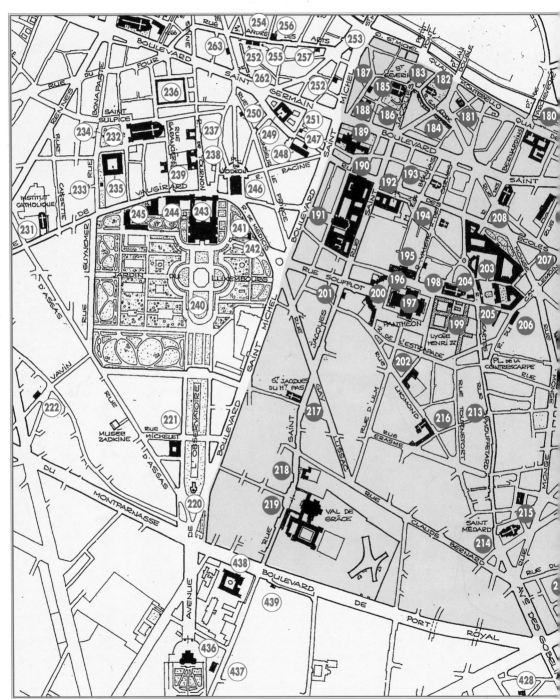

5th Arrondissement

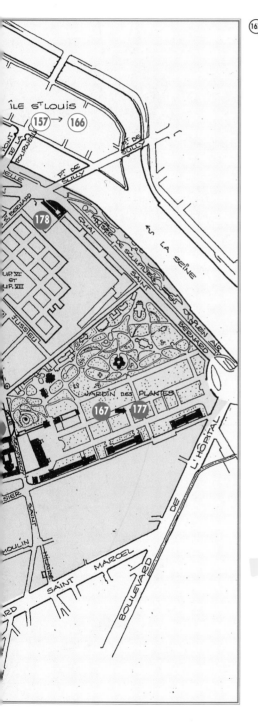

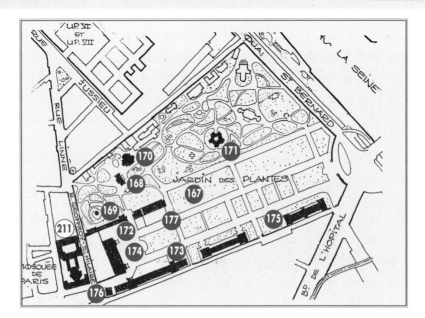

167 Jardin des Plantes

LOCATION: Place Valhubert, rue Buffon, rue
Cuvier, and rue Geoffroy-Saint-Hilaire
MÉTRO STATION: Gare d'Austerlitz
PATRON: Guy de La Brosse, médecin de
Louis XIII (1633–40), Fagon (1693), and the
comte de Buffon (1739–88)

The buildings indicated on the map of the complex are:

168 Former Hôtel de Magny: Pierre Bullet, architect (c. 1700)

169 Belvédère: Edme Verniquet, architect (1787)

170 Grand Amphithéâtre: Edme Verniquet, architect (1787); modified by Auguste Molinos (1794)

171 Rotonde des Éléphants: Auguste Molinos (c. 1810)

172 Greenhouses (rectangular): Charles Rohault de Fleury (1834–36)

173 Galerie de Minéralogie: Charles Rohault de Fleury (1836)

174 Galerie of Zoologie: Jules André (1877–89); remodeled by Chemetov and Huidobro (1994)

175 Galerie de Paléontologie: Fernand Dutert (1894–95)

176 House of Buffon (built c. 1770; Buffon resided here 1771–78)

177 Jardin d'Hiver (winter garden): René Berger (1937)

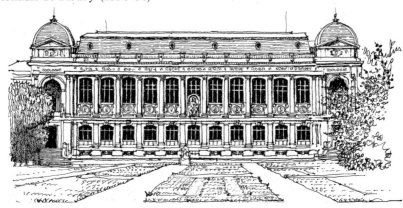

Galerie de Zoologie

The Jardin Royal des Herbes Médicinales (royal garden of medicinal herbs) was opened to the public in 1640. The best known and most active of its directors was comte de Buffon, who headed it from 1739 to 1788, doubling its area by appropriating the land lying between the original garden and the Seine. Bernardin de Saint-Pierre succeeded Buffon as director in 1789, shortly before the establishment was rechristened the Musée National d'Histoire Naturelle.

The menagerie of the Jardin des Plantes was initially a pound created in 1793, in the wake of new regulations restricting private ownership of unleashed and wild animals. The last animals to remain at the royal menagerie of Versailles were also transferred here.

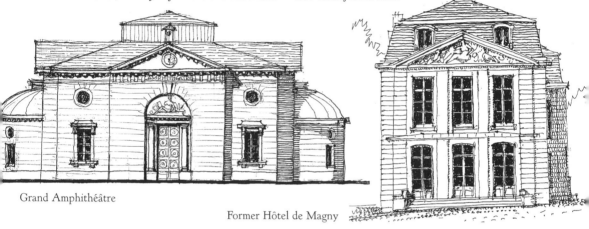

Grand Amphithéâtre

Former Hôtel de Magny

LOCATION: 23, quai Saint-Bernard
MÉTRO STATION: Jussieu
PATRONS: Nineteen Arab states and the French government
ARCHITECTS: Jean Nouvel, Henri Bernard, Pierre Soria, and Gilbert Lezènes. Winning competition design selected in 1981; under construction 1982–87

Institut du Monde Arabe 🔢178

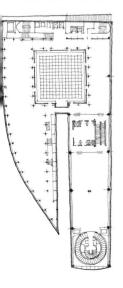

The building is sliced into two parts by a narrow opening that leads to a central patio. The northern façade consists largely of glass; the southern façade, by contrast, is built from aluminum elements (inspired by Arab art) whose transparency varies in response to shifting intensities of light by means of photoelectric cells. The roof terrace affords a beautiful view of Notre-Dame de Paris.

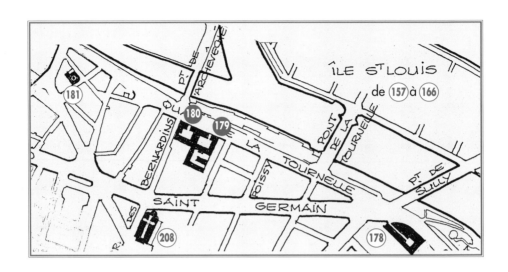

🕙 Hôtel de Miramion

LOCATION: 47, quai de la Tournelle
MÉTRO STATION: Maubert-Mutualité
PATRON: Christophe Martin, conseiller d'État
ARCHITECT: Unidentified (1630–31)

This building was acquired in 1675 by Madame de Miramion to serve as a residence for the congregation of the Filles de Sainte-Geneviève. In 1810, it was occupied by the central pharmacy of Parisian hospitals, and it was linked to the neighboring hôtel after the latter's east wing was destroyed in 1812. It now houses the Musée de l'Assistance Publique.

Court façade

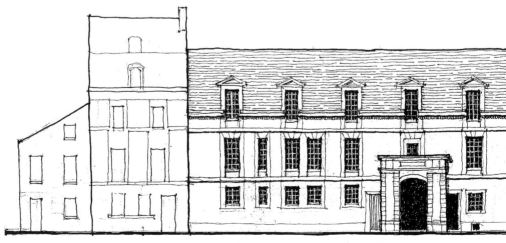

Façade at 47, quai de la Tournelle

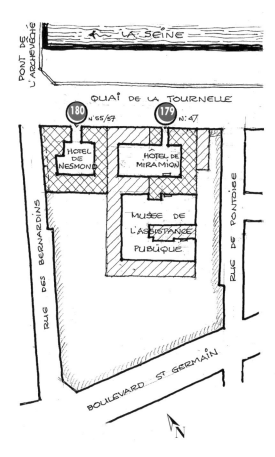

The first documented residence on the site dates from the 13th century, but it was rebuilt and/or remodeled several times, notably by François de Nesmond. After the Revolution, there was another series of alterations. Things came to a head in 1847, when an explosion in a distillery on the premises seriously damaged the buildings. They were finally remodeled between 1971 and 1976 as an apartment complex. The noble portal and entrance pavilions still convey something of the ensemble's original splendor.

LOCATION: 55, quai de la Tournelle
MÉTRO STATION: Maubert-Mutualité
PATRONS: Many, including François de Nesmond, who acquired the hôtel in 1643 and remodeled it

Hôtel de Nesmond 180

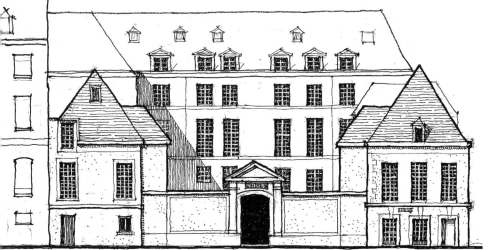

Façade at 55, quai de la Tournelle

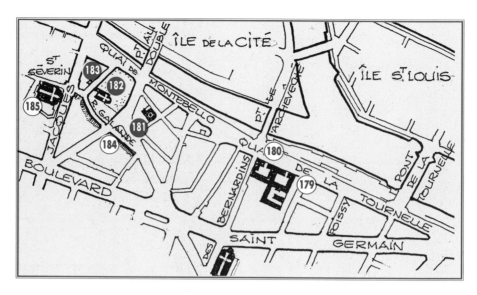

 Former Faculté de Médecine

LOCATION: 13–15, rue de la Bûcherie (corner rue de l'Hôtel-Colbert)
MÉTRO STATION: Maubert-Mutualité
PATRON: The medical school, which occupied this site between 1472 and 1775
ARCHITECT: Barbier de Blignères (amphitheater, 1743–45)

Founded by Philippe le Bel in 1331, the medical school moved to this quarter early in the 15th century. The anatomy amphitheater, illustrated at left, was inaugurated in 1745 by Jacques Benigne de Winslow, professor at the science academies of Paris and Berlin.

Abolished during the Revolution, the medical school was later reestablished and housed in the building on the rue des Cordeliers (now rue de l'École-de-Médecine), already home to the surgery school (see entries 247 and 249).

Saint-Julien-le-Pauvre

LOCATION: 1, rue Saint-Julien-
le-Pauvre
MÉTRO STATIONS: Maubert-
Mutualité; Saint-Michel-Notre-Dame
PATRONS: The Benedictine monks of
Longpont (c. 1165–1220)

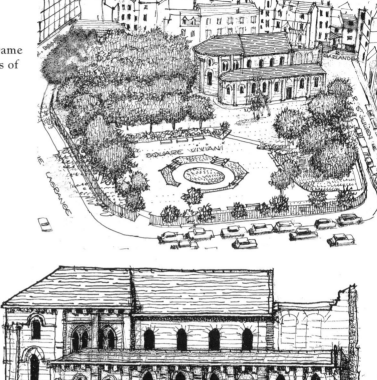

*Several chapels occupied this site
in succession before construction
of the present church, which is
contemporary with Notre-Dame
de Paris. In 1651, it was in such
disrepair that two bays had to be
removed and the façade rebuilt.
Seven years later, it lost its status
as a priory and became a
dependent chapel of Saint-
Séverin. Finally, in 1889 it was
ceded to the Greek Malachite
faith, which requires a barrier
(iconostasis) between the nave
and the chancel.*

Saint-Julien-le-Pauvre,
north façade

Hôtel de Laffémas

LOCATION: 14, rue Saint-Julien-le-Pauvre,
opposite the church
MÉTRO STATIONS: Maubert-Mutualité; Saint-
Michel-Notre-Dame
PATRON: Isaac de Laffémas, lieutenant civil
de Paris (c. 1640)

*This residence has been extensively rebuilt, but the
magnificent portal, with its relief depicting a
personification of Justice, is original. It is situated
immediately opposite the entry to Saint-Julien-
le-Pauvre.*

159

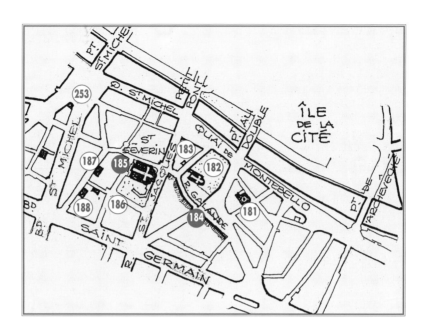

184 Rue Galande

LOCATION: Between rue Saint-Jacques
and rue Lagrange
MÉTRO STATION: Maubert-Mutualité

The rue Galande follows the
path of an old Roman road linking Lyons to Lutetia. It was laid
out in 1202 and still features
some 16th- and 17th-century
houses of interest, though extensively rebuilt.

The drawing at right represents some of the buildings
between the rue Dante and
the rue Lagrange (nos. 27–39),
the most picturesque part of the
street. Note especially no. 31,
with its gabled façade. Likewise
no. 65 (17th century) and the
restaurant at no. 46, whose interior retains a window from the
Saint-Blaise chapel (13th century).

Saint-Séverin

LOCATION: Rue des Prêtres-Saint-Séverin
MÉTRO STATION: Saint-Michel
CONSTRUCTION: 13th–14th centuries. All that survives from the early period are the tower, three bays of the central nave, and the supports between the right side aisles. The church was ravaged by fire shortly before 1450, necessitating a partial reconstruction in the late 15th century. Construction of the apse and the ossuary began in 1489; that of the side chapels continued from 1498 to 1520. The Communion chapel by Jules Hardouin-Mansart dates from 1673.

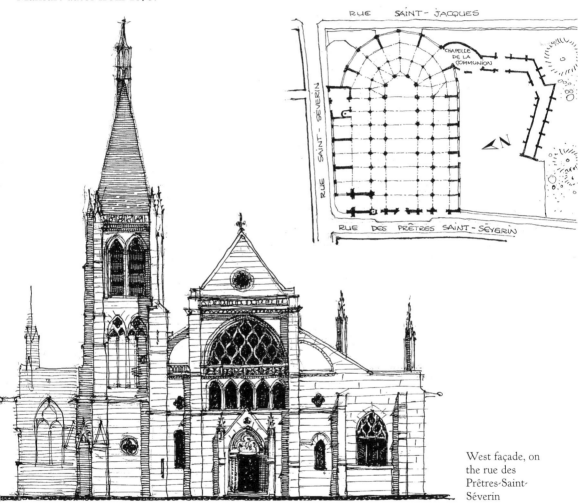

West façade, on the rue des Prêtres-Saint-Séverin

The church of Saint-Séverin was built in the 13th century on the site of an oratory destroyed by the Normans. It was enlarged in the 14th century, then partially rebuilt in the 15th century after a fire. It is notable for its great width in proportion to its length. The west portal was moved here from the church of Saint-Pierre-aux-Boeufs (13th century) on the Île de la Cité, demolished in 1837 when the rue d'Arcole was laid out. To the south is the vaulted gallery of the ossuary (15th century), where remains from common paupers' graves were deposited. A small garden now occupies the site of the cemetery.

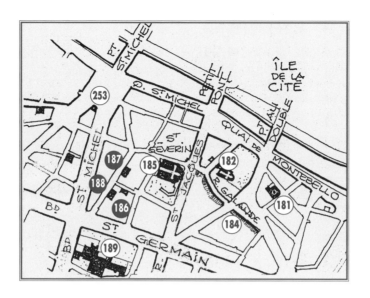

Saint-Séverin Quarter

This quarter boasts many picturesque streets bordered by old houses that have been remodeled to varying degrees over the centuries.

Among these streets, the most noteworthy are the rue Saint-Séverin, rue de la Huchette, rue de la Harpe, and rue de la Parcheminerie.

186 Rue de la Parcheminerie, no. 29

LOCATION: Between rue Saint-Jacques and rue de la Harpe
MÉTRO STATION: Cluny-La Sorbonne

This street owes its name to the presence, until the late 15th century, of many parchment merchants. The hôtel at no. 29 was built in 1736 for Claude Dubuisson, inspector at the coin exchange. It is a fine example of the Louis XV style.

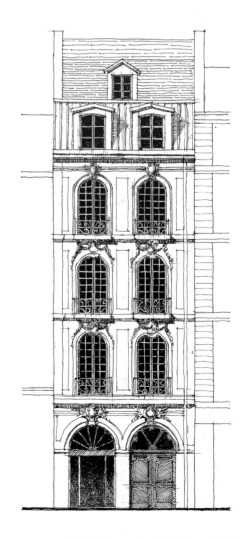

Rue de la Harpe, no. 35

LOCATION: Between boulevard Saint-Germain and rue Saint-Séverin
MÉTRO STATION: Cluny-La Sorbonne

This house, built in 1730 by Charles Bernard, is known as the Maison Rondet or the Maison de la Rose Rouge (house of the red rose). Note the abundant decoration of the arches and windows on the entresol level.

Rue de la Harpe, no. 45

LOCATION: Between boulevard Saint-Germain and rue Saint-Séverin
MÉTRO STATION: Cluny-La Sorbonne

This residence, known as the Maison Juliennet, dates from about 1740. Unfortunately, the ground-floor façade has been mutilated by the installation of shop windows within the arches next to the entrance.

189 Cluny Baths

LOCATION: Corner of boulevard Saint-Michel and boulevard Saint-Germain. Entry through the Musée de Cluny (see opposite)
MÉTRO STATION: Cluny-La Sorbonne
DATE: Late 2nd–early 3rd century CE

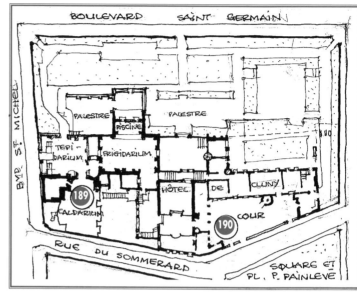

View of the *frigidarium* (note consoles shaped like ships' bows)

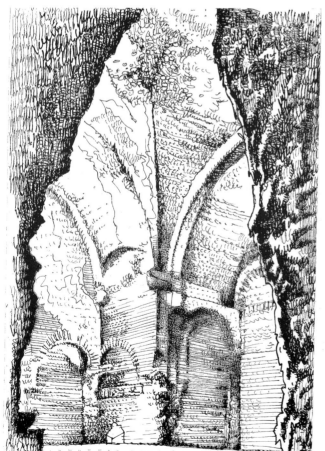

The Cluny baths are now part of the Musée de Cluny, some of whose buildings were erected on its foundations. The remains date from the 2nd or early 3rd century CE and were built of brick and stone, like all the Roman baths from the period. Only the frigidarium *retains its vault, which rests on consoles shaped like ships' bows, suggesting that the baths were built for the Parisian* nautae, *or navigators. Near the* frigidarium *(cold baths) are remains of the* tepidarium *(warm baths) and the* calidarium *(hot baths). The facility boasted a system whereby heat emanated from the floor and basement* (hypocaustum). *On display in the* frigidarium *are four blocks from the Pillar of the* Nautae, *whose reliefs represent Roman and Gallic divinities side by side.*

LOCATION: 6, Place Paul-Painlevé
MÉTRO STATION: Cluny-La Sorbonne
PATRON: Jacques d'Amboise, abbé de Cluny
(construction 1485–1510)
Remodeled and enlarged by Albert Lenoir
beginning in 1843; museum opened in 1844

Hôtel and
Musée de Cluny

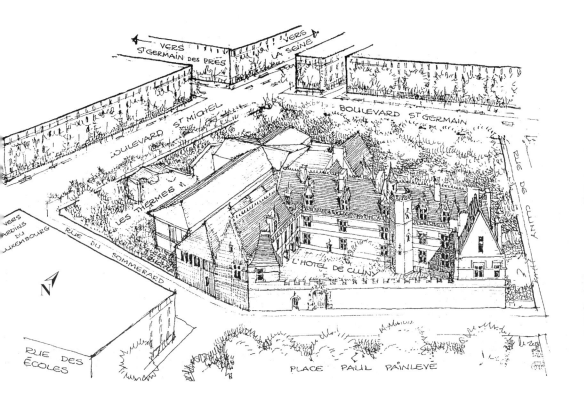

The building is configured around a trapezoidal courtyard entered at 6, Place Paul-Painlevé. Aside from the Hôtel de Sens, this is the only Gothic residence to be seen in Paris. It was built at the end of the period in which the Gothic style was used for civil buildings. The crenellations derive from defensive architecture, but their use here is purely decorative.

During and after the Revolution, when it was appropriated by the state, the Hôtel de Cluny was much disfigured. In 1832, it was acquired by Alexandre du Sommerard, a great collector of medieval and Renaissance artifacts. First the city, then the state, assumed ownership of the house, which became a museum. Notable among its collections are several sculpted heads from the Galerie des Rois (gallery of kings) of Notre-Dame de Paris, lost during the Revolution but rediscovered in 1977.

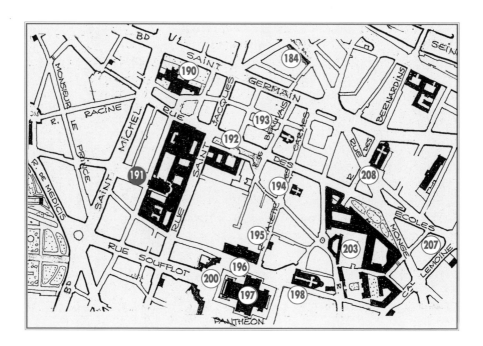

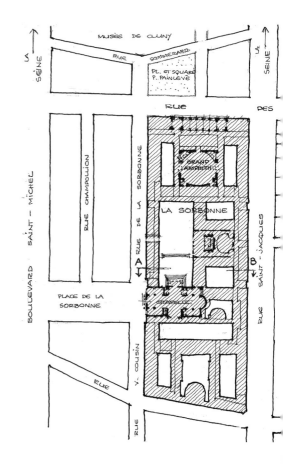 ⓵⁹¹ Sorbonne

LOCATION: Large quadrangle between the rue de la Sorbonne, rue des Écoles, rue Saint-Jacques, and rue Cujas
MÉTRO STATION: Cluny-La Sorbonne
DATES: Institution founded in 1253 by Robert de Sorbon. Cardinal Richelieu reconstructed its buildings beginning in 1626. The Third Republic rebuilt the complex (excluding the chapel) between 1885 and 1901.

Chapel
PATRON: Cardinal Richelieu
ARCHITECT: Jacques Lemercier (1635–42)

New Sorbonne
PATRON: The French government, at the initiative of President Jules Ferry
ARCHITECT: Henri-Paul Nénot (1881–1901)

The Sorbonne was founded in 1253 by the master of theology Robert de Sorbon, who wanted to house and educate students too poor to pay for their studies. The college developed rapidly, becoming quite large. In 1626, Cardinal Richelieu commissioned the architect Jacques Lemercier to rebuild the complex, including the magnificent chapel that still stands, the only portion from the period to survive.

The chapel has two entrances: one to the west, opening onto the Place de la Sorbonne; and another to the south, opening onto a large courtyard. It is covered by a dome erected between 1641 and 1645, the fifth such structure to rise in Paris.

In 1881, President Jules Ferry decided to rebuild the facilities and entrusted the project to the architect Henri-Paul Nénot. Noteworthy in the new complex are two large amphitheaters; one of them, accommodating 2,700, is decorated with a mural by Pierre Puvis de Chavannes representing the sacred wood of the arts and sciences. The chapel is accessible only when it is housing temporary exhibitions.

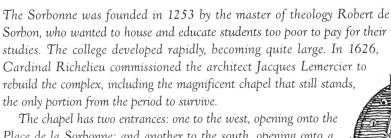

Façade on the Place de la Sorbonne. The buildings on either side of the chapel are not pictured.

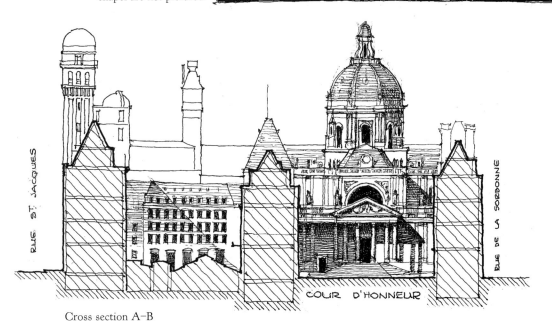

Cross section A–B

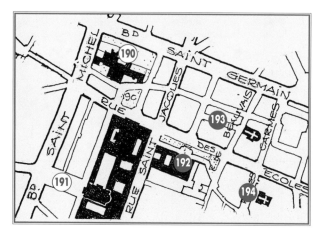

Collège de France

LOCATION: 11, Place Marcelin-Berthelot (rue des Écoles)
MÉTRO STATION: Maubert-Mutualité
PATRON: François I, who founded the institution in 1530
ARCHITECTS: Buildings of 1610 rebuilt by Jean-François Chalgrin (1774–80). Extensions by Paul Letarouilly (1831–32); then Albert and Jacques Guilbert and Leconte (1928–33); finally Leconte (1941–52)

Façade on the Place Marcelin-Berthelot (rue des Écoles)

The Collège de France, originally the Collège Royal, was founded in 1530 by François I at the urging of Guillaume Budé, a great humanist who sought to revive the pedagogical methods of the ancients. The original buildings, dating from the 1610s, were rebuilt for the first time by François Chalgrin in an austere idiom (see drawing). Then Letarouilly added the buildings arranged around the two courtyards opening onto the rue Saint-Jacques. Finally, new buildings were erected to the rear between 1928 and 1952.

Chapel of the Collège de Beauvais

LOCATION: 9 bis, rue Jean-de-Beauvais
MÉTRO STATION: Maubert-Mutualité
PATRON: Jean de Dormans, bishop of Beauvais, who died just before work was begun
ARCHITECT: Raymond du Temple (1374–80)

This chapel, known as the Chapelle de Beauvais, is all that survives of the Collège de Beauvais, whose other buildings were razed in 1881. Like the college complex as a whole, it was designed by Raymond du Temple, but its façade was disfigured in the 18th and 19th centuries. The mosaic above the entrance dates from 1926. Since 1892, the building has been a Romanian Orthodox chapel.

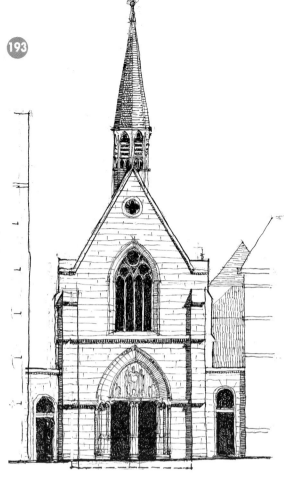

Saint-Éphrem

LOCATION: 17, rue des Carmes
MÉTRO STATION: Maubert-Mutualité
PATRON: The abbé de Vaubrun
ARCHITECT: Pierre Boscry (1738)

This church was built to serve as the chapel of the Irish College, then located on the site (now at 5, rue des Irlandais in the same arrondissement; see entry 202).

Pierre Boscry, its architect, was much influenced here by Italian Baroque models, notably in the concave pediment above the entry (whose sculpture was damaged during the Revolution). The chapel now serves a Syrian Catholic congregation and is dedicated to Saint Éphrem.

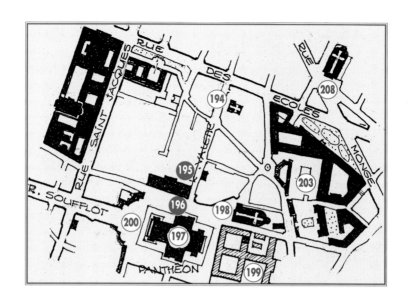

Rue Valette, no. 7

LOCATION: Near the Place du Panthéon
MÉTRO STATION: Luxembourg (northern exit)
PATRON: Frédéric Léonard, royal printer (1673–77)

At the time of writing, this hôtel's foundations were being consolidated, apparently as part of a larger restoration effort. The building prefigures the architecture of the Place des Victoires and the Place Vendôme, with which it shares several features: ground-floor arcades, continuous rustication, and colossal pilasters.

LOCATION: 8–10, Place du Panthéon
MÉTRO STATION: Luxembourg (northern exit)
ARCHITECT: Henri Labrouste (1844–50)

Bibliothèque 196
Sainte-Geneviève

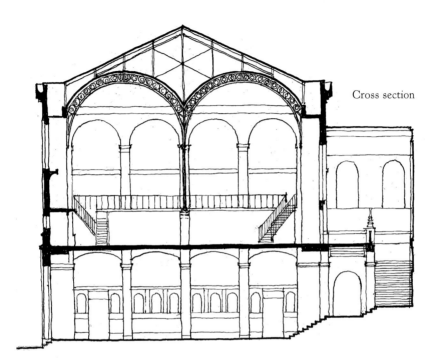

Cross section

Façade on the Place du Panthéon

The design of this library was immensely influential because of Labrouste's use of a metal structural armature, still unusual at the time.

This armature, highlighted in the drawing at the top of this page, consists of two parallel sequences of cast-iron arches supporting barrel vaults running the length of the building and supported by a row of slender cast-iron colonettes. The building's function is indicated by 810 names of writers and scientists engraved in the stone façade.

⑲⑦ Panthéon

LOCATION: Place du Panthéon
MÉTRO STATION: Luxembourg (northern exit)
PATRON: Louis XV
ARCHITECTS: Jacques-Germain Soufflot (from
1757 to his death in 1780). Final stages of
construction overseen by Maximilien Brébion
and Jean-Baptiste Rondelet

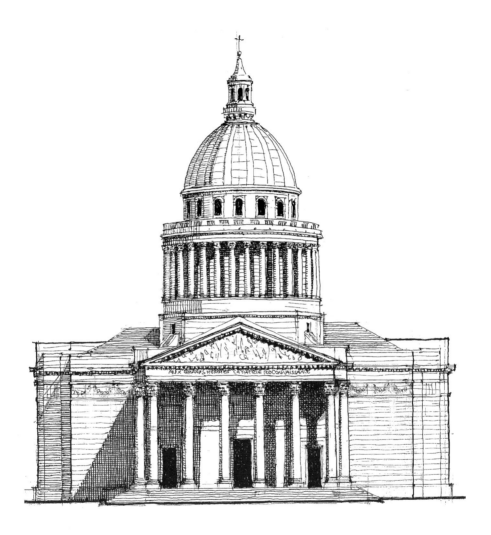

The church of Sainte-Geneviève, which in 1791 became the Panthéon, was built in order to carry out a sacred vow, sworn by Louis XV during a serious illness, to mark his recovery.

The new building replaced an old abbey church whose bell tower (the Tour Clovis) survives within the walls of the Lycée Henri-IV (see entry 199).

Construction began in 1757–58, but the first stone was laid by Louis XV only in 1764, the presence of underground quarries having complicated the laying of the foundations—and greatly increased related expenditures.

In plan, Soufflot's design takes the form of a Greek cross. The entrance is marked by a monumental portico, and a dome rises above the crossing. Soufflot arrived at the final form of the dome only after a series of studies giving it increasingly larger dimensions; it was greatly influenced by the dome of Saint Paul's cathedral in London.

Cracks appeared in the piers during construction, prompting a heated public debate about the building's solidity. Soufflot died before it was completed, and his collaborator Rondelet continued the work, reinforcing the piers in the process. The dome was completed in 1790, in the middle of the Revolution. The following year, the Constituent Assembly voted to transform the church into a "necropolis of great men"—hence the use of the term pantheon. All Christian imagery was removed and the windows were bricked up, which grossly disfigured the original design by betraying its lightness (traces of the windows are still visible on the outer walls).

The first "great man" to be buried in the new necropolis was the comte de Mirabeau, the most important figure in the early years of the Revolution, but a few years later he was expelled, along with Jean-Paul Marat, another revolutionary leader.

In 1806, the Panthéon reverted to its original intended function as a church, but it became the Panthéon again in 1831—and in turn a church again in 1852.

It was definitively redeclared the Panthéon in 1885, the year of the grandiose funeral of Victor Hugo, who was laid to rest among its other notables.

The pediment sculpture changed in tandem with these shifts. In 1791, the original sacred composition was replaced by a secular one; in 1830, this was in turn replaced by a group, The Nation Distributing Crowns to the Great Men, by the sculptor David d'Angers.

André Malraux was the last of the "great men" to be buried in the Panthéon.

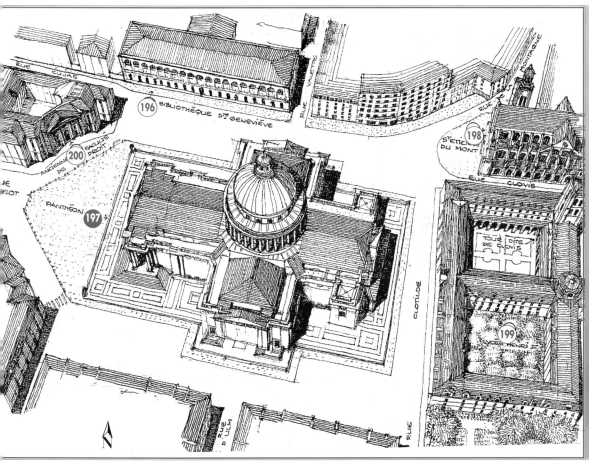

198 Saint-Étienne-du-Mont

LOCATION: Place Sainte-Geneviève (contiguous with the Place du Panthéon)
MÉTRO STATION: Luxembourg; Cardinal-Lemoine
ARCHITECT: Originally, Étienne Viguier (1492), but construction was protracted and overseen by a succession of architects (lower levels of bell tower, c. 1492–1500; choir, c. 1530–40; choir screen, 1530–45; nave, c. 1545–85; façade, by Claude Guérin, 1610–22; upper portion of bell tower, 1624; portal on left elevation, 1630). Victor Baltard (façade restored, 1861–65)

This church is very original, not because of its structure, still resolutely Gothic, but because of its later Renaissance façade. Crowned by a triangular gable, the façade consists of three superimposed pediments inspired by Italian Renaissance models. The foundation stone of the façade was laid by Marguerite de Valois in 1610.

Saint-Étienne-du-Mont also boasts a celebrated stone choir screen, the only one from this period to survive in Paris. It consists of a central low arch, richly carved, flanked by two spiral stairs encircling two of the building's pillars.

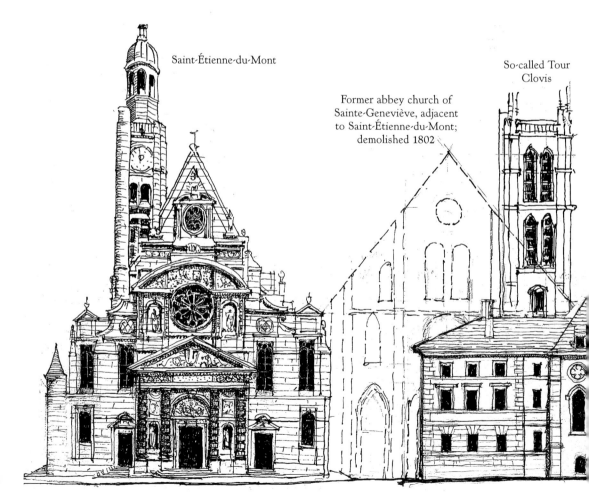

Saint-Étienne-du-Mont

Former abbey church of Sainte-Geneviève, adjacent to Saint-Étienne-du-Mont; demolished 1802

So-called Tour Clovis

Lycée Henri-IV 199

LOCATION: 23, rue Clovis and rue Clotilde
MÉTRO STATION: Cardinal-Lemoine
PATRON: According to tradition, Clovis
founded a basilica here, c. 507 (destroyed).
About 1150, the monks of Saint-Victor
established an abbey on the site named after
Sainte Geneviève.
DATES: So-called Tour Clovis (Clovis tower):
lower portion, 11th century; upper portion,
15th century. Kitchens: 12th century.
Refectory: 13th century. Cloister rebuilt in
the 18th century

The Lycée Henri-IV complex incorporates surviv-
ing portions of the old abbey of Sainte-Geneviève.

The tower mistakenly named after the Frankish
king Clovis is in fact the surviving bell tower of the
abbey church, the church itself having been demol-
ished in 1802 and replaced by the church of
Sainte-Geneviève, which became the Panthéon
after the Revolution.

During the Revolution, the government also
declared the abbey national property, and it became
a school in 1796. The adjacent streets are named
after Clovis and Clotilde as a reminder that this
famous royal couple was buried in the basilica
founded on the site in 507.

Former cloister of the abbey

Lycée Henri-IV

175

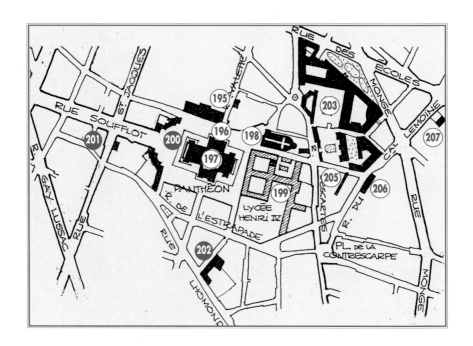

200 Former Law School

LOCATION: 12, Place du Panthéon (see aerial view, page 173)
MÉTRO STATION: Cardinal-Lemoine
ARCHITECT: Jacques-Germain Soufflot (1771–74)

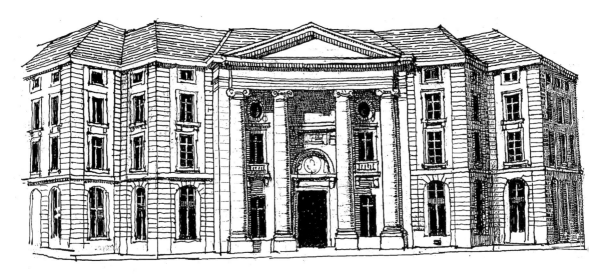

The architect of the Panthéon, Jacques-Germain Soufflot, had envisioned a semicircular square in front of it bordered by two buildings with concave façades. Only this one, to the north, intended to house the law school, was built before the Revolution. The one to the south, which houses the mairie (town hall) of the 5th arrondissement, was built in 1850, along lines almost identical to the first.

House of Lepas-Dubuisson

LOCATION: 151 bis, rue Saint-Jacques
MÉTRO STATION: Luxembourg (northern exit)
PATRON AND ARCHITECT: Charles-Nicolas
Lepas-Dubuisson, beginning in 1718

The façade of this building boasts a superb balcony, supported by carved consoles, with a magnificent wrought-iron railing.

Charles-Nicolas Lepas-Dubuisson was the son of the master mason who built the chapel of the Foreign Missions (see entry 306). He himself built the hôtels at 118 and 120, rue du Bac (entry 305).

LOCATION: 5, rue des Irlandais
MÉTRO STATION: Luxembourg
ARCHITECT: Bélanger (1755–69), unrelated to
the better-known François-Joseph Bélanger

Irish College

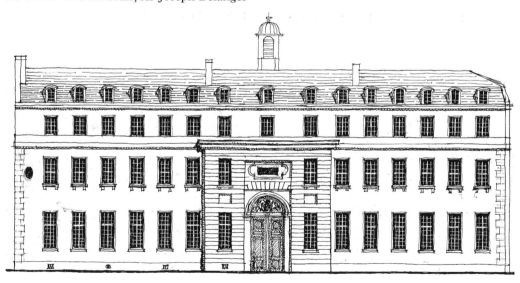

The Irish College was first located on the rue des Carmes, where its old chapel survives as the church of Saint-Éphrem (entry 194). The move was effected after disputes made it necessary to establish distinct institutions for the education of laymen and future priests. The building on the rue des Irlandais, whose beautiful façade has recently been cleaned, still houses a community of Irish students.

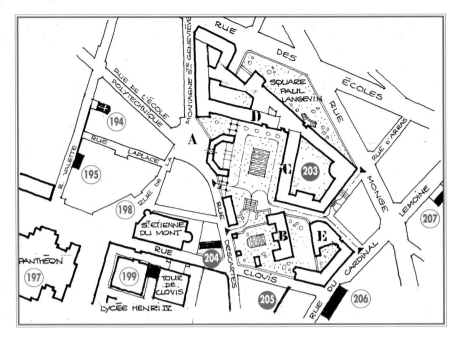

A. Portal at 5, rue Descartes
B. Former residence of the director of the school (now Ministère de la Recherche)
C. Foch building
D. Joffre building
E. Physics building

Former École Polytechnique

LOCATION: Rue Descartes and rue d'Arras (see map above)
MÉTRO STATION: Cardinal-

Portal at 5, rue Descartes (1837)

The École Polytechnique, a prestigious Parisian college, moved to Palaiseau in 1976, when its old facilities were reassigned to various government services, most notably the Ministry of Research and Technology.

Part of the courtyards of the complex have recently been transformed into a public garden with a reflecting pool. As indicated in the map above, the opening of this garden has created a picturesque walk linking the rue Descartes to the rue du Cardinal-Lemoine.

Presbytery ⑳ of Saint-Étienne-du-Mont

LOCATION: 30, rue Descartes
MÉTRO STATION: Cardinal-Lemoine
PATRON: The duc Louis d'Orléans,
son of the regent
ARCHITECT: Perhaps Gilles-Marie
Oppenord (c. 1740)

Now a presbytery, this structure, originally near the abbey of Sainte-Geneviève, was built by the duc Louis d'Orléans (known as Louis the Pious) to serve as his residence during his final years.

View of the southern façade from the rue Clovis

Remains of the Wall ⑳ of Philippe Auguste

LOCATION: 3–5, rue Clovis
MÉTRO STATION: Cardinal-Lemoine
PATRON: Philippe Auguste in 1190, on the
occasion of his departure on the Crusades

With those now part of the Lycée Charlemagne (see entry 148), these are the largest remains of the Wall of Philippe Auguste to survive in Paris.

The wall, visible in cross section from the rue Clovis, is some 33 feet high and 3 feet thick at the base.

This cross section reveals the wall's manner of construction, consisting of a layer of rough stone infill between two outer layers of dressed stone.

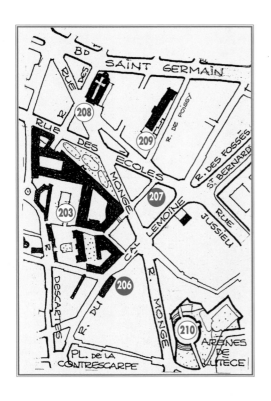

⓻ Former Scottish College

LOCATION: 65, rue du Cardinal-Lemoine
MÉTRO STATION: Cardinal-Lemoine
PATRON: Robert Barclay (1662–72)

The unorthodox treatment of the façade's central bay was prompted by a lowering of the level of the street by several feet in 1685, shortly after the building's completion, necessitating construction of a second entry below the first one.

A chapel on the main floor (initially the ground floor) contains the tomb of James II, king of England, who died in exile at Saint-Germain-en-Laye in 1701.

LOCATION: 49, rue du Cardinal-Lemoine
MÉTRO STATION: Cardinal-Lemoine
PATRON: Charles II Le Brun, nephew of the famous painter
ARCHITECT: Germain Boffrand (1700)
SCULPTOR: Anselme Flamen (pediments on both façades).
Since 1912 this building has housed the Office d'Habitations
à Bon Marché (HBM), now the Office d'Habitations à
Loyers Modérés (HLM).

Hôtel Le Brun

Forecourt façade

This hôtel, one of the earliest works of the architect Germain Boffrand, was built for a nephew of the painter Charles Le Brun who bore the same name.

Magnificently proportioned, it features seven window bays; in both court and garden façades the three central bays are contained within a projecting frontispiece with a triangular pediment containing sculpture.

The composition within the court-side pediment represents the arms of the Le Brun family supported by unicorns. The composition within the garden-side pediment shows a personification of Immortality presenting Minerva with a portrait of Le Brun.

Trellised arcades along the street serve to separate the hôtel visually from adjacent buildings in a modern style.

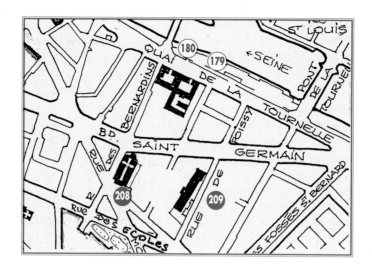

⑳ Saint-Nicolas-du-Chardonnet

LOCATION: 30, rue Saint-Victor
MÉTRO STATION: Maubert-Mutualité
ARCHITECTS: The master mason Charles Comtesse (bell tower, 1625); François Levé and Michel Noblet (1656–67); participation of Charles Le Brun (west portal façade and decoration of a chapel, c. 1665); Charles Halley (façade, 1934)

Façade before 1934

Present façade

This site, previously known for its thistles (chardons, *hence the name of the church*), was occupied in succession by a 13th-century chapel and a 15th-century church, for which the present bell tower was erected.

The church was rebuilt beginning in 1656 by François Levé and Michel Noblet, architects in the king's service. The painter Charles Le Brun, a member of the congregation, provided designs for the portal on the rue des Bernardins.

The first two bays of the nave were added later, between 1707 and 1715. The façade was built only in 1934.

The interior decor of the present church is magnificent, and it contains Le Brun's tomb, realized by the sculptor Antoine Coysevox.

West portal

LOCATION: 18–24, rue de Poissy
MÉTRO STATION: Cardinal-Lemoine
PATRON: The college of Bernardine monks, beginning in 1246. The refectory, the only surviving portion of the convent, dates from the second half of the 13th century.

Refectory of the 209 Bernardine Monks

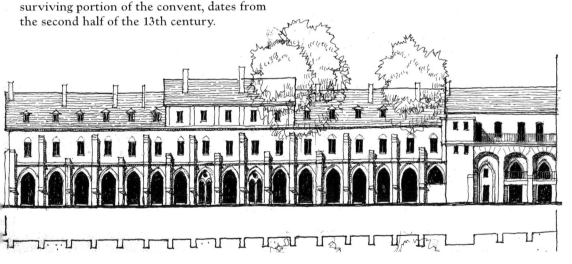

This building, which consisted of a basement storeroom, a ground-floor refectory, and dormitories on the floor above, is all that survives of the convent of the Bernardine monks, destroyed between 1806 and 1855 during the construction of the rue de Pontoise and rue de Poissy, then of the boulevard Saint-Germain.

The old cellar is a magnificent vaulted room.

The firemen's barracks that had been housed here since 1850 has recently been moved, and there are plans to open the building to the public.

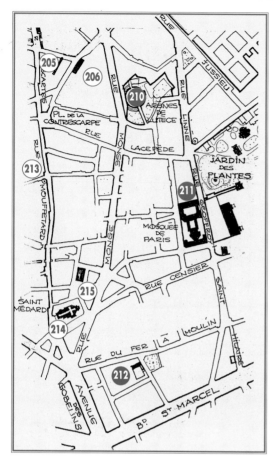

The so-called Arena of Lutetia (or Lutèce) is actually an amphitheater that served as both an arena and a theater.

The structure was built toward the end of the 1st century CE and could accommodate about 15,000 spectators.

The invasions of the 3rd century spelled ruin for the arena: its stones were reused and its remains were gradually buried, to such an extent that they virtually disappeared until 1869.

That year, construction of the rue Monge led to rediscovery of the site, occasioning a heated debate about its preservation. The remains were finally uncovered and restored in 1918, although buildings along the rue Monge still stand over part of them.

210 Arena of Lutetia (Lutèce)

LOCATION: 6, rue des Arènes
MÉTRO STATION: Monge

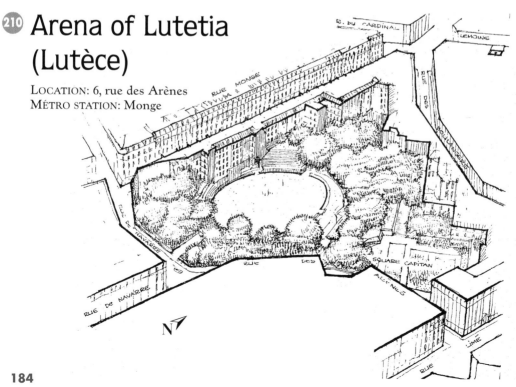

Paris Mosque

LOCATION: 1, Place du Puits-de-l'Hermite
MÉTRO STATION: Censier-Daubenton
PATRON: The French government, in
collaboration with several Moslem countries
ARCHITECTS: C. Heubès, R. Fournez, and
M. Mantout (1922–26)

The architects employed artists, craftsmen, and mate-
rials from countries in the Maghreb so as to faithfully
re-create the Moslem art of that region of northwest
Africa. The complex, the Institut Franco-Musulman,
consists of three distinct parts, corresponding respec-
tively to religious, cultural, and commercial activities.

In the center is the sanctuary and prayer hall,
which can accommodate 500 worshipers. This hall
opens onto a marble patio in whose center is a basin
with a fountain. The complex is dominated by the tra-
ditional minaret.

LOCATION: 13, rue Scipion
MÉTRO STATION: Censier-Daubenton
PATRONS: Maurice Bullioud (1532); then the banker Scipion
Sardini (c. 1565)
ARCHITECT: Unidentified
SCULPTOR: Probably Girolamo Della Robbia (façade medallions)

Hôtel Scipion

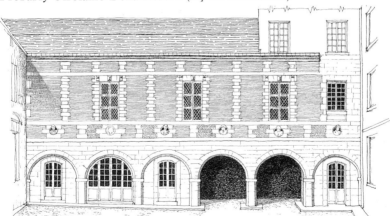

The entrance to this residence, originally situated
on the banks of the Bièvre, is now at 13, rue
Scipion. One must enter the courtyard to see, to the
right, this very beautiful Renaissance hôtel built of
stone and brick, one of the earliest examples of such
construction in Paris. The ground floor features six
round-arch arcades and, above, a band decorated
with magnificent terra-cotta medallions attributed
to Girolamo Della Robbia. The building now hous-
es the central pharmacy of the hospitals of Paris.

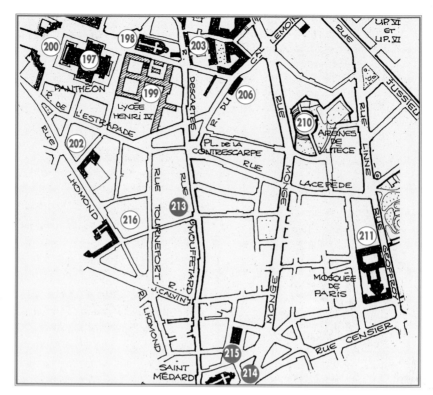

The Saint-Médard Quarter and the rue Mouffetard

The Bourg Saint-Médard was in existence by the 12th century, when its territory and its church belonged to the abbey of Sainte-Geneviève. Situated outside the Wall of Philippe Auguste, it was not encompassed by the city limits until the reign of Louis XV. The rue Mouffetard, which links Saint-Médard to the Place de la Contrescarpe, is one of the liveliest and most picturesque streets in Paris.

213 Fontaine du Pot-de-Fer

LOCATION: 60, rue Mouffetard, and 1, rue du Pot-de-Fer.
MÉTRO STATION: Censier-Daubenton

This structure, built in 1671, is so large because it was once part of a château-d'eau, or urban reservoir. It may have been designed by Michel Noblet.

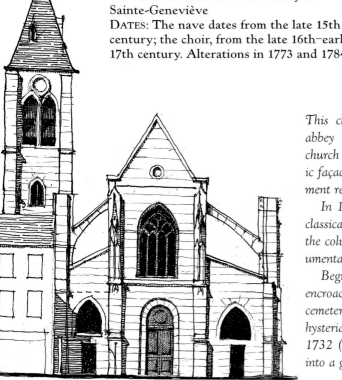

LOCATION: 141, rue Mouffetard
MÉTRO STATION: Censier-Daubenton
PATRONS: The monks of the abbey of
Sainte-Geneviève
DATES: The nave dates from the late 15th
century; the choir, from the late 16th–early
17th century. Alterations in 1773 and 1784

Saint-Médard  214

This church, previously a dependency of the abbey of Sainte-Geneviève, became a parish church in 1665. In 1773, its Flamboyant Gothic façade was "simplified" and its Gothic ornament removed.

In 1784, in accordance with prevailing neoclassical taste, the architect Petit-Radel fluted the columns of the choir. He also added a monumental Lady Chapel to the church's apse.

Beginning in 1868, some of the buildings encroaching on the church were razed, and its cemetery—famous for the scenes of collective hysteria that took place there between 1727 and 1732 (the "convulsionaries")—was transformed into a garden square.

Place du Marché-des-Patriarches 215

LOCATION: Behind and north of the church of Saint-Médard
MÉTRO STATION: Censier-Daubenton
PATRON: The City of Paris (competition held in 1980)
ARCHITECTS: Robert Gransjean, Jean-Philippe Pargade, and Gérard Viard

Here is a fine example of the integration of a modern structure into an old quarter. In its volume and orientation, this small apartment complex recalls the market that it replaced (known as the Marché des Patriarches).

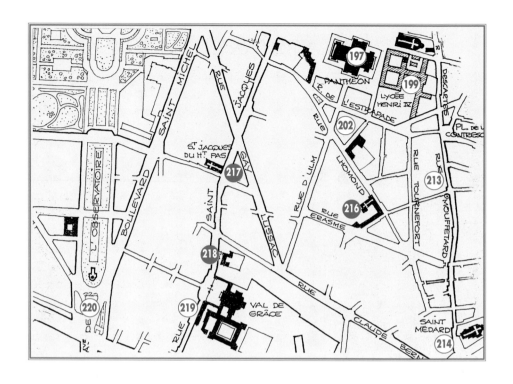

⓶⓵⓺ Congrégation du Saint-Esprit

LOCATION: 30, rue Lhomond (corner of rue Rataud)
MÉTRO STATION: Monge
PATRON: The Congregation of the Holy Spirit, founded in 1703 to train missionary seminarians
ARCHITECTS: The master mason René Baudouin (building on corner of rue Rataud, 1732–35).
Nicolas Le Camus de Mézières (chapel, 1769). Jean-François Chalgrin (completion of chapel and
building on rue Lhomond, 1782)
SCULPTOR: François-Joseph Duret (relief on chapel façade entitled *Missionaries to India
Preaching and Baptizing,*1776)

Façade on the
rue Lhomond

Saint-Jacques-du-Haut-Pas

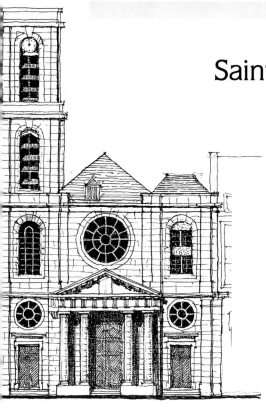

LOCATION: 252, rue Saint-Jacques
MÉTRO STATION: Luxembourg (southern exit)
ARCHITECTS: A master mason in 1630; then
Daniel Gittard (nave and façade beginning in
1675, church consecrated in 1684)

The 17th-century church of Saint-Jacques-du-Haut-Pas took its name from the order of Hospitalers of Altopascio (that is, "Haut Pas," or "high pass"). In the 12th century, the order had founded a nearby lodge for pilgrims on their way to Santiago de Compostela, the renowned cathedral in northwestern Spain said to house the remains of the apostle Saint James the Greater.

Begun in 1630, construction of Saint-Jacques-du-Haut-Pas proceeded slowly and then was interrupted due to a lack of funds. It resumed in 1675, but, money again falling short, the second tower of the façade was never built. The Lady Chapel dates from 1690 and the Catechism Chapel from 1850.

Schola Cantorum 218

LOCATION: 269, rue
Saint-Jacques
MÉTRO STATION:
Port-Royal
PATRONS: The
English Benedictines
(1674–77)

Façade on the rue Saint-Jacques (with adjacent buildings fronting the street shown in dotted lines)

The building, formerly an English Benedictine monastery, still belongs to the English Catholic community, but it has been leased to the Schola Cantorum, a famous music conservatory, since 1900. The projecting garden wing dates from the 18th century.

Val-de-Grâce

LOCATION: 277 bis, rue Saint-Jacques
MÉTRO STATIONS: Luxembourg; Port-Royal
PATRON: Anne of Austria, who laid the foundation stone of a convent building in 1624 (construction of the church began much later, in 1645)
ARCHITECTS: François Mansart (1645–46); then Jacques Lemercier (1646–48). Construction interrupted (1653; Lemercier died 1654). Pierre Le Muet (1654) in collaboration with Gabriel Le Duc; construction all but completed at the death of Anne of Austria (1666; Le Muet died 1669)

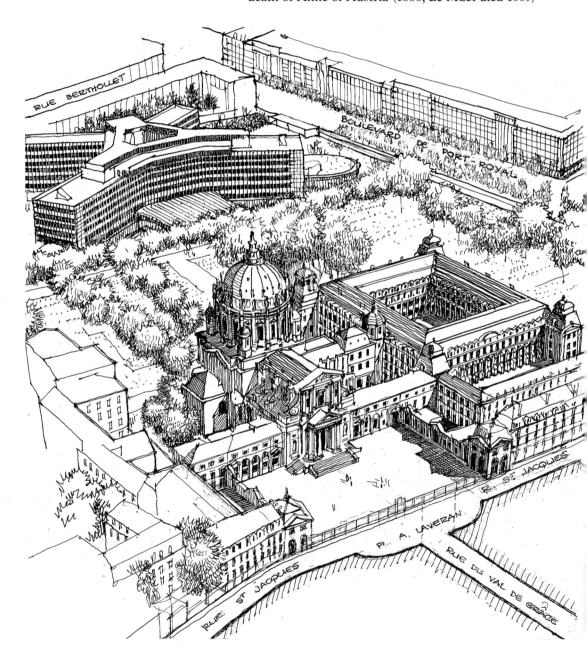

Anne of Austria was behind the installation of the Benedictines of the Val-de-Grâce on the rue Saint-Jacques. Louis XIV, however, was responsible, if only indirectly, for this religious community's magnificent church: his birth (September 5, 1638) necessitated the fulfillment of the vow sworn earlier by Anne of Austria to build a church if she was blessed with a son.

The first stone was not laid, however, until nearly seven years later (April 1, 1645). Thus began the realization of a vast program including not only the church but also a new convent. Its realization was initially entrusted to François Mansart, but Anne of Austria, impatient with the slow pace of the work, soon replaced him with Jacques Lemercier.

After Lemercier's death, the project was entrusted to Pierre Le Muet and Gabriel Le Duc, who designed the dome. This was greatly influenced by Roman architecture, notably the dome of Saint Peter's basilica, although there are significant differences between the two designs.

The interior of the church is richly decorated: especially noteworthy are the baldachin with serpentine columns over the main altar (Le Muet and Le Duc), the frescoes in the dome by Pierre Mignard, and sculpture by Michel Anguier.

After closure of the convent during the Revolution, it became a military hospital (1795). The buildings in the complex have just been restored.

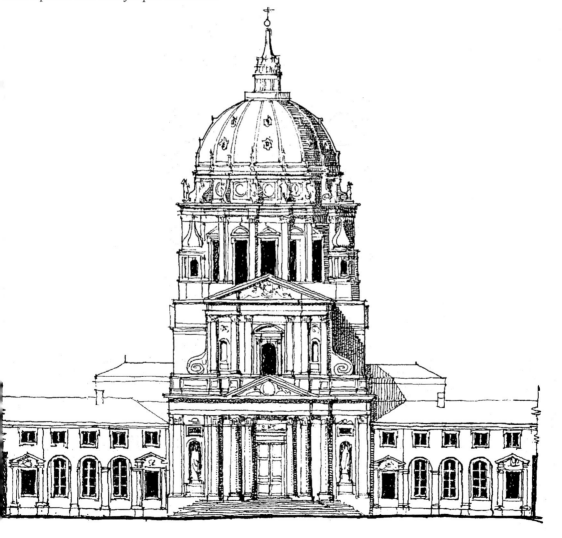

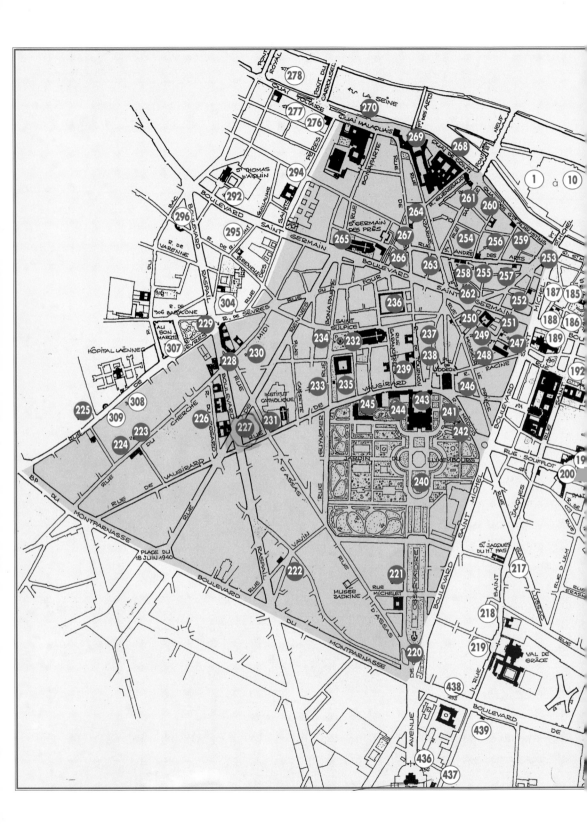

6th
Arrondissement

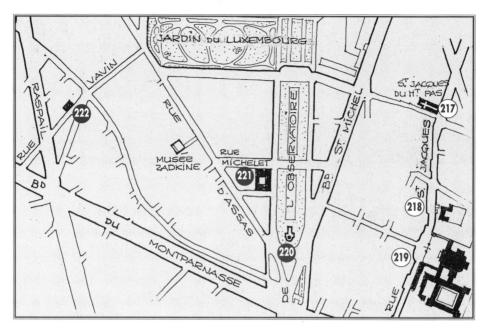

220 Fontaine de l'Observatoire

LOCATION: Gardens of the avenue de l'Observatoire
MÉTRO STATION: Port-Royal
ARCHITECT: Gabriel Davioud (1873)
SCULPTORS: Jean-Baptiste Carpeaux (figures representing the Four Parts of the Globe), Eugène Legrain (globe), Emmanuel Frémiet (horses and dolphins)

When the jets are operating, the fountain creates a remarkable impression of power and movement.

Institut d'Art et d'Archéologie

LOCATION: 3, rue Michelet and
avenue de l'Observatoire
MÉTRO STATION: Port-Royal
ARCHITECT: Paul Bigot (1927)

A wide gulf separates this building from those realized during the same period by Robert Mallet-Stevens, Le Corbusier, and many others. Even so, the design is not without qualities, notably in the virtuosic use of the deep red brick.

The frieze on the lower portion of the building recalls that of the Parthenon, but it incorporates compositions drawn from a diverse array of periods and regions.

Rue Vavin, no. 26

MÉTRO STATIONS: Vavin; Notre-Dame-des-Champs
PATRONS AND ARCHITECTS: Henri Sauvage and Charles Sarazin
(1912–14)

The architect Henri Sauvage (1873–1932) produced many inventive designs, notably that of the Samaritaine department store (see entry 12).

With his colleague Charles Sarazin, he obtained authorization from the city to build stepped apartment buildings at two locations: rue des Amiraux (see entry 517) and rue Vavin (see drawing at right).

In the latter instance, the necessary licenses were twice refused, but finally a compromise was reached and construction proceeded.

The building remains in excellent condition, thanks to its white ceramic facing.

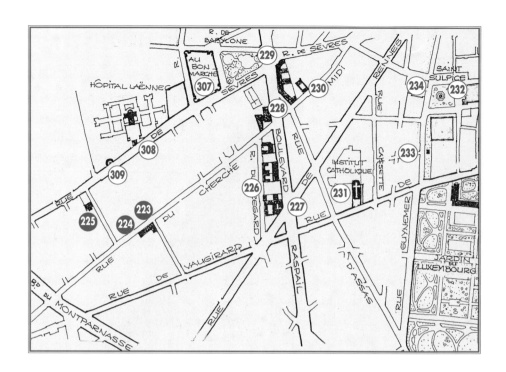

 ~~223~~ Musée Hébert

LOCATION: 85, rue du Cherche-Midi, and 2, rue Ferrandi
MÉTRO STATION: Saint-Placide

This building, the former Hôtel de Montmorency-Bours, known as the Petit Hôtel de Montmorency, was built in 1743. It consists of several adjacent structures that were subsequently consolidated.

Note the statue of the Madonna on the corner as well as the old plaques bearing the names of the streets.

Embassy of Mali 224

LOCATION: 89, rue du
Cherche-Midi
MÉTRO STATION: Saint-Placide
PATRON: The comte de Mont-
morency-Bours
ARCHITECT: Claude Le Chauve
(1757)

*This residence was built by the
comte de Montmorency-Bours,
who already owned the adjacent
hôtel (see previous entry). To dis-
tinguish the present building from
its neighbor, he called this one the
Grand Hôtel de Montmorency.*

Hôtel de Choiseul-Praslin 225

LOCATION: 2–4, rue Saint-Romain,
and 111, rue de Sèvres
MÉTRO STATION: Vaneau
PATRON: The comtesse de Choiseul
ARCHITECT: Sulpice Gaubier (1732)

Façade of 111,
rue de Sèvres

*Now hedged in by buildings, this hôtel, which has
lost its garden, was very nearly destroyed. It is now
restored, and the façade on the rue de Sèvres (originally the court façade) is especially beautiful.*

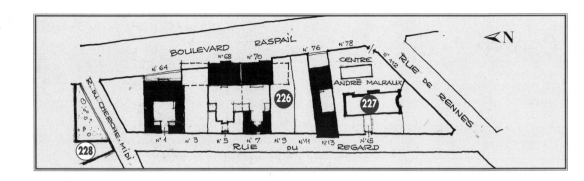

226 Hôtels, rue du Regard

LOCATION: The rue du Regard is parallel to boulevard Raspail and links the rue de Rennes to the rue du Cherche-Midi.
MÉTRO STATION: Saint-Placide

Entrance pavilion of 7, rue du Regard

The façades of nos. 64, 68, 70, and 76, boulevard Raspail do not align with the street; the opening up of the boulevard entailed destruction of the gardens of these residences, whose entrances are at the indicated numbers of the rue du Regard (see drawing). The hôtels originally situated at nos. 3, 9, and 11 were demolished.

All of them were built by a Carmelite congregation situated nearby (rue de Vaugirard), which leased them. Designed by the architect Victor Thierry Dailly, they date from 1728 and 1740.

No. 1, known as the Hôtel de Dreux-Brézé

(or Petit Hôtel de Verrue), has a beautiful porte cochere.

The service buildings of no. 5, known as the Hôtel de Croÿ, have been replaced by an apartment building incorporating the original porte cochere.

No. 7 was truncated to accommodate the boulevard Raspail. Like its neighbor at no. 5, it now houses the offices of the Caisse Nationale de Retraite du Bâtiment et des Travaux Publics (department of unused buildings and public works).

No. 13, which boasts a beautiful entrance pavilion, now houses the Sisters of Providence.

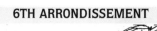

㉗ Centre André-Malraux

LOCATION: Corner of boulevard
Raspail and rue de Rennes, and 15,
rue du Regard
MÉTRO STATIONS: Rennes; Saint-
Placide

*The center is housed in the former
Crédit Municipal building (1887),
built on the site of the Hôtel de la
Guiche (1754), some elements of
which were incorporated into it (see
plan below).*

View from C in the plan
Elevation at A was moved to B

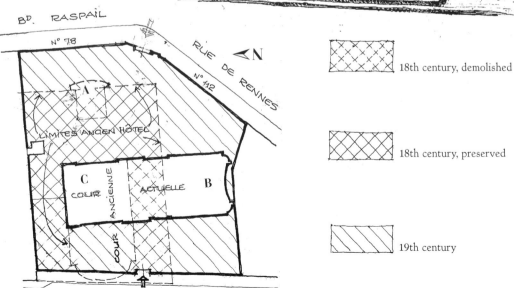

18th century, demolished

18th century, preserved

19th century

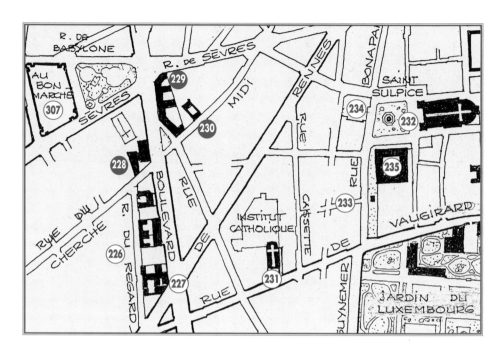

228 Maison des Sciences de l'Homme

LOCATION: 54, boulevard Raspail
MÉTRO STATION: Rennes
ARCHITECTS: H. Beauclair, P. Depondt, and M. Lods (1968)

The architects opted to express the mode of construction in the façade: the metal armature is readily apparent, as are the mobile shutters that punctuate its surface.

Unfortunately, the nine floors along the boulevard Raspail tower above the neighboring buildings; the five floors along the rue du Cherche-Midi are more deferential to the urban context.

Lutetia Hotel

LOCATION: 43, boulevard Raspail
MÉTRO STATION: Sèvres-Babylone
ARCHITECTS: Louis Boileau and Henri
Tauzin (1907–11)
SCULPTOR: Léon Binet

This public hotel is situated on the corner of the rue de Sèvres and the boulevard Raspail. Its architecture, which features carefully integrated sculptural elements, is characteristic of stylistic tendencies pervasive at the beginning of the 20th century.

Most of the decorative motifs are of vegetal inspiration, with vines predominating. The entrance retains its original decor. The hotel now has approximately 300 rooms

Hôtel de Marsilly 230

LOCATION: 18, rue du Cherche-Midi
MÉTRO STATION: Saint-Sulpice
PATRON AND ARCHITECT: Claude Bonnot (1738)

In designing this hôtel for himself, the architect took particular care with the motif above the portal, which consists of a Rococo cartouche surmounted by a cornice on consoles supporting two stone vases.

Inside, the staircase boasts a magnificent wrought-iron railing.

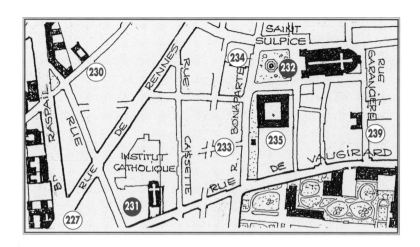

 231 Saint-Joseph-des-Carmes

LOCATION: 70, rue de Vaugirard (the church is within the precinct of the Institut Catholique but is accessible from the rue de Vaugirard)
MÉTRO STATIONS: Rennes; Saint-Placide
PATRON: The congregation of Discalced Carmelites, founded in 1611
ARCHITECT: Unidentified (built 1613–20)

Saint-Joseph-des-Carmes, whose foundation stone was laid by Marie de Médicis in 1613, is the chapel of the convent of the Discalced (unshod) Carmelites, founded in 1611, the surviving buildings of which are now occupied by the Institut Catholique. Its dome was the second to be built in Paris, having been preceded by that of the Petits-Augustins, now situated within the complex of the École des Beaux-Arts. The dome of the Carmelite chapel is a rudimentary wooden structure, but it was modeled after Italian masonry domes.

The convent was the site of tragic events during the Revolution, when it served as a prison: on September 2, 1792, more than a hundred priests were massacred here at the insistence of a mob that had forced the doors.

LOCATION: Place Saint-Sulpice
MÉTRO STATION: Saint-Sulpice
ARCHITECTS: Christophe Gamard (initial design and construction, from 1646). Daniel Gittard (second phase of design and construction, 1660–78), completed by Gilles-Marie Oppenord (1719–36). Jean-Nicolas Servandoni (façade, 1732–66). Oudot de Maclaurin (south tower, 1766–70). Charles De Wailly (Lady Chapel, 1774). Jean-François Chalgrin (balustrade and north tower, 1777–80)

Saint-Sulpice ⓶⓷⓶

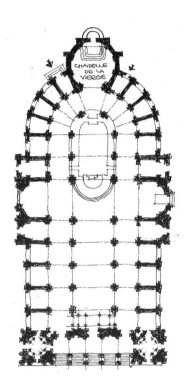

Five principal architects worked successively on this church. Although construction began in 1646, a lack of funds brought work to a halt in 1678, by which time only the choir had been completed.

Construction resumed in 1719 under the direction of Gilles-Marie Oppenord, who completed everything but the façade. A competition held in 1732 for the design of the façade was won by Jean-Nicolas Servandoni. Upon his death in 1766, its construction was overseen by Oudot de Maclaurin, who modified Servandoni's design and decided not to rebuild the pediment after it was destroyed by lightning. As a result of criticism of the tower

design, work was entrusted to Jean-François Chalgrin, who modified the north tower by applying a new stone revetment over the old, adding columns, and increasing its height.

When he was about to commence similar modification of the south tower, funds ran out, and the work was never done, which explains the asymmetry of the present façade.

The architect De Wailly also contributed to the work by rebuilding, in 1774, the Lady Chapel, which had been damaged by fire. The rear of the chapel is supported by a curious masonry corbel visible from the rue Garancière.

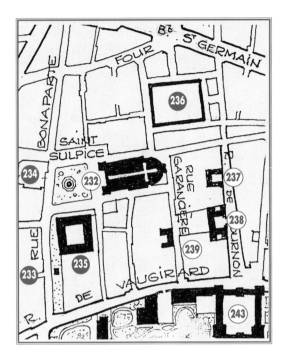

The Fontaine de la Paix (fountain of peace) was originally in the Place Saint-Sulpice; being deemed too small for that site, it was moved to the Marché Saint-Germain in 1842 and to its present location in 1935.

233 # Fontaine de la Paix

LOCATION: Allée du Séminaire (opposite 92, rue Bonaparte)
MÉTRO STATION: Saint-Sulpice
PATRON: Napoléon I
ARCHITECTS: A. Détournelle and A. Voinier (1806)

234 # Fontaine des Quatre-Évêques

LOCATION: Place Saint-Sulpice
MÉTRO STATION: Saint-Sulpice
ARCHITECT: Ludovico Visconti (1847)
SCULPTORS (in order of the works listed below): Jean-Jacques Feuchère, L. Desprez, J. Faguinet, and F. Lannot

Ludovico Visconti clearly modeled his design after the Fontaine des Innocents (see entry 37), but he increased its scale, producing a ponderous result. Furthermore, the four statues of bishops (Bossuet, Fléchier, Massillon, and Fénelon) lack the grace of the nymphs of Jean Goujon.

LOCATION: 9, Place Saint-Sulpice
MÉTRO STATION: Saint-Sulpice
ARCHITECT: Étienne-Hippolyte Godde (1820)

Former Seminary 235 of Saint-Sulpice

As the first seminary of Saint-Sulpice was destroyed beginning in 1808 to make way for the Place Saint-Sulpice, the state helped pay for reconstruction of a new one, entrusting its design to the architect Godde, the author of several neoclassical churches in Paris. It was occupied by the seminari- ans until the separation of church and state, decreed in 1905.

Godde modeled his building after Italian palazzi, but the result is nonetheless austere and massive. The building now houses offices of the Ministry of Finance.

LOCATION: Rue Clément, rue Félibien, rue Lobineau, and rue Mabillon
MÉTRO STATION: Mabillon
ARCHITECTS: Jean-Baptiste Blondel and Auguste Lusson (1813–18). O.-C. Cacoub (reconstruction of original design with modifications, 1994–96)

Marché Saint-Germain 236

Built on the site of the old Saint- Germain fair, this market, whose demolition was begun several years ago, has finally been rebuilt in accordance with its original appearance, at least on the out- side. Various public facilities have now been incorporated into the building.

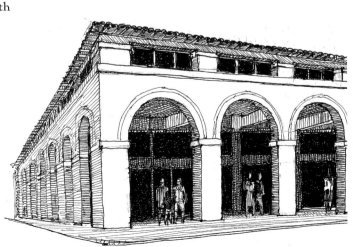

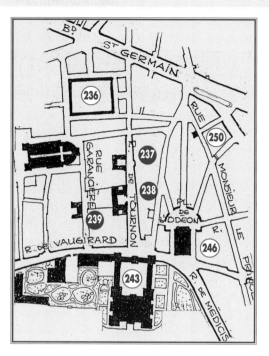

㉓⑦ Hôtel de Brancas

LOCATION: 6, rue de Tournon
MÉTRO STATIONS: Odéon; Luxembourg
PATRON: Jean Terrat, marquis de Chantosme
ARCHITECT: Pierre Bullet (c. 1706–10)

The drawing at the bottom of this page shows the monumental portal on the rue de Tournon (with its allegorical figures of Prudence and Justice). The drawing above it represents the central block, which boasts a magnificent staircase.

The residence is now the property of the Institut Français d'Architecture, which maintains an exhibition space nearby.

Court façade

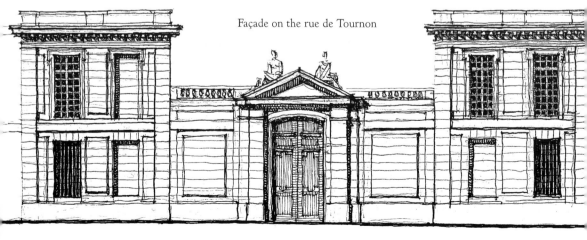

Façade on the rue de Tournon

LOCATION: 10, rue de Tournon
MÉTRO STATIONS: Odéon; Luxembourg
PATRONS: Concino Concini (1607), the future maréchal d'Ancre; then duc Louis-Jules de Nivernais (1783)
ARCHITECTS: Francesco Bordoni (1607); then Marie-Joseph Peyre, who rebuilt the residence in 1783

Hôtel du Maréchal-d'Ancre 238
(Barracks of the Garde Républicaine)

Remodeled several times, this residence is most noteworthy for its fine neoclassical portal, built in 1783 by Marie-Joseph Peyre. The building is now occupied by the Garde Républicaine.

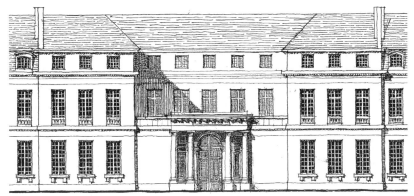

LOCATION: 8, rue Garancière
MÉTRO STATION: Saint-Sulpice
PATRON: René de Rieux, bishop and comte de Léon
ARCHITECT: Robelini (?) or Robelin (1640)

Hôtel de Sourdéac 239

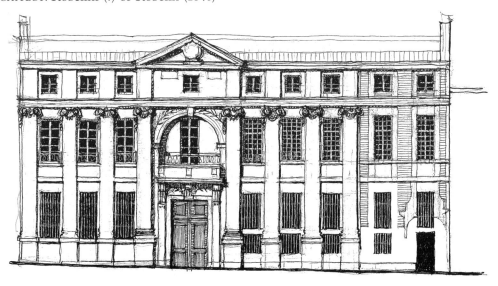

This hôtel has two notable features: the colossal order of its façade, rare in Paris at the time, and the use of Ionic capitals with ram-horn volutes.

ⓔ Luxembourg Gardens

LOCATION: Bordered by Boulevard Saint-Michel, rue de Vaugirard, rue Guynemer, rue Auguste-Comte, rue de Médicis
MÉTRO STATIONS: Luxembourg; Notre-Dame-des-Champs
PATRON: Marie de Médicis
LANDSCAPE DESIGNERS: Nicolas Deschamps, Jacques Boyceau, Alexandre Francine (17th century); then Jean-François Chalgrin (late 18th century, after demolition of the Carthusian monastery)

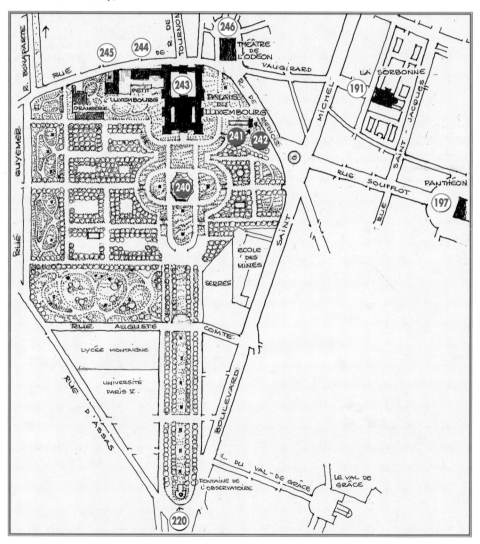

The Luxembourg gardens are in large part the gardens of the palace that Marie de Médicis built for herself beginning in 1615. They were modified after the Revolution by J.-F. Chalgrin, who profited from the demolition of the Carthusian convent to extend the perspective as far as the Observatoire. Save for their periphery, the gardens are in the classic French formal style. In addition to the fountains discussed below, they boast many statues that make them a veritable museum of 19th-century French sculpture.

Fontaine Médicis

LOCATION: Northeast area of the gardens
MÉTRO STATION: Luxembourg
PATRON: Marie de Médicis
ARCHITECT: Salomon de Brosse (attributed, c. 1620)
SCULPTOR: Auguste-Louis-Marie Ottin (1866)

This fountain dates from the original palace gardens, but it was initially configured as an artificial grotto. Its attribution to Salomon de Brosse, architect of the palace, is now contested. Restored by J.-F. Chalgrin about 1800, the fountain was shifted slightly by Alphonse de Gisors to accommodate the rue de Médicis (1861). Subsequently, it received the new statues that now decorate it, as well as a pool.

Note the curious perspectival effect resulting from the slope of the pool's edges.

Fontaine du Regard

LOCATION: Attached to the back of the Fontaine Médicis
MÉTRO STATION: Luxembourg
SCULPTORS: Achille Valois (Leda relief, 1807) and Jean-Baptiste Klagmann (naiads on the pediment, 1864)

This fountain, sometimes called the Leda Fountain, was erected in 1807 at the corner of the rue de Vaugirard and the rue du Regard, hence its name.

The laying out of the rue de Rennes entailed its displacement, and it was the architect Alphonse de Gisors who attached it to the back of the Fontaine Médicis in 1864.

243 Palais du Luxembourg

LOCATION: 15, rue de Vaugirard
MÉTRO STATIONS: Odéon; Luxembourg
PATRON: Marie de Médicis
ARCHITECTS: Salomon de Brosse
(1615–30). Alphonse de Gisors (assembly hall, 1835–41)

Façade on the boulevard de Vaugirard

In 1612, Marie de Médicis, the widow of Henri IV, acquired the Hôtel de Luxembourg, the building now known as the Petit Luxembourg (see next entry). Her intention was to build a new palace nearby, and she instructed her architect, Salomon de Brosse, to design it in a style recalling that of the Palazzo Pitti in Florence, her former home. He indeed used rustication in the Italian style, but he also honored the classic "between court and garden" formula of Parisian hôtel design.

It was for this palace that Marie de Médicis commissioned the famous cycle by Peter Paul Rubens tracing her life in twenty-four paintings (now in the Louvre). She did not long enjoy her palace, for an uprising against her, known as the Day of the Dupes (November 10, 1630), obliged

her to flee, and she never returned.

After her death in 1642, the palace became the property of Gaston d'Orléans, and then of several members of the royal family in succession. In 1791, it was declared national property and was made into a prison.

In 1799, it became home to the French Senate, and the necessary alterations were entrusted to Jean-François Chalgrin.

Between 1835 and 1841, the architect Alphonse de Gisors built a new assembly hall and enlarged the building; he added a new block to the rear (facing the pool), reproducing the original garden façade. He also built an orangery, which functioned as the Musée du Luxembourg until 1937.

Petit Luxembourg ⑳

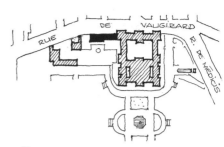

LOCATION: 17, rue de Vaugirard. The façade can be glimpsed from the Luxembourg gardens
MÉTRO STATION: Luxembourg
PATRON: Alexandre de la Tourette (early 16th century). Acquired by Marie de Médicis (1612). Remodeled by architect Germain Boffrand (c. 1710)

This building is the old Hôtel de Luxembourg that Marie de Médicis acquired in 1612 prior to building her new palace nearby. In 1627, she gave it to Cardinal Richelieu, who in turn presented it to his niece. In the 1710s, the building was remodeled and redecorated for Anne of Bavaria by Germain Boffrand. Since 1816, it has been the residence of the president of the Senate.

Convent of the Filles du Calvaire ㉔

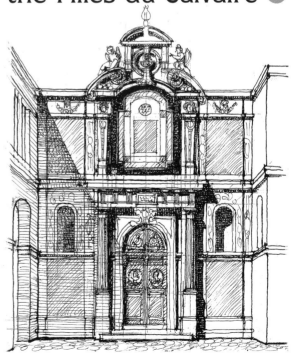

LOCATION: Remains are visible at 17 bis, boulevard de Vaugirard
MÉTRO STATION: Luxembourg
PATRON: The Benedictine congregation of Notre-Dame-du-Calvaire, founded in 1622 by Marie de Médicis

Most of the convent of the Daughters of Calvary, whose first stone was laid in 1625, is destroyed. All that survives, situated within the walls of the Petit Luxembourg, are a portion of the cloister, now remodeled as a winter garden, and the façade of the church, rebuilt in 1840 by Alphonse de Gisors at 17 bis, rue de Vaugirard (see drawing).

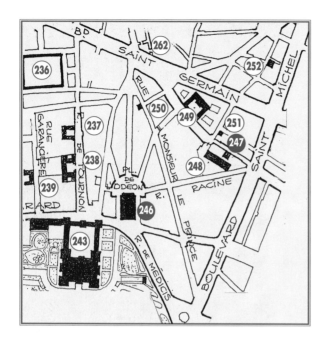

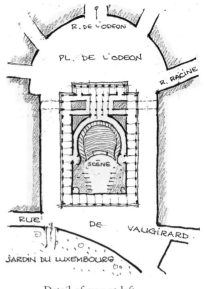

Detail of map at left

246 # Théâtre de l'Odéon

LOCATION: Place de l'Odéon
MÉTRO STATION: Odéon
PATRON: Louis XVI
ARCHITECTS: Marie-Joseph Peyre and
Charles De Wailly (1779–82)

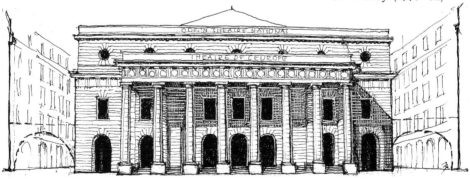

Demolished arch   Façade on the Place de l'Odéon   Demolished arch

The theater and its adjacent semicircular plaza occupy the former site of the Hôtel de Condé and its gardens, acquired by Louis XVI with the intention of building a new theater for the Comédie-Française. He entrusted its design to Peyre and De Wailly, stipulating that it was to hold an audience of 1,900, making it the largest theater in the city at the time.

The architects devised façades that are sober and even austere. Some years later, they also erect-ed the buildings of the semicircular plaza, designed to harmonize with the theater. They even linked the theater to nearby buildings with arches, envisioning the establishment of cafés there for use by patrons during the intermissions. The arches were demolished in 1818.

Two successive fires destroyed the original interiors (1799, 1818), but on both occasions the exteriors were rebuilt in accordance with the initial design.

LOCATION: 5, rue de l'École-de-Médecine
MÉTRO STATION: Odéon
PATRON: Confraternity of Barber-Surgeons
ARCHITECTS: Charles and Louis Joubert (1691–95)

Académie de Chirurgie, 247
First Amphitheater

Drawing after Jacques-François Blondel (1752–56)

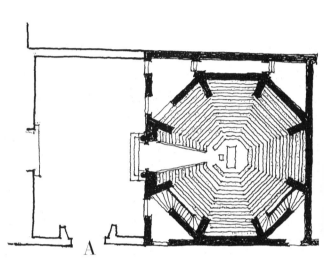

A

Portal at 6, rue de l'École-de-Médecine
(corresponds to A in plan above)

Before the Revolution, medicine and surgery were rival professions with separate training schools. In Paris, the school of medicine was on the rue de la Bûcherie and the surgery school was in the present quarter. The first amphitheater of the Académie Royale de Chirurgie (royal academy of surgery) was built between 1691 and 1695 (see drawing above). Its elevations, dome, and portal recall the anatomy amphitheater on the rue de la Bûcherie (see entry 181), whose function was similar.

After construction of the new venue (see entry 249), this first amphitheater became a drawing school (1775). It now belongs to the modern language institute of the University of Paris (Paris-III).

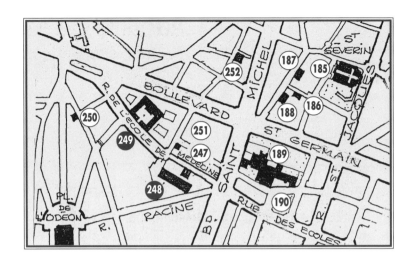

Refectory of the Franciscans

LOCATION: 15, rue de l'École-de-Médecine
MÉTRO STATION: Odéon
PATRONS: The Franciscan monks
DATE: late 14th century

This refectory was part of the Franciscan monastery in Paris, founded in the 13th century. After a period of prosperity, the monastery declined and was even deserted by the monks just prior to the Revolution. Curiously, the Revolution gave it renewed life, for the building became headquarters of the Club des Cordeliers, founded by the revolutionary leader Camille Desmoulins.

The monastery church was demolished in 1802, and the refectory is all that now remains of the complex. It consists of a large hall on the ground floor (the refectory) and two additional floors, one of which is under the eaves and is served by a spiral stair in the turret.

The ground-floor hall is now used for temporary exhibitions.

LOCATION: 12, rue de l'École-de-Médecine
MÉTRO STATION: Odéon
PATRON: Académie de Chirurgie, which became the Faculté de Médecine in 1808
ARCHITECTS: Jacques Gondoin (1776–86). Léon Ginain (extensions on three sides, 1878–1900)

Faculté de Médecine ⓶⓸⓽
(Former Académie de Chirurgie)

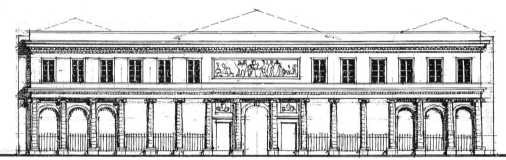

Cross section A–B

Façade on the rue de l'École-de-Médecine

After the *Académie Royale de Chirurgie (royal academy of surgery)* was founded in 1748, new quarters were commissioned from the architect *Jacques Gondoin, who designed them in a neoclassical style inspired by Roman architecture.*

The court façades are punctuated by Ionic columns. The location of the amphitheater is signaled by a Corinthian peristyle surmounted by a pediment. Within, it is covered by a coffered half-dome whose central oculus recalls the Pantheon in Rome.

The schools of surgery and medicine merged in 1794, becoming the École de Santé (school of health); this arrangement was confirmed by Napoléon in 1808, but he rechristened the consolidated institution the Faculté de Médecine (school of medicine).

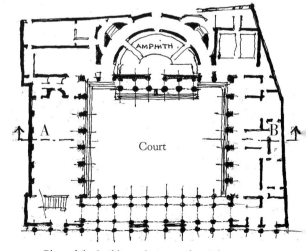

Plan of the buildings dating to the 18th century

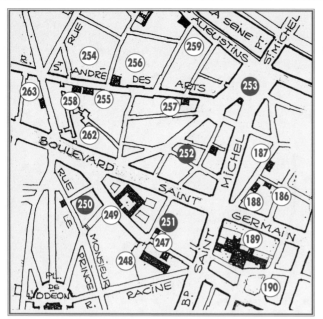

250 Hôtel Darlons

LOCATION: 4, rue Monsieur-le-Prince
MÉTRO STATION: Odéon
PATRON: Pierre Darlons (early 18th century)

This magnificent portal is certified as an historical monument.

251 Rue Hautefeuille, no. 21

MÉTRO STATION: Saint-Michel

This 16th-century octagonal turret is one of very few corner turrets to survive in Paris. The others are located as follows: rue Pavée (Hôtel de Lamoignon; see entry 120); corner of the rue Saint-Paul and rue des Lions (see entry 150); 5, rue Hautefeuille (Hôtel des Abbée de Fécamp; see entry 252); 54, rue Vieille-du-Temple (Hôtel d'Hérouet; see entry 93).

Hôtel des Abbés de Fécamp

LOCATION: 5, rue Hautefeuille
MÉTRO STATION: Saint-Michel
PATRON: Superior of the abbey of Fécamp
(1292), but the hôtel was rebuilt c. 1520–30
and the tower dates from this period.

The abbots of Fécamp possessed a Parisian residence of which all that remains is the building
shown in the drawing; its picturesque corner turret (early 15th century) is one of very few that
survive in Paris (see previous entry).

Legend has it that the building's past residents include Diane de Poitiers and the lover
of the marquise de Brinvilliers, the notorious
poisoner.

Fontaine Saint-Michel

LOCATION: Place Saint-Michel
MÉTRO STATION: Saint-Michel
ARCHITECT: Gabriel Davioud (1858–60)

The Saint-Michel fountain was created within the
context of the large-scale urbanist initiatives undertaken in the city in the mid-19th century.

Situated on the axis of the Pont Saint-Michel,
it occupies the entire gable wall of a building,
which explains its large size.

The statue in the center of the composition is by
Francisque-Joseph Duret; it represents the arch-
angel Michael crushing the Devil.

Place Saint-Michel opens onto the much more
intimate Place Saint-André-des-Arts, which occupies the site of a church of that name demolished
in 1809.

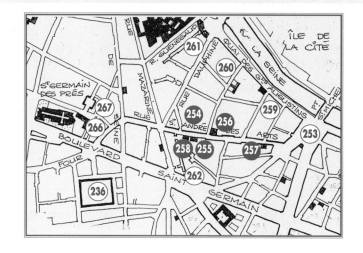

254 Rue Saint-André-des-Arts

LOCATION: Links the Place Saint-André
des-Arts to the Carrefour de Buci
MÉTRO STATIONS: Saint-Michel; Odéon

*From the Middle Ages, the rue Saint-André-des-
Arts was an important thoroughfare, for it led to
the abbey of Saint-Germain. It remains a lively
street linking the Place Saint-Michel to the Saint-
Germain-des-Prés quarter. It boasts several remarkable buildings, at the following numbers:*

*No. 27: Maison Simonnet, with a very beautiful
balcony (entry 257);
No. 47: So-called Hôtel de la Vieuville (entry 255);
No. 49: Hôtel dating from 1730–40 (entry 258);
No. 52: Maison Cotelle (entry 256).*

255 So-called Hôtel de la Vieuville

LOCATION: 47, rue Saint-André-des-Arts
MÉTRO SATIONS: Saint-Michel; Odéon
PATRON AND ARCHITECT: Jacques-
Richard Cochois (1740)

Maison Cotelle 256

LOCATION: 52, rue Saint-André-des-Arts
MÉTRO STATIONS: Saint-Michel; Odéon
ARCHITECT: François Debias-Aubry
(1737–39)

Maison Simonnet 257

LOCATION: 27, rue Saint-André-des-Arts
MÉTRO STATIONS: Saint-Michel; Odéon
ARCHITECT: Claude-Louis Daviler (1748)

Rue Saint-André-des-Arts, no. 49 258

MÉTRO STATIONS: Saint-
Michel; Odéon

*This hôtel was built about
1730–40. It is adjacent to
the Hôtel de la Vieuville
(entry 255).*

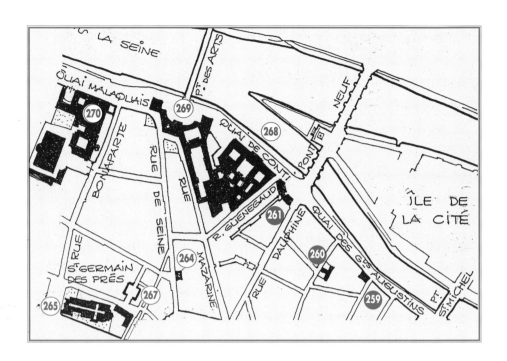

㉕㊉ Hôtel de Montholon

LOCATION: 35, quai des Grands-Augustins, and 2, rue Séguier

MÉTRO STATION: Saint-Michel

PATRON: Renée de Florette, wife of Jérôme de Montholon (?), maître d'hôtel of the regent, Anne of Austria

ARCHITECT: Unidentified (built c. 1650)

This residence, on the corner of the quai des Grands-Augustins and the rue Séguier, was occupied in 1740 by the famous printer François Didot.

The rue Séguier, formerly known as the rue Pavée (hence the address inscribed on the hôtel façade), boasts two remarkable portals, at no. 16 (Hôtel Séguier) and no. 18 (Hôtel d'Aguesseau).

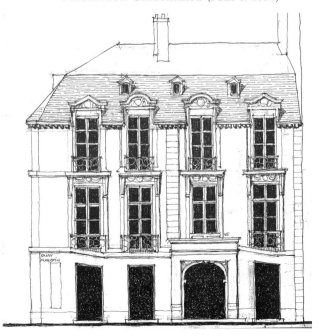

So-called Hôtel d'Hercule

LOCATION: 5–7, rue des Grands-Augustins
MÉTRO STATION: Saint-Michel
PATRON: Jean de la Driesche (first hôtel, late 15th century; destroyed); then, probably, Antoine Duprat (late 16th century)
ARCHITECT: Unidentified

The name "Hercules" ascribed to this residence, whose history is complex, is really that of the residence that preceded it. The ornamental detailing of the façade is quite original, especially the window treatments on the third floor, which incorporate motifs found nowhere else in Paris. As indicated by a plaque at the entrance to no. 7, between 1936 and 1955 this was home to Pablo Picasso; Guernica, *one of his most famous works, was painted here.*

Rue de Nevers

LOCATION: Begins at 1–3, quai de Conti, passing beneath a building that faces the Pont-Neuf
MÉTRO STATION: Pont-Neuf
ARCHITECT: Joseph Marrast (1930)

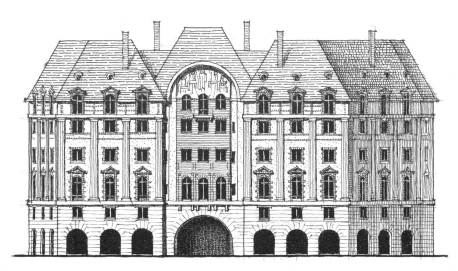

The rue de Nevers is one of the narrowest streets in Paris. Beginning at an arch passing below the building at 1–3, quai de Conti, it terminates at a surviving fragment of the Wall of Philippe Auguste. The brick-and-stone riverfront façades were conceived to harmonize with the original buildings of the Place Dauphine.

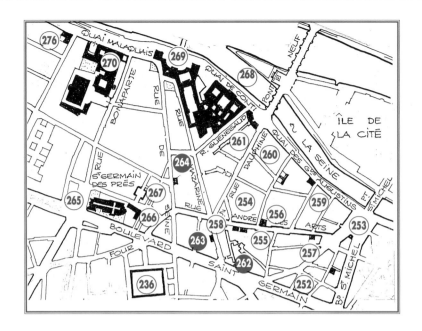

Cour de Rohan

LOCATION: Four possible modes of access (see map): rue Saint-André-des-Arts; rue de l'Ancienne-Comédie; boulevard Saint-Germain; rue du Jardinet
MÉTRO STATION: Odéon

The name "Rohan" is a corruption of "Rouen," applied to a residence originally belonging to the archbishops of that city. Its former site is now occupied by three picturesque sequential courtyards.

LOCATION: 14, rue de l'Ancienne-Comédie
MÉTRO STATION: Odéon
ARCHITECT: François d'Orbay (1688–89)
SCULPTOR: Étienne Le Hongre (reclining Minerva from the original pediment, the balance of which was removed when the theater was abandoned in 1770)

Hôtel des (263) Comédiens du Roy

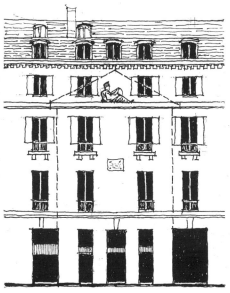

Present state

Original state

Rue de Seine, no. 57 (264)

MÉTRO STATIONS: Saint-Germain-des-Prés; Odéon
PATRON AND ARCHITECT: Pierre-Jean Varin (1740)

The architect took particular care with the proportions of this building, which he built for himself. He also worked on the Hôtel de Jaucourt (entry 31), a collaboration with Pierre Desmaisons.

Saint-Germain-des-Prés

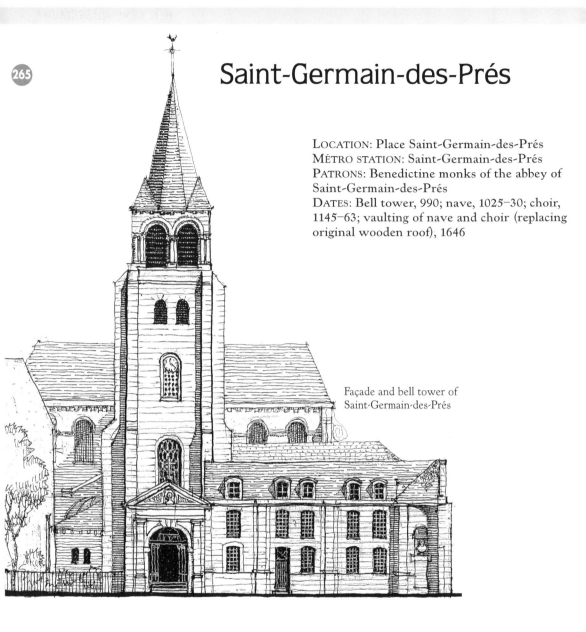

LOCATION: Place Saint-Germain-des-Prés
MÉTRO STATION: Saint-Germain-des-Prés
PATRONS: Benedictine monks of the abbey of
Saint-Germain-des-Prés
DATES: Bell tower, 990; nave, 1025–30; choir,
1145–63; vaulting of nave and choir (replacing
original wooden roof), 1646

Façade and bell tower of
Saint-Germain-des-Prés

Saint-Germain-des-Prés was originally the church of a Benedictine abbey established on the site in the 6th century, around a first basilica built in 558–59 to house relics of Saint Vincent. Saint Germain, bishop of Paris, was buried there in 576.

The oldest parts of the present church (bell tower and nave) were built c. 990–1030. A new choir was consecrated in 1163 by Pope Alexander III.

In the 13th century, Pierre de Montreuil built a Lady Chapel and several convent buildings (destroyed).

In the 14th century, the walls around the abbey

were rebuilt; they were not demolished until the 17th century.

During the Revolution, the abbey was closed and pillaged. For a time, a saltpeter factory was even installed in the church, which was subsequently abandoned. Disfigurement continued with demolition of the Lady Chapel in 1800 and of the two central towers, on the verge of collapse, in 1822. The final blow came during the Second Empire with the opening up of the boulevard Saint-Germain, which entailed demolition of the abbey prison, built in 1635.

LOCATION: 2, rue de l'Abbaye
MÉTRO STATION: Saint-Germain-des-Prés
PATRON: Charles de Bourbon, abbé de Saint-Germain-des-Prés
ARCHITECT: Guillaume Marchant (1586–90)

Palais Abbatial 266

Façade on the
rue de l'Abbaye

The Palais Abbatial was built of stone and brick, like many noble buildings of the late 16th and early 17th centuries. Cardinal de Fürstenberg, who resided here at the end of the 17th century, added service buildings; situated on axis with the palace, the present Place de Fürstenberg and the buildings fronting it belonged to this complex.

The square's modest size, its trees, and its central lamp make it one of the most agreeable spots in Paris. The Musée Delacroix is located at no. 6, in the studio occupied by the painter at the end of his life.

LOCATION: Between the rue Jacob and
rue de l'Abbaye
MÉTRO STATION: Saint-Germain-des-Prés

Place de Fürstenberg 267

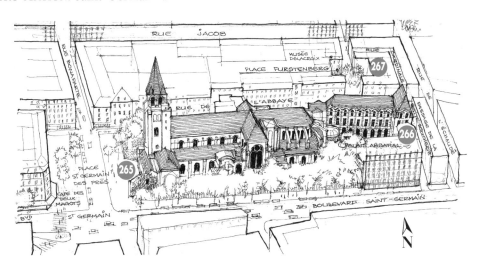

Hôtel des Monnaies

LOCATION: 11, quai de Conti
MÉTRO STATIONS: Saint-Germain-des-Prés;
Pont-Neuf
PATRON: The Royal Mint
ARCHITECT: Jacques-Denis Antoine (1771–75)

This building, originally the royal mint, now houses a workshop for coins minted in precious metals, a workshop for medals, and the Musée de la Monnaie de Paris (museum of the Paris mint).

Two prestigious residences preceded the Hôtel des Monnaies on this site: the Hôtel de Nesles and the Hôtel de Conti. The latter was demolished to make way for the new mint, previously housed in cramped quarters across the Seine on a street still called the rue de la Monnaie (west of the Samaritaine department store).

It was Louis XV who chose the new site and

entrusted the commission to the architect Antoine, who drafted an original project for the mint in the western hôtel of the Place Louis XV (now the Place de la Concorde). His definitive design was conceived such that the offices and reception rooms occupy a riverfront building that masks a network of workshops beyond.

The Hôtel des Monnaies is a building characterized by sobriety and nobility. The six allegorical statues on the attic of the central frontispiece are keyed to its official function, representing Prudence, Strength, Justice, Abundance, Commerce, and Peace.

LOCATION: 23, quai de Conti
MÉTRO STATIONS: Saint-Germain-des-
Prés; Pont-Neuf
PATRON: Cardinal Mazarin, under the
terms of his will
ARCHITECT: Louis Le Vau (1663–70,
construction completed 1688)

Institut de France

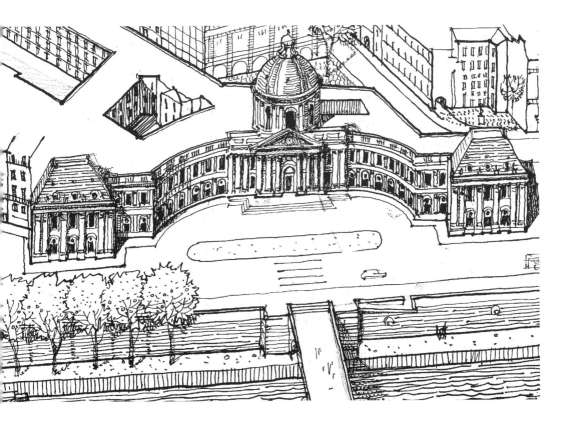

The Collège des Quatre Nations, whose former quarters now house the Institut de France, was founded by Cardinal Mazarin, who bequeathed a large sum for construction of an appropriate venue. The school was intended to educate students from the four "nations," or provinces, absorbed by France during Mazarin's ministry: Alsace, Artois, Pignerol (Piémont), and Roussillon.

Louis XIV commissioned the architect Le Vau to design the building, which is on axis with the Cour Carrée of the Louvre. In the center of the composition is the chapel, crowned by a dome whose proportions harmonize perfectly with those of the design as a whole. Construction began in 1663, but the building was not occupied until 1688, after Le Vau's death (1670).

During the Revolution, the college was closed (1790), and in 1805 Napoléon decided to make the building the seat of the Institut de France, established by the Convention in 1795. To this end, the chapel was transformed into an assembly hall. Mazarin's tomb, moved during the Revolution, was reinstalled in its original site in the vestibule of the chapel in 1962.

Façade on the quai de Conti

Detail of the frontispiece

Institut de France

Façade on the Place de l'Institut

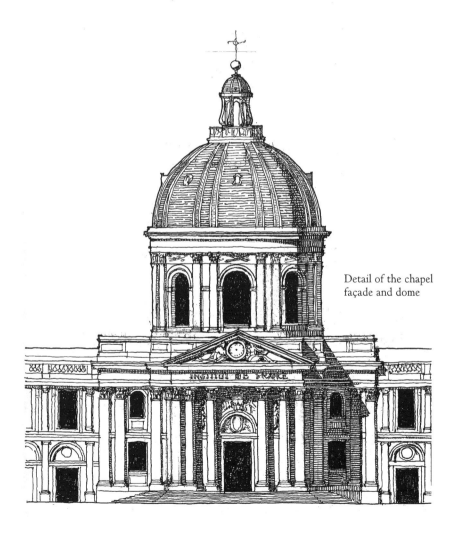

Detail of the chapel
façade and dome

École des Beaux-Arts

LOCATION: 14, rue Bonaparte and 11–17, quai Malaquais
MÉTRO STATION: Saint-Germain-des-Prés

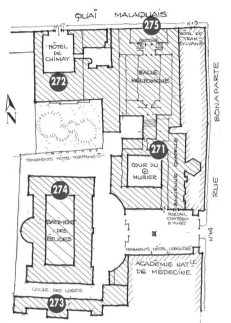

Château
d'Anet

The École des Beaux-Arts occupies the site of the convent of the Petits-Augustins, whose only surviving portions are the convent church (entry 271) and the cloister (renamed the Cour du Mürier, or court of the mulberry tree, after Felix Duban's renovations). The so-called Chapelle des Louanges (chapel of praise), adjacent to the church, is covered by the oldest dome in Paris.

During the Revolution, the convent was closed (1791) and designated a depot for works of art, mostly sculpture; its director, Alexandre-André Lenoir, subsequently transformed the holdings placed in his care into the Musée des Monuments Français.

In 1816, Lenoir's museum was closed and its facilities ceded to the École des Beaux-Arts. The remodeling was entrusted first to Debret (Loges building), then to Duban (Palais des Études; build-

École des Beaux-A

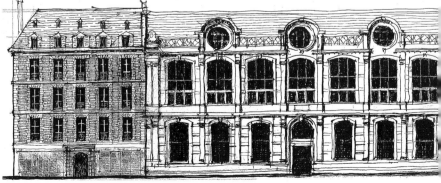

Hôtel de Transylvanie

Building by Duban, 1858–62

ing on the quai Malaquais housing, among other things, the Melpomène exhibition hall). In 1884, the school acquired the Hôtel de Chimay, which now houses administrative offices and ateliers.

The school's courtyards showcase fragments of several important buildings, notably the Château d'Anet, the Hôtel Le Gendre, and the Hôtel de la Trémoille (forecourt); and the Hôtel de Torpanne (opposite the garden façade of the Hôtel de Chimay).

Former Church and Cloister
MÉTRO STATION: Saint-Germain-des-Prés
PATRONS: The Augustinian monks, whose convent (built 1608–17) was founded by Marguerite de Valois, first wife of Henri IV

Hôtel de Chimay
MÉTRO STATION: Saint-Germain-des-Prés
PATRON: The duc de Bouillon
ARCHITECT: François Debias-Aubry (1740–56)
Built on the site of the Hôtel de La Bazinière, designed in part by François Mansart

Loges Building
MÉTRO STATION: Saint-Germain-des-Prés
ARCHITECT: François Debret (1820–29)

Contained the *loges*, or carrels, within which students had to remain while completing works for the institution's most important competitions, notably the Prix de Rome

Palais des Études
MÉTRO STATION: Saint-Germain-des-Prés
ARCHITECT: Félix Duban (1839)

Building on the Quai Malaquais
MÉTRO STATION: Saint-Germain-des-Prés
ARCHITECT: Félix Duban (1858–62)
Houses the Melpomène exhibition hall

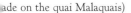

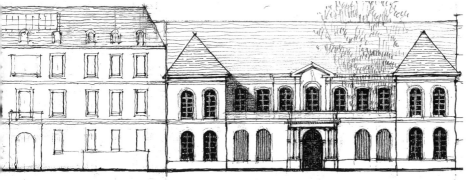

Palais des Études

ade on the quai Malaquais)

Hôtel de Chimay

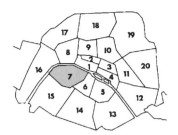

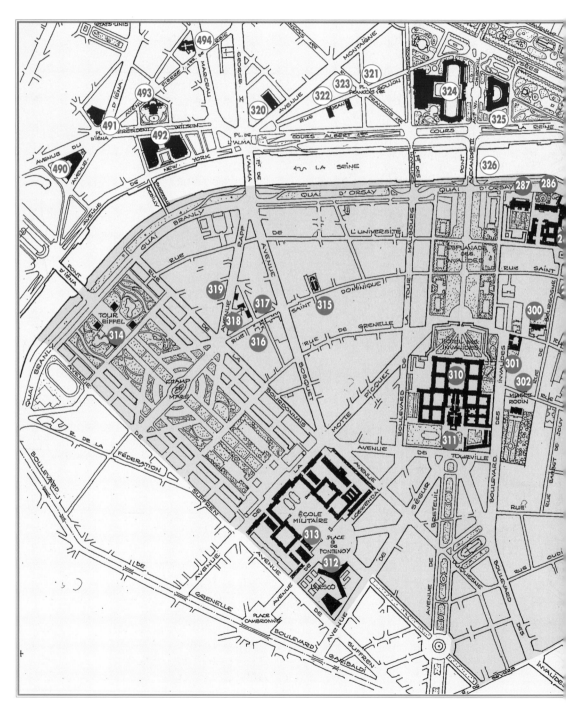

7th Arrondissement

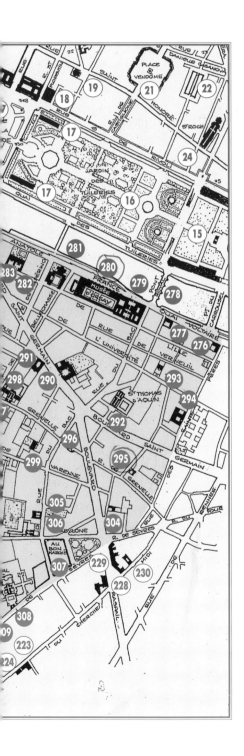

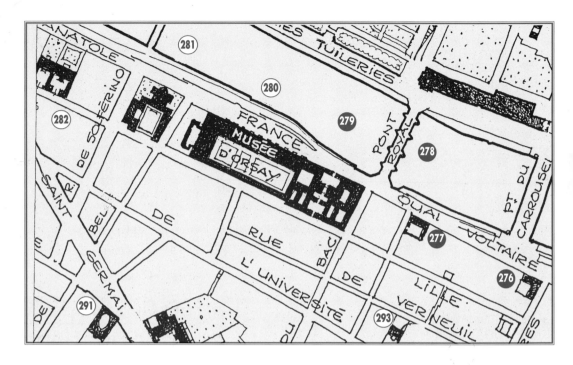

② Hôtel de Tessé

LOCATION: 1, quai Voltaire
MÉTRO STATION: Saint-Germain-des-Prés
PATRON: The comtesse de Tessé
ARCHITECT: Louis Le Tellier (1768)

Classical hôtel design typical of its period.

Hôtel de Villette ②

LOCATION: 27, quai Voltaire, and 1, rue de Beaune
MÉTRO STATION: Rue-du-Bac

Voltaire spent his last weeks here, between February and May 30, 1778, the date of his death. To commemorate this event, the quai des Théatins was rechristened the quai Voltaire.

Hôtel de Tessé

Hôtel de Villette

LOCATION: Links the 1st and 7th arrondissements
MÉTRO STATION: Rue-du-Bac
PATRON: Louis XIV
ARCHITECTS: Jacques IV Gabriel (1685–89), working from designs by Jules Hardouin-Mansart

Pont Royal ②⑦⑧

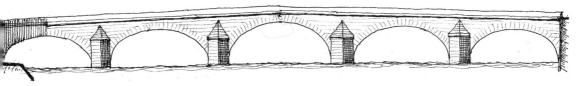

This bridge was financed by Louis XIV, which explains its name. In 1838, its inclines were reduced by removing some of the masonry. It is now a certified national monument.

LOCATION: 1–3, quai Anatole-France; 2–4, rue du Bac; 52–56, rue de Lille
MÉTRO STATION: Musée d'Orsay
PATRON: The Caisse des Dépôts (state deposit and consignment bank), which remodeled and enlarged two 18th-century hôtels damaged by fire during the Commune of 1871
ARCHITECTS: Either Eudes or Julien (reconstruction, late 19th–early 20th centuries). Recent work by Pierre Riboulet

Caisse des Dépôts ②⑦⑨ et Consignations

Façade on the quai Anatole-France

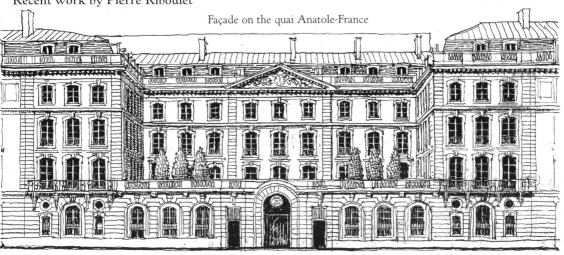

Almost nothing survives of the original 18th-century hôtels, although the present building is in imitation Louis XV style. The ensemble was recently restored and the ground-floor rooms remodeled. As a result, the rue de Lille and quai Anatole-France sides are now linked by tastefully appointed interior courtyards. One of them (Seine side) is decorated with a sculpture by Jean Dubuffet entitled Réséda (1988, conceived 1972).

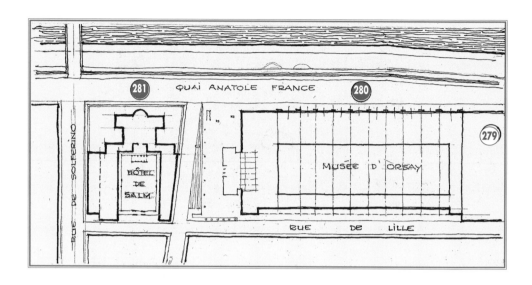

280 Musée d'Orsay

LOCATION: Quai Anatole-France
MÉTRO STATIONS: Solférino; Musée-d'Orsay
PATRONS: Chemins de Fer d'Orléans (railroad station). The French government (museum)
ARCHITECTS: Victor Laloux (railroad station, 1898–1900). R. Gardon, P. Colbac, and J.-P. Philippon (museum, 1983–86). Gae Aulenti (museum interiors, 1983–86)

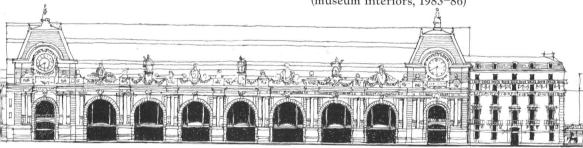

The Musée d'Orsay is housed within the former Gare d'Orsay railroad station (1900), itself built on the site of the Palais d'Orsay (1838), which burned during the Commune (1871). The ruins of the palace were left standing until 1897, when the land was purchased by the Orléans railroad company as the site for a station more centrally located than the Gare d'Austerlitz, owned by the same firm.

After a competition, the new station's design was entrusted to the architect Victor Laloux, who devised a building with an imposing metal arma-ture that was hidden from the viewer on the street by a monumental stone façade decorated with sculpture. The design also featured a large public hotel, likewise of metal-frame construction, with 600 rooms.

The station opened in 1900 and continued to serve the principal train lines until 1939. There-after, it was progressively abandoned, and eventu-ally its demolition was envisioned. Finally, the deci-sion was made to transform the structure into a showcase for 19th-century art. The new museum was inaugurated in December 1986.

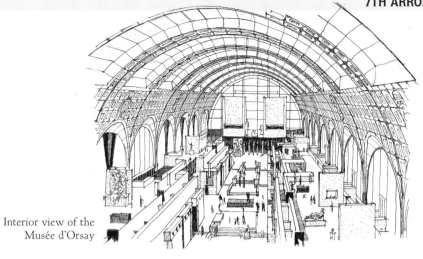

Interior view of the
Musée d'Orsay

LOCATION: 64, rue de Lille
MÉTRO STATIONS: Solférino; Musée-d'Orsay
PATRON: Friedrich de Salm-Kyrbourg
ARCHITECTS: Pierre Rousseau (original
building, 1782–87). Lejeune (extension along
the rue de Solférino, 1866–70)
SCULPTORS: Philippe-Laurent Roland and
Jean-Guillaume Moitte

Hôtel de Salm ㉛
(Palais de la Légion d'Honneur)

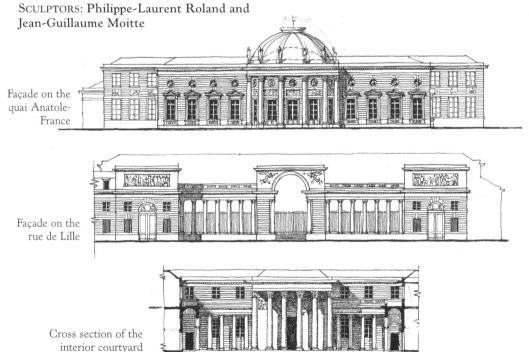

Façade on the
quai Anatole-
France

Façade on the
rue de Lille

Cross section of the
interior courtyard

Prince Friedrich de Salm-Kyrbourg did not long enjoy his residence, completed in 1787, for he was guillotined during the Revolution. The building was acquired in 1804 by the grand chancellory of the Légion d'Honneur (legion of honor) to serve as its *administrative headquarters; it now also houses the museum of the Légion d'Honneur. The residence was burned in 1871 during the Commune but was restored much as before, save for the cupola, whose height was increased, and the interiors.*

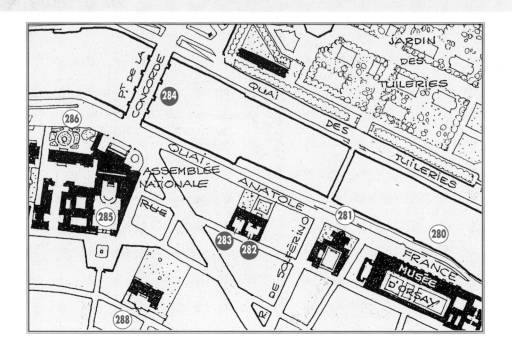

⑱ Hôtel
de Beauharnais
(Hôtel de Torcy)

LOCATION: 78, rue de Lille (garden façade
visible from the quai Anatole-France)
MÉTRO STATION: Assemblée-Nationale
PATRONS: Germain Boffrand, who sold it
upon completion to the marquis de Torcy.
Acquired by Eugène de Beauharnais in 1803
ARCHITECT: Germain Boffrand (1714–15)

Hôtel ⑱
de Seignelay
(Ministry of Commerce)

LOCATION: 80, rue de Lille (garden façade
visible from the quai Anatole-France)
MÉTRO STATION: Assemblée-Nationale
PATRONS: Germain Boffrand, who sold it in
1718 to the comte de Seignelay
ARCHITECT: Germain Boffrand (1714–15)

Hôtel de Beauharnais   Garden façades   Hôtel de Seignelay

These two residences were built by the architect Germain Boffrand, who sold them upon completion, one to the comte de Seignelay and the other to the marquis de Torcy. Their façades are quite similar and they form a handsome ensemble—which was even more harmonious originally, for their rooflines were consistent (indicated in drawing opposite). In 1804, Eugène de Beauharnais, who then owned one of the residences, added an Egyptian entry portico to commemorate the Egyptian campaign in which he had taken part. Needless to say, the result mars the harmony of the façade. Since 1814, the Hôtel de Beauharnais has been the residence of the German ambassador. The Hôtel de Seignelay now houses the French Ministry of Commerce.

Hôtel de Beauharnais, Egyptian entry portico

LOCATION: Links the Place de la Concorde to the Left Bank
MÉTRO STATIONS: Assemblée-Nationale; Concorde
ARCHITECT: Jean-Rodolphe Perronet (design, 1777; construction, 1788–91)

Pont de la Concorde

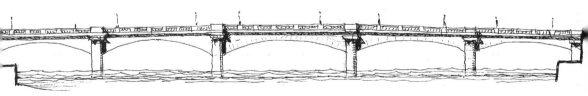

The bridge was begun in 1788 and completed in 1791, when the Revolution was in full swing. For symbolic reasons, and doubtless to save money as well, stones from the Bastille were incorporated into the structure.

The columns terminating each of the piers were originally intended to support decorative metal pyramids, but in the end this scheme was judged too expensive. Napoléon decided to adorn the pedestals with busts of generals of the empire who had perished in battle; carving began, but the Restoration intervened and the commission was canceled. In 1830, after another change of government, twelve different monumental statues were installed; these were removed in 1836 and have never been replaced. The bridge was widened in 1931.

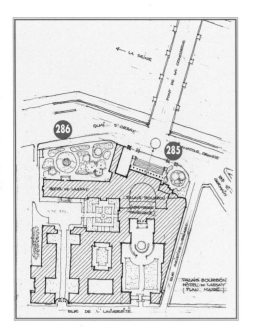

285 Palais Bourbon
(National Assembly)

LOCATION: 126–128, rue de l'Université; 29–35, quai d'Orsay

MÉTRO STATION: Assemblée-Nationale

PATRON: Originally, Louise-François de Bourbon (daughter of Louis XIV and Madame de Montespan), 1722

ARCHITECTS: Giovanni Giardini (original residence, 1722); then, after his death, Pierre Cailleteau, known as Lassurance (1722–24); then, after his death, Jean Aubert and Jacques V Gabriel (1724; work completed 1730). Jacques Gisors and Emmanuel Leconte (Salle des Cinq-Cents [hall of the five hundred], 1795). Bernard Poyet (riverfront façade, designed to harmonize with the Madeleine, 1806). Jules de Joly (later modifications, notably, remodeling of the assembly hall, 1828)

Palais Bourbon, façade, on the quai Anatole-France

Built for the duchesse de Bourbon, this palace was sold in 1764 to the prince de Condé, who four years later acquired the adjacent Hôtel de Lassay. During the Revolution, the Palais Bourbon was confiscated by the state and designated the seat of the Council of Five Hundred, for which a large semicircular meeting hall was added in 1795. In 1807, Napoléon decided to build a new river façade on axis with, and in the same style as, the church of the Madeleine across the Seine. This was not an easy task, for the new axis, that of the intervening Pont de la Concorde, diverged significantly from that of the Palais Bourbon (see map above). In 1828, a new assembly hall was commissioned from the architect Joly, who opted for a semicircular plan largely consistent with the outline of the first one. This room remains the meeting hall of the French National Assembly.

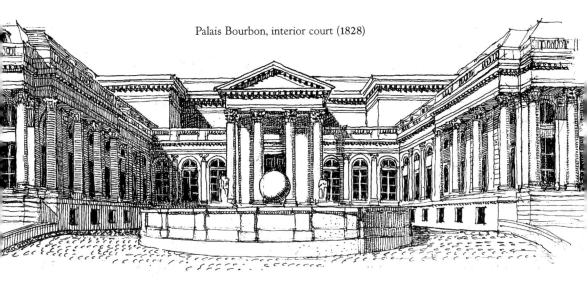

Palais Bourbon, interior court (1828)

LOCATION: 128, rue de l'Université. The hôtel is
connected to the Palais Bourbon by a gallery
MÉTRO STATION: Assemblée-Nationale
PATRON: The marquis Armand de Lassay (1722)
ARCHITECTS: Same as for the Palais Bourbon, 1722–28
(see entry 285)

Hôtel de Lassay

*This hôtel, built for the marquis de Lassay, was
acquired in 1768 by the prince de Condé, who
already owned the adjacent residence. Like the
Palais Bourbon, the Hôtel de Lassay originally had
only one floor. The upper level, which incorporates
decorative elements from the original roof treatment, was added in 1854.*

*Linked to the National Assembly by a gallery,
the building is now the official residence of the president of the Assembly.*

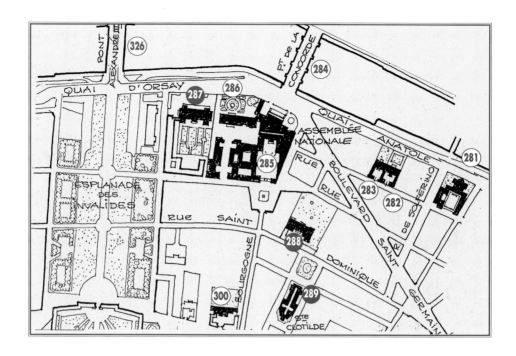

287 Ministry of Foreign Affairs

LOCATION: 37, quai d'Orsay
MÉTRO STATION: Invalides
PATRON: The French government
ARCHITECT: Jacques Lacornée
(1845–54)

Façade on the quai d'Orsay

This ministry, often referred to simply as the "quai d'Orsay," is housed in an exceptionally long building in a late neoclassical idiom. The rather dense ornament on the façade includes white marble medallions, above the main-floor windows, that were to have been carved with the arms of nations friendly to France. Given the mutability of such alliances, it is easy to understand why they were finally left blank.

On the orders of Napoléon III, who became emperor in 1852, while work was under way, the interiors were given opulent decoration.

LOCATION: 14, rue Saint-Dominique
MÉTRO STATION: Solférino
PATRON: François Duret for the marquise de Prie
ARCHITECT: François-Debias Aubry (1724–25)

Hôtel de Brienne (288)
(Ministry of Defense)

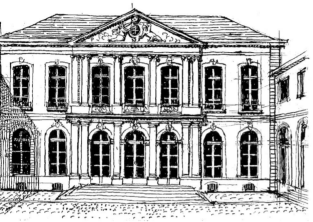

Forecourt façade

The hôtel is now named after Loménie de Brienne, secretary of state for war, who acquired it in 1776. Many illustrious figures have resided here, notably Laetitia, the mother of Napoléon I, and General Charles de Gaulle (August 1944–January 1946). In commemoration of de Gaulle's residency, a cross of Lorraine was carved on the pediment of the forecourt façade. Since 1817, the hôtel has been the official residence of the French minister of armed forces.

Sainte-Clotilde (289)
(Basilica Sainte-Clotilde-Sainte-Valère)

LOCATION: 23 bis, rue Las-Cases
MÉTRO STATION: Solférino
ARCHITECT: François-Christian Gau
(1846–53); then, after his death, Théodore
Ballu (1853–57)

An architect born in Cologne who settled in France, Christian Gau was doubtless the first to propose the construction in Paris of a neo-Gothic church. His design occasioned much criticism during both its design phase (which was prolonged) and its construction. Although derided as a "gauthique" pastiche, it inaugurated, in Paris and elsewhere, a long series of neo-Gothic churches.

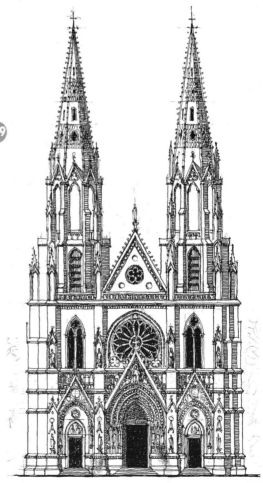

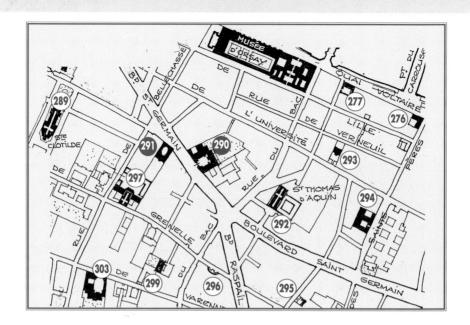

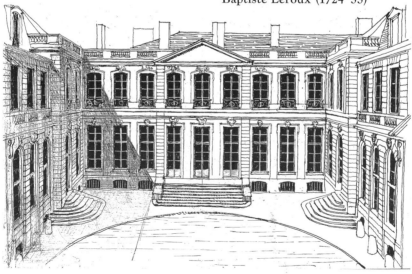 Hôtel de Roquelaure

LOCATION: 246, boulevard Saint-Germain
MÉTRO STATION: Rue-du-Bac
PATRON: The duc de Roquelaure
ARCHITECTS: Pierre Cailleteau, known as
Lassurance (1724); then, after his death, Jean-
Baptiste Leroux (1724–33)

Forecourt
façade

The rather severe façades of this hôtel are the work of Lassurance, but its interiors were realized by Jean-Baptiste Leroux after his colleague's death. The original decoration of the vestibule and a cabinet survive.

In 1808, the Hôtel de Roquelaure was consoli-

dated with the adjacent Hôtel de Lesdiguières. In 1832, the complex became home to the Council of State, then, in 1839, to the Ministry of Public Works. It now houses the Ministry of Equipment and Transport.

Hôtel Amelot de Gournay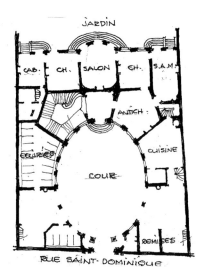

LOCATION: 1, rue Saint-Dominique
MÉTRO STATION: Solférino
PATRONS: Germain Boffrand; then
Michel Amelot de Gournay, who
acquired the hôtel in 1713
ARCHITECT: Germain Boffrand (1712)

Court
façade

This hôtel has several original features, most notably an oval forecourt. Boffrand's use of a colossal order that rises the full height of the court *façade gives the central block exceptional dignity. The garden façade also features a central curved wall, this one convex (see plan above).*

② Saint-Thomas-d'Aquin

LOCATION: Place Saint-Thomas-d'Aquin
MÉTRO STATION: Rue-du-Bac
PATRONS: The Dominican monks
ARCHITECTS: Pierre Bullet (1683–88); frère Claude Navan (façade, 1770)

This church, begun in 1683, was that of the Dominican novitiate, located on this site since 1631. Due to a shortage of funds, the monks' choir was not built until 1722 and the façade in 1770. The façade, similar to that of Saint-Roch, is typical of the purified Baroque idiom favored at the time.

The church became a Temple of Peace during the Revolution but was restored to the Catholic Church in 1802. Its interior is richly decorated, boasting a ceiling fresco painted by François Lemoyne in 1724 (chapel of Saint Louis, the former monks' choir).

② Hôtel de Sénectère
(Ministry of Crafts)

LOCATION: 24, rue de l'Université
MÉTRO STATION: Rue-du-Bac
PATRONS: Thomas Gobert (1685); then comte Henri-Charles de Sénectère (1772)
ARCHITECTS: Thomas Gobert (1685); then Nicolas Ducret and Denis-Claude

The façade pictured in the drawing, with its curving porch, dates from the remodeling effected in 1772, after the hôtel was acquired by the comte de Sénectère. The façade fronting the street was remodeled in 1837.

Forecourt façade

LOCATION: 28, rue des Saints-Pères
MÉTRO STATION: Saint-Germain-des-Prés
PATRON: Jacques Frécot de Lanty, conseiller
au Parlement; then Jacques Brochet de
Saint-Prest
ARCHITECT: Jacques-Denis Antoine (1772)

Hôtel de Fleury 294
(School of Civil Engineering)

Façade on the rue des Saints-Pères

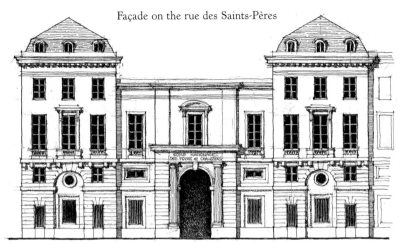

The architect of this hôtel also designed the prestigious Hôtel des Monnaies (see entry 268). Unfortunately, his conception for the Hôtel de Fleury was greatly altered in 1831, when the building became the École Nationale des Ponts et Chaussées (school of civil engineering). The width of the façade on the rue des Saints-Pères was doubled, with unfortunate results. The sketch above represents the street façade reduced to its original width, but the second floor of the three central bays is a later addition.

Maison de Verre 295

LOCATION: 31, rue Saint-Guillaume,
in the courtyard
MÉTRO STATIONS: Saint-Germain-
des-Prés; Sèvres-Babylone
PATRON: Dr. Jean Dalsace
ARCHITECT: Pierre Chareau (1931)

This house caused quite a stir when it was built, largely because its façades are faced integrally with prefabricated glass bricks. Further innovations were introduced within, notably movable walls and ceilings.

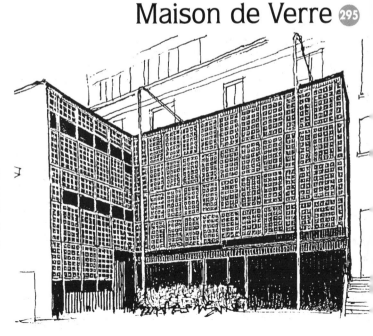

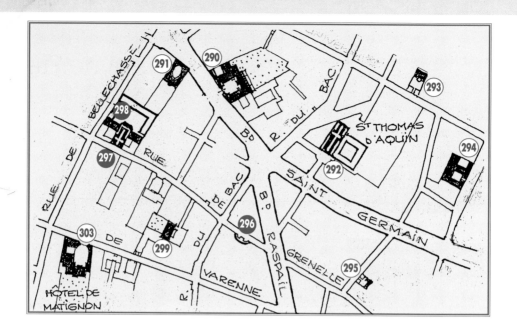

Fontaine des Quatre-Saisons

LOCATION: 57–59, rue de Grenelle
MÉTRO STATION: Rue-du-Bac
PATRON: The City of Paris
DESIGNER: The sculptor Edme
Bouchardon (1739–45)

Despite its grandiose proportions, this magnificent fountain remains relatively little known, for it is situated in a narrow street that prevents its being viewed from a proper distance, despite the concave plan adopted by Bouchardon.

The central frontispiece is decorated with a seated figure of the City of Paris, flanked by reclining figures of the Seine and the Marne Rivers. Lateral niches are occupied by personifications of the Four Seasons, below which are four masterly bas-reliefs representing putti engaged in corresponding seasonal occupations.

The two buildings illustrated on this page originally belonged to the same ensemble: the convent of the nuns of Pentemont, whose mother house was located in the Beauvais region. Initially lodged in a former convent, the nuns

Protestant Church 297 of Pentemont

LOCATION: 104–106, rue de Grenelle
MÉTRO STATION: Solférino
PATRONS: Nuns of the abbey of Notre-Dame de Pentemont
ARCHITECT: Pierre Contant d'Ivry
(1747–77, work completed 1783)

Façade on the rue de Grenelle

Abbaye 298 de Pentemont
(Veterans' Administration)

LOCATION: 37, rue de Bellechasse
MÉTRO STATION: Solférino
PATRONS: Nuns of the abbey of Notre-Dame de Pentemont
ARCHITECT: Pierre Contant d'Ivry
(1747–77, work completed 1783)

decided to have the complex rebuilt. Work began in 1747 and continued for more than thirty-five years. The drawing above represents the chapel (now the Protestant church of Pentemont), which features a Greek-cross plan and a pendentive cupola over the crossing. After being confiscated by the state during the Revolution, the convent buildings were put to various uses. Notably, they served as a barracks for the Cent-Gardes, a designation that occasioned the construction of new buildings.

In 1844, the chapel became a Protestant church, and Victor Baltard, entrusted with the remodeling, opted to suppress the central door to accommodate an organ. The convent buildings now house the French Veterans' Administration.

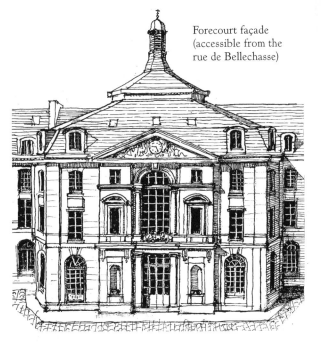

Forecourt façade (accessible from the rue de Bellechasse)

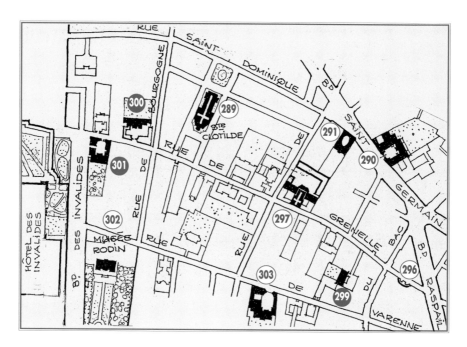

299 Hôtel de Gallifet

(Italian Cultural Institute)

LOCATION: 73, rue de Grenelle and 50, rue de Varenne (public entrance)
MÉTRO STATION: Varenne
PATRON: Simon de Gallifet
ARCHITECT: Étienne-François Legrand (1784)

Garden façade

This hôtel was originally entered from the rue du Bac; its present portal at 73, rue de Grenelle, dates only from 1837. Seized during the Revolution, the building was remodeled in 1794 to house the Ministry of Foreign Affairs, of which Talleyrand was minister from 1797 to 1807. The heirs of the comte de Gallifet regained possession in 1822; they later sold the portion situated on the rue du Bac, which explains the creation of the portal on the rue de Grenelle. The building now houses the Institut Culturel Italien, whose entrance is located at 50, rue de Varenne.

LOCATION: 138–140, rue de Grenelle
MÉTRO STATION: Varenne
PATRON: The duc de Noirmoutiers
ARCHITECT: Jean Courtonne (1720–23)

Hôtel de Noirmoutiers ③⓪⓪

Forecourt
façade

The presence of the Hôtel de Noirmoutiers is marked on the rue de Grenelle by a monumental portal flanked by Ionic columns supporting a curved entablature. Its court façade is extremely refined, incorporating a central frontispiece surmounted by a pediment (which has lost its sculp- *ture) and an elegant balcony supported by carved consoles.*

Originally, as with the Hôtel de Matignon (also designed by Courtonne, see entry 303), the beginning of the roof was masked by a balustrade.

LOCATION: 127, rue de Grenelle (corner of the boulevard des Invalides)
MÉTRO STATION: Varenne
PATRON: The comte and comtesse du Châtelet-Losmont
ARCHITECT: Mathurin Cherpitel (1770–76)

Hôtel du Châtelet ③⓪①

Forecourt
façade

The monumental portal and large semicircular courtyard culminating in a façade dominated by an imposing Corinthian colonnade give this hôtel an air of exceptional grandeur and nobility. During the Revolution, it was confiscated and its owner *sent to the scaffold. After serving for a time, beginning in 1796, as the École des Ponts et Chaussées (school of bridges and roadways), it has been put to various uses. Since 1907, it has housed the Ministry of Labor.*

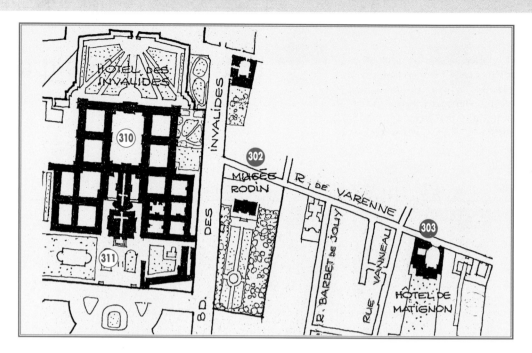

Musée Rodin

(Hôtel Peyrenc de Moras
or Hôtel de Biron)

LOCATION: 77, rue de Varenne
MÉTRO STATION: Varenne
PATRON: The financier Abraham Peyrenc
de Moras
ARCHITECTS: Jean Aubert and Jacques V Gabriel
(1727–32)

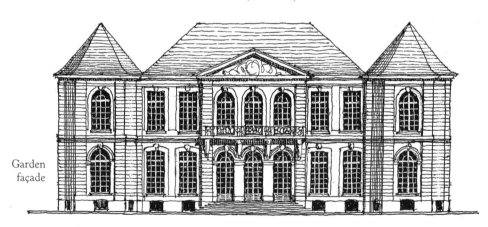

Garden
façade

There are two good reasons to visit this hôtel: it is one of the most beautiful in Paris, and it is devoted to the sculptor Auguste Rodin. The financier Abraham Peyrenc de Moras, enriched by the speculations of the banker John Law, built this residence, his third in Paris. It was later purchased in succession by the duchesse du Maine and the maréchal de Biron (1753) and came to be known as the Hôtel de Biron.

From 1829 to 1902, it served as a residence for young girls; the chapel on the rue de Varenne dates from this period. In 1904, the French state became the owner and began to rent portions of it to artists. Rodin resided here from 1908 until his death in 1917. Since he bequeathed all the work then in his possession to the government, the state chose to restore the hôtel and transform it into the Musée Rodin. Several of the artist's larger works are on display in the gardens, which have also been restored.

LOCATION: 57, rue de Varenne
MÉTRO STATION: Varenne
PATRON: Chrétien-Louis de Montmorency-
Luxembourg, prince de Tingry; then, from 1723,
Jacques de Matignon, comte de Thorigny
ARCHITECT: Jean Courtonne (1722–23)

Hôtel de Matignon

Forecourt façade

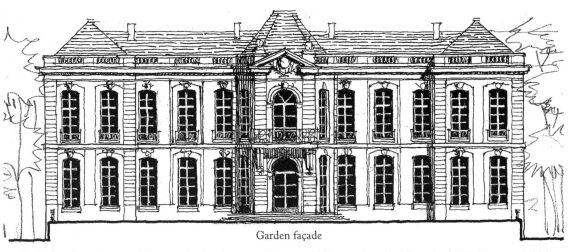

Garden façade

Built for the prince de Tingry, the hôtel was sold, while construction was still under way, to Jacques de Matignon, who entrusted completion of the work to the architect Jean Mazin.

The plan above shows how Courtonne deftly negotiated a shift in axis between the court and garden façades, the latter being much wider than the former. Similar dispositions were subsequently adopted in many Parisian town houses.

Talleyrand resided here in 1810. Between 1888 and 1914, it housed the Austro-Hungarian embassy. Subsequently purchased by the French government, in 1935, it was designated the official residence of the president of the Council of State; since 1958, it has been the residence of the prime minister.

The hôtel boasts one of the most beautiful private gardens in Paris, extending to the rue de Babylone.

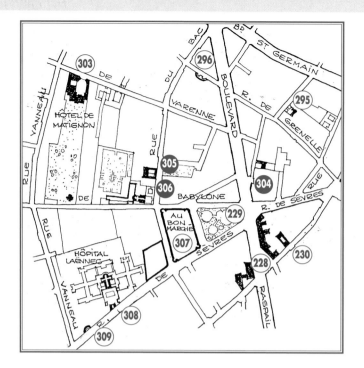

304 Institut d'Études Politiques

LOCATION: 9, rue de la Chaise
MÉTRO STATION: Sèvres-Babylone
PATRON: Gaillard de Beaumanoir
ARCHITECT: Alexandre-Louis De Labrière (c. 1775)

This small, little-known hôtel, which houses the Institut d'Études Politiques, boasts a façade notable for its harmonious proportions and is a certified national monument. Nos. 7 and 11, rue de la Chaise are by the same architect.

MÉTRO STATION: Vaneau
PATRON: Congregation of Foreign Missions
ARCHITECT: Nicolas Lepas-Dubuisson (1714)

Rue du Bac, nos. 118 and 120

305

From the beginning, these two paired residences, known collectively as the Hôtels Clermont-Tonnerre, were meant to be leased. Chateaubriand, who spent the last decade of his life in no. 120 (1838–48), was their most illustrious tenant. The architect of the two buildings was the son of the master mason who built the chapel of the Seminary of Foreign Missions, situated at 128, rue du Bac (see following entry). Both hôtels feature remarkable portals.

Portal of no. 118

LOCATION: 128, rue du Bac
MÉTRO STATION: Vaneau
PATRON: Congregation of Foreign Missions
ARCHITECT: Pierre Lambert (1683)
BUILDER: The master mason Lepas-Dubuisson (1683–89)

Chapel of the Seminary of Foreign Missions

306

The Seminary of Foreign Missions was created in the 17th century to train priests for foreign missionary work, especially in East Asia. The first lots were acquired in this quarter around 1650, or roughly thirty years before construction of the chapel. The grille to the right of the chapel leads to a large garden (not visible from the street) and the Grand Logis (large dormitory), an austere three-story building dating from 1732.

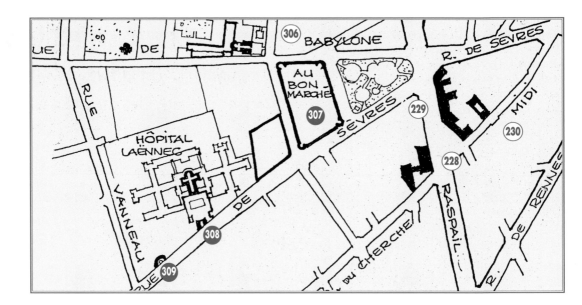

Le Bon Marché

LOCATION: 22–36, rue de Sèvres, rues Velpeau and Babylone
MÉTRO STATION: Sèvres-Babylone
PATRONS: Aristide and Marguerite Boucicaut (first store, 1852; destroyed)
ARCHITECTS: Alexandre Laplanche (first phase, 1869–72). Louis-Charles Boileau (later phases: rue Velpeau, 1872–74; rue de Sèvres, 1879–87, with metal frame by Gustave Eiffel). Hippolyte Boileau (new store west of the rue du Bac, 1920–23)

Building in 1872

In 1852, Aristide Boucicaut opened a small store on the corner of the rue de Sèvres and the rue du Bac. Systematically reinvesting his profits, he set about acquiring the surrounding propety. In 1869, he built a new store, designed along conventional structural lines, on the corner of the rue de Sèvres and the rue Velpeau (see drawing above).

Beginning in 1872, two additions were built, the second of which incorporated a metal frame designed by Gustave Eiffel (begun 1879). This part of the store boasted a magnificent monumental stairway, unfortunately destroyed in the course of work carried out between 1987 and 1991.

Chapel of the  Laënnec Hospital
(Former Hospice des Incurables)

LOCATION: 42, rue de Sèvres
MÉTRO STATION: Vaneau
PATRON: Establishment of the origi‑
nal hospice was made possible by
several bequests and gifts, notably
from Abbot François Joulet de
Châtillon (1625) and Cardinal de La
Rochefoucauld (1634).
ARCHITECT: Christophe Gamard
(1633–40)

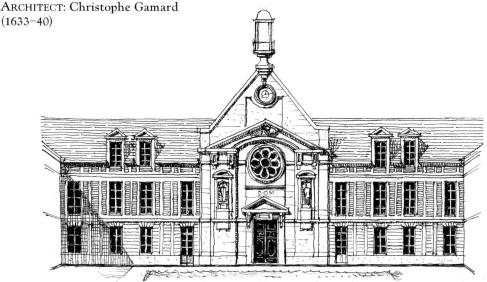

This chapel was built for the Hospice des Incu‑
rables (patients with incurable illnesses), other por‑
tions of which also survive, although they are
obscured by more recent construction (see the La

Rochefoucauld and Gamard courtyards). The
buildings that flank the chapel are of recent vintage,
but their brick‑and‑stone façades harmonize with
the original structure.

Fontaine du Fellah

LOCATION: Rue de Sèvres, left of
the entry to the Laënnec Hospital
MÉTRO STATION: Vaneau
SCULPTOR: Pierre Beauvallet
ARCHITECT: Nicolas Bralle
(1806–7)

The style of the Fellah fountain reflects the French
vogue for Egyptian art after Napoléon's Egyptian
campaign (1798–99). Fellah is an Egyptian word
for peasant or worker, most often associated in Ori‑
entalist iconography with the task of water carrier.

³¹⁰ Hôtel des Invalides

LOCATION: Esplanade des Invalides
MÉTRO STATIONS: Varenne; Latour-Maubourg
PATRON: Louis XIV
ARCHITECTS: Libéral Bruant (main building,
1671–76). Libéral Bruant, realized by Jules
Hardouin-Mansart (Soldier's Church,
1676–78). Dome Church: see following entry.

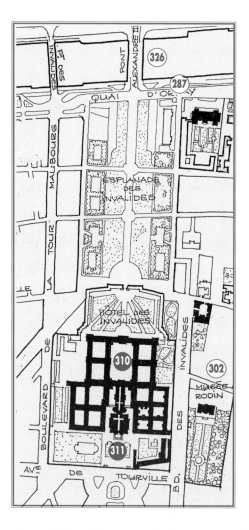

the church (now known as the Soldiers' Church), whose design he modified to accommodate the projected Dome Church (see next entry).

The main façade of the complex is some 656 feet long. It is organized around a large portal crowned by a rounded arch framing an equestrian statue of Louis XIV by Guillaume Coustou (as recarved in 1815). This portal provides access to a majestic courtyard often used for military drills.

Note the lucarne (dormer) windows of the façade: each one is different, although they all incorporate helmets and shields—with one notable exception. The fifth lucarne to the right of the central portal features the head of a wolf. This is a play on the name of the minister of war who oversaw construction of the complex: Louvois, which corresponds in French to le loup voit ("the wolf sees").

Louis XIV, rightly concerned about the fate of disabled soldiers without resources, decided to erect a large residential complex for them on the Grenelle Plain. He entrusted its design to Libéral Bruant, who had previously begun work on the chapel of the Salpétrière hospital (see entry 426).

In 1676, work was entrusted to Jules Hardouin-Mansart, who remained in charge until completion of the project. He honored Bruant's plans, save for

Detail of the façade opposite above

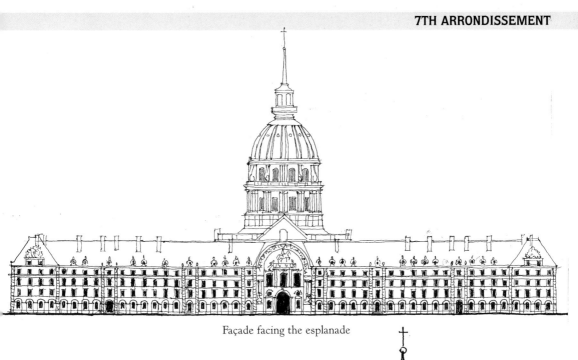

Façade facing the esplanade

LOCATION: Place Vauban;
also accessible from the
Hôtel des Invalides
MÉTRO STATION: Varenne
PATRON: Louis XIV
ARCHITECT: Jules Hardouin-
Mansart (1679–1708)

Dome ③⑪ Church of the Invalides

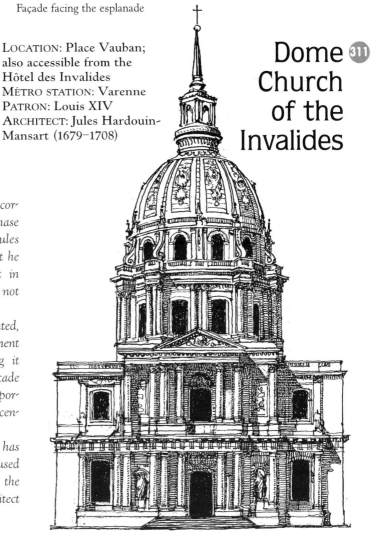

The Dome Church of the Invalides cor-responds in large part to a second phase of construction envisioned by Jules Hardouin-Mansart from the moment he assumed supervision of the project in 1676, although apparently it was not begun until 1679.

It is much more richly ornamented, but serves as a perfect visual complement to the adjacent complex, providing it with a welcome vertical accent. Its façade is dominated by the dome, whose propor-tions harmonize beautifully with the cen-tral portal composition.

Since 1840, the Dome Church has contained the tomb of Napoléon, housed in an impressive crypt visible from the main floor and designed by the architect Louis Visconti.

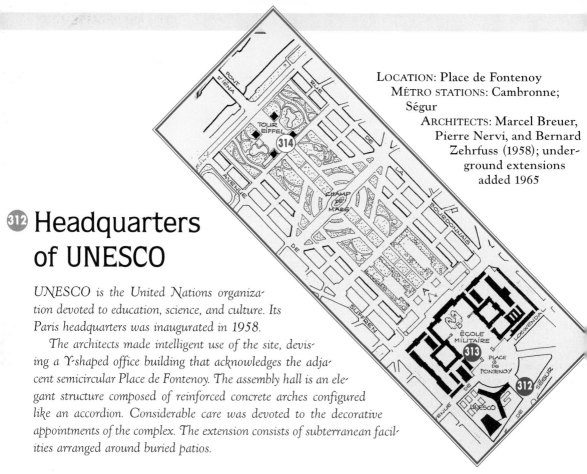

⓷⑫ Headquarters of UNESCO

⓷⑫ Headquarters of UNESCO

LOCATION: Place de Fontenoy
MÉTRO STATIONS: Cambronne; Ségur
ARCHITECTS: Marcel Breuer, Pierre Nervi, and Bernard Zehrfuss (1958); underground extensions added 1965

UNESCO is the United Nations organization devoted to education, science, and culture. Its Paris headquarters was inaugurated in 1958.

The architects made intelligent use of the site, devising a Y-shaped office building that acknowledges the adjacent semicircular Place de Fontenoy. The assembly hall is an elegant structure composed of reinforced concrete arches configured like an accordion. Considerable care was devoted to the decorative appointments of the complex. The extension consists of subterranean facilities arranged around buried patios.

View from A in the map above (with the UNESCO complex at the rear)

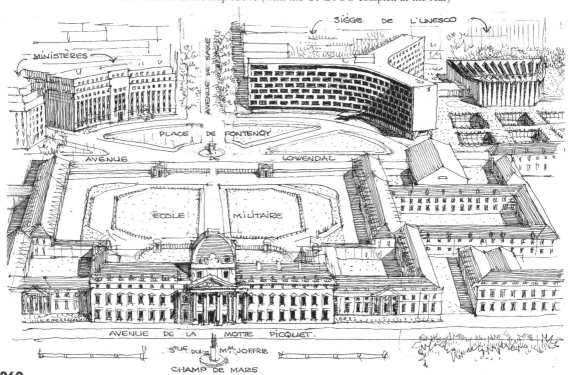

LOCATION: 43, avenue de la Motte-Picquet
MÉTRO STATION: École-Militaire
PATRON: Louis XV, at the prompting of Joseph
Pâris- Duverney and Madame de Pompadour
ARCHITECTS: Jacques-Ange Gabriel (initial phase,
1752–73). Étienne-Louis Boullée, then Alexan-
dre-Théodore Brongniart (second phase,
1780–88)

École Militaire

Façade on the Champs-de-Mars

Joseph Pâris-Duverney, intendant aux armées, per-
suaded Louis XV, with the help of Madame de
Pompadour, to establish an officers' school for the
children of noble families without fortune. A vast
expanse of land was acquired for its buildings and
drill grounds (the future Champ-de-Mars).

The king's principal architect, Jacques-Ange
Gabriel, was entrusted with the project, which
rivaled the Hôtel des Invalides in size. The school's
most famous alumnus was Napoléon, who gradu-
ated in 1786 with the rank of artillery lieutenant.

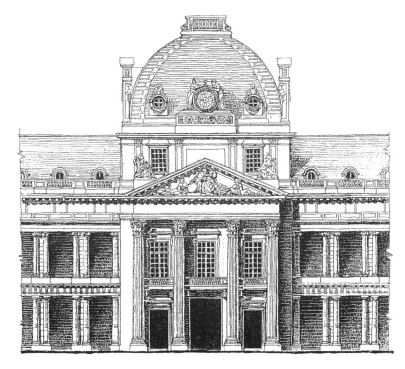

Forecourt façade

Eiffel Tower

LOCATION: Champ-de-Mars
MÉTRO STATION: Champ-de-Mars-Tour-Eiffel
ENGINEER-DESIGNER: Gustave Eiffel (1887–89)

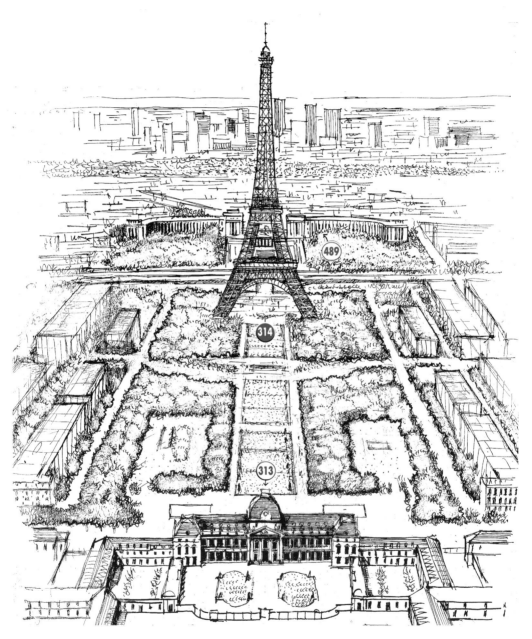

The Eiffel Tower resulted from a competition for the design of a 984-foot tower (300 meters) for the Exposition Universelle of 1889. The project of the engineer Gustave Eiffel was chosen from the 700 submissions, and very few problems arose in the course of construction. Most intellectuals of the day vigorously objected to the design, but the tower quickly became an emblem of the city, and it is now one of the most popular tourist sites in the world.

Saint-Pierre-du-Gros-Caillou

LOCATION: 92, rue Saint-Dominique
MÉTRO STATION: École-Militaire
ARCHITECT: Étienne-Hippolyte Godde (1822–29)

This was the first of three neoclassical churches erected in Paris by the architect Étienne-Hippolyte Godde, the second being Notre-Dame-de-Bonne-Nouvelle and the third Saint-Denis-du-Saint-Sacrement (entries 64 and 104). Like the other two, its plan is basilican, and its façade features a pedimented colonnade. The overall effect is quite austere.

Fontaine de Mars

LOCATION: 129–131, rue Saint-Dominique
MÉTRO STATION: École-Militaire
PATRON: Napoléon I
SCULPTOR: Pierre Beauvallet
ARCHITECT: Nicolas Bralle (1806)

This fountain takes its name from one of its reliefs, which represents Mars, the god of war, accompanied by Hygeia, the goddess of health. When first placed in operation (1806), it was provided with water from the Seine by the Gros-Caillou fire pump. The arcaded buildings surrounding the fountain postdate it (1858). The same collaborators designed the Fellah fountain on the rue de Sèvres (entry 309), which is quite different in character.

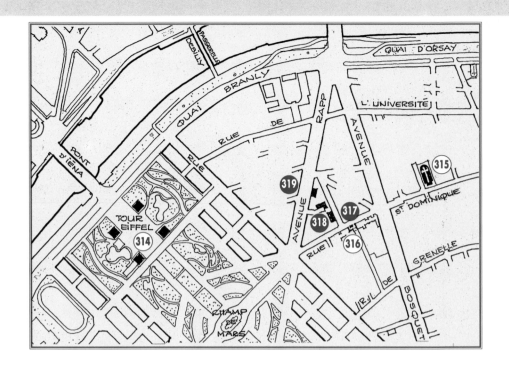

③⑰ Lycée Italien Léonard-de-Vinci

LOCATION: 12, rue Sédillot
MÉTRO STATION: École-Militaire
ARCHITECT: Jules Lavirotte
(1899)

The architect Jules Lavirotte is, after Hector Guimard, the best-known advocate of Art Nouveau in France. Over a very brief span of time he built three structures in the same quarter. The earliest, an Italian secondary school, is still relatively restrained (see drawing at left): its façade blends elements inspired by 18th-century models with Art Nouveau forms that become more emphatic in the later buildings (see next two entries).

Square Rapp, no. 3 ③¹⁸

LOCATION: Accessed through the alley
between 33 and 35, avenue Rapp
MÉTRO STATION: École-Militaire
PATRON AND ARCHITECT: Jules Lavirotte
(1899–1900)

*This building was erected a year after the one on
the rue Sédillot (see previous entry). Here Lavirotte
gave much freer rein to his penchant for exuberant
decoration. Note especially the eccentric turret supported by a column.*

Avenue Rapp, no. 29 ③¹⁹

MÉTRO STATION: École-Militaire
PATRON: The ceramist Alexandre Bigot
ARCHITECT: Jules Lavirotte (1901)
FAÇADE FACING: Alexandre Bigot (glazed
ceramic elements).

*Lavirotte's gift for exuberant
forms attained its zenith in this
façade, whose bravura set piece is
the doorway pictured at right.
The building won a municipal
competition for the finest façade
of 1901.*

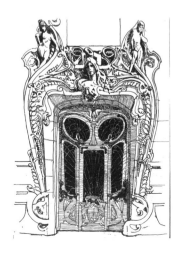

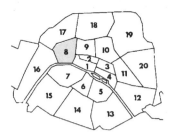

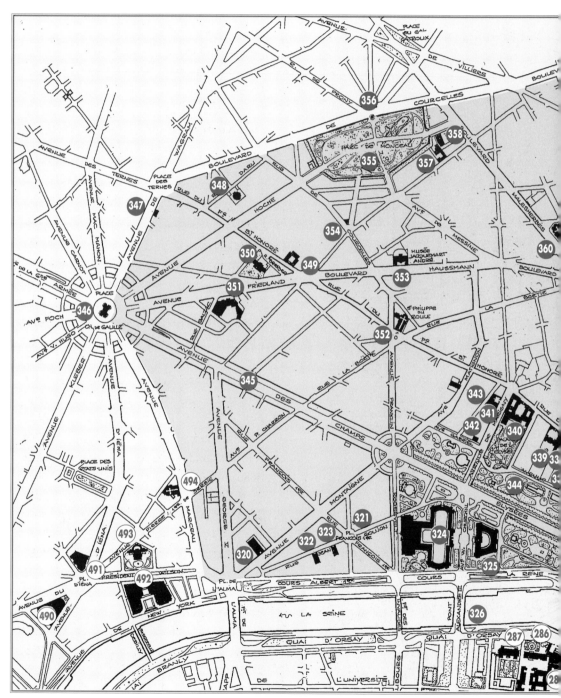

8th Arrondissement

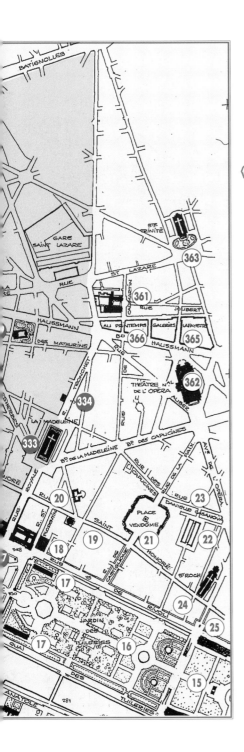

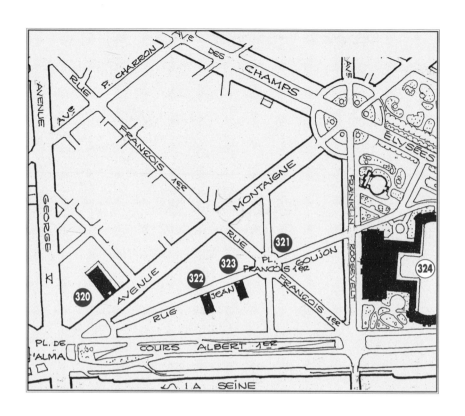

ⓈⒺⒺ Théâtre des Champs-Élysées

LOCATION: 13–15, avenue Montaigne
MÉTRO STATION: Alma-Marceau
PATRON: Gabriel Astruc
ARCHITECTS: Auguste and Gustave
Perret, largely adhering to a design by
Henry van de Velde (1911–13)

After the withdrawal of the architect Henry van de Velde, the Perret brothers, who had been serving as contractors, took over the project. They honored the basic configuration of his design but took maximum advantage of new developments in reinforced-concrete construction. The result was a magnificent theater with incomparable acoustics.

Place François-Ier

321

LOCATION: Center of a triangle formed
by avenue Montaigne, avenue Georges V,
and the Seine
MÉTRO STATION: Franklin-Roosevelt

*This square was designed at the same
time as the adjacent quarter, in accordance with a royal ordinance of
1822. The streets created or developed in tandem with the project were
named after figures and events from the reign of
François I. The fountain, designed by Gabriel
Davioud (1865), is one of the two originally in*
*front of the Madeleine. It was moved here in 1909;
the second was remounted in the Square de La
Tour-Maubourg (7th arrondissement).*

Notre-Dame-de-la-Consolation

322

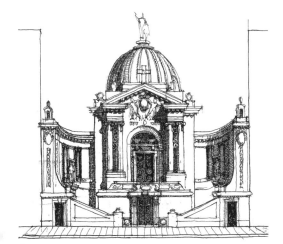

LOCATION: 23, rue Jean-Goujon
MÉTRO STATION: Alma-Marceau
PATRONS: Financed by subscription
ARCHITECT: Albert-Désiré Guilbert (1900)

*This church was erected as a memorial to the 135
persons killed in the 1895 fire in the Bazar de la
Charité, located in the same street. One of the victims was the duchesse d'Alençon, sister of the
empress of Austria. The architect adopted a neo-
Baroque style so overloaded that to modern eyes
it borders on caricature.*

Armenian Church

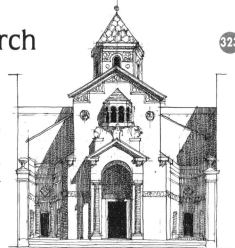

323

LOCATION: 15, rue Jean-Goujon
MÉTRO STATION: Alma-Marceau
ARCHITECT: Albert-Désiré Guilbert (1903)

*Apparently, contemporaries found nothing objectionable in the
design of Notre-Dame-de-la-Consolation (see previous entry),
for shortly thereafter the same architect was entrusted with the
design of this Armenian church in the same street. The latter
evidences an analogous striving for "monumental" effect within the confines of a narrow site.*

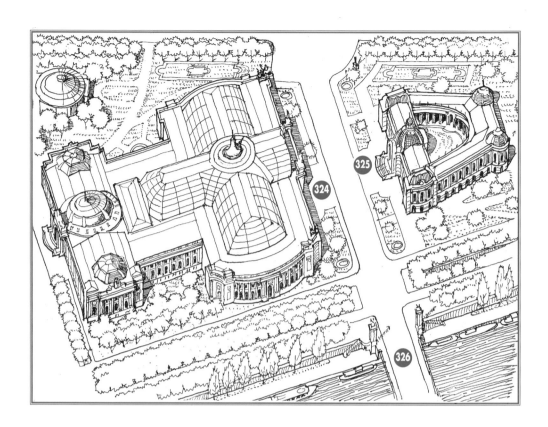

Grand Palais

LOCATION: Avenue Winston-Churchill.
MÉTRO STATION: Champs-Élysées-Clemenceau
PATRONS: Organizers of the Exposition Universelle of 1900
ARCHITECTS: Henri Deglane, Albert Louvet, and Albert
Thomas, under the supervision of Charles Girault (1897–1900)

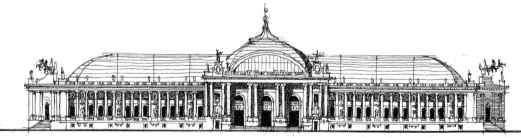

The Grand Palais was built for the Exposition Universelle of 1900. Its enormous but elegant metallic structure is hidden by a classical stone façade designed by Henri Deglane. The entrances are decorated with monumental sculptures, the most famous of which are the quadrigas of the lateral entrances by the sculptor Georges Récipon.

The dimensions of the Grand Palais are impressive: the façade on the avenue Winston-Churchill is 787 feet long, and the top of the dome is 144 feet above the ground.

The building is used as a venue for temporary exhibitions, but since 1937 its western portion has housed the Palais de la Découverte, a museum devoted to scientific discoveries.

Petit Palais ③²⁵

LOCATION: Avenue Winston-Churchill, opposite the Grand Palais
MÉTRO STATION: Champs-Élysées-Clemenceau
PATRON: Organizers of the Exposition Universelle of 1900
ARCHITECT: Charles Girault (1897–1900)

Unlike the Grand Palais, the Petit Palais was built primarily to function as a permanent museum. It now houses the art collections of the City of Paris. Its architect, Charles Girault, was also responsible for supervising work on the Grand Palais. He engaged a number of important sculptors and painters to decorate the building.

Pont Alexandre-III ③²⁶

LOCATION: Links the 7th and 8th arrondissements
MÉTRO STATIONS: Champs-Élysées-Clemenceau; Invalides
ENGINEERS: Jean Résal and Amédée Alby (1896–1900)
ARCHITECTS: Cassien-Bernard and Gaston Cousin
SCULPTORS: A group of seventeen, the most famous of whom are named below

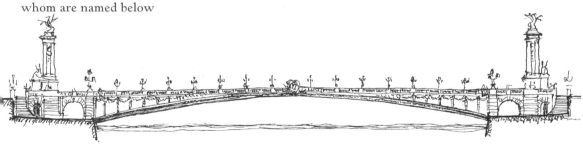

The first stone of this bridge was laid on October 7, 1896, in the presence of Nicholas II, in anticipation of the Exposition Universelle of 1900. It is supported by a single metal span that the engineers kept as low as possible to avoid obstructing the view of the Invalides.

Each entry to the bridge is flanked by imposing columns supporting equestrian groups in gilt bronze. The bridge platform is richly decorated with motifs inspired by marine flora and fauna. The seventeen sculptors who collaborated on the project included Jules Dalou, Emmanuel Frémiet, and Georges Récipon.

Place de la Concorde

LOCATION: Between the Tuileries gardens and the Champs-Élysées
MÉTRO STATION: Concorde
PATRON: The City of Paris, which held a competition in 1748 for a royal square; Louis XV assisted by making a gift of most of the land
ARCHITECT: Jacques-Ange Gabriel (design approved 1755; work completed 1772). Jacques-Ignace Hittorff (alterations, 1830–44)

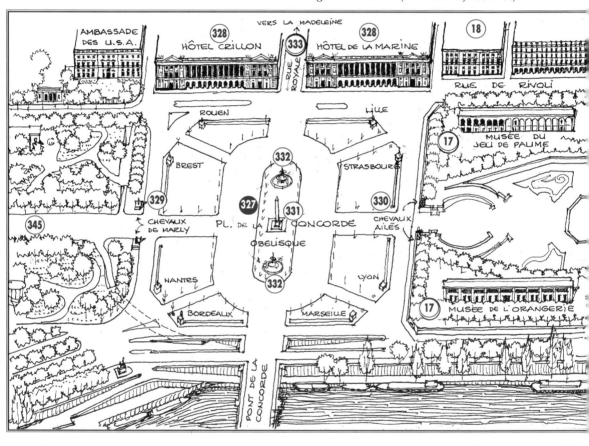

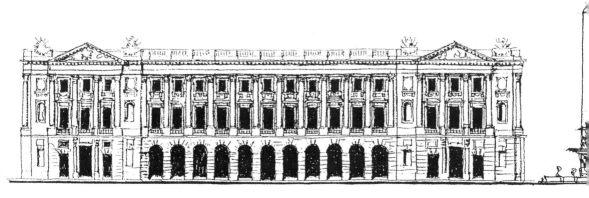

During the reign of Louis XV, the City of Paris resolved to create a royal square in his honor like those built under the reigns of Henri IV (the present Place des Vosges) and Louis XIV (Place des Victoires, Place Vendôme). After a preliminary competition, the site was selected and an architect chosen: Jacques-Ange Gabriel. A statue of Louis XV was commissioned from the sculptor Edme Bouchardon and installed in 1763.

Unlike the other royal squares, the Place Louis XV was largely left open to its surroundings: Gabriel's two magnificent buildings occupy only one side of it. Originally, it was delimited by moats, balustrades, and sentry boxes (see drawing below). Statues envisioned for the roofs of the sentry boxes were not executed; the personifications of French cities currently in place date from the following century, during the reign of Louis-Philippe.

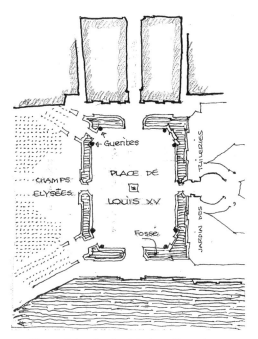

Plan and details of original configuration

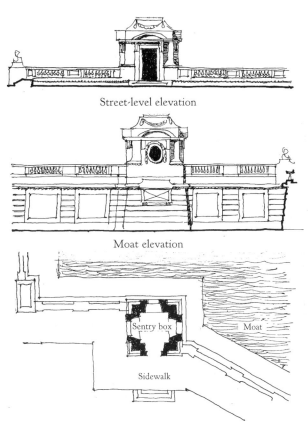

Street-level elevation

Moat elevation

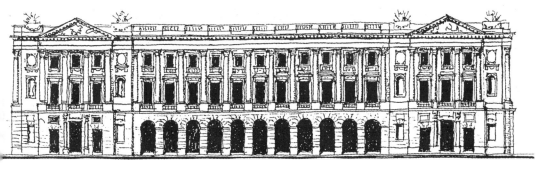

328 Colonnaded Buildings

LOCATION: On the northern side of the square
MÉTRO STATION: Concorde
ARCHITECT: Jacques-Ange Gabriel (1766–75)

The design of this square marks a significant departure from precedent: rather than incorporating profitable buildings around the perimeter, as in the city's other royal squares, at the Place de la Concorde the views of the Tuileries, the Seine, and the Champs-Élysées were left unimpeded. Gabriel's façade designs consciously evoke Claude Perrault's Louvre colonnade. Each of the two buildings features terminal projecting frontispieces flanking a central recessed colonnade. The proportions are beautifully gauged throughout, and the play of light and shadow over the building's carefully wrought detailing makes the result a magnificent background for the square.

The building on the left (see page 272), initially subdivided into several residences, now houses, among other tenants, the Hôtel Crillon and the Automobile-Club de France. The building on the right (see page 273), originally the royal furniture storehouse, is now the Ministère de la Marine.

29 # The Marly Horses

LOCATION: Place de la Concorde
MÉTRO STATION: Concorde
SCULPTORS: Guillaume Coustou
(Marly Horses, 1745). Antoine
Coysevox (Winged Horses, 1702)

The two sculpture groups known as the Marly Horses, which flank the entrance to the Champs-Élysées, were carved in 1745 by Guillaume Coustou. Across the square, two groups of Winged Horses, carved in 1702 by Antoine Coysevox and installed at the entrance to the Tuileries in 1717, depict Mercury and Fame. All four originals are now in the Louvre, and copies stand in the square.

The Winged 330 Horses

Obelisk

LOCATION: Center of the
Place de la Concorde
MÉTRO STATION: Concorde

331

The obelisk in the center of the square was given to Louis-Philippe in 1831 by the viceroy of Egypt. From the Temple of Ramses at Luxor and dating from the 12th century BCE, the obelisk was erected here in 1836.

32 # Fountains

LOCATION: Place de la Concorde
MÉTRO STATION: Concorde
ARCHITECT: Jacques-Ignace Hittorff

The two fountains were designed by Jacques-Ignace Hittorff, who redesigned the square beginning in 1830. Hittorff was also responsible for installing the rostral columns and the personifications of French cities now atop the sentry boxes.

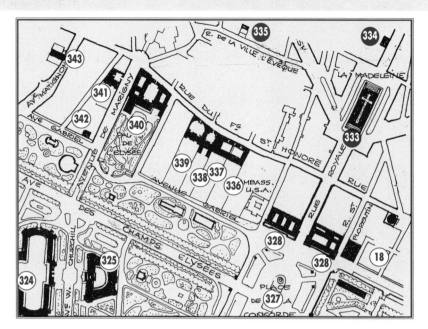

333 Church of the Madeleine

LOCATION: Place de la Madeleine
MÉTRO STATION: Madeleine
PATRON: Napoléon I (who envisioned it as a temple glorifying his armies)
ARCHITECTS: Pierre Vignon (1807); then, after his death in 1828, Jean-Marie Huvé (completed 1842)

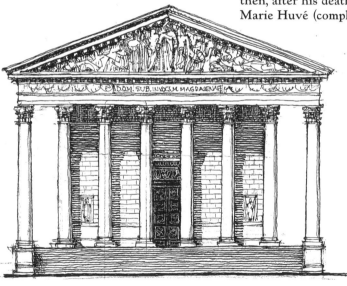

As early as 1761, the architect Contant d'Ivry designed a domed church for this site. Construction began but was interrupted by the Revolution, and none of several revisions of his project was realized. In 1806, Napoléon I decided to build, on the same site, a monument dedicated to the Grande Armée. He ordered the demolition of what had already been built and entrusted the new project to the architect Vignon, whose design resembled a Greek temple. After the fall of Napoléon, Louis XVIII commissioned the same architect to transform his building into a Catholic church—an unusual undertaking, given that the building had been designed to evoke a pagan temple.

Hôtel de Pourtalès

LOCATION: 7, rue Tronchet
MÉTRO STATION: Madeleine
PATRON: The comte James
Alexandre de Pourtalès
ARCHITECT: Félix Duban (1836)

This town house, somewhat overwhelmed by taller buildings on either side, no longer receives the attention it deserves. Designed by Félix Duban, who was also responsible for several buildings in the complex of the École des Beaux-Arts, this hôtel was freely inspired by Italian Renaissance palazzi. A wing that originally housed a picture gallery has not survived.

LOCATION: 16, rue de la Ville-l'Évêque
MÉTRO STATION: Madeleine
PATRON: The banker André-Claude-Nicolas Alexandre
ARCHITECT: Étienne-Louis Boullée (1763)

Hôtel Alexandre 335

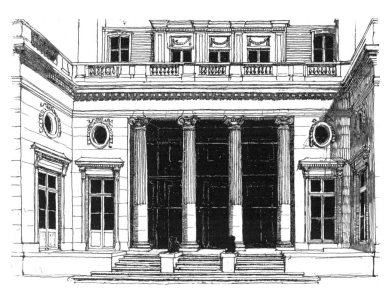

This residence is one of the few surviving works by Étienne-Louis Boullée (1728–1799), an architect of utopian tendencies who built little and devoted himself primarily to teaching. He is perhaps best known for visionary designs, such as his famous spherical cenotaph commemorating Sir Isaac Newton. The Hôtel Alexandre, which dates from the beginning of his career, is still classical in conception.

No. 33, Cercle de l'Union Interalliée · · · Nos. 35–37, British chancellory

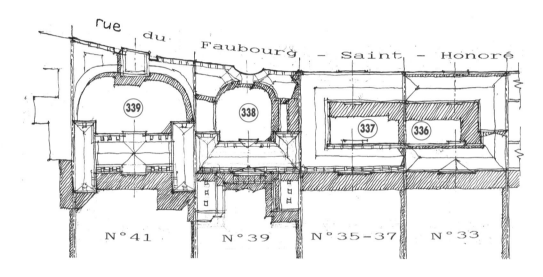

rue du Faubourg – Saint – Honoré

(339) · (338) · (337) · (336)

N°41 · N°39 · N°35–37 · N°33

(336) # Cercle de l'Union Interalliée
(Originally the Hôtel Levieux, then the Hôtel Nathaniel de Rothschild)

LOCATION: 33, rue du Faubourg-Saint-Honoré
MÉTRO STATIONS: Madeleine; Concorde
PATRON: Anne Levieux, sister of Louis Chevalie
patron of the adjacent hôtel (nos. 35–37)
ARCHITECTS: Initially the contractor Pierre
Grandhomme (1715–16); finally Robillard and
Émile Petit (1870)

No. 41, Hôtel Edmond de Rothschild · · · No. 39, British embassy

ue du Faubourg-Saint-Honoré

No. 39, British embassy   No. 41, Hôtel Edmond de Rothschild

LOCATION: 35–37, rue du Faubourg-Saint-Honoré
MÉTRO STATIONS: Madeleine; Concorde
PATRON: Louis Chevalier, président de la cour du
Parlement
DESIGNER: The developer Pierre Grandhomme
(1715–16)

British Chancellory ⒀⒊⒎
(Former Hôtel
Chevalier de Montigny)

LOCATION: 39, rue du Faubourg-Saint-Honoré
MÉTRO STATIONS: Madeleine; Concorde
PATRON: Paul-François de Béthune-Charost,
future duc de Béthune
ARCHITECT: Antoine Mazin (1720)

British Embassy ⒀⒊⒏
(Former Hôtel
de Béthune-Charost)

*The residence was purchased in 1803 by Pauline Borghese, sister of Napoléon I,
who remodeled it. In 1814, after the abdication of Napoléon, it was acquired by the
British government to serve as the residence of its ambassador.*

LOCATION: 41, rue du Faubourg-Saint-Honoré
MÉTRO STATIONS: Madeleine; Concorde
PATRON: Edmond de Rothschild, after his pur-
chase in 1876 of the Hôtel Pontalba (Visconti,
architect), which he drastically remodeled
ARCHITECT: Félix Langlais (1878)

Hôtel Edmond ⒀⒊⒐
de Rothschild
(Originally Hôtel de Pontalba,
then the residence of the Ameri-
can Ambassador)

cing the avenue Gabriel

Nos. 35–37, British chancellory   No. 33, Cercle de l'Union Interalliée

340 Palais de l'Élysée

LOCATION: 55–57, rue du Faubourg-Saint-Honoré
MÉTRO STATION: Champs-Élysées-Clemenceau
PATRON: The comte d'Évreux
ARCHITECTS: Claude-Armand Mollet (1718–20).
Pierre Cailloeteau (later alterations)

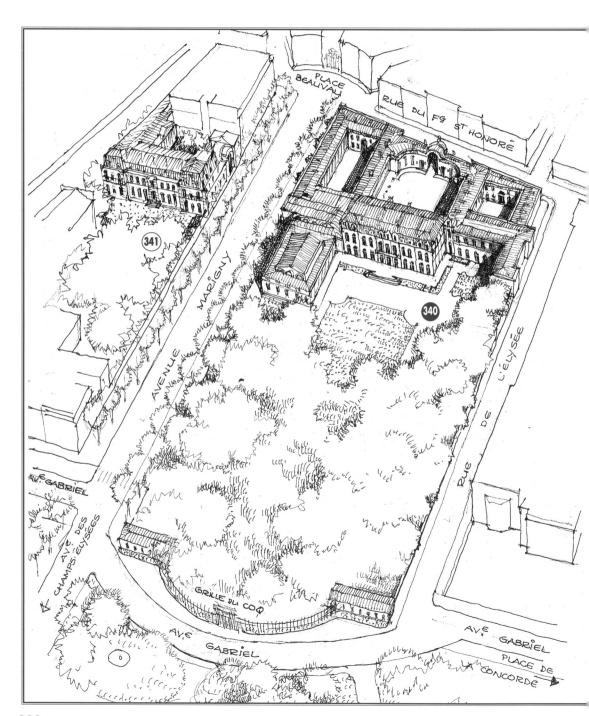

Garden façade

Built in 1718 for the comte d'Évreux, this hôtel later became the Parisian residence of Madame de Pompadour, who commissioned the architect Jean Cailleteau, known as Lassurance the Younger, to make alterations. After several more changes of ownership, it was purchased in 1805 by Napoléon I for his sister Caroline, wife of the comte de Murat. It served as a residence for Napoléon himself, and on June 22, 1815, after the Battle of Waterloo, he signed his abdication here. The Élysée palace has been the official residence of the president of the French republic since 1873.

Façade on the rue du Faubourg-Saint-Honoré

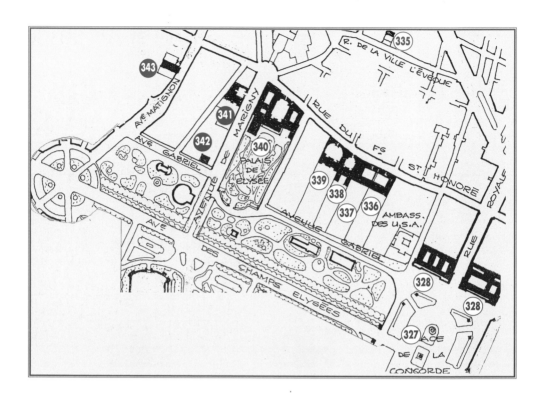

So-called Hôtel de Marigny

LOCATION: 23, avenue de Marigny
MÉTRO STATION: Champs-Élysées-Clemenceau
PATRON: Gustave de Rothschild (1873–83); then his son Robert, beginning in 1911 (interior decor, gardens)
ARCHITECTS: Alfred-Philibert Aldrophe (building, 1873–83). Jean-Charles Moreux (gardens, 1928)

Garden façade

Hôtel d'Argenson

LOCATION: 38, avenue Gabriel
MÉTRO STATION: Champs-Élysées-
Clemenceau
PATRON: Widow of the marquis d'Argenson
ARCHITECT: Jean-Philippe Lemoine de
Courzon (1780)

*Modification of the original attic story has not sig-
nificantly compromised the harmonious proportions of this classic hôtel. The viewer should try to
imagine it without the buildings that flank it today
and set amid similar hôtels likewise overlooking the
gardens of the Champs-Élysées.*

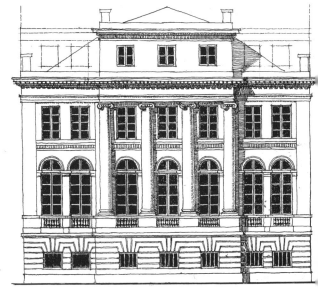

Façade on the avenue Gabriel

LOCATION: 23, avenue Matignon (garden
façade), and 25, avenue Matignon (court façade)
MÉTRO STATION: Franklin-Roosevelt
PATRON: The architect Louis-Marie Colignon,
who upon its completion leased it to the
marquis de La Vaupalière
ARCHITECT: Louis-Marie Colignon (1768)

Hôtel de La Vaupalière

South façade,
original garden
façade

*Although readily visible and situated on a busy
avenue, this magnificent town house is not as well
known as it should be. It lies perpendicular to
avenue Matignon, even extending slightly into it.
Entering the courtyard at no. 25, one can see the
façade that faced the forecourt, originally accessed
from the avenue du Faubourg-Saint- Honoré
(roughly at the site of no. 85). The garden façade,
which dates from the end of Louis XV's reign, is in
the restrained style conventionally associated with
his successor. The court façade was remodeled in
the 19th century.*

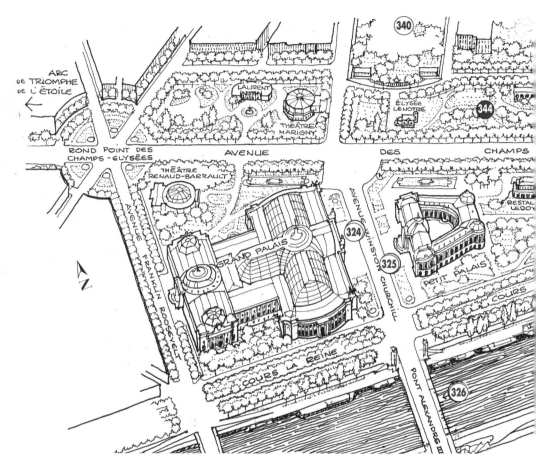

The design of the gardens of the Champs-Élysées, which extend from the Rond-Point des Champs-Élysées to the Place de la Concorde, was entrusted to the architect Jacques-Ignace Hittorff beginning in 1834, then to Adolphe Alphand beginning in 1858.

The gardens are subdivided into units (carrés) as follows: on the left side as one descends from the Rond-Point, one encounters in succession the Carré Marigny, the Carré de l'Élysée, and the Carré des Ambassadeurs; on the right side, the Carré de Géorama (a name no longer used).

For each of these units, Hittorff devised an English garden, a fountain, and theaters or restaurants. The principal surviving buildings are as follows: Restaurant Laurent, Théâtre Marigny (rebuilt c. 1880 by Garnier), Restaurant Élysée-Lenôtre, Espace Cardin (former Théâtre des Ambassadeurs), and Théâtre du Rond-Point Renaud-Barrault (former Palais des Glaces).

Of the buildings that do not survive, it is worth noting the Cirque d'Été, subsequently rechristened the Cirque de l'Impératrice and the Cirque National before being demolished around 1900.

These amenities made the gardens of the Champs-Élysées a fashionable center of entertainment and sociability under the Second Empire.

LOCATION: From the Place de la Concorde to Rond-Point des Champs-Élysées, on either side of the avenue des Champs-Élysées
MÉTRO STATIONS: Concorde; Champs-Élysées-Clemenceau

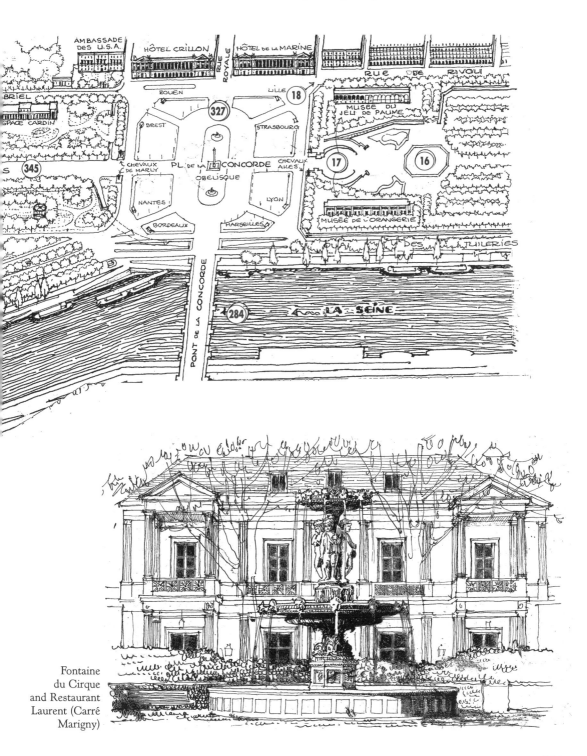

Fontaine
du Cirque
and Restaurant
Laurent (Carré
Marigny)

Champs-Élysées

LOCATION: Links the Place Charles-de-Gaulle (formerly Place de l'Étoile) to Place de la Concorde
MÉTRO STATIONS: Charles-de-Gaulle-Étoile; Georges V; Franklin-Roosevelt; Champs-Élysées-Clemenceau; Concorde

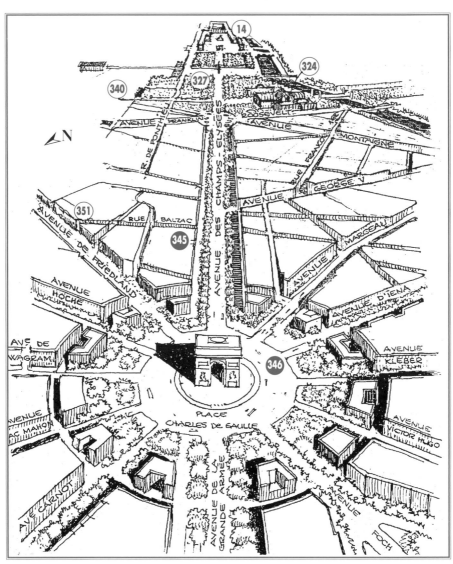

Marie de Médicis began to develop this area by creating, in 1616, the carriage promenade known as the Cours-la-Reine along the Seine. In 1667, the perspective from the Tuileries was lengthened by André Le Nôtre, who created a planted promenade; early in the 18th century, this was extended as far as the Étoile hill. Development of the quarter proceeded slowly until the Second Empire, when commercial venues and residences sprang up along the avenue. The only residences that survive are the Hôtel de Païva (no. 25) and the Hôtel Le Hon (on the Rond-Point).

In subsequent years the avenue des Champs-Élysées, devoted to business, tourism, and entertainment, has become one of the most prestigious addresses in the world.

LOCATION: Place Charles-de-Gaulle (formerly Place de l'Étoile)
MÉTRO STATION: Charles-de-Gaulle-Étoile
PATRON: Napoléon I
ARCHITECT: Jean-François Chalgrin (1806); work completed in 1836, after Chalgrin's death (1811)
SCULPTORS: François Rude, Antoine Étex, and Jean-Pierre Cortot (four groups at the monument's base)

Arc de Triomphe

In 1805, Napoléon I decided to mark the western entry into Paris with a triumphal arch glorifying the armies of the empire. Its design was entrusted to Jean-François Chalgrin, who took as his model the Arch of Titus in Rome but opted for a colossal scale: the monument is roughly 148 feet wide and 164 feet high. The first stone was laid in 1806, but work largely came to a halt in 1814; it resumed in 1823 and was completed in 1836.

Each of the four pillars is decorated with a monumental group in high relief, the most famous of which was executed by François Rude: The Departure of the Volunteers, better known as

The Marseillaise.

At the end of World War I, the Arc de Triomphe was chosen as the site for the Tomb of the Unknown Soldier, marked by a Flame of Memory that is relit each night. When the arch was built, the Place de l'Étoile—étoile means "star"—did not feature the twelve radiating avenues that exist today: the last seven of them were created by Baron Haussmann in 1854, under the Second Empire. He had a series of residences, dubbed the "Hôtels des Maréchaux," erected around the perimeter along with a circular street so their entrances would not be situated directly on the Place.

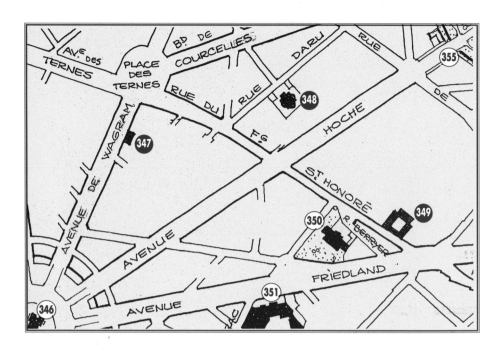

347 Céramic Hôtel

LOCATION: 34, avenue de Wagram
MÉTRO STATION: Ternes
ARCHITECT: Jules Lavirotte (1904)
SCULPTOR: Laphilippe
FAÇADE FACING: Alexandre Bigot (polychrome glazed earthenware tiles)

The façade of this building postdates by several years that of the one at 29, avenue Rapp (see entry 319), also designed by Lavirotte. Often cited as an exceptional example of Parisian Art Nouveau architecture, this won the municipal prize for the best façade of 1905. The name "Céramic Hôtel" is not original.

Saint-Alexandre-Nevski
(Russian Cathedral)

348

LOCATION: 12, rue Daru
MÉTRO STATION: Ternes
ARCHITECTS: Kuzmin and Stroehm (1859–61)

The Russo-Byzantine style of this church, quite unusual for Paris, is the work of Kuzmin, first architect to the Russian imperial court. Its Greek-cross plan and interior disposition were designed in accordance with Russian Orthodox ritual.

The mosaic on the tympanum of the façade reproduces a mosaic in the 6th-century church of Sant'Apollinare Nuovo in Ravenna.

LOCATION: 208, rue du Faubourg-Saint-Honoré
MÉTRO STATION: Ternes
PATRON: The financier Nicolas Beaujon
ARCHITECT: Nicolas-Claude Girardin (1784–85)

Hospice Beaujon **349**
(Centre Beaujon)

The wealthy financier Nicolas Beaujon, after having built an extravagant garden folly on adjacent lands (no longer extant), decided to establish nearby, as an act of charity, a school and hospice for indigent children. The result was an austere edifice consisting of four blocks enclosing a central court. Classrooms were on the ground floor and dormitories on the floors above. During the Revolution, the structure was transformed into a hospital and remained one until 1936.

The building, whose façade and portal are certified national monuments, now houses training workshops and recreation facilities known collectively as the Centre Beaujon.

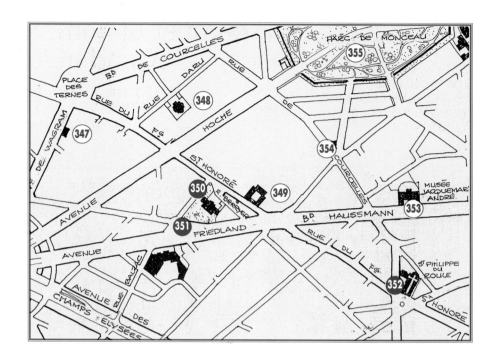

Hôtel Salomon de Rothschild

LOCATION: 9–11, rue Berryer (garden façade visible from avenue de Friedland)
MÉTRO STATION: Charles-de-Gaulle-Étoile
PATRON: The baronne Salomon de Rothschild
ARCHITECTS: Léon Ohnet; then, after his death, Justin Ponsard (1872–78)

In 1922, the baronne Salomon de Rothschild bequeathed to the state the town house she had built on land formerly occupied by Beaujon's gar- *den folly (entry 349). It is now headquarters of the Fondation Nationale des Arts Graphiques et Plastiques, which sponsors temporary exhibitions.*

LOCATION: 27, avenue de Friedland
MÉTRO STATION: Charles-de-Gaulle-
Étoile
PATRON: The comte Nicolas de
Potocki (1878–84). Enlarged in 1923
by the Paris Chamber of Commerce
ARCHITECT: Jules Reboul (1878–84)

Chamber of Commerce 351 and Industry
(Former Hôtel Potocki)

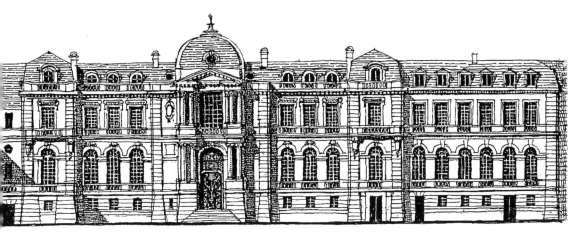

Even after discounting the additions built by the Chamber of Commerce, the dimensions of this former residence are imposing. The opulence of the interior decoration is also impressive. The central frontispiece crowned by a dome houses a monumental staircase richly adorned with marble.

LOCATION: 154, rue du Faubourg-Saint-
Honoré
MÉTRO STATION: Saint-Philippe-du-Roule
ARCHITECT: Jean-François Chalgrin (1774–84)

Saint-Philippe-du-Roule 352

Saint-Philippe-du-Roule was among the first 18th-century churches to adopt the basilican plan of the earliest Christian sanctuaries. Its façade likewise evokes Roman antiquity, featuring a portico whose pediment is decorated with a relief by Francisque-Joseph Duret representing Religion. The church was enlarged in 1845 by Étienne-Hippolyte Godde (ambulatory and Lady Chapel) and again in 1853 by Victor Baltard (Catechism Chapel).

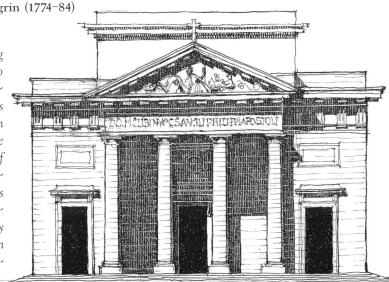

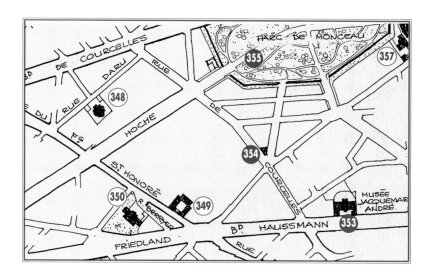

353 Musée Jacquemart-André

LOCATION: 158, boulevard Haussmann
MÉTRO STATION: Miromesnil
PATRON: Édouard André
ARCHITECT: Henri Parent (1864–75)

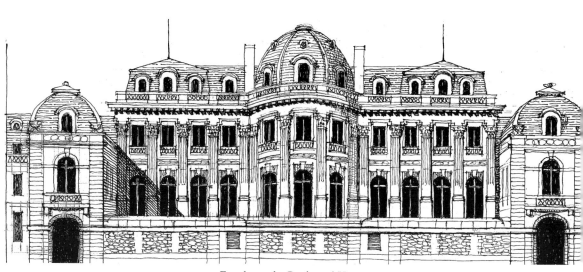

Façade on the Boulevard Haussmann

Édouard André, son of a banker, was an avid art collector, and he commissioned Henri Parent to design a large town house for his collection. He later married Nélie Jacquemart, who assisted him in seeking out works of art. It was she who bequeathed the residence and its collections to the Institut de France; hence the name of the museum established as a result of this gift. The museum's holdings are strongest in Italian Renaissance and 18th-century works.

C. T. Loo Building

LOCATION: 48, rue de Courcelles
MÉTRO STATION: Courcelles
PATRON: C. T. Loo (apartment building and art gallery)
ARCHITECT: Fernand Bloch (1926)

The gallery of East Asian art that was the building's raison d'être still exists.

Parc Monceau ⁣355

LOCATION: Four entrances (see map on page 294)
MÉTRO STATION: Monceau
PATRON: Louis Philippe d'Orléans; then Napoléon III
DESIGNERS: Louis de Carmontelle (1778), then Adolphe Alphand (1861)

In 1778, the duc de Chartres (the future Philippe Égalité) entrusted the design of the gardens of his Folie de Chartres to the artist Louis de Carmontelle, who gave free rein to his imagination, devising a pool, river, and follies in the picturesque mode, some of which survive (colonnade, pyramids). In 1783, after enlarging the property, the future duc d'Orléans commissioned the English landscapist Thomas Blaikie to recast the ensemble as an English garden. Appropriated by the state after the Revolution, it reverted to the Orléans family under the Restoration. In 1860, the property was purchased by the state; half of the land was divided into lots for development, but the balance was recast as a public park by the civil engineer Adolphe Alphand. Inaugurated by Napoléon III on August 13, 1861, it remains all but unchanged since that time.

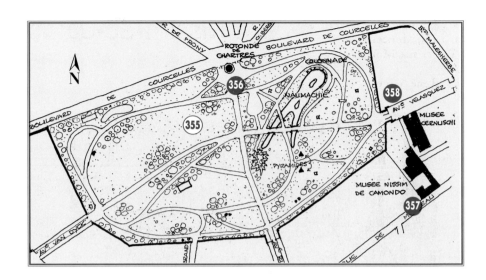

Rotonde de Chartres

LOCATION: Boulevard de Courcelles, at an entrance to the Parc Monceau
MÉTRO STATION: Monceau
PATRON: The City of Paris (part of the Wall of the Farmers General)
ARCHITECT: Claude-Nicolas Ledoux (1784–87)

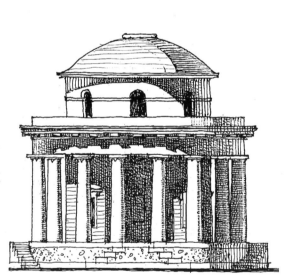

Original state

Present state

This structure was one of the barrières, or collection gates, of the Wall of the Farmers General, erected around Paris to facilitate the collection of entry duties levied against merchandise entering the city. Only four of these structures survive: the

Rotonde de Chartres (pictured above), the Rotonde de la Villette (entry 518), the Barrière d'Enfer (entry 448), and the Barrière du Trône (entry 412).

LOCATION: 63, rue de Monceau
MÉTRO STATION: Monceau
PATRON: The comte Moïse de
Camondo
ARCHITECT: René Sergent
(1911–14)

Musée Nissim-de-Camondo 357

The comte Moïse de Camondo built this hôtel to house his collection of works of art from the 18th century, instructing his architect to emulate the architecture of that century, especially the Petit Trianon. In 1935, he bequeathed the ensemble to the Union des Arts Décoratifs, and it was named the Musée Nissim-de-Camondo in memory of his son, who was killed during World War I.

All the works in the museum—paintings, furniture, tapestries, and so on—are exhibited so as to evoke 18th-century hôtel interiors.

Musée Cernuschi 358

LOCATION: 7, avenue Vélasquez
MÉTRO STATION: Monceau
PATRON: The financier Henri
Cernuschi
ARCHITECT: Williams Bouwens
van der Boijen (1873)

Henri Cernuschi built this hôtel to house his collection of Asian art. The entire ensemble was bequeathed to the City of Paris, which designated it a museum (inaugurated 1898).

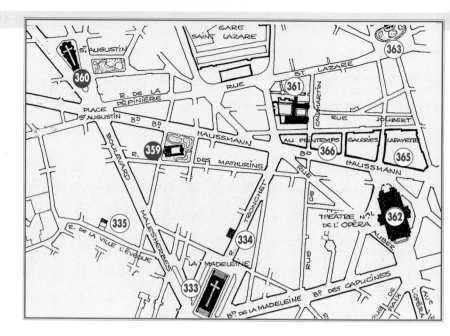

③⁵⁹ Expiatory Chapel

LOCATION: Square Louis XVI, boulevard Hauss-
mann, rue des Mathurins, rue d'Anjou, rue Pasquier
MÉTRO STATIONS: Saint-Augustin; Saint-Lazare
PATRON: Louis XVIII
ARCHITECT: Pierre Fontaine (1818–26)
SCULPTORS: François-Joseph Bosio and Jean-Pierre
Cortot

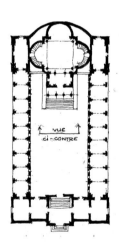

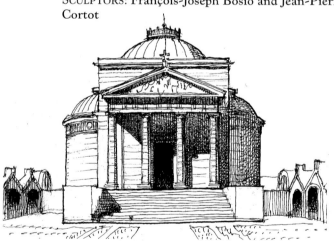

This was once the site of a small cemetery in which
were buried Louis XVI, Marie-Antoinette, and
other victims of the revolutionary guillotine, as well
as the Swiss Guards killed defending the Tuileries
during the riot of August 10, 1792.

In 1815, at the beginning of the Restoration,
Louis XVIII had the bodies of his brother, Louis
XVI, and Marie-Antoinette transferred to the basilica of Saint-Denis. He then ordered the construction of an expiatory chapel on the site, commissio-

ning its design from the architect Pierre Fontaine
(for once working independently of his associate
Charles Percier, whose political convictions preclu-
ded his collaboration on the project).

The statues inside the chapel are by François-
Joseph Bosio (Louis XVI) and Jean-Pierre Cortot
(Marie-Antoinette).

The curious enclosure that now surrounds the
chapel is not original; initially, the chapel was situated at the end of a long tree-lined promenade.

LOCATION: 46, boulevard Malesherbes
MÉTRO STATION: Saint-Augustin
ARCHITECT: Victor Baltard (1860–71)

Saint-Augustin

The church of Saint-Augustin was designed by Victor Baltard, architect of the Paris central market (*Les Halles*, destroyed). His task was difficult, for the plot was narrow and tapering (see plan above). He turned its shape to advantage, placing a large dome at the far end, above the high altar.

The structural frame of the church is metal; this made it possible to lighten the outer walls, for they do not bear the weight of the roof. This was the second church in Paris to use such a technique, the first being Saint-Eugène-et-Sainte-Cécile in the 9th arrondissement (see entry 379).

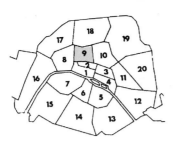

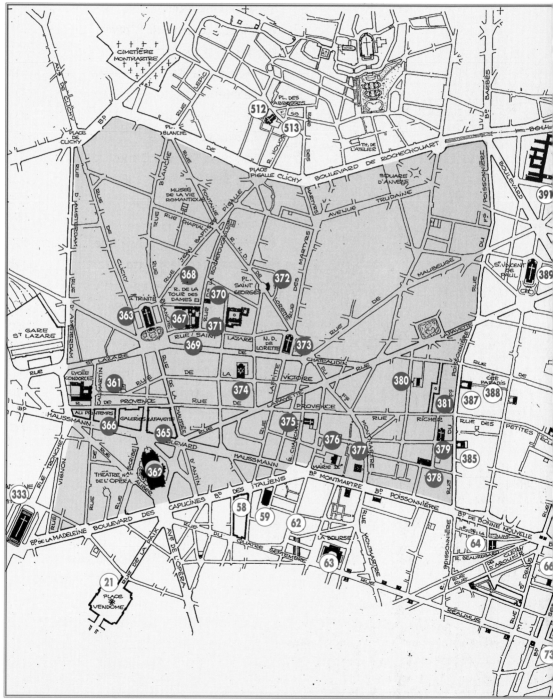

9th Arrondissement

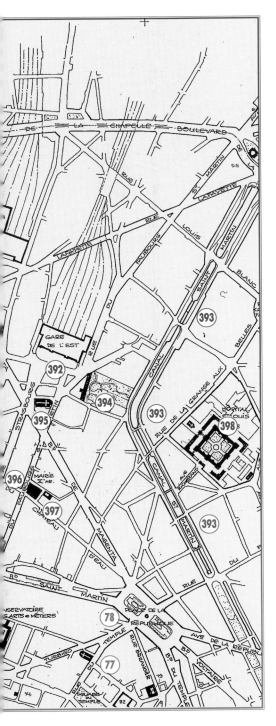

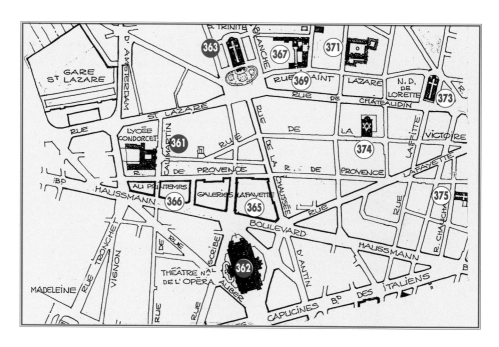

361 Lycée Condorcet and Church of Saint-Louis-d'Antin

LOCATION: 63–65, rue Caumartin
MÉTRO STATIONS: Saint-Lazare; Havre-Caumartin
PATRON: The Capuchin order
ARCHITECT: Alexandre-Théodore Brongniart (1781–83)

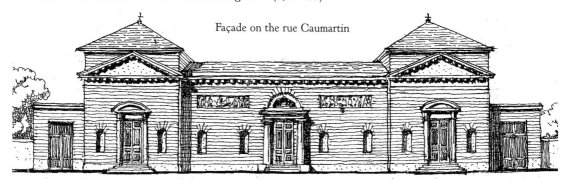

Façade on the rue Caumartin

The Lycée Condorcet occupies the buildings of a former Capuchin convent; the adjacent church was originally its chapel. The façade on the rue Caumartin consists of a central block and two lateral pavilions, of which the left one now belongs to the church of Saint-Louis-d'Antin. The old cloister, now the school's courtyard, features baseless columns inspired by the Greek Doric order.

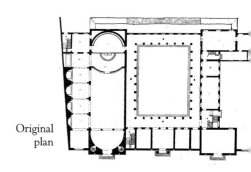

Original plan

Théâtre National de l'Opéra

LOCATION: Place de l'Opéra
MÉTRO STATION: Opéra
PATRON: The City of Paris,
which organized a design
competition in 1860
ARCHITECT: Charles Garnier
(1862–75)

Construction of the Paris Opéra was a prestige initiative launched by Napoléon III. The program called for an enormous structure, and the final realization is accordingly grandiose. The stage, service facilities, and reception areas take up a proportionately large area in comparison with the theater proper, which seats about 2,100.

The building's ornament is very rich, incor-porating colored stones and marbles. The grand stairway and foyer are renowned for the opulence of their decoration. Sculpture is abundant, and it was for this building that Jean-Baptiste Carpeaux realized one of his most celebrated works: The Dance, originally on the right of the main façade (now a copy; original in the Musée d'Orsay).

Church of the Trinity

363

LOCATION: place d'Estienne-d'Orves
MÉTRO STATION: Trinité
ARCHITECT: Théodore Ballu (1861-67)

Parisian religious architecture evolved quite rapidly in the mid-19th century. After a neoclassical period in the early decades (see Notre-Dame-de-Lorette, 1823, entry 373), neo-Gothic and neo-Romanesque styles became prevalent. This church, however, was inspired by French Renaissance models. The architect devoted considerable attention to the exterior detailing as well as the approach. The main entrance is through a monumental porch served by a double ramp and two curving stairways. The three fountains in front of the façade symbolize Faith, Hope, and Charity.

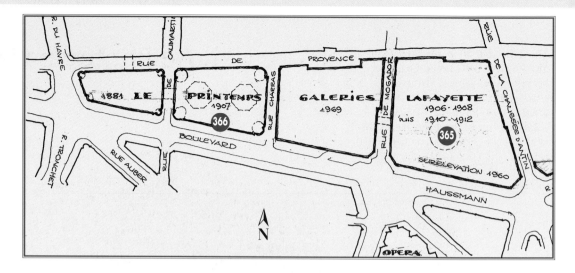

OPÉRA

364 The Grands Magasins

Many factors led to the creation in Paris of the first Grands Magasins, or department stores, including the definitive abolition after the Revolution of the craft guilds that had previously controlled the selling of fabricated products; the creation in the late 18th and early 19th centuries of covered passages that accustomed clients to finding diverse merchandise under one roof; the introduction of public transport that made it easier for Parisians to reach distant parts of the city; and the creation of railroads that brought potential new clients into the center of Paris.

Au Printemps and Galeries Lafayette were not the first Parisian department stores, but they underwent exceptionally rapid growth due to their proximity to the grands boulevards, the Opéra, and the Saint-Lazare railway station.

Of the city's first department stores, the most notable were (beginning with the earliest): Les Magasins Réunis, Place de la République (1866; see entry 78); La Belle Jardinière, now Conforama, corner of quai de la Mégisserie and rue du Pont-Neuf (1866–68); Le Bon Marché, founded by Aristide Boucicaut, corner of rue de Sèvres and rue du Bac (1869; see entry 307).

The Bazar de l'Hôtel de Ville (1904) and the Samaritaine (1906) postdate Au Printemps (1881) but predate the Galeries Lafayette (1906–7). See below.

365 Galeries Lafayette

LOCATION: 38–46, boulevard Haussmann
MÉTRO STATION: Chaussée-d'Antin
PATRONS: Alphonse Kahn and Théophile Bader (first store, 1895; destroyed)
ARCHITECTS: Georges Chédanne (boulevard Haussmann, 1906–7). Ferdinand Chanut (rear addition between rue de Mogador and rue de la Chaussée-d'Antin, 1910–12; display windows, 1926). Pierre Patout (some façades, 1932–36). Two floors added to 1906–7 building in 1960; block between rue de Mogador and rue Charras demolished and rebuilt in 1969

The large glass dome designed by Ferdinand Chanut survives, but the monumental stairway beneath it was destroyed in 1974.

LOCATION: 64–70, boulevard Haussmann
MÉTRO STATION: Havre-Caumartin
PATRON: Jules Jaluzot (first store, 1865;
destroyed)
ARCHITECTS: Paul Sédille (1881, after fire
destroyed the first store). René Binet
(addition on corner of rue Caumartin
and Rue Charras, 1905). Georges Wybo
(1912 and 1921–24, when fire
necessitated reconstruction)

Au Printemps

Present state

Original state

*The drawings represent the store built in
1881. The one at left depicts its original
appearance; the one above shows it as it
is today, after the construction of
additional floors. In designing the
addition erected in 1905, the architect
René Binet basically respected the design
of his colleague Paul Sédille but
accorded greater prominence to the
corner towers.*

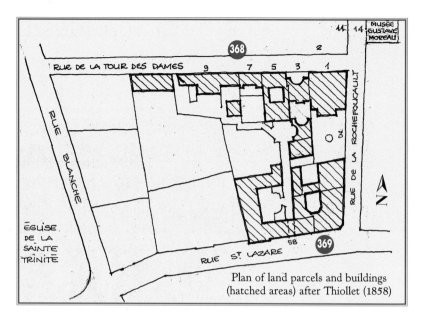

Plan of land parcels and buildings
(hatched areas) after Thiollet (1858)

367 La Nouvelle Athènes

LOCATION: Originally consisted of the developed lots indicated in the map above, contained within the block defined by the present rue de la Tour-des-Dames, rue de La Rochefoucauld, and rue Saint-Lazare
MÉTRO STATION: Trinité
PATRONS: The architect Auguste Constantin and investors (buildings erected 1820–35)

The quarter known as La Nouvelle Athènes (the New Athens) was created on land formerly occupied by the gardens of the Hôtel de Valentinois.

The developers set out to sell lots to prominent figures and to build the residences. A list of the residences and other buildings appears opposite.

Façades on rue de

No. 1
Hôtel de Mlle Mars

No. 3
Hôtel de Mlle Duchesnois

No. 5
House of Horace Vernet

Hous

Rue de la Tour-des-Dames

LOCATION: Connects rue Blanche to rue de La Rochefoucauld
MÉTRO STATION: Trinité

No. 1 (and no. 3, rue de La Rochefoucauld): Hôtel de Mademoiselle Mars, designed by Ludovico Visconti (1820)
No. 3: Hôtel de Mademoiselle Duchesnois, designed by Auguste Constantin (1820)
No. 5: House of the painter Horace Vernet, designed by Louis-Pierre Haudebourt (1822)
No. 7: House of the painter Paul Delaroche, designed by Auguste Constantin (1835)
Nos. 9–9 bis: Hôtel de Talma (house of the celebrated actor François-Joseph Talma), designed by Charles Lelong (1820); building much modified
No. 2: Hôtel de Lestapis (not part of core development but built in the same period, 1822–23)

Hôtel de Mlle Mars, garden façade

Rue Saint-Lazare, no. 58

MÉTRO STATION: Trinité

The polychrome façade of this building, erected c. 1820, has just been restored. Paul Delaroche resided here as well as at 7, rue de la Tour-des-Dames. The porch of this building leads to a dead-end alley from which one can glimpse the garden façades of 3–9, rue de la Tour-des-Dames.

ur-des-Dames, nos. 1–9 bis

7
Delaroche

Nos. 9–9 bis
Hôtel de Talma

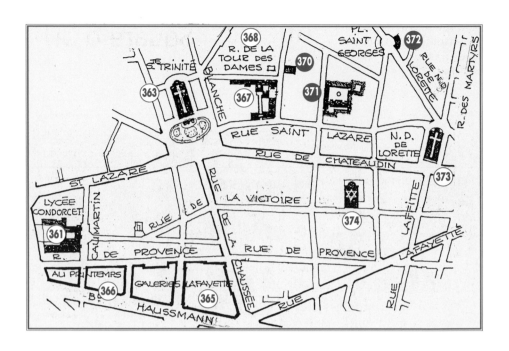

 Musée Gustave-Moreau

LOCATION: 14, rue de La Rochefoucauld
MÉTRO STATION: Trinité
PATRONS: The painter's parents; then the painter himself, who added two floors and had the façade redesigned
ARCHITECT: Albert Lafon (façade, 1895)

Before his death in 1898, Gustave Moreau decided to bequeath his house and the works it contained to the French state. The two upper floors, which housed his studio, became a museum in 1902; their rooms are arranged in accordance with instructions left by the artist

LOCATION: Entered at no. 20, rue Taitbou
MÉTRO STATION: Saint-Georges
PATRON AND ARCHITECT: The English architect
Edward Crésy (1829)

Square d'Orléans

Frédéric Chopin, George Sand, the elder Alexandre Dumas, and many other celebrated figures have resided in this peaceful enclave. The fountain in the center of the main courtyard dates from 1855

Place Saint-Georges Apartment Building

LOCATION: 26, Place Saint-Georges
MÉTRO STATION: Saint-Georges
ARCHITECT: Édouard Renaud (1840–42)

At a time when rental buildings tended to be simple, Renaud set out to make "his" building resemble a lavish town house. The abundant decoration is of French Renaissance inspiration. The building became a prestigious address, one of the most expensive in Paris. The future marquise de Païva lived here prior to the construction of her own residence on the Champs-Élysées. Also noteworthy on the Place Saint-Georges is no. 27, headquarters of the Dosne-Thiers Foundation; it was built in 1873 on the site of the Thiers residence, destroyed in 1871 by the Communards.

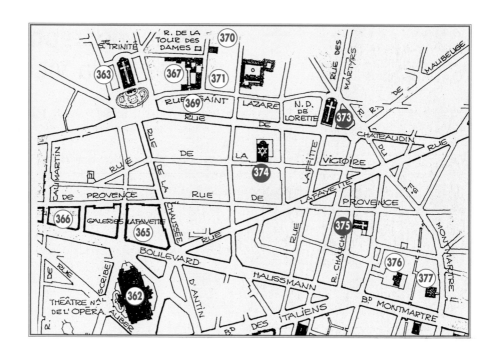

③⑦③ Notre-Dame-de-Lorette

LOCATION: 18 bis, rue de Châteaudun
MÉTRO STATION: Notre-Dame-de-Lorette
ARCHITECT: Hippolyte Lebas (1823)

For this church the architect adopted a neoclassical style, still fashionable some forty years after the construction of Jean-François Chalgrin's church of Saint-Philippe-du-Roule (see entry 352). Like that building, it features a basilican plan and culminates in a domed hemicycle. The façade is dominated by a Corinthian portico whose pediment contains Homage to the Virgin, *a relief by Charles Leboeuf-Nanteuil.*

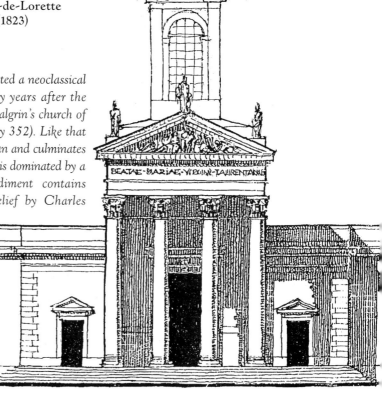

Synagogue on the rue de la Victoire (374)

LOCATION: 44, rue de la Victoire
MÉTRO STATION: Notre-Dame-de-Lorette
PATRONS: The Jewish consistory of the City of Paris
ARCHITECT: Alfred-Philibert Aldrophe (1867–76)

This synagogue is the largest in France. It was designated a certified public monument in 1987. The disposition of its façade corresponds to the interior, which features a wide central nave and two side aisles surmounted by two levels of galleries.

LOCATION: 16, rue Chauchat
MÉTRO STATION: Le-Peletier
PATRON: Initially, the City of Paris
ARCHITECTS: Adrien-Louis Lusson (depot, 1821–25). François-Charles Gau (remodeling as a Lutheran church, 1841–42)

Lutheran Church of the Redemption (375)

The surprising appearance of this Lutheran church results from its having been designed as a depot for a neighboring tollhouse. Furthermore, its architect, A.-L. Lusson, although a student of Charles Percier, was a great admirer of Claude-Nicolas Ledoux, whose influence is apparent here. When the building was transformed into a Lutheran church, the architect Gau enriched the façade by adding a portico with a rounded pediment.

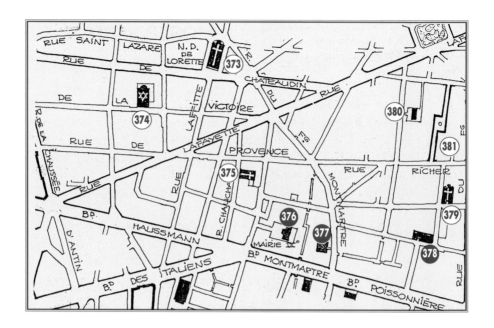

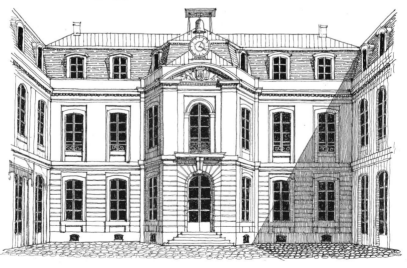 376 Mairie of the 9th Arrondissement

(Former Hôtel d'Augny)

LOCATION: 6, rue Drouot
MÉTRO STATION: Richelieu-Drouot
PATRON: The fermier-général d'Augny
ARCHITECT: Charles-Étienne Briseux
(1748–52); wings erected 1870

This residence, built for the farmer-general of Augny, became in 1836 the property of the banker Aguado, who remodeled it. It was eventually acquired by the City of Paris, which made it the mairie (town hall) of the 2nd arrondissement, redesignated the 9th arrondissement in 1860, after several outlying areas were incorporated into the city.

LOCATION: 7, rue du Faubourg-Montmartre
MÉTRO STATION: Rue-Montmartre
PATRONS: Édouard and Camille Chartier
(1898–99)

Restaurant Chartier 377

Restaurant Chartier is what was known as a bouillon, *an inexpensive restaurant catering to the city's working population. Such establishments proliferated at the end of the 19th century, when astute entrepreneurs opened series of them that were the ancestors of today's restaurant chains. Their interiors were rather richly appointed, offering less lavish imitations of more exclusive restaurants. That of Restaurant Chartier miraculously survives more or less intact.*

LOCATION: 14, rue Bergère
MÉTRO STATION: Bonne-Nouvelle
PATRON: Comptoir National
d'Escompte
ARCHITECT: Édouard Corroyer
(1881)

Banque Nationale de Paris 378
(Former Comptoir National d'Escompte)

This building is, with the Crédit Lyonnais headquarters (see entry 58), prototypical of the prestige structures erected by Parisian banks in the late 19th century to impress their clients and win their confidence. The architect judiciously placed the entrance not in the center of the building but on axis with the rue Rougemont, which maximizes its visual impact.

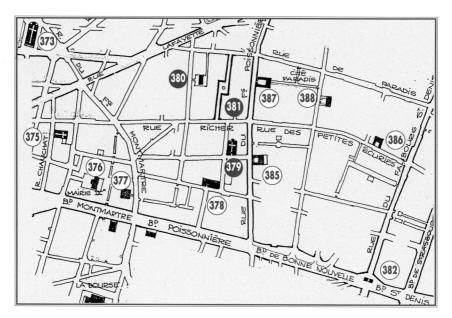

379 Saint-Eugène-et-Sainte-Cécile

LOCATION: 6, rue Sainte-Cécile
MÉTRO STATION: Bonne-Nouvelle
ARCHITECTS: Louis-Adrien Lusson and
Louis-Auguste Boileau (1855)

Funds being quite limited, the architects decided to use a metal structural frame, the first time such a solution was adopted in a Parisian church. The cast-iron columns supporting the lancet arches of the roof are remarkably delicate.

LOCATION: 32, rue de Trévise, and 13, rue Bleue
MÉTRO STATION: Cadet
PATRON: The public-works developer René Bony
ARCHITECT: Jules de Joly (1826)

Hôtel Bony

West façade on
the garden

This charming little town house is accessible either from the alley beginning at 13, rue Bleue (the sole entry before the rue de Trévise was constructed), or from the rue de Trévise (go through the courtyard at no. 32). One can also walk around the building to view the original court façade. Jules de Joly, the architect, also collaborated on the remodeling of the National Assembly in 1828 (see entry 285).

LOCATION: 8, rue Richer, and 5, rue Bleue
MÉTRO STATION: Cadet
PATRON: A private developer (1840)
ARCHITECTS: Lebaudy, Panier, and Merintier

Cité de Trévise ③⑧①

This residential complex, designed in a neo-Renaissance style, was built on the site of the Hôtel Margantin. In its center is a small square containing a fountain decorated with three nymphs.

In a gesture typical of the period, all fifteen of the houses in the development were given different designs.

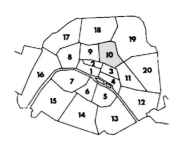

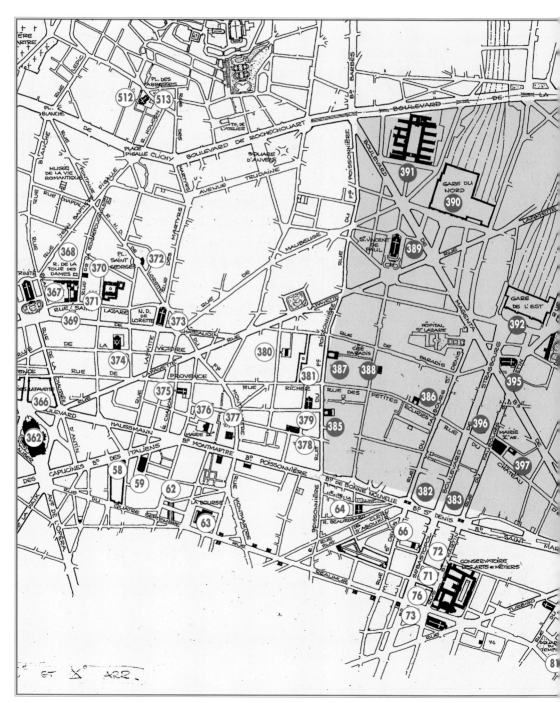

10th Arrondissement

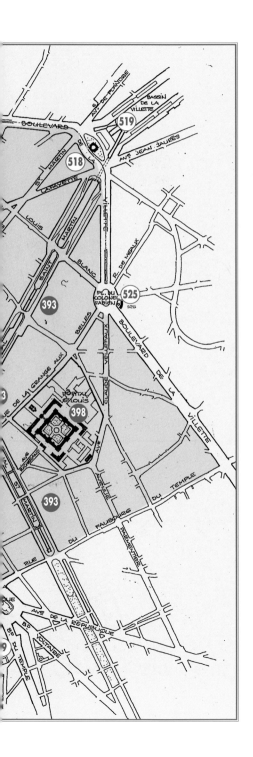

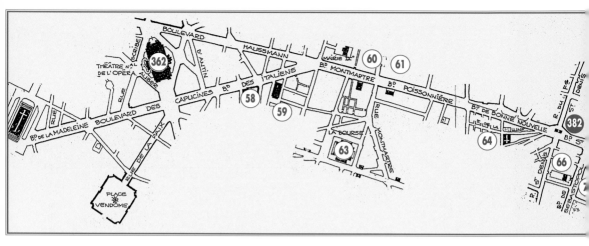

Les Grands Boulevards

The grands boulevards *follow the traces of the fortifications erected first between 1365 and 1395, during the reigns of Charles V and Charles VI, and completed during the reigns of Charles IX and Louis XIII.*

These wide avenues traverse several arrondissements, and their character varies from quarter to quarter. The principal buildings along these spacious avenues are discussed under the heading of the relevant arrondissement. Their respective entry numbers are indicated in the map above.

Originally, the term boulevard *designated the sentry walks of military ramparts; it was retained when the Parisian fortifications were replaced by broad thoroughfares.*

In 1670, Louis XIV, after having consolidated France's borders, decided to make Paris an open

city. First the ramparts between the Bastille and the Porte Saint-Denis were demolished, followed in 1676 by those between the Porte Saint-Denis and Porte Saint-Honoré (behind the present Madeleine).

The boulevards became fashionable places for promenades, and beautiful hôtels rose along them. Development became increasingly dense, and by the 19th century the boulevards boasted a great many taverns, theaters, and restaurants. The increasingly mixed character of the crowds drawn by these establishments alienated more fashionable Parisians, who began to favor other parts of the city. Many restaurants and theaters still line the boulevards, but their golden age is a thing of the past.

Porte Saint-Denis and Porte Saint-Martin in the early 19th century

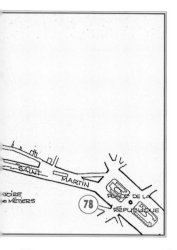

Porte Saint-Denis ⑧⑫

LOCATION: Boulevard Saint-Denis
MÉTRO STATION: Strasbourg-Saint-Denis
ARCHITECT: François Blondel (1672)
SCULPTORS: François Girardon; then Michel Anguier

This gate was commissioned by the City of Paris to commemorate Louis XIV's victories in the Rhine campaign. The reliefs above the central arch evoke The Crossing of the Rhine *(on the southern side) and* The Taking of Maastricht *(northern side).*

LOCATION: Boulevard Saint-Martin
MÉTRO STATION: Strasbourg-Saint-Denis
ARCHITECT: Pierre Bullet (1674)

Porte Saint-Martin ⑧⑬

This gate was commissioned by the aldermen of the city to commemorate Louis XIV's taking of Besançon and other victories.

The four reliefs flanking the central arch are as follows: northern side, on the left, The Taking of Limburg *(Pierre Legros) and on the right,* The Defeat of the German Armies *(Gaspard Marsy); southern side, on the left,* The Breaking of the Triple Alliance *(Étienne Le Hongre) and on the right,* The Taking of Besançon *(Martin Desjardins).*

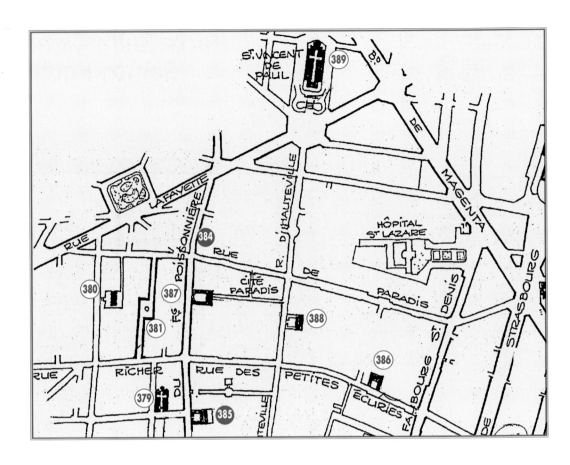

384 The Faubourg Poissonnière

LOCATION: Links boulevard Poissonnière
to boulevard de Magenta
MÉTRO STATION: Poissonnière

Walking down the rue du Faubourg-Poissonnière today, one finds it difficult to imagine this and the adjacent streets lined by beautiful town houses, for most of them have disappeared or been disfigured by subsequent artisanal and commercial tenants.

To envision this quarter as it appeared in the early 19th century, focus on the few surviving hôtels *and try to block out the later buildings that now surround them: in the 9th arrondissement, Hôtel Bony (entry 380); in the 10th arrondissement, Hôtel Benoist de Sainte-Paulle (entry 385), Hôtel de Botterel-Quintin (entry 386), Hôtel Titon (entry 387), and Hôtel de Bourrienne (entry 388).*

LOCATION: 30, rue du Faubourg-Poissonnière
MÉTRO STATION: Bonne-Nouvelle
PATRON: François Benoist de Sainte-Paulle (1773); then
Jean-François Caron (1776)
ARCHITECTS: Samson-Nicolas Lenoir, known as Lenoir
Le Romain (main block, 1773). Antoine-François Peyre,
known as Peyre the Younger (projecting wings, 1778)

Hôtel Benoist de ㉟ Sainte-Paulle

Façade on the rue du Faubourg-Poissonnière

This is the largest surviving hôtel in the Faubourg Poissonnière. The entrance to the structure on the street leads to a forecourt enclosed by what were originally service buildings. At its rear is the main block, whose façade features a monumental portico with four columns. As indicated in the drawing above, two stories have been added to the structure's lateral bays.

The property of Air France for many years beginning in 1946, the building has recently been restored and divided into apartments.

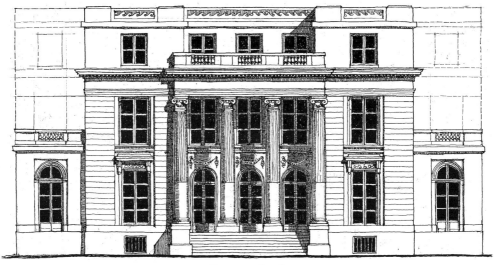

Forecourt façade

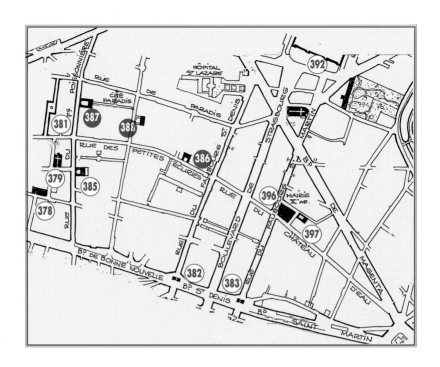

Hôtel de Botterel-Quintin

LOCATION: 44, rue des Petites-Écuries (at rear of court)
MÉTRO STATION: Bonne-Nouvelle
PATRON: Charles-André de la Corée (1782), who resold it to the comte de Botterel-Quintin in 1785
ARCHITECT: François-Victor Pérard de Montreuil (1782)

The main block in the sketch is situated at the rear of the fore-court, separated from the street by a building on which addition-al stories have unfortunately been constructed.

The interiors of this hôtel are quite remarkable, especially that of the original dining room, which is oval. Some authors have attributed the decor to François-Joseph Bélanger.

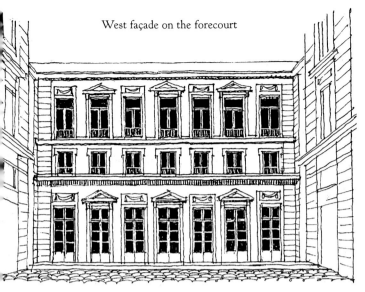

West façade on the forecourt

Hôtel Titon 387

LOCATION: 58, rue du Faubourg-Poissonnière
MÉTRO STATION: Poissonnière
PATRON: Antoine François Frémin, conseiller du Parlement de Paris; then Marie-Anne Coulbeau, who sold it to Jean-Baptiste Maximilien Titon, magistrate in the Parlement of Paris
ARCHITECT: Jean-Charles Delafosse (1776–83)

Two stories were added to the building fronting the street as well as the two side wings in the early 19th century. The interesting court elevations of these additions feature alternating windows and niches in the antique style. A new story was added to the main block a bit later; it repeats the elevation of the ground floor below, to rather cumbersome effect (see drawing above). The garden façade is visible from the alley of the Cité du Paradis, accessible from the nearby rue de Paradis.

LOCATION: 58, rue de Hauteville
MÉTRO STATION: Poissonnière
PATRON: Originally Madame Préponnier (1789–90), who was followed by several owners. The residence takes its name from the secretary of Napoléon I, Louis Fauvelet de Bourrienne, who acquired it in 1801.
ARCHITECT: Célestin-Joseph Happe (1789–98). Étienne-Chérubin Leconte (redesign of garden façade, early 19th century)

Hôtel de Bourrienne 388

Aside from the addition of eaves, the main building now appears much as it did in the 19th century. It also retains its interior decor dating from the Directory; the ground-floor rooms may be visited upon request.

Garden façade

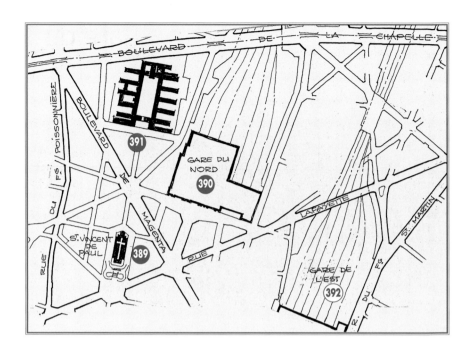

⓷⑧⑨ Saint-Vincent-de-Paul

LOCATION: Place Franz-Liszt
MÉTRO STATION: Poissonnière
ARCHITECT: Jean-Baptiste Lepère
(1824–31); then Jacques-Ignace Hittorff
(1831–44)

The church of Saint-Vincent-de-Paul marks a transition between the neoclassical religious architecture of the early 19th century and the unorthodox idiom that succeeded it (see Saint-Augustin and the church of the Trinity, entries 359 and 363). The basilican plan and the entry porch are neoclassical, but the towers are quite different in character.

LOCATION: Place de Roubaix
MÉTRO STATION: Gare-du-Nord
ARCHITECT: Jacques-Ignace Hittorff (1861–64)

Gare du Nord

So rapidly did rail traffic increase that the need to replace the first train station on this site, erected in 1846, was apparent as early as 1854. The new station was designed in an emphatically monumental style. Its stone façade, richly decorated with sculpture, bears little relation to the glass-and-metal train sheds just beyond, which are remarkable for the lightness of their construction.

LOCATION: 2, rue Ambroise-Paré
MÉTRO STATION: Barbès-Rochechouart
PATRON: The préfet Claude-Philippe-Barthelot Rambuteau, thanks to a bequest from the comtesse de Lariboisière
ARCHITECT: Pierre Gauthier (1846–53)

Hôpital Lariboisière

The cholera epidemic of 1832 led to the construction of new hospitals whose designs took new account of hygienic factors. The Lariboisière hospital was one of them. It consists of six pavilions arrayed around a large central courtyard and linked by a peripheral gallery.

The chapel, situated on the courtyard's central axis, houses the funerary monument of the comtesse de Lariboisière, a work by the sculptor Charles de Marochetti.

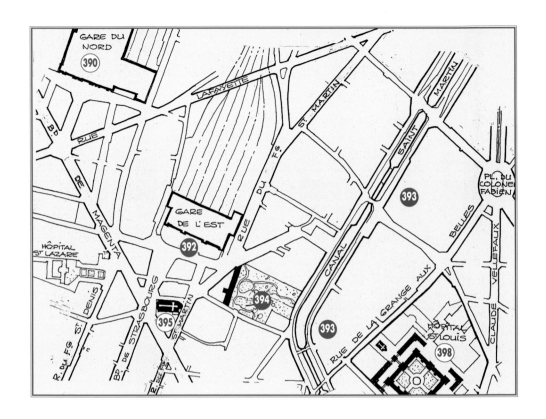

392 Gare de l'Est

LOCATION: Place du 8-Mai-1945
MÉTRO STATION: Gare-de-l'Est
PATRON: Chemins de Fer de l'Est
ARCHITECTS: François-Alexandre
Duquesney (1847–50). Addition by
the engineer Bertaut (1924–31)

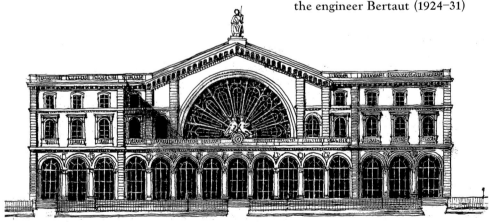

Originally this train station consisted only of what is now its left wing, facing the boulevard de Sébastopol. Its size was doubled between 1924 and 1931, which entailed changing the course of the rue Faubourg-Saint-Martin and demolishing some of the old Recollects convent (entry 394).

Canal ③⑨③
Saint-Martin

LOCATION: Between the La Villette basin to the north and the Arsenal basin to the south
CONSTRUCTION: Planned in 1802, realized 1822–25

The Saint-Martin canal was created under the Restoration to link the Seine to the Ourcq canal. It connects with the Arsenal basin to the south by way of a tunnel that passes beneath the Place de la Bastille. To the north, it flows into the La Villette basin. Its nine locks, humpbacked pedestrian bridges, and the trees lining its embankments give the canal a picturesque character ideally suited to promenades, but half of its original course from the Place de la Bastille to the rue du Faubourg-du-Temple is now covered over.

LOCATION: 148, rue du Faubourg-Saint-Martin, and 8, rue des Récollets
MÉTRO STATION: Gare-de-l'Est
PATRONS: The monks of the Franciscan Recollects community
CONSTRUCTION: The earliest buildings date from about 1620; they are now much altered, and part of the complex was demolished in 1926 to accommodate the addition to the Gare de l'Est.

Former Convent ③⑨④
of Recollects

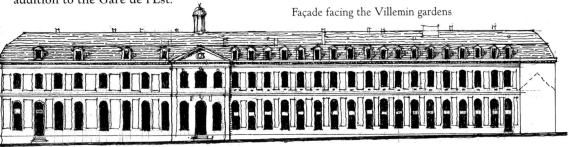

Façade facing the Villemin gardens

The Franciscan Recollect monks first occupied this site in the early 17th century and commenced construction of their convent about 1620. During the Revolution, the complex was transformed into a hospice for those with incurable illnesses; in 1860, it became a military hospital, taking the name Villemin in 1913.

The hospital abandoned the complex in 1968, and four years later the army followed suit. For a time, the buildings housed the Paris-Villemin architecture school (UP-I). Their future has been much discussed but remains uncertain.

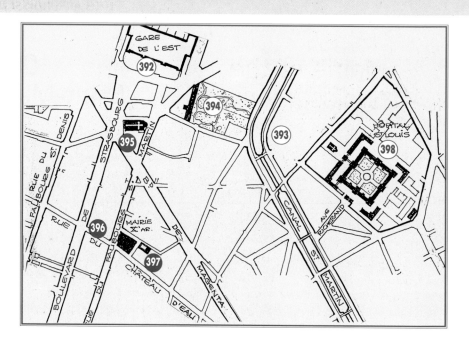

395 Saint-Laurent

LOCATION: 68, boulevard de Strasbourg
MÉTRO STATION: Gare-de-l'Est
CONSTRUCTION: 15th and 16th centuries; classical façade added, 1620 (destroyed 1863); Lady Chapel, 1712; present neo-Gothic façade, 1867
ARCHITECTS: Unidentified for the original structure. Antoine Le Pautre (façade, 1620; destroyed). Simon Constant-Dufeux (façade, completed 1867)

In the 19th century, after the construction of the boulevard de Magenta and the boulevard de Strasbourg, the classical façade of the church of Saint-Laurent lay recessed from the ideal street alignment, a discrepancy that Baron Haussmann found objectionable. In 1863, he had the façade demolished and ordered the construction of an additional bay and a neo-Gothic façade. The new composition, surmounted by a spire, was completed in 1867.

1620

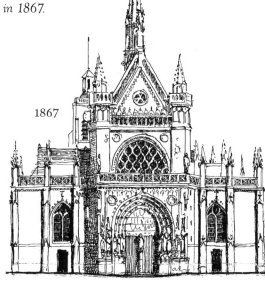

1867

Mairie of the 10th Arrondissement

396

LOCATION: 72–74, rue du Faubourg-Saint-Martin
MÉTRO STATION: Château-d'Eau
ARCHITECT: Eugène Rouyer (1892–96)
DECORATOR: Antoine Margotin

Construction of this mairie followed a competition won by the architect who had placed second in the competition for the reconstruction of the Hôtel de Ville, and there is a certain resemblance between the two buildings. Despite an overabundance of decoration typical of its period, the building is not without grandeur, notably in its large central hall.

Hôtel Gouthière **397**

LOCATION: 6, rue Pierre-Bullet
MÉTRO STATION: Château-d'Eau
PATRON: The engraver Pierre Gouthière
ARCHITECT: Joseph Métivier (1772–80)

This small town house, situated just behind the mairie of the 10th arrondissement, now houses the Hector-Berlioz music conservatory. Recently restored, it is a small marvel that can be admired from the forecourt as well as from the entrance hall. Two sphinxes guard the entrance stair.

Hôpital Saint-Louis

LOCATION: 40, rue Bichat
MÉTRO STATION: Goncourt
PATRON: Henri IV
ARCHITECTS: Claude Vellefaux and Claude
Chastillon (1607–11)

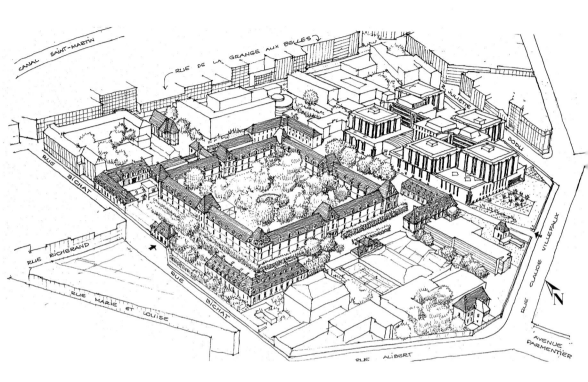

The Saint-Louis hospital is a magnificent example, too little known, of the brick-and-stone idiom known as the Louis XIII style (in fact, construction of the complex began under Henri IV).

The hospital was intended to combat epidemics, especially those of the plague, which raged at the time. The ill were brought together here not only to facilitate their care but also—and perhaps above all—to isolate them. The latter motivation explains the hospital's placement far outside the city limits of the day.

Furthermore, in plan the hospital rather resembles an internment camp, for, prior to entering, one encountered, in turn, a wall surrounding the grounds with only one entry, to maximize control, and an outer area defined by L-shaped buildings for the staff (during epidemics, all access to the exterior was forbidden, even to doctors and surgeons). Finally, one entered a central square quadrangle enclosed by buildings for the sick. Again to facilitate control during epidemics, patients were housed exclusively on the upper floor. Under normal circumstances, however, they had access to the garden within the central quadrangle. The chapel, meant to be accessible save during epidemics, straddled the outer wall.

The hospital is a fine example of a rational plan conceived for a precise purpose. The identity of its designer or designers is a matter of disagreement. Claude Chastillon was probably responsible for the original plan, but Claude Vellefaux, at the very least, oversaw its realization.

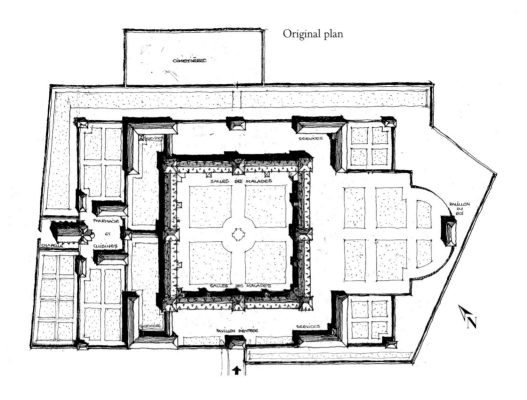

Original plan

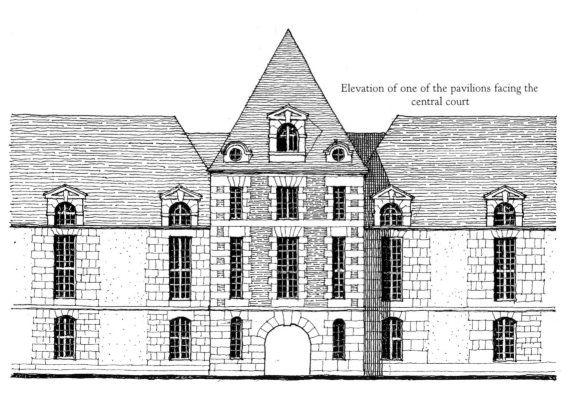

Elevation of one of the pavilions facing the central court

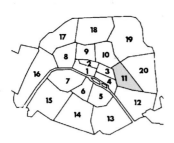

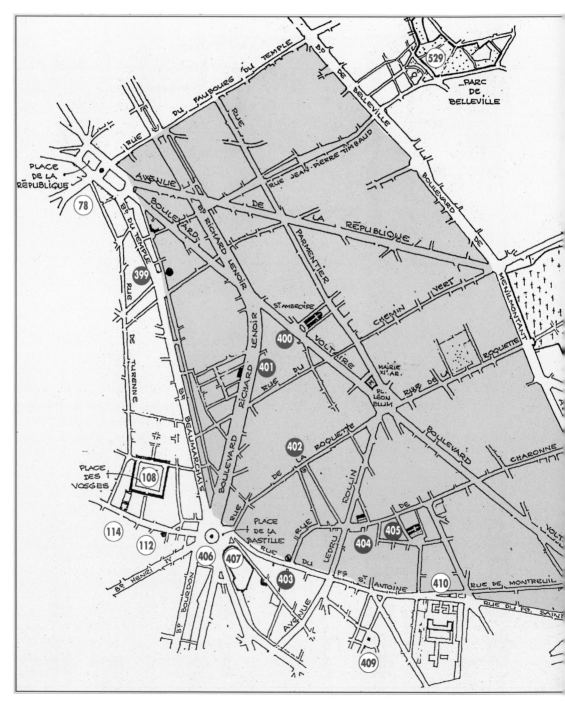

11th Arrondissement

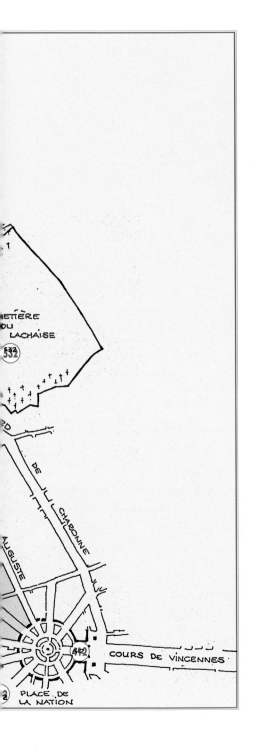

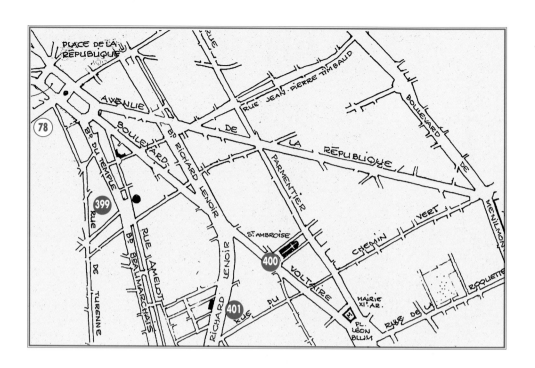

399 Cirque d'Hiver

LOCATION: 110, rue Amelot
MÉTRO STATION: Filles-du-Calvaire
PATRON: Louis Dejean, owner of the Cirque
des Champs-Élysées (destroyed)
ARCHITECT: Jacques-Ignace Hittorff (1852)

Jacques-Ignace Hittorff, who had already built the Cirque des Champs-Élysées, devised for this building a circular plan about 135 feet in diameter with no internal supports. It could originally accommodate about 4,000 spectators, but fire regulations have necessitated a reduction of this figure by half. Hittorff, an advocate of polychromy in architecture, decorated the façade with two friezes against colored grounds. The entrance is marked by two equestrian sculpture groups.

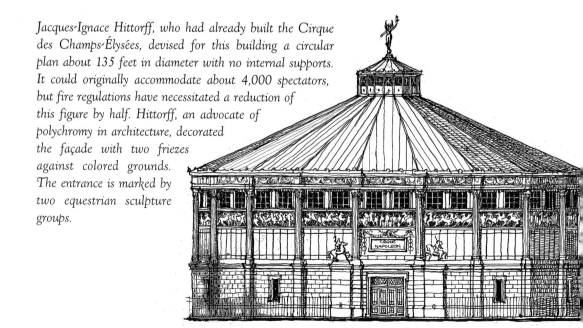

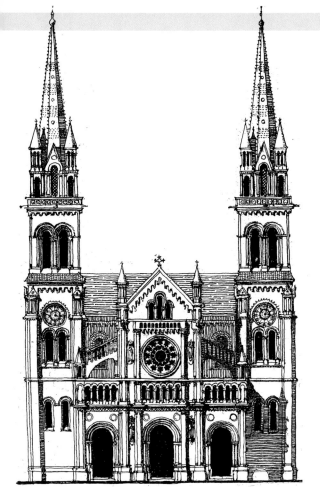

Saint-Ambroise

LOCATION: 71 bis, boulevard Voltaire
MÉTRO STATION: Saint-Ambroise
ARCHITECT: Théodore Ballu (1865)

Théodore Ballu drew upon Romanesque and Gothic models in this design, but he displayed less imagination here than in his contemporary church of the Trinity (entry 363). The part of the façade between the towers is too wide, disturbing its overall harmony.

Boulevard Richard-Lenoir, nos. 57–59

MÉTRO STATION: Richard-Lenoir

This hôtel is a late example of the Louis XVI style (it was built c. 1815). The rather ordinary rear façade is quite different from the one depicted here.

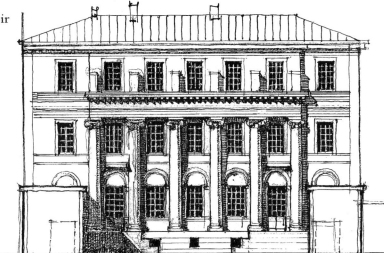

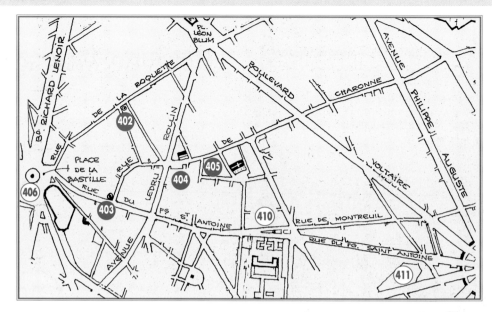

Fontaine de la Roquette

LOCATION: 70, rue de la Roquette
MÉTRO STATION: Bastille

403 Fontaine Trogneux

LOCATION: 61, rue du Faubourg-Saint-Antoine, ,and 1, rue de Charonne
MÉTRO STATION: Ledru-Rollin
ARCHITECT: Jean Beausire (1719–21).
Rebuilt according to the original design in 1807

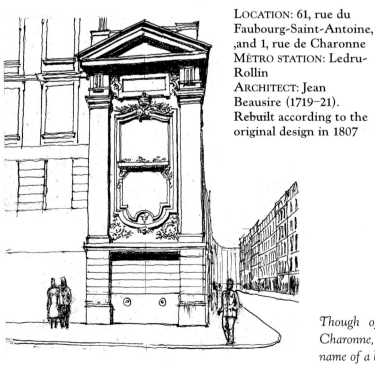

The Roman numerals on the pediment of this fountain indicate the date 1846, but its construction actually began in 1839. The keystone above the central niche is decorated with the arms of the City of Paris.

Though officially christened the Fontaine de Charonne, this fountain is better known by the name of a brewery formerly located in the quarter.

LOCATION: 51–53, rue de Charonne (façades visible from the cul-de-sac Charles-Dallery)
MÉTRO STATION: Ledru-Rollin
PATRON: Jacques Nourry, secrétaire des commandements of the duc d'Orléans
ARCHITECT: Pierre Delisle-Mansart, nephew of François Mansart (c. 1660)

Hôtel de Mortagne

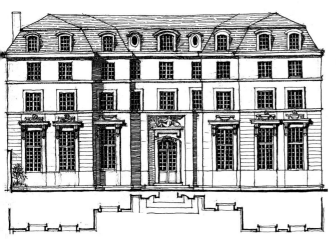

This residence is known by three names: Folie Nourry, for its original patron, Jacques Nourry; Hôtel de Mortagne, after its owner in 1711; and, finally, Hôtel de Vaucanson, after the celebrated fabricator and collector of automata who leased it for a time (1746). The building has been subjected to many unfortunate alterations, and a recent structure now masks the façade on the rue de Charonne. It is still visible, however, from the nearby cul-de-sac, and it retains its elegant ground-floor window heads.

LOCATION: 36, rue Saint-Bernard
MÉTRO STATION: Ledru-Rollin

Sainte-Marguerite 405

Erected as a chapel in 1627, this building was gradually enlarged and became an independent parish church in 1712. Its most notable feature is the chapel of the Souls in Purgatory, built between 1760 and 1765 under the supervision of the architect Victor Louis. Its remarkable illusionist decor, *painted by Paolo Antonio Brunetti, evokes a classical basilica. In the past, this church was almost entirely surrounded by a cemetery, only a small portion of which survives. The legend that the dauphin was buried here after he died in the prison of the Temple on June 8, 1795, is without foundation.*

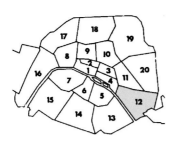

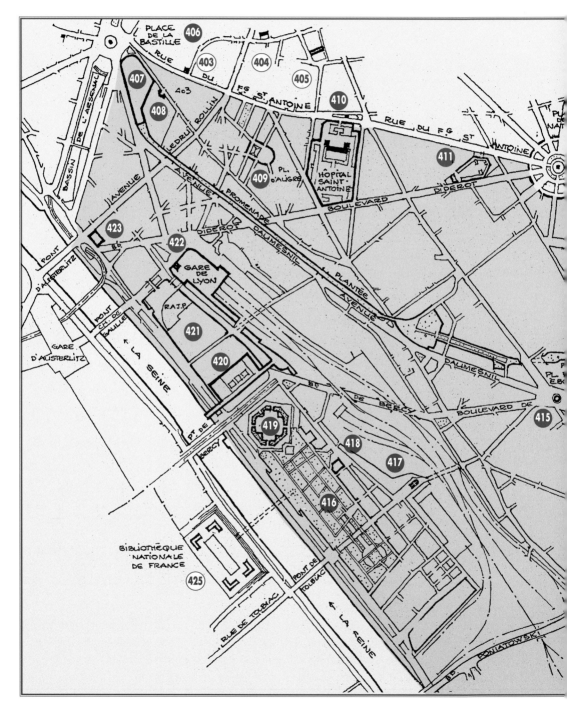

12th Arrondissement

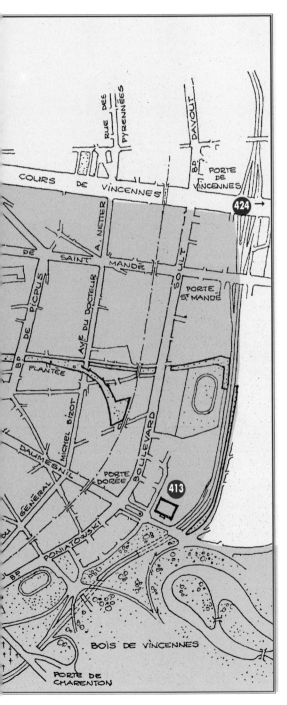

⓭ Place de la Bastille and July Column

LOCATION: Straddles boundaries of the 4th, 11th, and 12th arrondissements
MÉTRO STATION: Bastille
FORTRESS OF THE BASTILLE: Built 1370–72, demolished 1789
PORTE SAINT-ANTOINE: Built 1584, demolished 1778
JULY COLUMN: Erected 1831–40

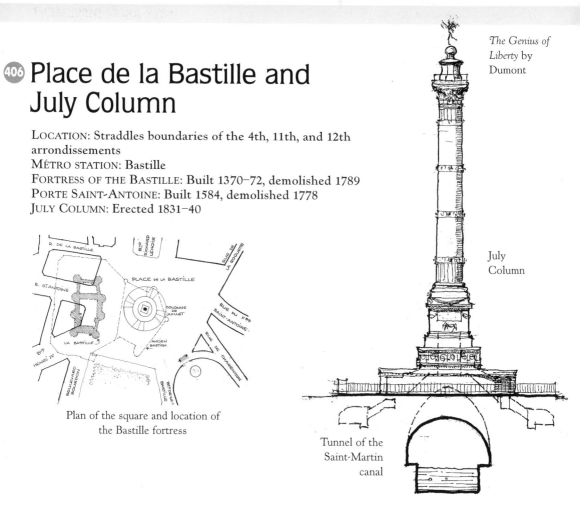

The Genius of Liberty by Dumont

July Column

Plan of the square and location of the Bastille fortress

Tunnel of the Saint-Martin canal

As its name indicates, the site of this square was formerly occupied by the fortress of the Bastille, which was demolished at the beginning of the Revolution in 1789. Charles V built the stronghold in 1370–72 to defend the city and especially the Hôtel Saint-Pol, his Parisian residence. It was also intended as a retreat for himself in the event of a Parisian uprising.

Louis XI transformed the Bastille into a prison, which gave it a sinister reputation among the Parisian population. That is why, when riots broke out in the faubourg Saint-Antoine on July 14, 1789, this symbol of oppression was the first target.

The small garrison could muster only meager resistance, and all hands were massacred, along with the governor of the prison. Soon thereafter, the edifice was demolished; many of its masonry blocks were preserved, carved into miniature Bastilles, and sold throughout France. Today, paving

stones record the former placement of the fortress.

After the Revolution, the terrain remained undeveloped until Napoléon I decided to transform it into a place decorated with a monumental fountain in the form of an elephant. He commissioned the architect Jean-Antoine Alavoine to build a full-scale plaster model on the site.

The fall of Napoléon caused the project to be abandoned, but the base was built and the plaster model remained in place, beside the base, until 1846.

In the meantime, King Louis-Philippe had risen to power, and from the moment of his accession he resolved to commemorate the Trois Glorieuses, the "three glorious days" of street fighting (July 28–30, 1830) that led to the fall of his predecessor, Charles X. Accordingly, he asked Alavoine, author of the elephant fountain, to design a memorial column that would rise from the base originally intended for the fountain. After Alavoine died in 1834, he was succeeded by Joseph-Louis Duc.

This column, realized in bronze, consists of twenty-one hollow cylindrical drums through the center of which rises a spiral stair. Light penetrates the interior through lion heads placed on collars circling the column. The culminating Genius of Liberty is by the sculptor Augustin-Alexandre Dumont.

Spaces within the base, which straddles the vaulted tunnel of the Saint-Martin canal, were remodeled to accommodate the remains of more than 500 victims of the revolution of 1830, later joined by those of victims of the revolution of 1848.

Opéra Bastille

LOCATION: Place de la Bastille
MÉTRO STATION: Bastille
PATRON: The French government, at the initiative of President François Mitterrand
ARCHITECT: Carlos Ott (building inaugurated 1989)

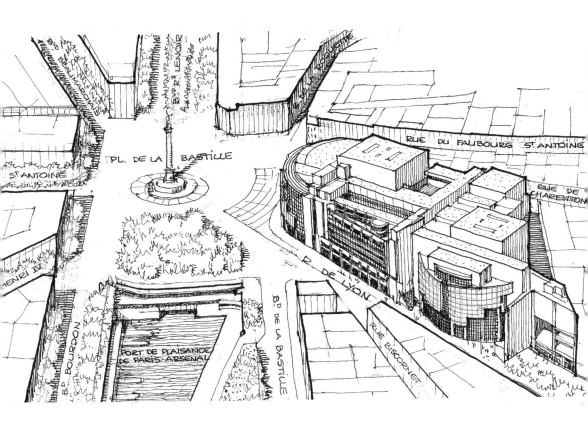

The international competition for the design of the Opéra Bastille was won by the Canadian Carlos Ott. The building was inaugurated on July 13, 1989, by President Mitterrand, but the first performance of an opera there—Les Troyens by Hector Berlioz—did not take place until March 17, 1990.

The main theater holds about 2,700. It is notable for the large size of the stage and the sophistication of its technical facilities. The building also houses an amphitheater for 500 and a workshop theater for 250.

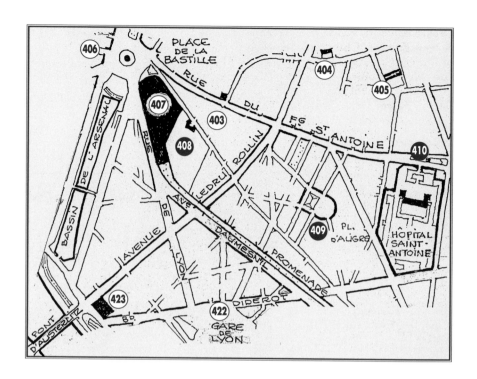

Entrance to the Hôpital des Quinze-Vingts

LOCATION: 26–28, rue de Charenton
MÉTRO STATION: Ledru-Rollin
PATRONS: Louis XIV for the barracks of the Black Musketeers, then Cardinal Rohan for the Maison des Quinze-Vingts (1780)
ARCHITECT: Robert de Cotte (1710)

The entrance to the Quinze-Vingts hospital is that of the old barracks of the Black Musketeers, decommissioned in 1775 and acquired in 1780 by Cardinal Rohan—later notorious for his involvement in the Diamond Necklace Affair—to house the Quinze-Vingts hospital for the blind.

All of the former barracks complex was demolished in 1959–65 except for the chapel and the entrance (right).

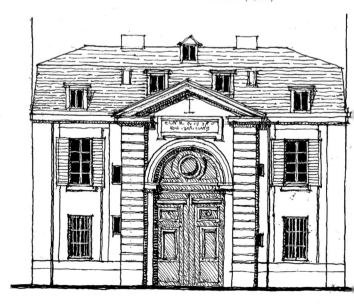

Place d'Aligre ⑨

MÉTRO STATION: Ledru-Rollin
PATRON: Jean-François Chomel de Seriville, who in 1776 acquired a large tract of land from the nuns of the Abbaye Royale de Saint-Antoine for residential development
ARCHITECTS: Samson-Nicolas Lenoir (first market, 1779).
Marc-Gabriel Jolivet (reconstruction, 1843)

Despite recent construction of dubious quality around their periphery, the Place d'Aligre and the Beauveau market remain picturesque thanks to the animated crowds that still frequent them.

Guardhouse

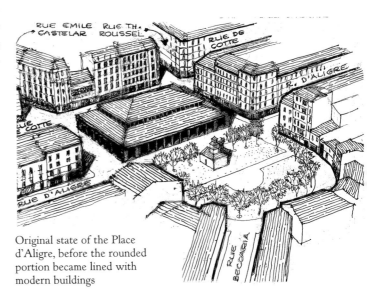

Original state of the Place d'Aligre, before the rounded portion became lined with modern buildings

Hôpital Saint-Antoine ⑩
(Pavillon de l'Horloge)

LOCATION: 184, rue du Faubourg-Saint-Antoine
MÉTRO STATION: Faidherbe-Chaligny
PATRON: Nuns of the Abbaye Royale de Saint-Antoine
ARCHITECTS: Samson-Nicolas Lenoir (design) and Claude-Martin Goupy (construction); alterations by Claude-Martin Goupy in 1767 (except for the wings, added in 1795)

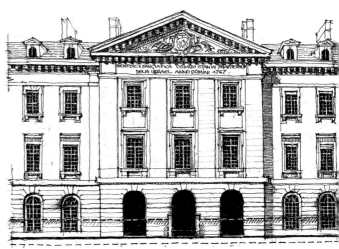

The Pavillon de l'Horloge, transformed into a hospital in 1795, is all that remains of the Abbaye Royale de Saint-Antoine.

Southern façade of the Pavillon de l'Horloge (facing the entrance)

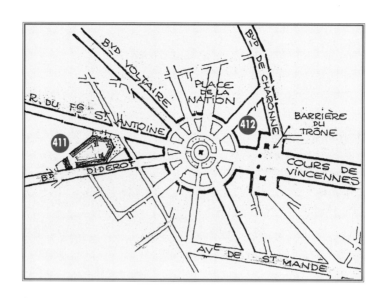

411 Fondation Eugène-Napoléon

LOCATION: 254, rue du Faubourg-Saint-Antoine
MÉTRO STATION: Nation
PATRON: Empress Eugénie
ARCHITECT: Jacques-Ignace Hittorff (1853–57)

The City of Paris was indirectly involved in this project, for Empress Eugénie requested that the funds allocated for the purchase of her wedding gift (a necklace) be used instead to build a school for the professional training of indigent young women. The school's chapel is in the center of the building, which occupies a lozenge-shaped plot.

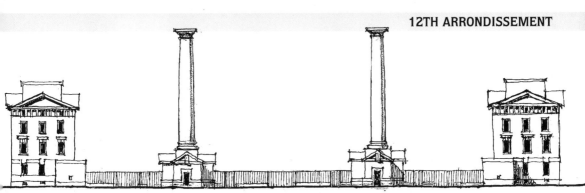

Original appearance of the Barrière du Trône, 1787

MÉTRO STATION: Nation
ARCHITECT: Claude-Nicolas Ledoux (tollhouse, 1785–87)
SCULPTOR: Jules Dalou (*The Triumph of the Republic*, installed in the center of the *place*, 1889–99)

Place de la Nation 412
(Barrière du Trône)

The Place de la Nation was previously known as the Place du Trône, after a monument erected on the occasion of the entry into Paris on August 26, 1660, of Louis XIV and his young wife, the infanta Marie-Thérèse. The present name dates from 1880.

The Barrière du Trône is one of four surviving tollhouses of the fifty in the Wall of the Farmers General, designed to facilitate the collection of duties levied against merchandise entering the city. Their design was entrusted to Claude-Nicolas Ledoux, who gave two of them an especially monumental character in light of their geographic importance: the Barrière de l'Étoile (destroyed); and the Barrière du Trône, which he punctuated with two monumental Doric columns.

The following elements were added during the reign of Louis-Philippe: fluting on the columns; sculpted decoration at the base of the columns; and statues at their summits representing Saint Louis and Philippe Auguste.

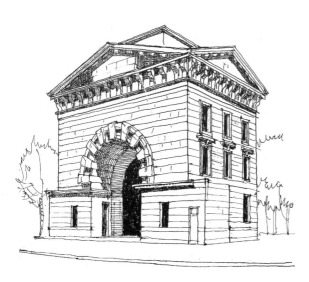

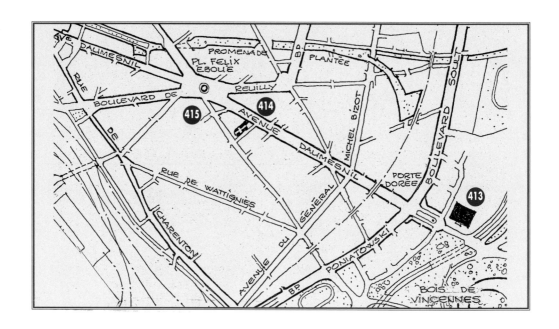

413 Musée National des Arts d'Afrique et d'Océanie

LOCATION: 293, avenue Daumesnil
MÉTRO STATION: Porte-Dorée
PATRON: The French government
for the Colonial Exposition of 1931
ARCHITECTS: Léon Jaussely and
Albert Laprade (1928–31)
SCULPTOR: Alfred
Janniot

This building, built for the Colonial Exposition of 1931, was originally the Palais (then Musée) de la France d'Outremer (French overseas territories). In 1960, after decolonization, it took its present name and was transformed accordingly.

The prominence accorded sculpture on the façade influenced the architects of the Palais de Tokyo (entry 492), who collaborated with the same sculptor, Alfred Janniot.

Saint-Esprit

LOCATION: 186, avenue Daumesnil
MÉTRO STATION: Daumesnil
ARCHITECT: Paul Tournon (1928–35)
FRESCOES: Artists working under the
direction of Maurice Denis

Paul Tournon modeled the sanctuary of this church after Saint Sophia in Istanbul, but he employed a building material that was new at the time, reinforced concrete. Although the eccentrically shaped plot featured only a narrow frontage on the avenue Daumesnil, this proved sufficient for an entrance vestibule, which Tournon crowned with a bell tower some 279 feet high.

Fontaine aux Lions

LOCATION: Place Félix-Éboué
MÉTRO STATION: Daumesnil
ARCHITECT: Gabriel Davioud (1887)
SCULPTOR: H.-A. Jacquemart

This fountain originally stood in the Place de la République. Deemed too small for that site, it was moved to the Place Félix-Éboué to make way for the gigantic Triumph of the Republic *by Jules Dalou.*

Parc de Bercy

416

LOCATION: Quai de Bercy
MÉTRO STATION: Bercy
ARCHITECTS: Marylène Ferrand, Jean-Pierre
Feugas, and Bernard Leroy
LANDSCAPE DESIGNERS: Yann Le Caisne,
Philippe Reguin (competition design 1987,
realization 1993–95)

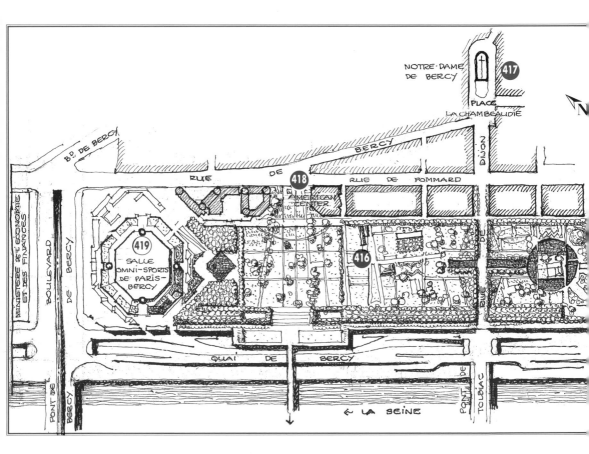

Early in the 19th century, the quai de Bercy became the center of the wine trade, for which many storage depots were built. The City of Paris came into possession of the land in 1878, from which time it could set about recasting the quarter whenever it deemed fit. The project finally began in the 1980s with construction of the Palais Omnisports de Paris-Bercy and the establishment of a coordinated development zone consisting of three distinct areas: in the center, along the Seine, the Parc de Bercy; north of the park, a residential zone with various social and cultural amenities; and to the east, a business quarter reserved for facilities relating to food and agriculture.

In 1987, a competition held for the design of the park was won by the three architects indicated above. The former Lheureux and Saint-Émilion wine warehouses on the tract were retained and restored to house restaurants, shops, and temporary exhibitions. In 1991, excavations undertaken in tandem with the project uncovered four oak dugout canoes dating from c. 4500–4300 BCE.

Notre-Dame-de-Bercy

LOCATION: 9, Place Lachambeaudie
MÉTRO STATION: Bercy
ARCHITECTS: A.-M. Chatillon (1823).
After a fire destroyed the church in
1871, it was rebuilt by A.-J. Hénard
in accordance with the original
design (1873).

Erected in what was an industrial area at the time, this church, restrained in design, is now situated in a quarter undergoing rapid development. The building resembles the neoclassical churches that began to appear in Paris after the construction of Saint-Philippe-du-Roule (entry 352). The statues in the niches flanking the entrance represent the apostles Peter and Paul.

American Center

LOCATION: 51, rue de Bercy
MÉTRO STATION: Bercy
PATRON: The American Center
ARCHITECT: Frank Gehry (1994)

Founded in 1931, the American Center, previously situated at 261, boulevard Raspail, sold that lot to the Fondation Cartier in 1987 (entry 449). For its new venue, located in a quarter undergoing rapid transformation, the institution turned to the American architect Frank Gehry, renowned for the freedom and ingenuity of his designs.

The building boasts all the facilities usually found in cultural centers of this kind: a theater, a cinema, a restaurant, an exhibition hall, and so on. Unfortunately, the new American Center did not prove as successful as expected, and a lack of funds obliged it to close its doors soon after completion, although it will soon house a cinema.

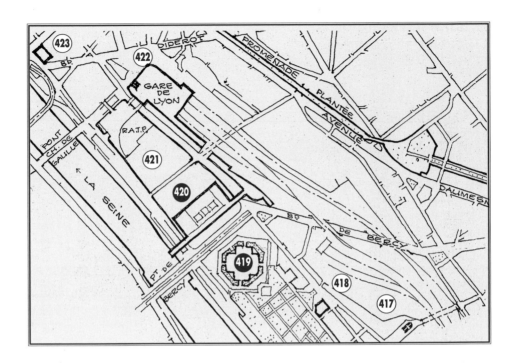

⑲ Palais Omnisports de Paris-Bercy

LOCATION: 8, boulevard de Bercy, and 89, rue de Bercy
MÉTRO STATION: Bercy
ARCHITECTS: Michel Andrault, Pierre Parat, and Aydin Guvan (1984)

In 1979, a design competition was organized for the Palais Omnisports, whose program stipulated a bicycle racetrack convertible to various other uses to be built on a site formerly occupied by the Bercy warehouses.

The winning design, quite original, called for exterior walls planted with grass. This end was achieved with a reinforced concrete structure supporting slopes of about 45° on each side; the outer surfaces were covered with lawns and the interior ones with stepped seating. The roof is supported by a three-dimensional metal armature with a span of about 262 feet whose only supports are four reinforced-concrete pillars. The stadium can accommodate 3,500 to 17,000 spectators, depending on the configuration chosen for a given performance or sports event.

LOCATION: 1, boulevard de Bercy
MÉTRO STATION: Bercy
ARCHITECTS: Paul Chemetov, Borja Huidobro,
and Émile Duhart Harosteguy (1989)

Ministry of Finance

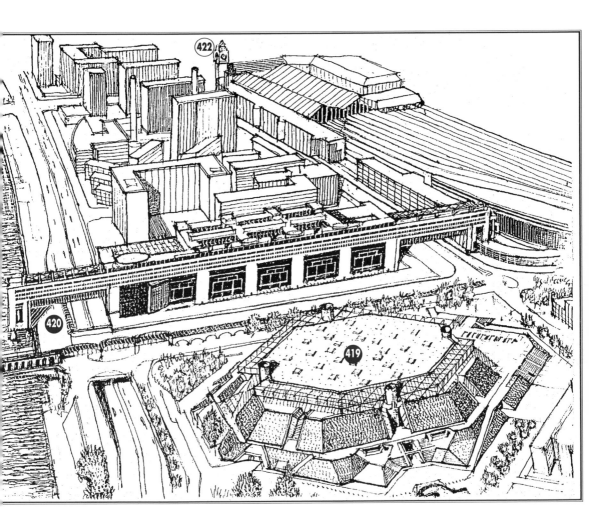

The Ministry of Finance previously occupied the Rivoli wing of the Louvre; it was displaced as part of the Grand Louvre project launched by President François Mitterrand.

The design of the new building was the result of a competition. The winning project features a very long structure whose silhouette brings to mind a bridge spanning the rue de Bercy (north side) and the quai de la Rapée (southern side), beyond which it plunges into the Seine.

Two buildings built for the army between 1815 and 1830 were integrated into the complex (139, rue de Bercy and the symmetrical structure on the quai de la Rapée). They both feature an arcaded ground floor and two upper floors.

421 Gare de Lyon–Bercy Quarter

LOCATION: Between the Gare de Lyon and the quai de la Rapée
MÉTRO STATION: Gare-de-Lyon

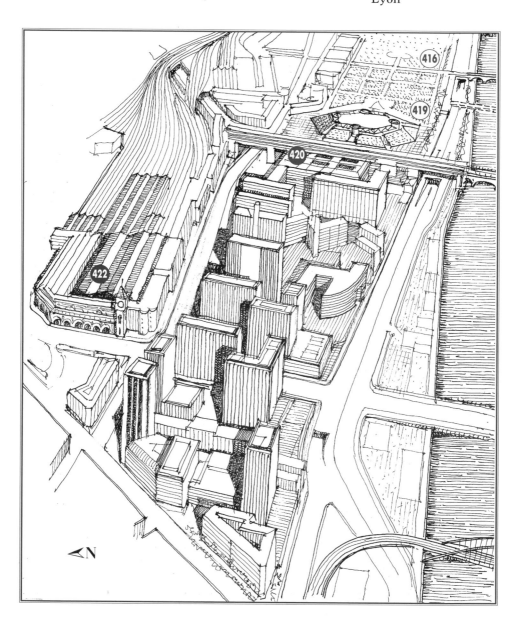

This new quarter was created in the 1970s by the construction of a group of office towers. It was completed recently by construction of a new Ministry of Finance (see previous entry) and a new headquarters for the RATP, the agency that operates the Paris métro system (semicircular building in the center of the ensemble with a very original exhibition space, designed by Pierre Sirvin).

Gare de Lyon (422)

LOCATION: 20, boulevard Diderot
MÉTRO STATION: Gare-de-Lyon
PATRON: The PLM Company (Paris-Lyon-Marseilles)
ARCHITECT: Marius Toudoire (1895–1902)

The Gare de Lyon is distinguished from other Parisian train stations by its commanding tower, which houses a clock whose faces are almost twenty feet in diameter. The tower's placement makes the façade asymmetrical, an unusual disposition up to that time. By contrast, the abundant decoration both inside and out is consistent with contemporaneous usage. The Gare de Lyon also boasts a restaurant overlooking the platforms, the Train Bleu, whose exuberant interior has been certified as a public monument. The frescoes in the departure hall date from the 1920s.

LOCATION: 94–96, quai de la Rapée
MÉTRO STATION: Quai-de-la-Rapée
ARCHITECT: Aymeric Zublena (1992)

Administrative Building (423)

Originally intended to house the Préfecture de Paris, in the end this building was occupied by the municipal services office (DASES). The site is exceptional in that it allows the viewer to withdraw sufficiently from the structure to take it in at a glance. Particularities of the terrain, however, led the architect to devise a curved façade that creates a small open space in front of the entrance. The space is emphasized by the placement of the elevator cages, which rise from it and thus become the dominant feature of the elevation.

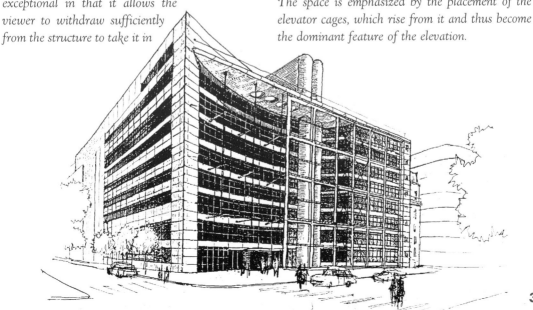

424 Château de Vincennes

LOCATION: Avenue de Paris, Vincennes
MÉTRO STATION: Château-de-Vincennes

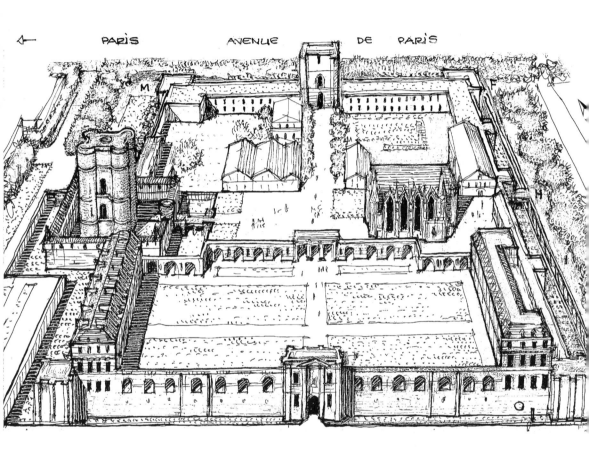

Excavations currently under way seem to indicate that it was Philippe Auguste who built the first château, now destroyed, during his reign (1180–1223); it occupied a square area measuring almost 200 feet per side in the northeast quadrant of the present enclosure.

Saint Louis, known to all French schoolchildren for having rendered justice under an oak at Vincennes, added to Philippe Auguste's château the Chapelle Saint-Martin, which was intended to

house a thorn from the crown of Christ; it was subsequently replaced by the present chapel (see opposite).

The château that now stands was built during the reigns of the first kings of the Valois dynasty: Philippe VI, Jean II le Bon, and Charles V. In the 17th century, the Château de Vincennes functioned as a prison and not as a royal residence, except during the minorities of Louis XIII, Louis XIV, and—in the early 18th century—Louis XV.

The Tower

Construction of the tower, or keep, began about 1360 and was completed in 1369. A powerful structure rising 170 feet above the ground (216 feet above the bottom of the moat), it features four corner turrets and is entered over a drawbridge. When new, it looked very much like the building we see today.

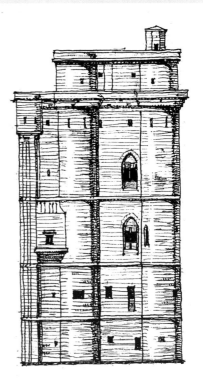

The Walls

Most of the defensive walls were built under Charles V in the 1370s. Enclosing an area 1,240 by 574 feet, they are ringed by a moat that was originally filled with water. The defensive towers once rose 138 feet above the ground (184 feet above the bottom of the moat). With the exception of the Tour du Village to the north, all of them were "decapitated" under the First Empire.

The Chapel

The chapel was begun during the reign of Charles V, but work was interrupted and did not resume until the 16th century; construction was completed during the reign of Henri II. Unlike Sainte-Chapelle on the Île de la Cité, it has only one level.

Pavillons du Roi et de la Reine

During the minority of Louis XIII, Marie de Médicis built, beginning in 1610, a pavilion whose width was doubled in 1654 by the architect Louis Le Vau; this building is the present Pavillon du Roi.

In 1658, the same architect built a symmetrical structure named the Pavillon de la Reine. He also designed the south portico (adjacent to the Tour de Bois) and the north portico (in the center near the chapel, flanked by arcades).

The Arsenal and the Barracks

Napoléon I transformed the château into a military arsenal and had the duc d'Enghien assassinated there (he was shot in the moat during the night of March 20–21, 1804). In 1840, the site became a military fort and the old château of Philippe Auguste was replaced by barracks.

During World War II the building was occupied by the Germans, who shot twenty-six hostages there on August 20, 1944, before blowing up the casemates and damaging the southern part of the château. The complex is currently being restored.

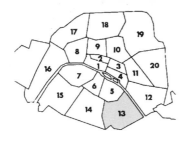

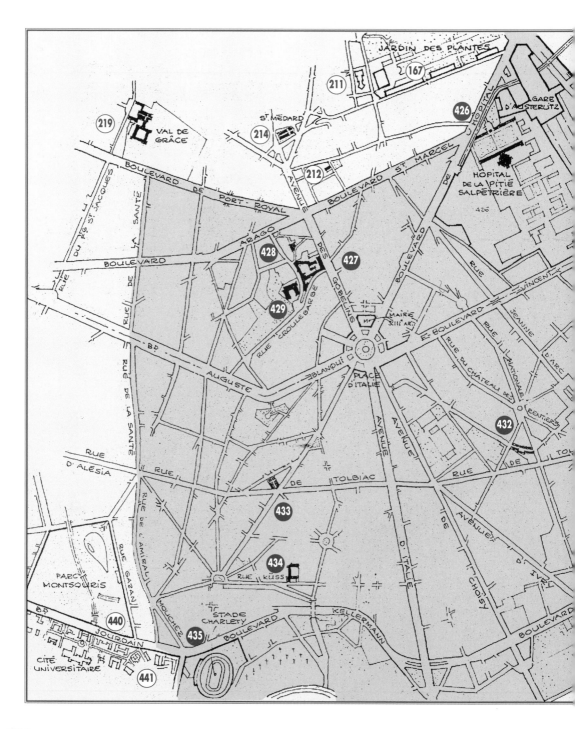

13th Arrondissement

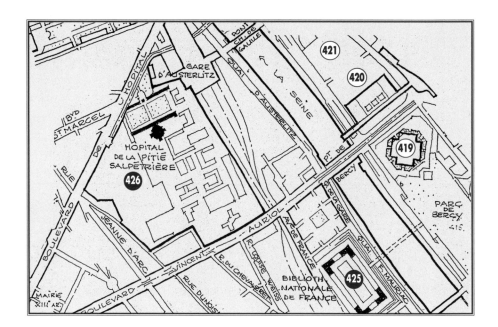

425 Bibliothèque Nationale de France

LOCATION: Quai François-Mauriac
MÉTRO STATION: Quai-de-la-Gare
PATRON: The French government, at the initiative of President François Mitterrand
ARCHITECT: Dominique Perrault, winner of a competition held in 1989 (construction 1993–97)

Since the French Revolution, the Bibliothèque Nationale de France, or French national library (formerly the royal library), located on the rue de Richelieu (see entry 51), has suffered from a chronic shortage of space. In July 1989, a national competition was held for a new building, and four designs were selected, including the one by Dominique Perrault that was eventually declared the winner.

The complex takes the form of an underground platform surrounding a large rectangular sunken patio—planted with lush vegetation—from whose corners rise four towers, L-shaped in plan and some 262 feet high. The two floors of the platform contain reading rooms overlooking the central patio as well as technical facilities in the areas lacking natural light, while the towers house offices (first seven floors) and bookshelves (upper floors).

The dimensions of the complex are impressive, and from the building's interior the patio rather resembles a public garden, although one without either public or noise. A pedestrian bridge across the Seine is envisioned that would link the library to the Parc de Bercy.

LOCATION: 47, boulevard de l'Hôpital
MÉTRO STATION: Austerlitz
PATRON: Louis XIV
ARCHITECTS: Louis Le Vau, Pierre Le Muet, and Antoine Duval (1657–70). Libéral Bruant (chapel, 1670–77). Germain Boffrand (new master plan, 1729)

Hôpital de la ⓐ Salpêtrière

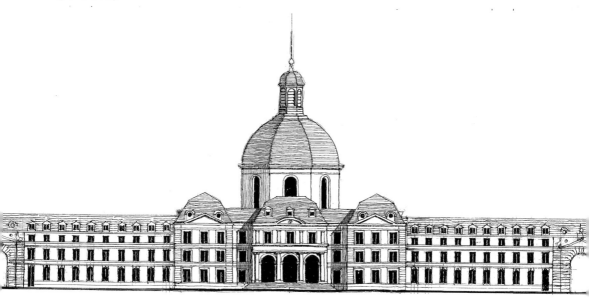

A proliferation of beggars, the disabled, and the ill in the streets of Paris prompted Louis XIV to establish a large general hospital for them. It initially occupied several existing buildings on this site, one of which was formerly a gunpowder mill; hence the name by which the hospital became known (salpêtrière means saltpeter works).

Design of the new complex was entrusted to Louis Le Vau, architect to the king, who was assisted in the task by his colleagues Le Muet and Duval. After Le Vau's death, construction of the chapel was entrusted to Libéral Bruant, who designed the building's dome and elevations. Its Greek-cross plan is quite original, making it possible for the congregation to be seated in four separate groups in the four arms, all with a view of the central altar below the dome.

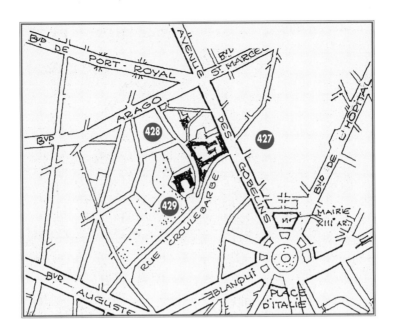

 427 Gobelins Manufactory

LOCATION: 42, avenue des Gobelins
MÉTRO STATION: Gobelins
PATRON: Jean-Baptiste Colbert, minister of Louis XIV
ARCHITECTS: Unidentified for the 17th-century work; Jean-Camille Formigé for the building on the avenue des Gobelins, built beginning in 1912

In 1662–67, Colbert founded the Manu-facture Royale des Meubles et Tapisseries de la Couronne (royal manufactory of fur-nishings and tapestries for the crown), which he housed on property belonging to a family of dyers, the Gobelins, whose name became that of the manufactory as well.

The original complex (see right) has sub-sequently been altered: in 1721, a chapel was added (it now projects into the rue Berbier-du-Mets, to the east); in 1871, some buildings were burned during the Commune and destroyed; between 1912 and 1918, a museum was built on the site of buildings demolished to accommodate a widening of the rue Mouffetard, rechristened the avenue des Gobelins.

The Gobelins complex in 1691
(plan after Sébastien Le Clerc)

LOCATION: 17–19, rue des Gobelins
and rue Gustave-Geoffroy
MÉTRO STATION: Gobelins
DATE: 15th century

So-called Hôtel de la Reine-Blanche

Many stories have been embroidered around this building, known by the evocative name Hôtel de la Reine-Blanche (town house of the white queen, or Queen Blanche). In fact, we do not know what queen this nickname designates or even if it refers to an actual personage. In any case, the building is picturesque and merits restoration.

LOCATION: 1–3, rue Berbier-du-Mets
MÉTRO STATION: Gobelins
PATRON: The French government
ARCHITECT: Auguste Perret (1935–37)

Mobilier National

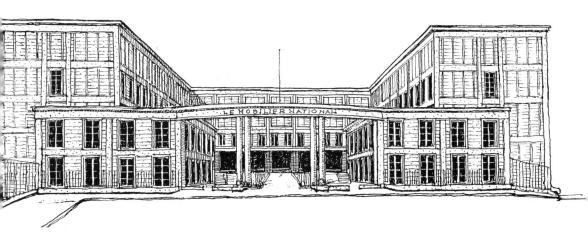

This building is a storehouse for furnishings used to decorate prestigious government offices. Its construction was occasioned by the Exposition Universelle of 1937, which necessitated the demolition of the previous storage facility on the quai Branly.

The building, designed by Auguste Perret, quite classical in its massing, employs materials and construction techniques consistently favored by this architect: an exposed skeleton of rough reinforced concrete and prefabricated concrete wall panels.

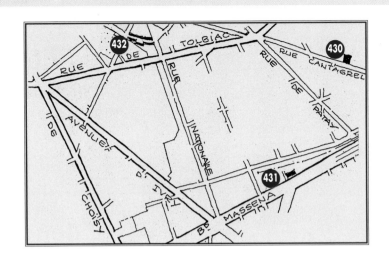

430 Salvation Army Hostel
(Cité de Refuge)

LOCATION: 12, rue Cantagrel
MÉTRO STATION: Boulevard-Masséna
PATRON: The Salvation Army, with assistance from the comtesse de Polignac
ARCHITECT: Le Corbusier (1929–33)

Original state of the façade, before the addition of a screen of sun breakers in 1952

This building was conceived to serve several functions performed by the Salvation Army for society's outcasts, including the provision of dormitory housing and of meals. It can accommodate 500 persons.

Le Corbusier encountered many difficulties in connection with this project, both before and after construction. His first designs were refused building licenses because they did not adhere to building codes. After construction, problems with the air-conditioning, a technology then in its infancy in France, necessitated modification of the façade (opening windows; a screen of sun breakers).

LOCATION: 26, boulevard Masséna
MÉTRO STATION: Porte-d'Ivry
PATRON: The sculptor Antonin Planeix
ARCHITECT: Le Corbusier (1924–28)

Villa Planeix

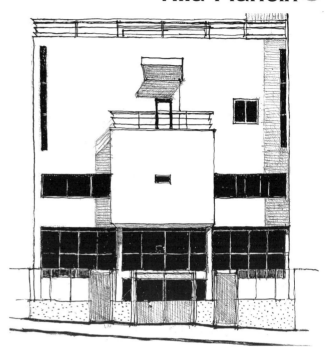

The sketch at right represents the street façade; the rear façade is visible from the rue Regnault. The building's exterior is largely intact, but the interiors of this house-atelier have now been subdivided into several apartment units.

LOCATION: Between rue Nationale and rue Baudricourt
MÉTRO STATION: Tolbiac
PATRON: Régie Immobilière de la Ville de Paris (RIVP)
ARCHITECT: Christian de Portzamparc and Georgia Benamo (1979)

Rue des Hautes-Formes

The supervisor of this project had envisioned the construction of two high apartment towers, but Christian de Portzamparc countered with a proposal for eight smaller buildings that, while costing about the same, would be much more human in scale.

The resulting complex signaled a fortunate shift in Parisian housing design, previously typified by massive apartment towers like those nearby in the same 13th arrondissement.

361

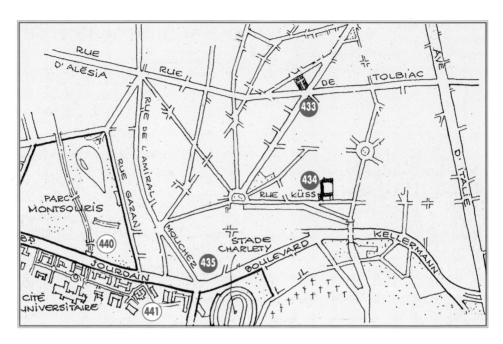

Sainte-Anne-de-la-Maison-Blanche

LOCATION: 186, rue de Tolbiac
MÉTRO STATION: Tolbiac
ARCHITECT: Prosper Bobin (1897–1912)

Like many churches of the period, this one was inspired—very freely—by Romanesque models. The porch imitates closely that of Saint-Trophime in Arles, here applied to a very different façade.

LOCATION: 8, rue Kuss
MÉTRO STATION: Maison-Blanche
ARCHITECT: Roger-Henri Expert
(1934)

Groupe Scolaire, rue Kuss 434

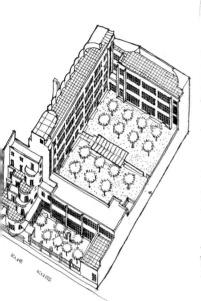

As with 3–5, boulevard Victor, by Pierre Patout (entry 462), the rue Kuss school is an interesting example of "ocean-liner" architecture of the 1930s.

The architects of these two buildings collaborated on the decoration of several ocean liners, notably the Normandie.

LOCATION: 83, boulevard Kellerman
MÉTRO STATION: Cité-Universitaire
ARCHITECTS: Henri and Bruno
Gaudin (1992–94)

Charlety Stadium 435

This complex includes the following features: a stadium seating 20,000; the headquarters of the French National Olympic Committee (at right); training grounds; and underground parking for 1,500 vehicles.

The seating tiers in the stadium and the roof protecting them are supported by a mixed structure, part concrete and part metal, of exceptional elegance.

Headquarters of the
French National
Olympic Committee

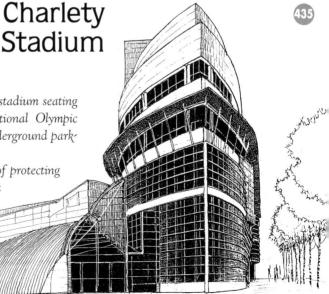

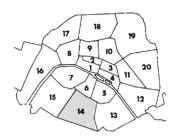

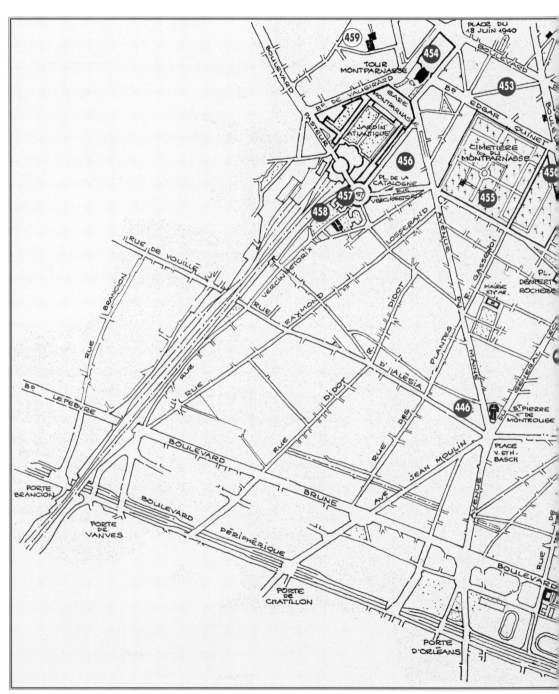

14th Arrondissement

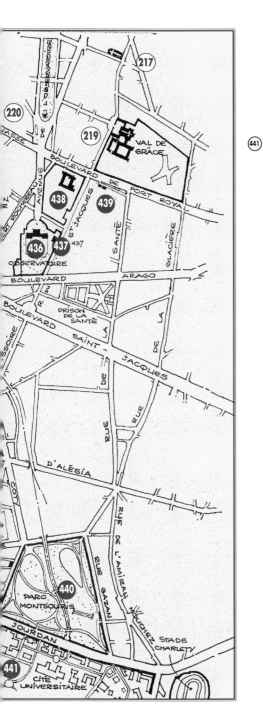

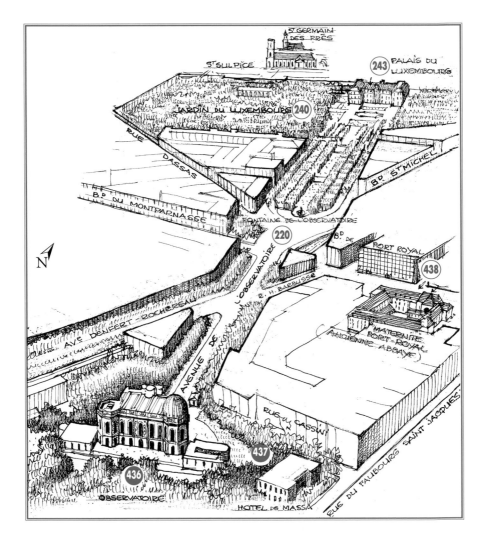

The map labels, reading throughout the illustration:

ST GERMAIN DES PRÈS

ST SULPICE

243 PALAIS DU LUXEMBOURG

JARDIN DU LUXEMBOURG 240

RUE D'ASSAS

B? ST MICHEL

B? DU MONTPARNASSE

FONTAINE DE L'OBSERVATOIRE

220

B? DE PORT ROYAL

438

N

AVE DENFERT ROCHEREAU

R. H. BARBUSSE

AVENUE DE L'OBSERVATOIRE

MATERNITÉ PORT ROYAL (ANCIENNE ABBAYE)

AVENUE DE

RUE DU CASSINI

RUE DU FAUBOURG SAINT JACQUES

437

436

OBSERVATOIRE

HÔTEL DE MASSA

436 Observatoire de Paris

LOCATION: 61, avenue de l'Observatoire
MÉTRO STATIONS: Saint-Jacques; Port-Royal
PATRON: Louis XIV
ARCHITECT: Claude Perrault (1667–72)

During the reign of Louis XIV, in 1667, Jean-Baptiste Colbert acquired the land for the observatory on an undeveloped site known as the Grand Regard (roughly, "grand view"). Design of the building was entrusted to the architect Claude Perrault, brother of Charles Perrault, the famous author of fairy tales.

The two axes of the building are aligned with the four points of the compass. The north-south axis corresponds to the Paris meridian, later demoted in favor of the Greenwich meridian.

The building consists of a rectangular structure to which two octagonal towers are attached. The eastern tower now features a cupola added in the 19th century to house a large telescope.

The façades of the building are quite restrained. The south façade features two relief trophies incorporating astronomical motifs. The north façade has a projecting frontispiece surmounted by a pediment whose sculpture has disappeared.

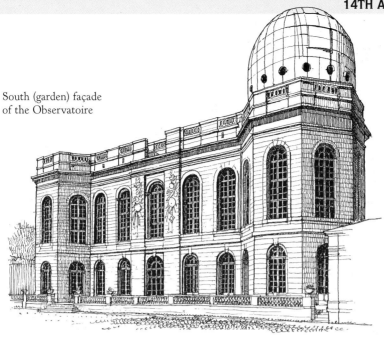

South (garden) façade
of the Observatoire

LOCATION: 38, rue du Faubourg-Saint-Jacques
MÉTRO STATION: Saint-Jacques
PATRON: The contrôleur des finances
Thiroux de Montsauge
ARCHITECT: Jean-Baptiste Le Boursier (1777–78).
Hôtel moved to this site in 1929.

Hôtel de Massa

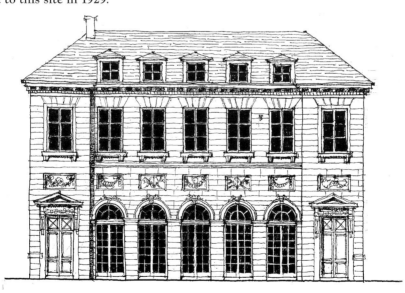

The Hôtel Massa was originally situated at 52–60, avenue des Champs-Élysées, at the corner of rue La Boétie. It was dismantled and rebuilt stone by stone on its present site. When the house was built (1777–78), the Champs-Élysées was still somewhat rustic, but this had certainly changed by 1929, when the building was unceremoniously displaced by real-estate developers. It is now surrounded by greenery once more and serves as the headquarters of the Société des Gens de Lettres.

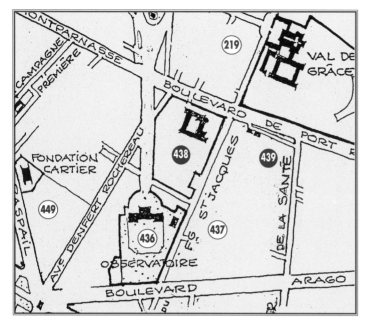

438 Abbey of Port-Royal

LOCATION: 123–125, boulevard de Port-Royal
MÉTRO STATION: Port-Royal
PATRON: The congregation of Cistercian nuns of
Port- Royal, beginning in 1626
ARCHITECT: Antoine Le Pautre (chapel, 1648–53)

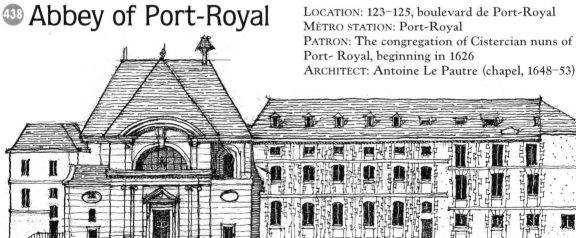

Façade on the boulevard de Port-Royal

The Cistercian abbey of Port-Royal des Champs, in the Chevreuse Valley, had flourished to such an extent under Mother Superior Angélique Arnauld that a new establishment was created in Paris in 1625–26, first in an extant building and then in new facilities. The young architect Antoine Le Pautre was chosen to design the chapel, whose cornerstone was laid in 1646.

The abbey of Port-Royal des Champs quickly became a center of Jansenism, eventually con-

demned by both the Church and Louis XIV, who ordered the complex demolished. By contrast, the abbey of Port-Royal de Paris, having become independent and more moderate, was spared. After the Revolution, Port-Royal de Paris became a prison, then a nursing facility. Since 1815, it has been a maternity hospital.

The convent buildings and the chapel, which survive, surround a magnificent cloister now incorporated into the hospital complex.

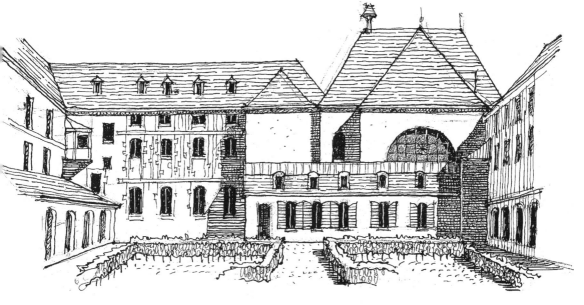

Cloister façade, Abbey of Port-Royal

LOCATION: 111, boulevard de Port-Royal
MÉTRO STATION: Port-Royal
PATRONS: Originally, the Capuchin monks of
Saint-Jacques (early 17th century; buildings
destroyed); then the Hospitals of the City
of Paris (beginning in 1785)
ARCHITECT: Eustache Saint-Fart (1785–92)
Only the portal survives.

Former Hospital for Venereal Diseases

Original state

Present state

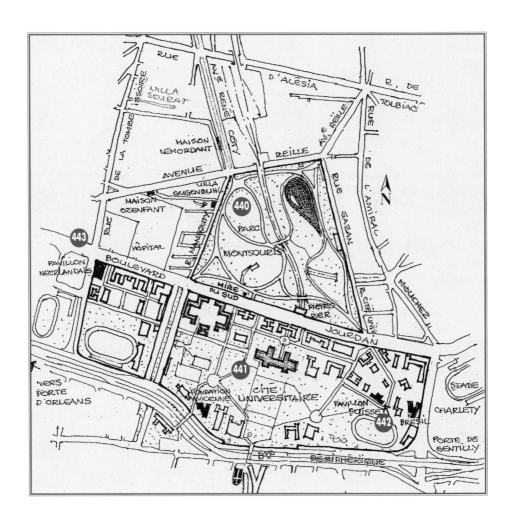

440 Parc Montsouris

LOCATION: Boulevard Jourdan, avenue Reille, and rue Gazan, among others
MÉTRO STATION: Cité-Universitaire
PATRON: Napoléon III, assisted by Baron Haussmann
DESIGNER: The civil engineer Adolphe Alphand (1867–78)

The Montsouris park was envisioned by Napoléon III and Baron Haussmann as a southern analogue to the Buttes-Chaumont park, but it is in fact much smaller (37 acres as opposed to 62 acres).

It was designed by Alphand on difficult terrain, riddled with old quarries and traversed by two railroad lines (the Sceaux-RER commuter line and the Petite Ceinture, accommodated with sunken and/or underground tracks). A large artificial lake (about two and a half acres) was built in the northern part of the park.

To the south, beside boulevard Jourdan, is a stone marker indicating the southern course of the meridian of Paris passing through the Observatoire (the northern marker is now in a private residence in Montmartre: 1, rue Girardon).

Cité Universitaire 441

LOCATION: 1–83, boulevard Jourdan
MÉTRO STATION: Cité-Universitaire
AREA: 109 acres
NUMBER OF DORMITORIES: 37, built between 1923 and
1961 (the most recent is the Résidence Avicenne)

The Cité Universitaire, immediately south of the Montsouris park (see map opposite), is situated on a plot of land roughly three-fifths of a mile long, parallel to boulevard Jourdan, formerly occupied by fortifications. It consists of thirty-seven dormitories for students from the French provinces as well as various foreign countries, the first of which to be built was the Fondation Émile et Louise Deutsch de La Meurthe (1923).

The most remarkable dormitory complexes are as follows: Pavillon Suisse (Swiss hostel), designed by Le Corbusier (1933, entry 442); Collège Néerlandais (Dutch college, entry 443), designed by Marinus Dudok (1929–38); Fondation Franco-Brésilienne (Franco-Brazilian foundation), designed by Lucio Costa and Le Corbusier (1959); and Résidence Avicenne, designed by C. Parent (1961).

Pavillon Suisse 442

LOCATION: In the Cité Universitaire
MÉTRO STATION: Cité-Universitaire
ARCHITECT: Le Corbusier (1933)

This building, inaugurated in 1933, illustrates the main principles of modern architecture advocated by its designer, Le Corbusier: the use of pilotis, or thin round posts, on the ground floor; the free plan, independent of structural supports; metal-and-glass curtain walls on the façades; and a furnished roof terrace (a solarium was planned).

Collège Néerlandais 443

LOCATION: In the Cité Universitaire
MÉTRO STATION: Cité-Universitaire
ARCHITECT: Marinus Dudok (1929–38)

Christened the Fondation Juliana, this building, notable for the purity of its forms, was designed by the great Dutch architect Marinus Dudok, likewise author of the town hall in Hilversum.

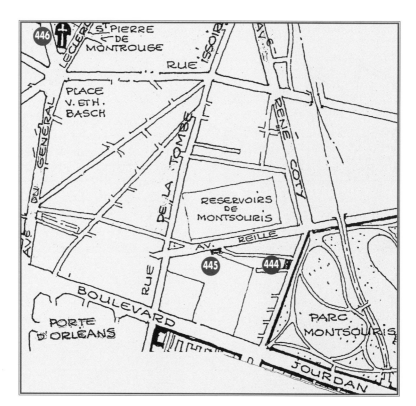

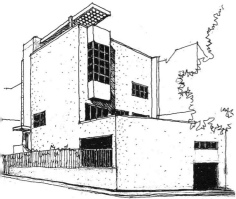

Original state

444 Guggenbühl House

LOCATION: 14, rue Nansouty
MÉTRO STATION: Cité-Universitaire
PATRON: The painter Walter Guggenbühl
ARCHITECT: André Lurçat (1927)

Present state

*In addition to the modifications indi-
cated in the two drawings, it is worth
noting that the original façade featured a two-toned color scheme: the
bow window and the vertical strip
above the entrance were white, while
the rest of the building was gray.*

Ozenfant House and Atelier

LOCATION: 53, avenue Reille
MÉTRO STATION: Cité-Universitaire
PATRON: The painter Amédée Ozenfant
ARCHITECTS: Le Corbusier and Pierre Jeanneret (1923)

This house, designed in collaboration with his cousin Pierre Jeanneret, was Le Corbusier's first building in Paris. It is consistent with his early writings, which called for an architecture consisting of simple forms and volumes.

These shed roofs have now been removed and replaced by a terrace.

LOCATION: Place Victor-Basch
MÉTRO STATION: Alésia
ARCHITECT: Émile Vaudremer
(1863–70)

Saint-Pierre-de-Montrouge

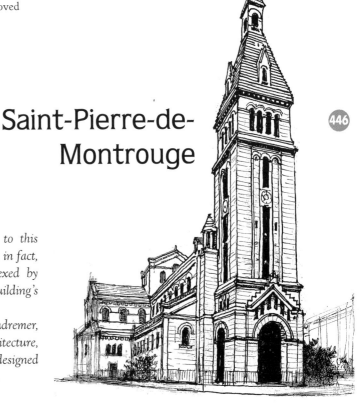

The place-name Montrouge attributed to this church is a potential source of confusion: in fact, the township of Montrouge was annexed by Paris in 1860, several years before the building's construction.

The church's architect, Émile Vaudremer, was freely inspired by Romanesque architecture, also his point of reference when he designed Notre-Dame-d'Auteuil some years later.

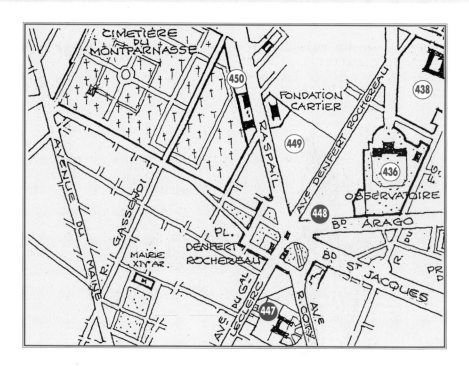

447 Hôpital La Rochefoucauld

LOCATION: 15, avenue du Général-Leclerc
MÉTRO STATION: Mouton-Duvernet
ARCHITECTS: Jacques-Denis Antoine (design), Charles-François Viel (construction, 1781–83)

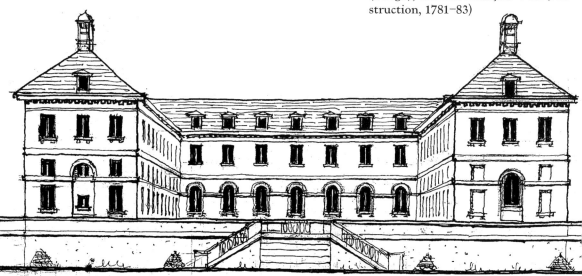

Garden façade (visible from avenue René-Coty)

This structure, originally designated the Maison Royale de Santé (royal house of health), was built a few years before the Revolution as a hospital for poor veterans and ecclesiastics. Often attributed to the architect Jacques-Denis Antoine (author of the Hôtel des Monnaies, entry 233), it may have been designed in its entirety by Charles-François Viel, responsible for several other hospital buildings.

MÉTRO STATION: Denfert-Rochereau
ARCHITECT: Claude-Nicolas Ledoux
(tollhouses, 1784–87)
SCULPTOR: Auguste Bartholdi (1880)

Place Denfert-Rochereau 448
(The Catacombs)

The Lion of Belfort in the center of the place is a bronze reduction of the lion carved in the side of the Rock of Belfort to commemorate the defenders of that city and their commander, Colonel Denfert-Rochereau, in the Franco-Prussian War of 1870. Flanking the avenue du Général-Leclerc are two tollhouses—originally known as the Barrière d'Enfer—designed by Claude-Nicolas Ledoux as part of the Wall of the Farmers General (see also entries 356, 412, and 518). The tollhouse at no. 1 houses the entrance to the catacombs, a network of old underground quarries used between 1786 and 1814 to store human remains moved from Parisian cemeteries that had been deconsecrated, for reasons of public hygiene, beginning with the cemetery of the Saints-Innocents.

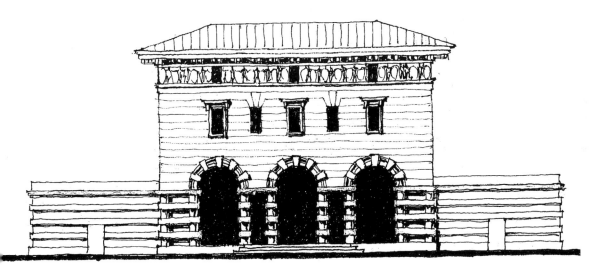

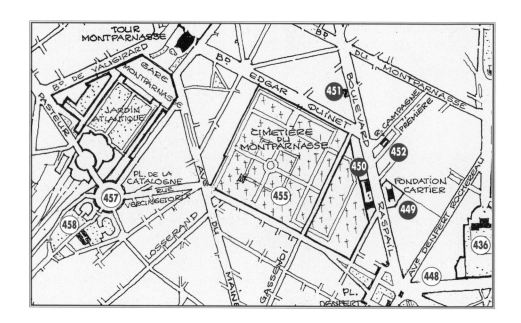

449 Fondation Cartier

LOCATION: 261, boulevard Raspail
MÉTRO STATIONS: Raspail; Denfert-Rochereau
PATRONS: GAN Vie and Cartier SA
ARCHITECTS: Jean Nouvel, Emmanuel Catani, and Associates (1992–94)
ENGINEERS: OVE ARUP (structure), Arnaud de Bussière and Associates (façades)

This building is the headquarters of Cartier France, whose previously dispersed offices are now housed under its one roof. The lower part of the structure is reserved for exhibition spaces, some of them underground, while the upper floors contain the company's offices.

Schematically, the building consists of a rectan-gular block whose glass-and-metal façade extends beyond its volume. Furthermore, an independent glass-and-metal screen stands be-tween the street and the building. As a result of these novel fea-tures, the trees in front of the structure appear to be integrated into it, as though encompassed by an enormous greenhouse.

LOCATION: 254–266,
boulevard Raspail
MÉTRO STATIONS: Raspail;
Denfert-Rochereau

École Spéciale d'Architecture

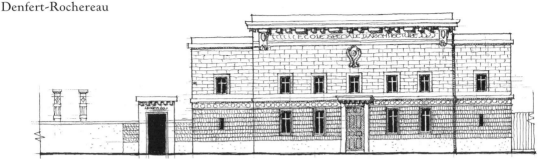

This architecture school was founded in 1865, but the building illustrated above dates from 1904. A new building, its design inspired by the Centre Georges-Pompidou, has since been erected on a site corresponding to 266, boulevard Raspail. The school's courtyard contains columns from the Tuileries palace (burned 1871; remains demolished 1882).

Boulevard Raspail, no. 216

MÉTRO STATION: Raspail
ARCHITECT: Bruno Elkouken (1932–34)

This building was quite advanced for its day and can justly be regarded as a pioneering work. Unfortunately, its architect built very little in Paris, his Jewish origins having obliged him to flee to the United States during World War II. However, another work by him can be seen at 146, boulevard Montparnasse (corner of rue Campagne-Première).

Rue Campagne-Première, no. 31

MÉTRO STATION: Raspail
ARCHITECT: André Arfvidson (1911)

This magnificent building contains duplex apartments for artists. The polychrome glazed earthenware tiles on the façade, notable for its harmonious color scheme, are the work of Alexandre Bigot. It won the prize for the best new façade in the city in 1911. The rear façade of the complex is visible from the passage d'Enfer.

⟨453⟩ Montparnasse

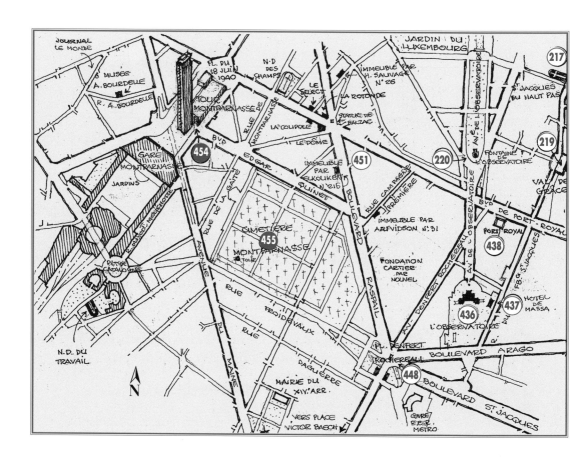

The Montparnasse quarter takes its name from an artificial hill, no longer extant, that was probably formed from earth excavated from neighboring underground quarries. A fashionable area for promenades during the Revolution, the quarter became popular with artists in the early 20th century. This development was due in part to the establishment nearby, in 1902, of the center for artists' housing known as La Ruche (formerly the wine pavilion at the Exposition Universelle of 1900; see entry 461). Poets and writers followed suit, and the quarter became famous in the 1920s, when it was frequented by Pablo Picasso, Amedeo Modigliani, Max Jacob, and many others.

World War II marked a clean break that became definitive in the 1960s, when the area was transformed by the Maine-Montparnasse development project (see entry 454). Other important initiatives followed, especially to the south of the Gare Montparnasse. Montparnasse nonetheless retains many theaters, movie houses, brasseries, and cabarets that continue to make it a favored area for leisure and entertainment.

Maine-Montparnasse Complex

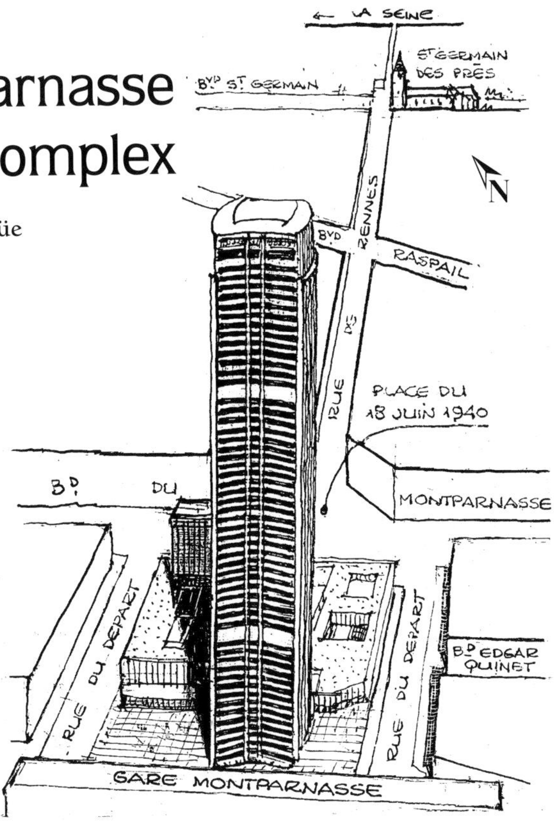

454

MÉTRO STATION: Montparnasse-Bienvenüe

Demolition of the old Montparnasse train station marked the start of the Maine-Montparnasse redevelopment project, implemented between 1961 and 1973. Its key elements were: construction of a new Gare Montparnasse surrounded by office and apartment buildings; construction of a large commercial center; and construction of the high office tower known as the Tour Montparnasse.

The Tour Montparnasse rises fifty-eight stories above ground level and is 690 feet high. The top floor has a viewing platform that offers splendid views of the city.

LOCATION: 3, boulevard Edgar-Quinet
MÉTRO STATIONS: Edgar-Quinet; Gaîté; Raspail

Cimetière de Montparnasse

455

Montparnasse cemetery, originally called the Cimetière du Sud (southern cemetery), was created in 1824, in the wake of the abolition of central Parisian cemeteries beginning in the 1780s.

Many famous people are buried here, among them Guy de Maupassant, Jean-Paul Sartre, Simone de Beauvoir, César Franck, and Camille Saint-Saëns.

Sculptors whose work can be seen here include Frédéric-Auguste Bartholdi (tomb of Gustave Jundt), Constantin Brancusi (the famous Kiss), and Auguste Rodin (several medallions, for example, on the tombs of César Franck and Jean-Baptiste Carpeaux).

The cemetery also contains an old windmill, known as the Moulin de la Charité, which probably dates from the 15th century. It has lost its sails and its swivel roof, but recent restoration has given its exteriors a new allure.

Moulin de la Charité

456 The "New" Montparnasse

MÉTRO STATION: Montparnasse-Bienvenüe
The quarter was transformed as a result
of the following: the Maine-Montparnasse
redevelopment project, 1961–73; reconstruction
of the Gare Montparnasse and planting of a garden
on a terrace spanning the tracks, 1987–94;
Guilleminot ZAC (see below), 1980–85;
Guilleminot-Vercingétorix ZAC;
and Gare de Vaugirard ZAC.

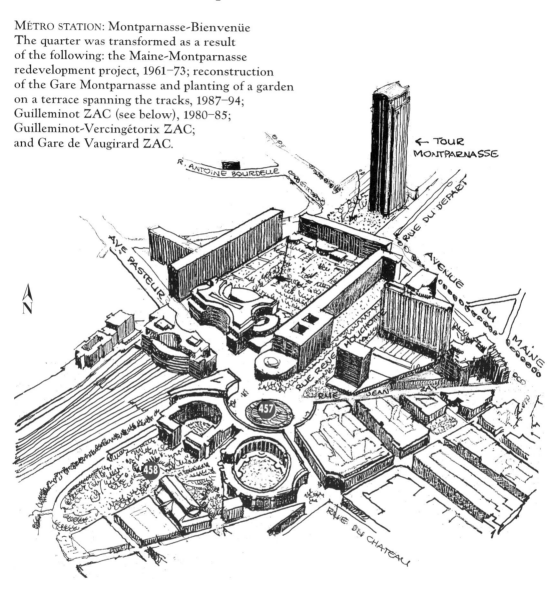

After completion of the Maine-Montparnasse project, the train station has undergone several trans-
formations: redesign of the platforms, tracks, and
public areas to accommodate the new TGV-
Atlantic high-speed train lines; and construction of
a roof over the departure platforms and tracks supporting a green area christened the Jardin de l'At-
lantique (Atlantic gardens).

As part of the same development, several buildings defining a new, circular place west of the station were built; plans to redevelop the areas west,
south, and east of the station led to the creation of
the three ZACs, or coordinated development zones,
listed above. This resulted in much new construction, the most important features of which are indicated in the drawing above.

MÉTRO STATION: Montparnasse-Bienvenüe

Place de la Catalogne ④⑤⑦

Two of the buildings fronting the Place de la Catalogne were designed by Ricardo Bofill, who disposed them as well around two inner courtyards, one of them oval and the other semicircular (respectively, the Place de Séoul and the Place de l'Amphithéâtre; see aerial view opposite). The entire

complex is in a neoclassical style. The other two buildings defining the place were designed by the architect Novarina.

The monumental circular fountain in the center is by the sculptor Shamaï Haber.

LOCATION: 59, rue Vercingétorix
MÉTRO STATION: Pernety
ARCHITECT: Jules Astruc
(1899–1902)

Notre-Dame-du-Travail ④⑤⑧

This church, originally surrounded by a workers' quarter, was dedicated to laborers throughout the world. For reasons both symbolic and financial (especially the latter), the architect decided to use primarily metal-frame construction, leaving the armature exposed on the church's interior. The façades, by contrast, are of traditional stone and brick construction.

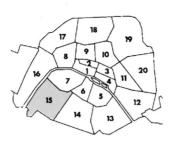

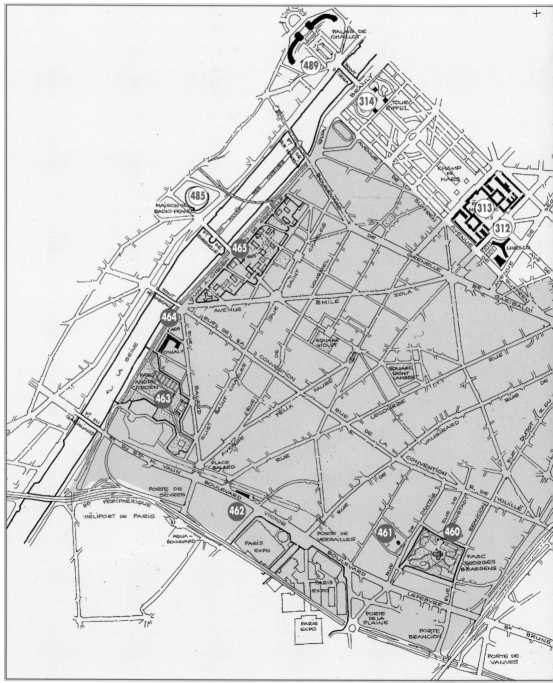

15th Arrondissement

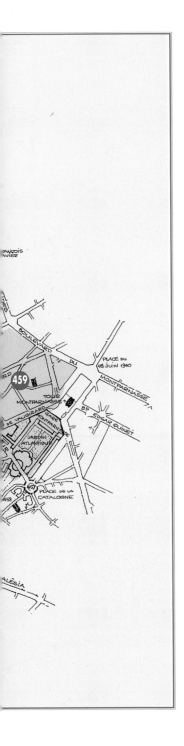

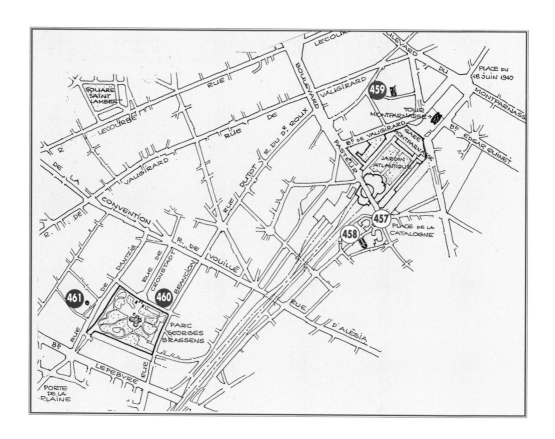

459 Musée Bourdelle

LOCATION: 14–16, rue Antoine-Bourdelle
MÉTRO STATIONS: Falguière; Montparnasse-
Bienvenüe
ARCHITECTS: H. Gaudruche (1949 and 1961).
Christian de Portzamparc (addition, 1991)

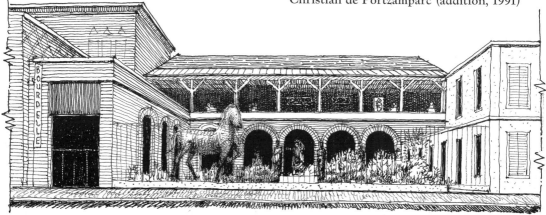

The Antoine Bourdelle museum occupies the sculptor's former house and studio, which were left to the city by his wife, who died in 1929. An addition designed by Christian de Portzamparc was completed in 1991.

Parc Georges-Brassens 460

LOCATION: Main entrance
on the rue des Morillons
MÉTRO STATIONS: Convention;
Portes-de-Vanves
ARCHITECTS: Ernest Moreau
(former abattoirs, 1894–97).
A. Ghiulamila, J.-M. Milliex, and D. Collin
(park, 1982–85)
SCULPTOR: Auguste-Nicolas Cain
(two bulls flanking the main entrance,
1898)

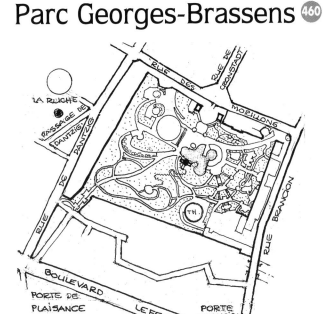

This park is named after the poet Georges Brassens, who lived in this quarter at the end of his life. Its site was formerly occupied by the Abbatoirs de Vaugirard, some elements of which survive, notably two pavilions and two sculptures of bulls flanking the main entrance and the clocktower beside the pool. The Carré Silvia-Montfort, south of the park, can be entered from the rue Brancion.

La Ruche 461

LOCATION: 2, passage de Dantzig
MÉTRO STATION: Porte-de-Versailles
PATRON: The artist Alfred Boucher (1900–1902)

The painter and sculptor Alfred Boucher acquired the wine rotunda of the 1900 Exposition Universelle, which he then rebuilt on land he had purchased on the passage de Dantzig to serve as an artists' residence. The new facility, opened in 1902, was soon nicknamed La Ruche (the beehive); its residents have included such famous artists as Amedeo Modigliani, Chaim Soutine, Marc Chagall, and Fernand Léger.

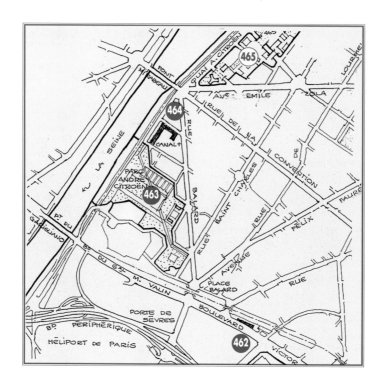

⑯ Boulevard Victor, nos. 3–5

MÉTRO STATION: Balard
ARCHITECT: Pierre Patout
(1934–35)

The architect Pierre Patout designed the interiors of several ocean liners, projects that required maximum efficiency in the use of space.

He was confronted with similar problems when designing this building, due to the exceptional narrowness of the site (ranging from 10 to 40 feet). The result is a remarkable building, in which Patout incorporated a three-level apartment for himself at its narrow end.

Parc André-Citroën

LOCATION: Main entrances on the rue Balard and quai André-Citroën
MÉTRO STATIONS: Balard; Boulevard-Victor
DESIGNERS: Alain Provost and Gilles Clément, landscape designers; Patrick Berger, Jean-Paul Viguier, and Jean-François Jodry, architects (1992)

The André-Citroën park resulted from a large urbanist program occasioned by the demolition of the Citroën factory. It is organized around a large central parterre bordered on one side by the Seine and on the other by a "peristyle" of water jets emerging from the paving stones. This line of foun-tains is flanked by greenhouses of impressive height.

Around this central motif are gardens of various kinds, each with its own theme or formal concept: a black garden, a white garden, a rock garden, and so on.

Headquarters of Canal Plus

LOCATION: 85–89, quai André-Citroën
MÉTRO STATION: Javel
PATRON: Canal Plus television
ARCHITECTS: Richard Meier and Partners (1991–92)

This building is both the headquarters and the broadcast center of the French television channel Canal Plus.

The broadcast studios are parallel to the rue des Cévennes, while the office block faces the Seine; both of these elements overlook a large glass atrium. Another wing on the rue Balard houses various subsidiary facilities.

As is his wont, Richard Meier opted for a white color scheme for the building's exterior.

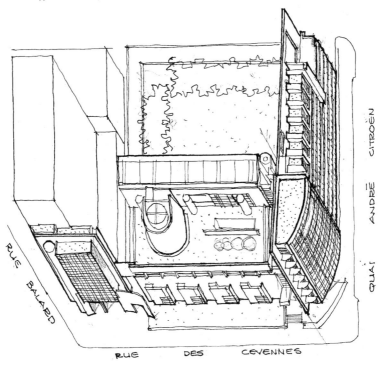

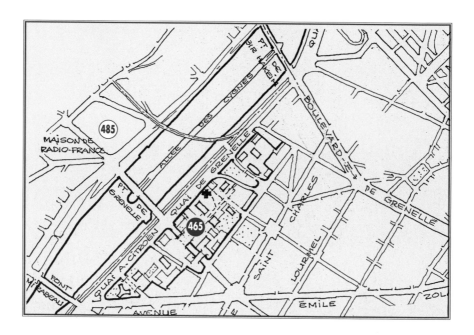

465 Front de Seine

LOCATION: Between avenue Émile-Zola and rue
du Docteur-Finlay
MÉTRO STATIONS: Bir-Hakeim; Charles-Michels
PATRON: Société d'Économie Mixte et d'Aménagement du XVe arrondissement
ARCHITECTS: Originally R. Lopez, H. Pottier,
and M. Proux, followed by many architects,
including Andrault and Parat for the Tour
Totem illustrated at right

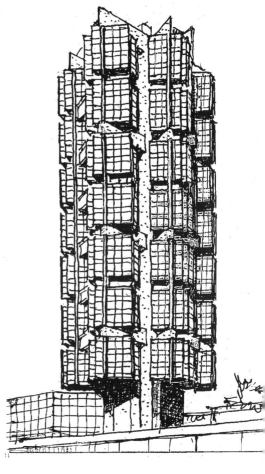

The development project known as Front de Seine
(Seine frontage) was initiated in the 1960s on a large
tract parallel to the river.

The overriding principle of its master plan was to
separate pedestrian from vehicular traffic. To this end,
a large elevated platform reserved for pedestrians was
built over much of the area, vehicular roadways being
relegated to the level below.

Some twenty buildings were erected above this platform, most of them towers with about thirty stories.
Most contain apartments or offices, but one of them
houses the Nikko Hotel.

Tour Totem
Architects: Michel Andrault and Pierre Parat, 1979
(apartments)

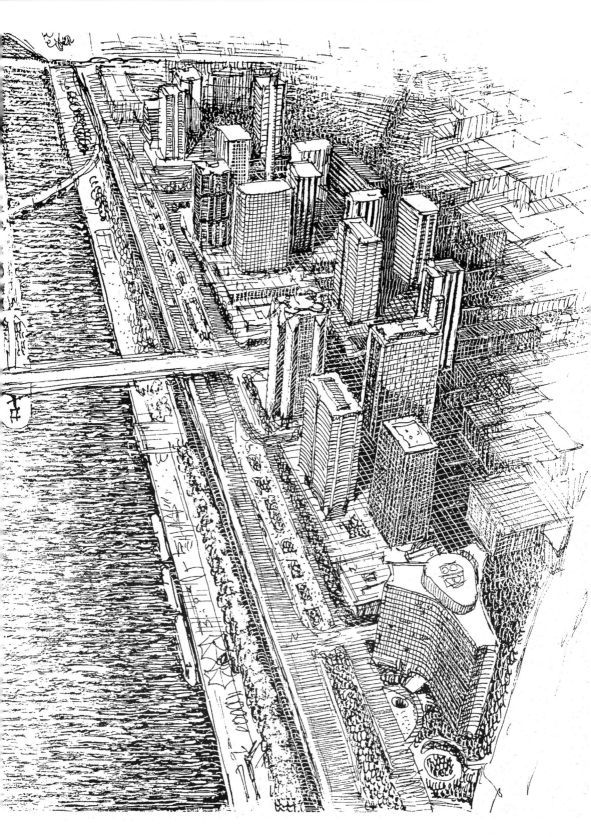

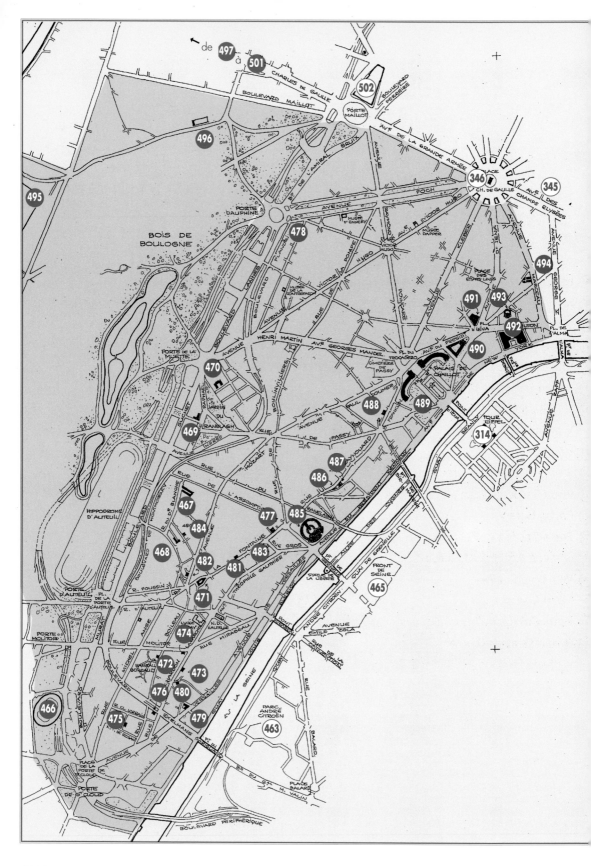

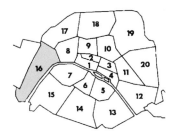

16th
Arrondissement

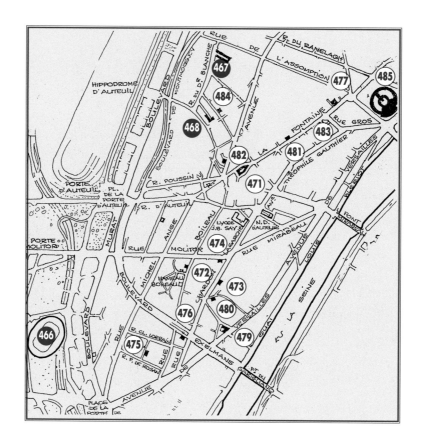

Parc-des-Princes

LOCATION: 24, rue du Commandant-Guilbaud
MÉTRO STATION: Porte-de-Saint-Cloud
ARCHITECT: Roger Taillibert (1972)
ENGINEER: R. Richard

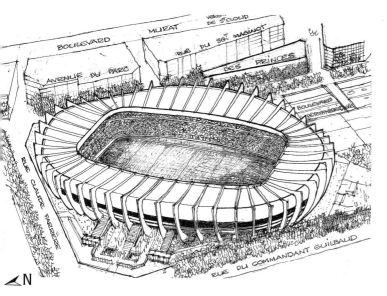

This stadium, designed by Roger Taillibert and R. Richard, can hold 50,000 spectators. The same prefabricated, reinforced-concrete brackets support both the roof and the tiered seats. Remarkable in shape as well as structural engineering, these brackets have overhangs ranging from 98 to 164 feet, depending on their placement.

Design and construction of the Parc-des-Princes stadium were complicated by the passage of the peripheral highway below the site.

Rue Mallet-Stevens

467

LOCATION: This dead-end street begins at 9, rue du Docteur-Blanche
MÉTRO STATION: Jasmin
PRINCIPAL PATRONS: No. 12: Robert Mallet-Stevens, architect. No. 8: Madame Reifenberg, pianist. No. 10: Joël and Jean Martel, sculptors. Nos. 3–5: Aliatani, filmmaker
ARCHITECT: Robert Mallet-Stevens (1926–27)

Present state
of no. 12

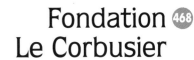

Original state of no. 12

Rue Mallet-Stevens exemplifies the ideas of its namesake architect, who, reacting against Art Nouveau, advocated the use of simple volumes in architecture. As Mallet-Stevens reserved no. 12 for his own office, there is reason to think that it best represents his taste (see drawing at left of its original state). Unfortunately, the street as well as its buildings have been disfigured over the years. The street was modified in 1951 and the buildings have been altered several times; the façades were designated national monuments in 1975.

Fondation Le Corbusier

468

LOCATION: 8–10, square du Docteur-Blanche (dead-end street beginning at 53, rue du Docteur-Blanche)
MÉTRO STATION: Jasmin
PATRONS: Raoul La Roche, industrialist, for one villa; Albert Jeanneret, musician and brother of Le Corbusier, for the other
ARCHITECT: Le Corbusier (1923)

The Fondation Le Corbusier now occupies these two adjacent medium-size residences, the Villa La Roche and the Villa Jeanneret. Le Corbusier prepared plans for a third villa facing the Villa Jeanneret, but it was never built. The rotunda on axis with the street was designed as a gallery for La Roche's painting collection.

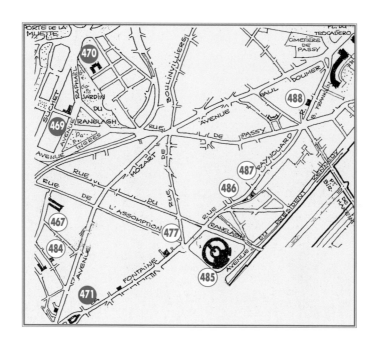

⑤ Musée Marmottan

LOCATION: 2, rue Louis-Boilly
(Jardins du Ranelagh)
MÉTRO STATION: Ranelagh

Façade on the rue Raphaël

Both this 19th-century hôtel and the core collection of the museum it now houses were donated to the Institut de France in 1932 by the art historian Paul Marmottan. The museum was subsequently enriched by several bequests, most notably sixty-five paintings by Claude Monet given to it by the artist's son. Thus, the museum's Impressionist works are now regarded as its most important holdings.

LOCATION: 2, rue André-Pascal
MÉTRO STATION: La Muette
PATRON: The baron Henri de Rothschild
(who wrote under the pseudonym André
Pascal)
ARCHITECT: Henri Hesse (1912–22)

Headquarters 470
of the OCDE

This château was built beginning in 1912 in the northern part of the park of the Château de la Muette, which was demolished in 1920. In 1949, it became the headquarters of the OCEE, known since 1961 as the OCDE (Organisation de Coopération et de Développement Économique).

The building, whose interiors are richly decorated, is connected by underground passages to new buildings on the other side of the rue André-Pascal; without architectural interest, they were built between 1950 and 1970.

Studio Building

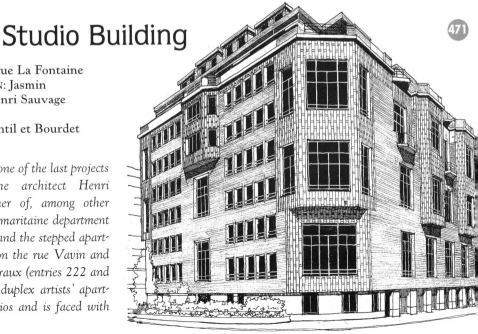

471

LOCATION: 65, rue La Fontaine
MÉTRO STATION: Jasmin
ARCHITECT: Henri Sauvage
(1926–28)
CERAMISTS: Gentil et Bourdet

This building is one of the last projects realized by the architect Henri Sauvage, designer of, among other buildings, La Samaritaine department store (entry 12) and the stepped apartment buildings on the rue Vavin and the rue des Amiraux (entries 222 and 517). It houses duplex artists' apartments with studios and is faced with ceramic tiles.

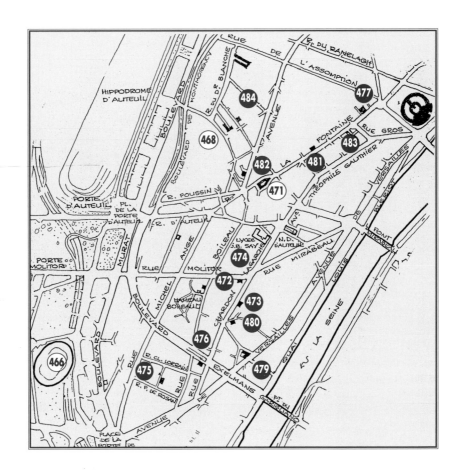

Work by the architect
Hector Guimard in the
16th arrondissement

The rue La Fontaine, mentioned above, boasts several works by the architect Hector Guimard, who built a great deal in the Auteuil quarter. This is thus an appropriate place to review briefly this architect's work in the 16th arrondissement.

Born in Lyon in 1868, Hector Guimard realized his first important work, the Villa Roszé (entry 479), in 1891, but only in 1898 did his personali-

ty blossom, on the occasion of the construction of a group of apartment buildings christened Castel Béranger (entry 475), which won the competition for the best façade erected in Paris in 1898. He then became the principal representative in France of the "Modern style," now known as Art Nouveau.

LOCATION: 34, rue Boileau
MÉTRO STATION: Chardon-Lagache
ARCHITECT: Hector Guimard (1891), his first important building

Villa Roszé 472

LOCATION: 41, Chardon-Lagache
MÉTRO STATION: Chardon-Lagache
PATRON: The Jassedé family, for whom
Hector Guimard designed the building
at 142, avenue de Versailles in 1904
ARCHITECT: Hector Guimard (1893)

Villa Jassedé 473

Guimard's characteristic style is not yet present in this building, but it already features his favorite materials.

LOCATION: 1 ter, rue Molitor
MÉTRO STATION: Chardon-Lagache
ARCHITECT: Hector Guimard (c. 1895)
1895)

Hôtel Delfau 474

LOCATION: 9, avenue de la Frillière
MÉTRO STATION: Exelmans
PATRON: Société d'Immeubles pour
l'Éducation et la Récréation de la
Jeunesse (society for buildings for the
education and recreation of youth)
ARCHITECT: Hector Guimard (1895)

Former École du 475
Sacré-Coeur

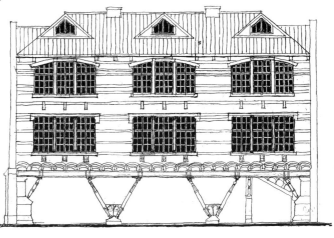

Hector Guimard here used the V-pole supports proposed by Viollet-le-Duc in one of his unrealized projects. The result is a very original building. The original interiors have been destroyed (the building now contains co-op apartments), but the original façade is intact.

476 Hôtel Carpeaux

LOCATION: 39, boulevard Exelmans
MÉTRO STATION: Exelmans
PATRON: The widow of the sculptor Jean-Baptiste Carpeaux
ARCHITECT: Hector Guimard (1895)

477 Castel Béranger

LOCATION: 14, rue La Fontaine
MÉTRO STATION: Kennedy-Radio-France
PATRON: The Fourniers
ARCHITECT: Hector Guimard (1895–98)

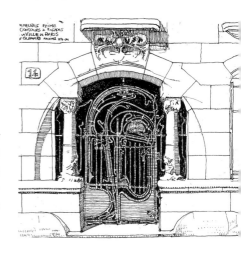

The cluster of buildings known as Castel Béranger is Hector Guimard's most important work, the one that made him famous. Influenced by his Belgian colleague Victor Horta, he designed its every detail in the style later known as Art Nouveau. The complex won the prize for the best façade erected in Paris in 1898.

478 Porte-Dauphine Métro Station

LOCATION: Avenue Foch (Porte Dauphine side)
ARCHITECT: Hector Guimard (1900–1904)

Hector Guimard is best known as the designer of 141 entrances to Parisian métro stations (1900–1904), all made of prefabricated cast-iron elements. Some of them were covered, but only two examples of this canopied design survive in Paris: this one, and one accessing the Abbesses métro station (18th arrondissement).

479 Jassedé Apartment Building

LOCATION: 142, avenue de Versailles, and 1, rue Lancret
MÉTRO STATION: Chardon-Lagache
PATRON: The Jassedé family, for which Guimard had previously designed a villa at 41, avenue Chardon-Lagache (1893)
ARCHITECT: Hector Guimard (1903–5)

The design of this building is already less exuberant than that of Castel Béranger. Even so, considerable attention was devoted to the detailing of the façade, and the handling of the corner is remarkable.

LOCATION: 8, villa de la Réunion
MÉTRO STATION: Chardon-Lagache
ARCHITECT: Hector Guimard (1905–8)

Villa Deron-Levent 480

Hôtel Mezzara 481

LOCATION: 60, rue La Fontaine
MÉTRO STATION: Michel-Ange-Auteuil
PATRON: The industrialist and textile
designer Paul Mezzara
ARCHITECT: Hector Guimard (1910)

In this residence, the architect reverted to an almost classical symmetry. Now owned by the Éducation Nationale, the building retains its original furnishings and has been certified a national monument.

Hôtel Guimard 482

LOCATION: 122, avenue Mozart
MÉTRO STATION: Michel-Ange-Auteuil
PATRON: Hector Guimard and his wife, Adeline, who provided most of the money
ARCHITECT: Hector Guimard (1909–12)

Hector Guimard designed this building for himself: it housed his office, his apartment, and an atelier for his wife, Adeline, a painter.

Buildings at the corner of rue La Fontaine and rue Gros 483

This complex of buildings was built between 1909 and 1912. Some of the structures planned along the rue Agar were not built. Miraculously, the splendid façade and interior decor of the small café-bar on rue La Fontaine survives.

MÉTRO STATION: Jasmin
ARCHITECT: Hector Guimard (1925–26)

Rue Henri-Heine, no. 18 484

This apartment house, one of the architect's last Parisian buildings, marks a transition between Art Nouveau and Art Deco.

485 Maison de la Radio

LOCATION: 116, avenue du Président-Kennedy
MÉTRO STATION: Kennedy-Radio-France
ARCHITECT: Henry Bernard (1955–62)

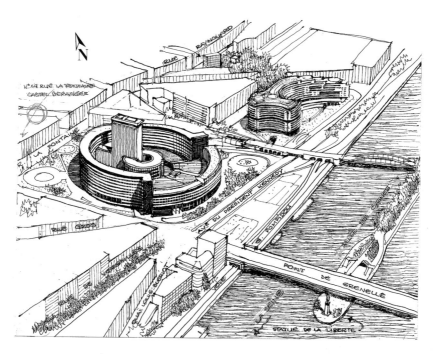

The building's circular form made it possible to isolate the broadcast studios from the noise of the street by placing them in the center. Four auditoriums with a capacity of 250 to 1,000 are accessible to the public (studios nos. 102 to 105, of which the largest is no. 104). The outer structures house offices; the central core also contains libraries of recordings and printed sources, and the tower houses the institution's archives.

486 Musée Balzac

LOCATION: 47, rue Raynouard
MÉTRO STATION: Kennedy-Radio-France

This museum occupies a house in which Honoré de Balzac lived between 1840 and 1847. It was originally a service building for a town house that does not survive. It is said that Balzac chose this house because at the time it had an exit on the rue Berton that facilitated quick escapes from his many creditors.

Rue Raynouard, nos. 51–55 487

MÉTRO STATION: Kennedy-Radio-France
PATRONS: Auguste and Gustave Perret
ARCHITECTS: Auguste and Gustave Perret (1932)

Two buildings by Auguste Perret are quite near each other. The earlier is the one on the rue Benjamin-Franklin, which dates from the beginning of the century (see next entry). The one on the rue Raynouard, more conventional, was built thirty years later to house the Perret brothers' offices and architectural firm as well as several apartments, including that of Auguste Perret himself.

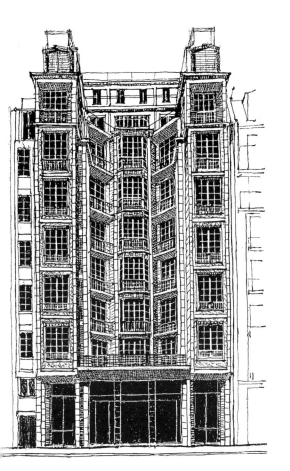

Rue Benjamin- 488 Franklin, no. 25 bis

MÉTRO STATION: Trocadéro
ARCHITECTS: Auguste and Gustave Perret (1902–3)

This building, erected early in the century, was quite innovative because it is supported by reinforced-concrete posts rather than the load-bearing walls that were then the norm. On the façade, the intervening areas are filled with reinforced-concrete panels faced with glazed earthenware tiles by Alexandre Bigot, some of which are shaped like flower petals.

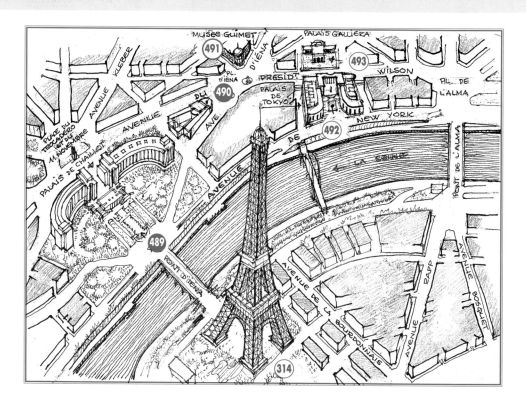

489 Palais de Chaillot

LOCATION: Place du Trocadéro et du 11-Novembre
MÉTRO STATION: Trocadéro
PATRON: The French government, for the Exposition Universelle of 1937
ARCHITECTS: Louis-Hippolyte Boileau, Jacques Carlu, and Léon Azéma (1935–37)

For reasons of economy, the architects were obliged to use the foundations of the Palais du Trocadéro built for the Exposition Universelle of 1878. Like the earlier building, the Palais de Chaillot features two large curved wings stretching across the summit of the Chaillot hill. The architects skillfully left a large open space between the wings, a decision permitting them to devise a central terrace offering magnificent views of the city. Below this terrace is a large theater; its original interiors were designed by Jean and Édouard Nierman, but it has since been remodeled several times. The terrace overlooks a large pool famous for its powerful jets of water.

The complex, which includes the Musée des Monuments Français, the Musée de la Marine, and the Théâtre de Chaillot, is richly decorated with sculpture. A large garden is situated at the feet of the buildings and around the adjacent pools; it was designed after the 1937 exposition by Roger Lardat.

LOCATION: 1, avenue d'Iéna
MÉTRO STATION: Iéna
PATRON: The French government, to house a museum of public works
ARCHITECT: Auguste Perret (1937–39). Enlarged 1960–62

Conseil Économique et Social

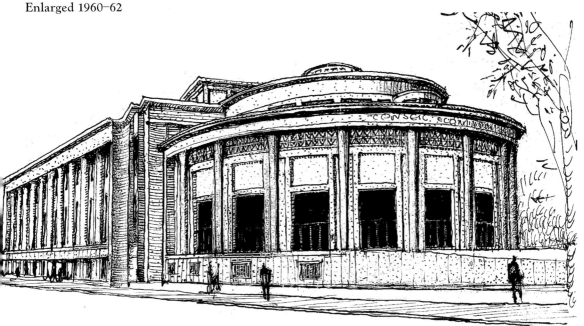

Façade on the Place d'Iéna

The Conseil Économique et Social (economic and social council) occupies a building originally intended to house a museum of public works. Its design was entrusted to Auguste Perret, perhaps as compensation for his vast project for the abandonment of the Palais de Chaillot in favor of a more practical design making use of the foundations of the old Palais du Trocadéro (see previous entry). Characteristically for Auguste Perret, the concrete was left rough, but much care was devoted to the choice of its constituent materials and the fabrication of the molds, with results that have a nobility exceptional for this material.

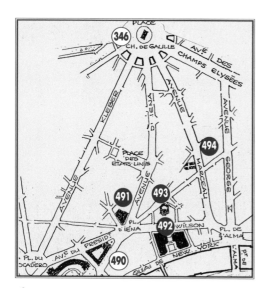

491 Musée Guimet

LOCATION: 6, Place d'Iéna
METRO STATION: Iéna
PATRONS: The industrialist Émile Guimet (collections) and the state (building)
ARCHITECT: Terrier (1888)

Émile Guimet had built a museum in Lyons to house the large collection of art objects he had acquired during his travels in the Far East. When he gave the collection to the state in 1855, the latter decided to move it to Paris and commissioned a building for it from Terrier. The result was a neo-Greek building housing Far Eastern artifacts.

492 Palais de Tokyo

LOCATION: 11–13, avenue du Président-Wilson
MÉTRO STATION: Iéna
PATRON: The City of Paris and the French government, for the Exposition Universelle of 1937
ARCHITECTS: J.-C. Dondel, A. Aubert, P. Viard, and M. Dastugue (1937)
SCULPTOR: Alfred Janniot (reliefs)

This building was erected for the Exposition Universelle of 1937 to house two art museums, one for the City of Paris and the other for the state. This program explains the disposition of the plan, with its two independent wings linked by a central portal.

The façades are decorated with reliefs by Alfred Janniot. In the center of the composition is a large statue by Antoine Bourdelle representing France. The east wing houses the Musée d'Art Moderne de la Ville de Paris, the west wing a museum of the cinema and the Fédération Européenne des

Métiers de l'Image et du Son (European federation of image and sound technicians).

LOCATION: 10, avenue Pierre-1er-de-Serbie
MÉTRO STATION: Iéna
PATRON: The duchesse de Galliera
ARCHITECT: Léon Ginain (1878–94)

Palais Galliera

For her palace, the duchesse de Galliera and her architect, Léon Ginain, opted for an Italian Renaissance style that may strike us today as rather brutal. The arches of the central pavilion frame three statues representing Painting, Architecture, and Sculpture. The building now houses the Musée de la Mode et du Costume (museum of fashion and costume).

LOCATION: 33, avenue Marceau
MÉTRO STATION: Alma-Marceau
ARCHITECT: Émile Bois (1931–38)
SCULPTOR: Henri Bouchard (tympanum)

Saint-Pierre-
de-Chaillot

This church was freely inspired by Romanesque models. It features a monumental bell tower and an exceptionally large tympanum whose sculpture depicts episodes from the life of Saint Peter.

495 Bagatelle

(Park and Château)

LOCATION: Bois de Boulogne, main entrance on the road to Sèvres at Neuilly
MÉTRO STATION: Pont-de-Neuilly
PATRONS: The comte d'Artois (1775), Lord Seymour (1835), then his son (1870), who added buildings (Trianon and guard-houses); finally, the City of Paris (1905)
ARCHITECT: François-Joseph Bélanger (château, 1775); Léon de Sanges (Trianon and guardhouses, 1872)

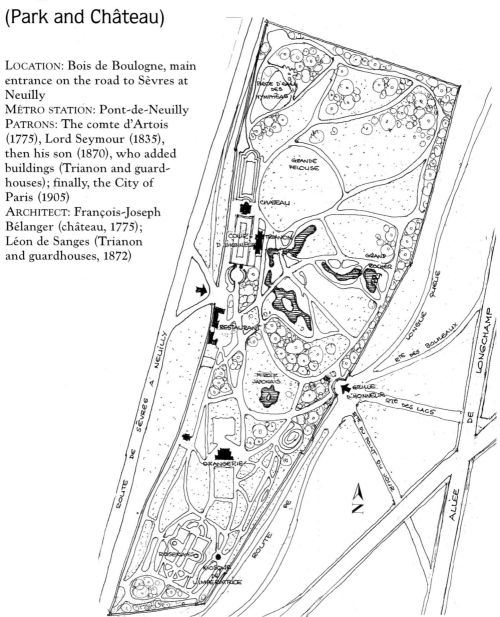

After acquiring the property in 1775, the comte d'Artois accepted a wager—which he won—that he could not build a château there in two months. The resulting building, designed by François-Joseph Bélanger, survives in good condition, although it was subsequently altered (the height of the attic level was increased, and a balustrade was added around the dome).

The last private owner of the property was Sir Henry Murray Scott, who added the Trianon and the two guardhouses. He sold it to the City of Paris in 1905, which converted it into a sixty-acre park and a venue for cultural and floral exhibitions.

Château de Bagatelle

LOCATION: Bois de Boulogne, 6, route du Mahatma Gandhi, near the Jardin d'Acclimatation
MÉTRO STATION: Les Sablons
ARCHITECT: Jean Dubuisson (1969)

Musée des Arts et (496) Traditions Populaires

The complex consists of a low three-story building (two of them under ground) surmounted by an eight-story vertical block with curtain walls (aluminum and gray-tinted glass). It was among the first structures of this type to be built in Paris. The museum is devoted primarily to French rural culture of past centuries.

497 The Défense Complex

LOCATION: To the west of Paris, two miles from the Porte Maillot
MÉTRO STATION: La Défense

The decision to develop the Défense complex was made in 1955, and in 1958 the project was entrusted to an entity known as the EPAD (Établissement Public pour l'Aménagement de la Défense). The first building to rise was the headquarters of the CNIT (Centre National des Industries et Techniques), a remarkable structure designed by Bernard Zehrfuss, Robert Camelot, and Jean de Mailly. The main feature of the master plan was the separation of pedestrian from vehicular traffic (the former on the surface, the latter below), made possible by the construction of an elevated deck almost half a mile long. This master plan was adopted in 1964, when the Esso building was built (now destroyed). Implementation of the project was slow and difficult, but improvements in transportation so increased sales to private developers that it was decided to expand the complex. The new master plan permitted the construction of much higher towers, but these "second-generation" structures prompted complaints from their office tenants about high rents and the lack of natural light entailed by their great width. The result was a "third generation" of towers, more isolated from one another, with thinner massing and ampler façades.

498 Nobel Tower

LOCATION: The Défense Complex
MÉTRO: La Défense
ARCHITECTS: Jean de Mailly and Jacques Depussé (1966)

The Nobel Tower (1966) belongs to the first generation of construction. Containing 70,000 square feet of office space on twenty-eight floors, it features a central structural-service core and a peripheral metal armature.

LOCATION: The Défense complex
MÉTRO STATION: La Défense
ARCHITECTS: Saubot and Jullien (1974)

Fiat Tower 499

The Fiat Tower (1974; now the Framatome Tower), designed by Roger Saubot and François Jullien (Skidmore, Owings and Merrill consultants), was among the first of the second-generation buildings in the complex. Some 570 feet high, its forty-four floors contain 108,000 square feet of open office space. Its façades are load-bearing concrete walls faced with black granite.

500 ELF Tower

LOCATION: The Défense complex
MÉTRO STATION: La Défense
ARCHITECTS: Saubot and Jullien (1985)

The ELF Tower, a third-generation construction in the Défense complex, has the same area and the same architects as the Fiat Tower (see entry 499), but its realization is very different. Its composition as three connected units permitted an ampler façade and, thus, better illumination.

LOCATION: The Défense complex
MÉTRO STATION: La Défense
PATRON: The EPAD (Établissement Public pour l'Aménagement de la Défense)
ARCHITECTS: Otto van Spreckelsen, then Paul Andreu (1983–89; competition held in 1982)

Arch of the Défense 501

The design of this building, conceived by the Danish architect Otto von Spreckelsen, was chosen in an international competition. Resembling an enormous hollowed cube (360 feet to a side), it contains more than 1,000,000 square feet of office space, making it a kind of inhabited triumphal arch. The building is faced with white marble and reflective glass. Exterior elevators whisk the public to a roof terrace offering a magnificent view of Paris and its environs.

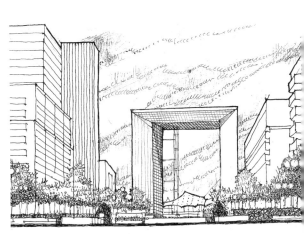

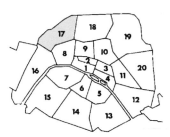

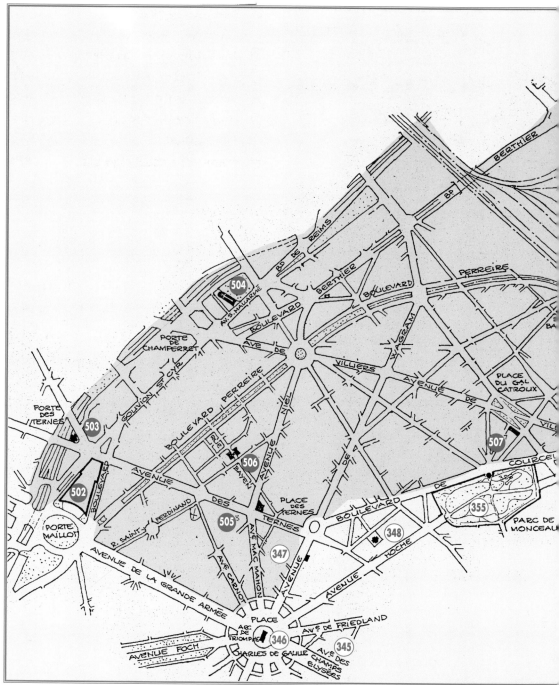

17th Arrondissement

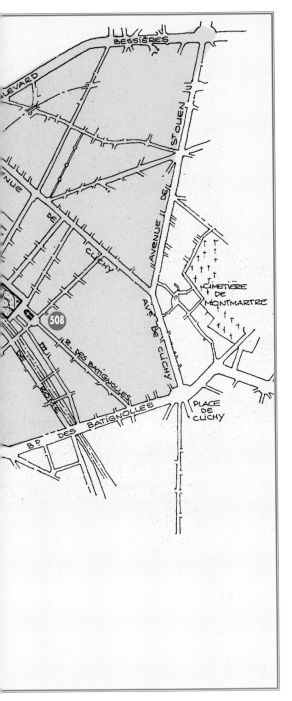

502 Palais des Congrès and the Concorde-Lafayette Hotel

LOCATION: 3, Place du Général-Koenig
MÉTRO STATION: Porte-Maillot
ARCHITECTS: G. Gillet, H. Guibout, and S. Maloletenkov (1971–74)

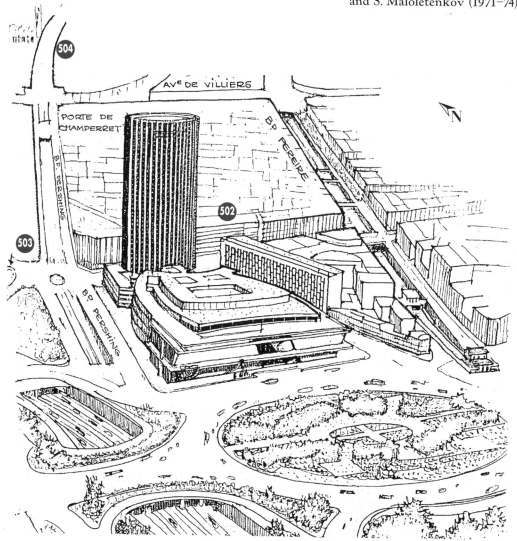

This vast complex, situated between the Porte Maillot and the Porte des Ternes, constitutes the Centre International de Paris. It contains: the Palais des Congrès, an assembly hall seating 3,500; the Concorde-Lafayette Hotel, with 1,000 rooms; a shopping center; 38,000 square feet of office space; and a parking garage for 3,000 vehicles.

The architects emphasized the contrast between the horizontal assembly building and the vertical hotel tower. Both structures have curving façades.

The façade facing the Porte Maillot is now being rebuilt in accordance with a new design.

Notre-Dame-de-la-Compassion 503

LOCATION: 2, boulevard Aurelle-de-Paladines, near the Concorde-Lafayette Hotel
MÉTRO STATION: Porte-Maillot

PATRON: Louis-Philippe, after the death of his eldest son, Ferdinand d'Orléans, in 1842
ARCHITECT: Pierre-Bernard Lefranc (1843)
STAINED-GLASS WINDOWS: Designed by Jean-Auguste-Dominique Ingres
MAUSOLEUM: Henri de Triqueti

This chapel was originally located on the site of the carriage accident that cost duc Ferdinand d'Orléans his life. The Porte Maillot development project entailed its displacement by several hundred feet in 1972.

The chapel's design is of Byzantine inspiration, and it has a Greek-cross plan.

Sainte-Odile 504

LOCATION: 2, avenue Stéphane-Mallarmé
MÉTRO STATION: Porte-de-Champerret
ARCHITECT: Jacques Barge (1934–46)

Dedicated to Saint Odile, patron saint of Alsace, this church was meant to evoke Rhenish models, but it seems to have been more directly inspired by Byzantine churches. The façades are made of Vosges sandstone and brick. The spire, often described as Futurist, is 236 feet high.

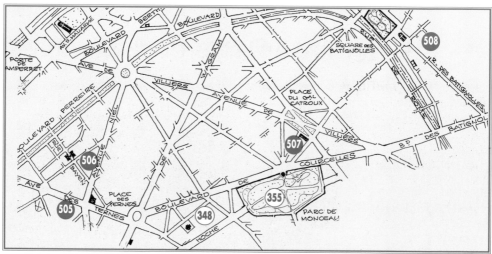

505 Avenue des Ternes, no. 28

MÉTRO STATION: Ternes
PATRON: M. Boisselat, owner of the store
À l'Économie Ménagère
ARCHITECT: Marcel Oudin (1912)

*The corner tower still bears the sign of the Magasins Réunis,
which acquired the building in 1914. It was restored in 1991
to house a bookstore.*

506 Château des Ternes

LOCATION: 17–19, rue Pierre-Demours, and
rue Bayen
MÉTRO STATION: Ternes
PATRONS: The treasurer Mirey de Pomponne, in 1715; then the architect Lenoir, in
1778, who divided the property into lots.
He created the rue Bayen, which passes
through the building.

*Although much altered, this building is still
quite charming.*

Hôtel Gaillard
(Banque de France)

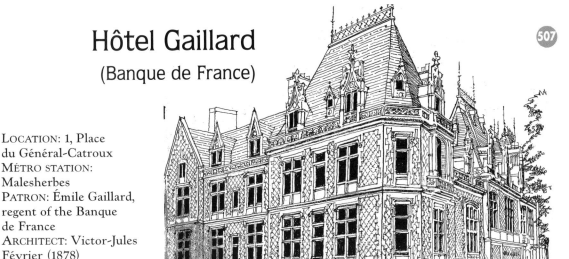

507

LOCATION: 1, Place
du Général-Catroux
MÉTRO STATION:
Malesherbes
PATRON: Émile Gaillard,
regent of the Banque
de France
ARCHITECT: Victor-Jules
Février (1878)

Émile Gaillard was an art collector, and he wanted to build a town house worthy of his collection. Accordingly, he instructed his architect to model the design after the Château de Gien and the Louis XII wing of the Château de Blois. The result is a building that now seems odd, but its brick architecture evidences remarkable craftsmanship.

Since 1919, the building has been the property of the Banque de France.

LOCATION: Place du Docteur-
Félix-Lobligeois
MÉTRO STATION: Rome
ARCHITECT: Auguste Molinos
(1826–29)

Sainte-Marie-des-Batignolles **508**

This building has an austerity typical of Parisian neoclassical churches: the pediment is unadorned and the bases of the Doric columns are as simple as possible. Its architect, Auguste Molinos, also designed the beautiful amphitheater in the Jardin des Plantes (entry 170).

The Square des Batignolles next to the church was designed, like many other parks of the period, by the civil engineer Adolphe Alphand; it dates from 1862, shortly after the Batignolles township was annexed by Paris (1860).

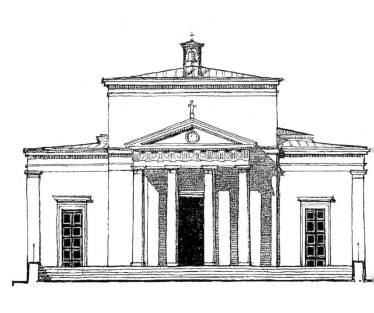

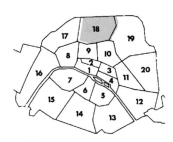

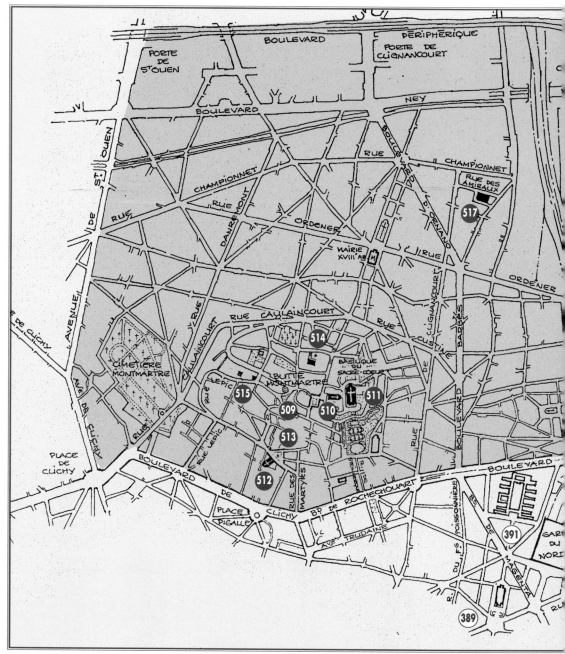

18th Arrondissement

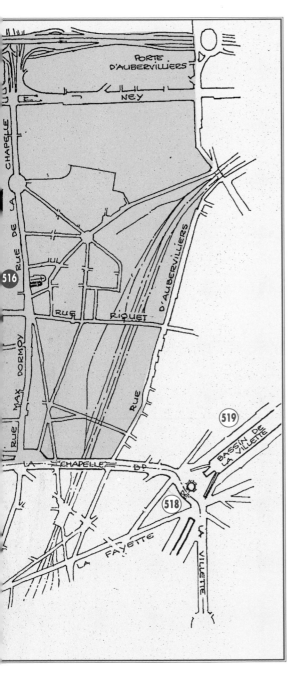

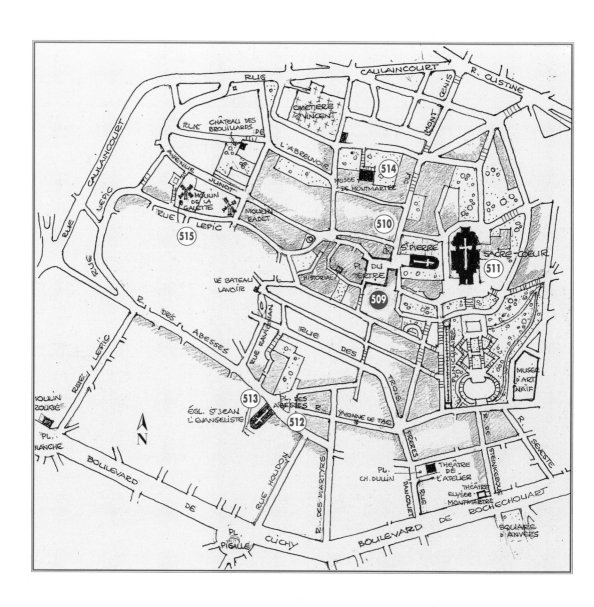

CIMETIÈRE ST VINCENT

CAULAINCOURT

R. CUSTINE

RUE

RUE

Château des Brouillards

L'ABREUVOIR

MONT

GENIS

Musée de Montmartre

514

AVENUE

JUNOT

CAULAINCOURT

RUE

MOULIN DE LA GALETTE

MOULIN RADET

RUE

LEPIC

510

RUE

LEPIC

515

SACRÉ-COEUR

St PIERRE

511

LE BATEAU LAVOIR

HISTORIAL

PL. DU TERTRE

509

R. DES

ABESSES

RUE

RAVIGNAN

RUE

DES

TROIS

FUNICULAIRE

MUSÉE D'ART NAÏF

MOULIN ROUGE

RUE

L'EPIC

PL. DES ABESSES

513

R.

512

ÉGL. ST JEAN L'ÉVANGÉLISTE

YVONNE LE TAC

R.

FRÈRES

N

PL. BLANCHE

RUE

HOUDON

R. DES MARTYRS

DANCOURT

R. DE

STEINKERQUE

RUE

SÉVESTE

THÉÂTRE DE L'ATELIER

PL. CH. DULIN

THÉÂTRE ÉLYSÉE MONTMARTRE

BOULEVARD

DE

CLICHY

PL. PIGALLE

BOULEVARD

DE

ROCHECHOUART

SQUARE D'ANVERS

ACCESS: Abbesses métro station
and funicular railway

The Montmartre Hill ⑤⁰⁹

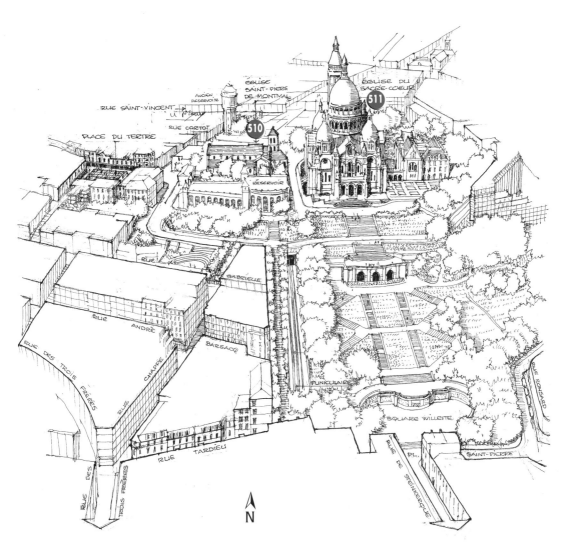

The Montmartre hill and the Belleville hill offer the highest vantage points in Paris. The origins of the name Montmartre are uncertain, but many scholars believe it derives from the Latin phrase mons Martyrium (hill of the martyr), a reference to Saint Denis, the first bishop of Paris, who according to legend was martyred here around 250 CE.

The Montmartre hill was the site, beginning in the 12th century, of an important Benedictine convent, but the building was progressively abandoned beginning in the 17th century and was destroyed at the time of the Revolution. The Montmartre township was annexed by Paris in 1860, along with several other peripheral communities. At that time, it still boasted some windmills and a few vineyards.

The hill's command of the city obviously gives it exceptional strategic importance. It was here, for example, that the Paris Commune began on March 18, 1871. At the end of the 19th century, the Montmartre hill began to attract many artists, but its picturesque sites are now frequented primarily by tourists.

510 Saint-Pierre-de-Montmartre

LOCATION: 2, rue du Mont-Cenis
ACCESS: Abbesses métro station and
funicular railway
PATRON: Louis VI, for the Benedictine nuns

Above:
view from the northeast
Below:
east elevation (left),
north elevation (right)

This church is, with Saint-Martin-des-Champs and Saint-Germain-des-Prés, one of the oldest churches in Paris. Its construction began shortly after Louis VI (Louis le Gros) and his wife, Adélaïde of Savoy, founded a Benedictine abbey in 1134. It was consecrated in 1147 by Pope Eugene III.

The vaults of the three first bays were rebuilt in the 15th century, and the façade, notably lacking in relief, dates from the 18th century. During the Revolution, the church became a Temple of Reason; in later years it was abandoned. Fortunately, it was restored at the beginning of the 20th century and reconsecrated in 1908.

Visible on the interior are four 6th-century marble columns, probably from a Merovingian chapel that occupied the site prior to the present building, and the tombstone of Adélaïde of Savoy. In 1954, stained-glass windows realized by Max Ingrand were installed. North of the church is a small cemetery dating from the Merovingian era.

Basilica of the Sacré-Coeur 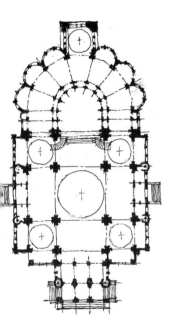 ⑤¹¹

LOCATION: Place du Sacré-Coeur
ACCESS: Abbesses métro station and funicular railway
PATRON: Cardinal Guibert, with funds collected under the auspices of a national vow
ARCHITECT: Paul Abadie until his death in 1884; then Honoré Daumet, Hervé Rauline, and, finally, Lucien Magne, who designed the tower. Built between 1876 and 1914

The silhouette of the Sacré-Coeur (Sacred Heart) has prompted much criticism, but like the Eiffel Tower it has become an emblem of Paris. After the Franco-Prussian War of 1870 and the uprising of the Commune that followed, a group of Christians led by two laymen, Alexandre Legentil and Hubert Rohault de Fleury, took a vow to build a church on this site. Their plans moved toward realization in 1873, when the National Assembly authorized the building's construction, but the entire project was financed with private funds.

Construction of Abadie's design, greatly influenced by the Romanesque church of Saint-Front in Périgueux, which he had restored, began in 1876. Its advance was hampered by difficulties in the foundation work, which in the end required shafts some 131 feet deep. Construction was completed in 1914, but the basilica was not inaugurated until 1919.

421

512 Saint-Jean-de-Montmartre

LOCATION: 19, rue des Abbesses
MÉTRO STATION: Abbesses
PATRON: Abbé Sobeaux
ARCHITECT: Anatole de Baudot, 1894–98,
then 1902–4

This church was built on terrain that posed formidable difficulties, being both steeply sloped and unstable. In light of these problems, the architect opted for a concrete structure, and, despite the novelty of this material, he instinctively put it to the best possible use. Shafts for the foundation were sunk almost forty feet deep, and the decline was exploited to accommodate a crypt whose upper floor is less than three inches thick. The walls, made of double layers of brick, are not load-bearing but help to stabilize the building. Incorporated into the concrete elements of the façade are ceramic tiles by Alexandre Bigot.

513 Entrance to the Abbesses métro station

LOCATION: Place des Abbesses
ARCHITECT: Hector Guimard (1900–1904)

Hector Guimard did not enter the 1899 design competition for the métro entrances, but he received the commission nonetheless, and 141 entrances were realized according to his plans. Eighty-six of them are still in place, including two with glass-roofed pavilions: the Dauphine station and this one, originally at the Hôtel de Ville station. All of them feature sinuous vegetal forms that, despite their eccentricity, could be readily standardized in cast iron.

Musée de 514 Montmartre

LOCATION: 12, rue Cortot
MÉTRO STATION: Lamarck-
Caulaincourt
PATRON: The comedienne
Rose de Rosimond (c. 1860)

This museum occupies the former country house of the theater personality Rose de Rosimond. The building has been enlarged several times since its construction. In 1922, it was purchased by the City of Paris, which had it restored to house the collections of the Société d'Histoire et d'Archéologie du Vieux Montmartre.

LOCATION: 77, rue Lepic
MÉTRO STATION: Abbesses
PATRON: Denis Guignard (mill, c. 1620),
then Nicolas Debray (Debray farm, c. 1810).
Multiple restorations

Moulin de la Galette 515

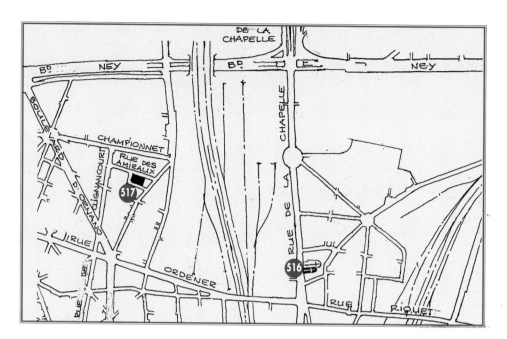

⑯ Saint-Denis-de-la-Chapelle

LOCATION: 16, rue de la Chapelle
MÉTRO STATION: Marx-Dormoy

The basilica of Sainte-Jeanne-d'Arc is at the left, the church of Saint-Denis-de-la-Chapelle at the right.

This church has been altered several times. The nave and side aisles date from the 13th century, the façade from the 18th century, and the choir from the 19th century. It is said that Joan of Arc came here to pray in 1429 before attacking Paris, which explains the presence of a statue (F. Charpentier, 1890) of her in front of the façade. It also explains the presence of the adjacent basilica of Sainte-Jeanne-d'Arc, a massive structure that overwhelms its more modest neighbor.

MÉTRO STATION: Simplon
PATRON: Office d'Habitation
à Bon Marché de la Seine
ARCHITECTS: Henri Sauvage
and Charles Sarazin
(designed 1909, built 1922–27)

Rue des Amiraux, no.13 517

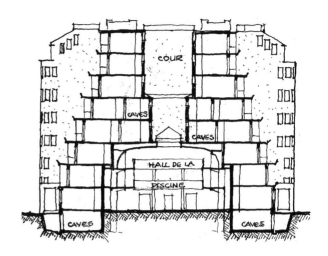

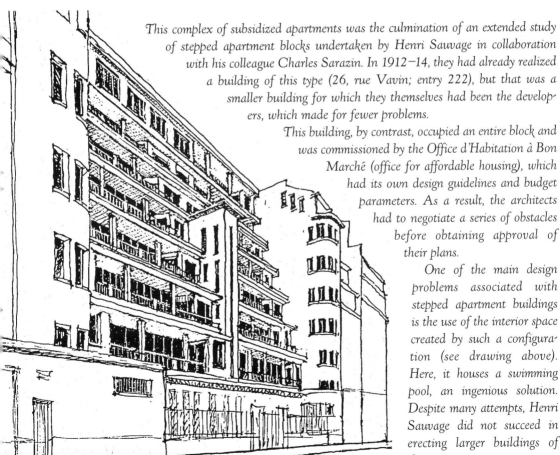

This complex of subsidized apartments was the culmination of an extended study of stepped apartment blocks undertaken by Henri Sauvage in collaboration with his colleague Charles Sarazin. In 1912–14, they had already realized a building of this type (26, rue Vavin; entry 222), but that was a smaller building for which they themselves had been the developers, which made for fewer problems.

This building, by contrast, occupied an entire block and was commissioned by the Office d'Habitation à Bon Marché (office for affordable housing), which had its own design guidelines and budget parameters. As a result, the architects had to negotiate a series of obstacles before obtaining approval of their plans.

One of the main design problems associated with stepped apartment buildings is the use of the interior space created by such a configuration (see drawing above). Here, it houses a swimming pool, an ingenious solution. Despite many attempts, Henri Sauvage did not succeed in erecting larger buildings of this type.

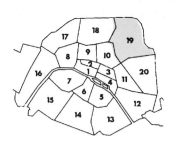

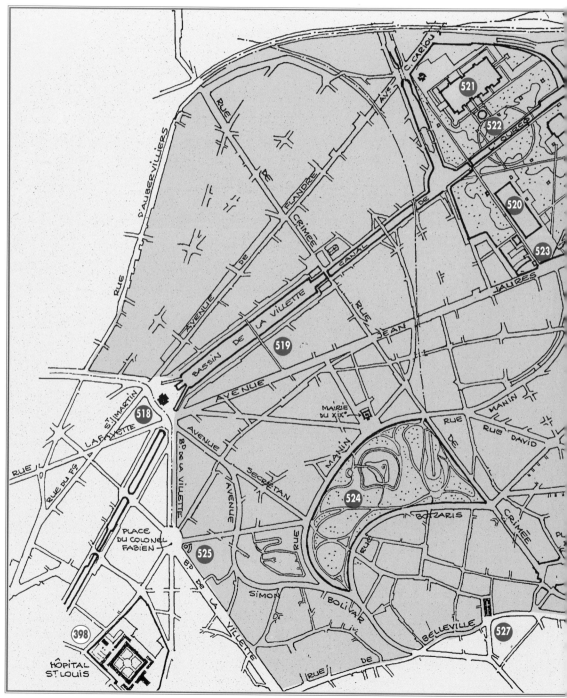

19th Arrondissement

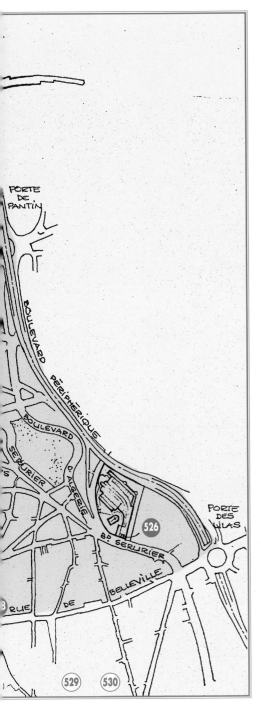

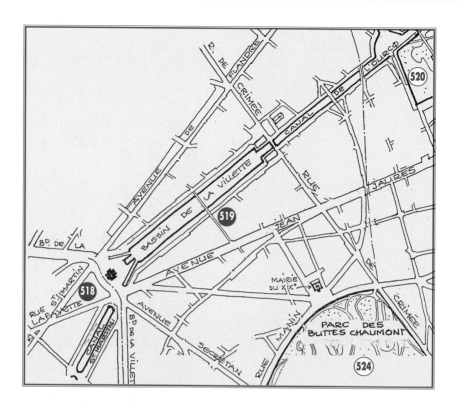

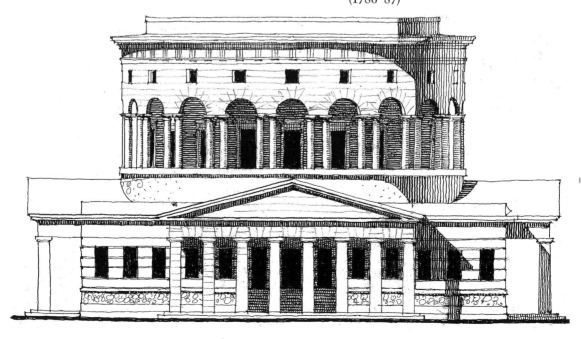

518 Rotonde de La Villette

LOCATION: Place de Stalingrad
MÉTRO STATION: Stalingrad
PATRON: The City of Paris (part of
the Wall of the Farmers General)
ARCHITECT: Claude-Nicolas Ledoux
(1786–87)

The Rotonde de La Villette was one of the tollhouses of the Wall of the Farmers General, already mentioned in connection with the Rotonde de Chartres (entry 356), a wall erected between 1784 and 1787 to facilitate the collection of duties levied against merchandise entering Paris.

Construction of the tollhouses was entrusted to Claude-Nicolas Ledoux, who shocked contemporaries with the originality and force of his designs. The Rotonde de La Villette is a fine example of the power of his architectural forms. Essentially, it consists of a rectangular building from whose center rises a large cylindrical structure surrounding an open court. Each of the building's four façades features massive pedimented porticoes.

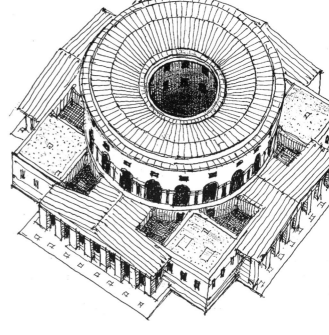

LOCATION: Between the Rotonde de La Villette and rue de Crimée
MÉTRO STATIONS: Jaurès; Stalingrad
PATRON: Napoléon I
ENGINEER: Pierre-Simon Gérard (1805–8)

Bassin de La Villette 519

The La Villette basin was excavated at the initiative of Napoléon I to facilitate distribution of water to the city from the Ourcq canal.

In its early years, it was a favored site for promenades and was plied by barges. Its attractions have again begun to lure strollers, and it sets off the Rotonde de La Villette to wonderful effect (see preceding entry).

The rue de Crimée crosses the basin over a curious hydraulic-lift bridge built between 1885 and 1889.

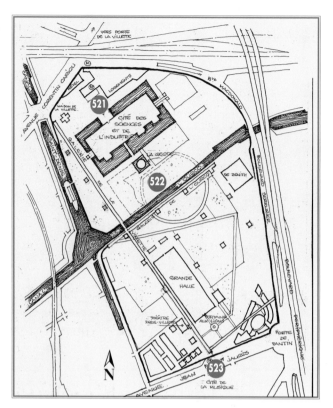

⑳ La Villette

LOCATION: Between the Porte de La Villette and the Porte de Pantin, on a site formerly occupied by abattoirs
MÉTRO STATIONS: Porte-de-La-Villette (to the north); Porte-de-Pantin (to the south)

㉑ Cité des Sciences et de l'Industrie

LOCATION: 30, avenue Corentin-Cariou
MÉTRO STATION: Porte-de-La-Villette
ARCHITECTS: Jean Semichon, then Adrien Fainsilber

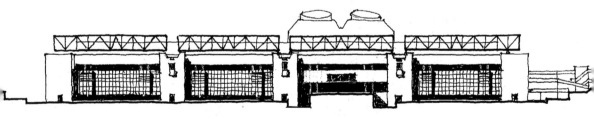

The site of the Cité des Sciences building was formerly occupied by the meat markets of the Abattoirs de la Villette, built in the 1960s but scarcely used prior to their demolition, changing economic circumstances having rendered them impractical.

This enormous structure, which encompasses an area of 886 by 360 feet, is covered by a metal-frame roof resting on widely spaced reinforced-concrete supports (each spanning unit measures 213 by 118 feet). It was designed by the architect Jean Semichon, and the museum installations inside were conceived by the architect Adrien Fainsilber.

The complex includes spaces for permanent and temporary exhibitions, a planetarium, a media center, a movie house, and a conference center.

LOCATION: Near the Cité des Sciences et de l'Industrie
MÉTRO STATION: Porte-de-La-Villette
ARCHITECT: Adrien Fainsilber

The Géode (522)

This is a cinema with a hemispherical screen that surrounds the viewer. The architect, Adrien Fainsilber, turned the building's spherical shape to account by facing it with stainless-steel mirrors and placing it in the center of a reflecting pool.

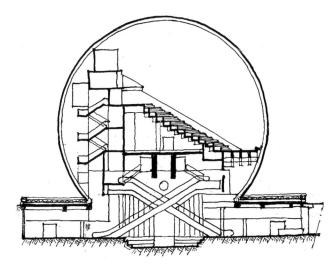

LOCATION: Avenue Jean-Jaurès
MÉTRO STATION: Porte-de-Pantin
ARCHITECT: Christian de Portzamparc

Cité de la Musique (523)

The buildings of the Cité de la Musique are situated on both sides of the court in front of the Grande Halle de La Villette. The western cluster houses the Conservatoire National de Musique and rehearsal rooms. The eastern cluster includes a concert hall, a museum of music, and a music school. This magnificent complex, opened in two stages (1995, 1997), was designed by Christian de Portzamparc.

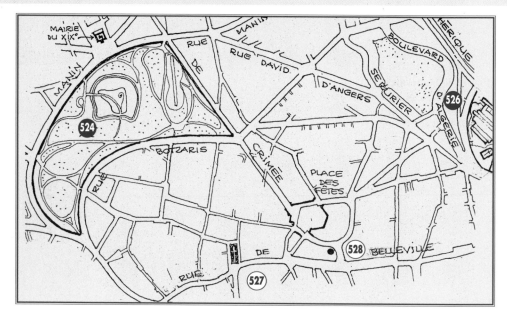

524 Parc des Buttes-Chaumont

LOCATION: Rue Manin, rue de Crimée, and rue Botzaris
MÉTRO STATIONS: Buttes-Chaumont; Botzaris
PATRONS: Napoléon III and Baron Haussmann
CIVIL ENGINEER: Adolphe Alphand (1864–67)
ARCHITECT: Gabriel Davioud

Before its transformation, the Buttes-Chaumont area was occupied by gypsum quarries and rubbish dumps. Work proceeded according to schedule, however, and the new park was inaugurated by Napoléon III in time for the Exposition Universelle of 1867. Rich in geographic incident and picturesque views, the park boasts a lake with a rocky island rising almost a hundred feet above the water. The latter is surmounted by a belvedere in the form of a small temple designed by Davioud. It can be reached by crossing a brick bridge, nicknamed the Pont des Suicidés (suicide bridge), and a suspended walkway.

LOCATION: 2, Place du Colonel-Fabien
MÉTRO STATION: Colonel-Fabien
PATRON: French Communist Party
ARCHITECTS: Oscar Niemeyer, Jean
Deroche, and Paul Chemetov (1965–71).
Dome added in 1980

Central Headquarters of the French Communist Party

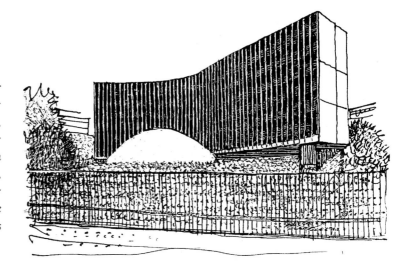

The Brazilian architect Oscar Niemeyer, working in collaboration with two French colleagues, intelligently exploited the triangular site by placing the main building, a curved office block, to the rear. The Central Committee's assembly hall, whose dome is readily visible, occupies the front of the plot.

LOCATION: 48, boulevard Serrurier
MÉTRO STATION: Porte-des-Lilas
ARCHITECT: Pierre Riboulet (1988)

Hôpital Robert-Debré 526

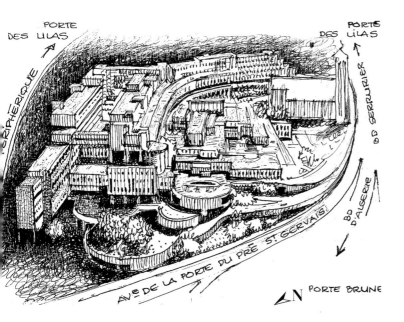

Pierre Riboulet exploited this site to magnificent effect, deftly arraying the complex's buildings over its sloping, curving terrain and facing their façades with white ceramic. Unfortunately, the final effect is compromised by the massive form of the church at the center of the composition, which had to be retained.

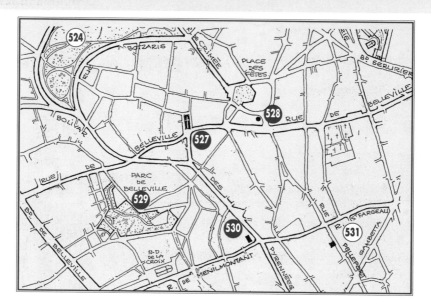

Belleville

Belleville (the name of the township prior to its annexation by Paris in 1860) is situated on a hill roughly as high as that of Montmartre (420 feet). It was once a rural community whose sunny slopes were conducive to the cultivation of vegetables and orchards. This changed suddenly in the 1850s as a result of Baron Haussmann's demolitions, which occasioned a massive displacement of the city's laboring population to its outskirts, notably Belleville.

The slopes of the Belleville hill still boast many picturesque streets and alleys, but quite a few disappeared beginning in the 1960s, notably around the Place des Fêtes, which is now disfigured by tall buildings.

⁵²⁷ Saint-Jean-Baptiste de-Belleville

LOCATION: 139, rue de Belleville
MÉTRO STATION: Jourdain
ARCHITECT: Jean-Baptiste Lassus (1854–57); then, after his death, Truchy (1857–59)

The construction of this church postdates that of Sainte-Clotilde, the first of the city's neo-Gothic sanctuaries, which was followed by many others in Paris as well as in the provinces.

The architect, Jean-Baptiste Lassus, was intimately familiar with the Gothic idiom, for he oversaw restoration of Saint-Germain-l'Auxerrois and then, in collaboration with Eugène Viollet-le-Duc, that of Notre-Dame de Paris.

LOCATION: Jardin du Regard de
la Lanterne
MÉTRO STATION: Place-des-Fêtes

Regard de la Lanterne (528)

The La Lanterne inspection pavilion was part of a water-supply system whose earliest elements were realized in the 12th century, probably by the monks of Saint-Martin-des-Champs for their abbey. It collected water from small wells gushing from the side of the Belleville hill. This structure, partly rebuilt in 1427, was given its present form in 1613.

Another such inspection pavilion, the Regard Saint-Martin, is located at 42, rue des Cascades; it belonged to a different supply system.

LOCATION: Rue des Couronnes, rue Piat, and rue
Julien-Lacroix
MÉTRO STATIONS: Jourdain; Pyrénées; Couronnes
ARCHITECT: François Debulois
LANDSCAPE DESIGNERS: API
Inaugurated 1988

Parc de Belleville (529)

The Belleville park, which encompasses about eleven acres, features a significant declivity, which the designers exploited by installing a long cascade fountain. The park's upper terrace (rue Piat side) offers a splendid view of Paris.

LOCATION: 119, rue de Ménilmontant (20th
arrondissement)
MÉTRO STATION: Jourdain
PATRON: Nicolas Carré de Beaudouin
ARCHITECT: Pierre-Louis Moreau-Desproux
(c. 1770)

Maison de Carré (530) de Beaudouin

This is one of the large pleasure houses built on the city's outskirts and known in the 18th century as folies. The many other folies erected on the hills of Belleville have disappeared, which makes this one especially precious. It was probably modeled after the villas of Palladio. Unfortunately, it is surrounded by an orphanage and is not visible from the street.

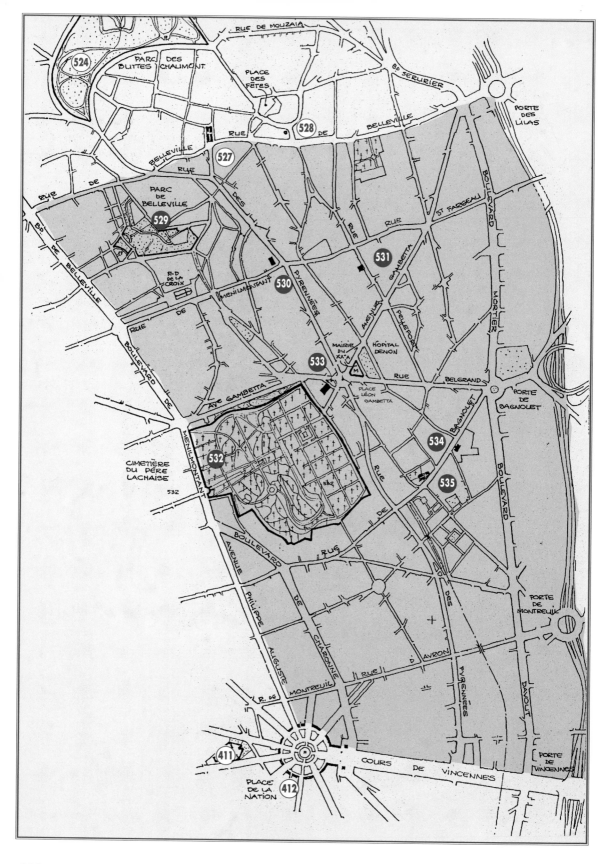

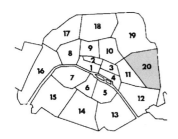

20th Arrondissement

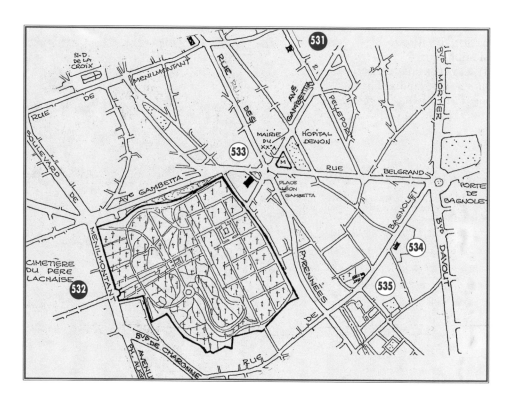

School at 99, rue de Pelleport

MÉTRO STATION: Pelleport
ARCHITECT: Francis Soler
(1988)

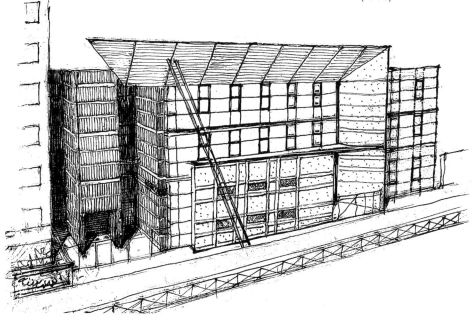

The design of this nursery school is exceptionally original. Its façade is faced with aluminum panels tinted gray and black.

Père-Lachaise Cemetery 532

LOCATION: Boulevard
de Ménilmontant
MÉTRO STATION: Père-Lachaise
DESIGNER: Alexandre-Théodore
Brongniart (1804). Main entrance by
Étienne-Hippolyte Godde (c. 1825)

This is the most famous cemetery in Paris, because of the large number of illustrious people buried within its green expanses. It was named after the Jesuit father La Chaise, confessor of Louis XIV, who lived on the property. The city acquired it in 1804 with the intention of transforming it into a cemetery.

Graves of La Fontaine and Molière

Tomb of Abélard and Héloïse

The cemetery was designed by the architect Brongniart (also responsible for the Palais de la Bourse, entry 63), whose original conception more closely resembles a shady park than a conventional burial ground. To make it more attractive, the administration had the remains of renowned figures moved there, such as Molière, La Fontaine, and Abélard and Héloïse, whose funerary monument was originally located in the gardens of Alexandre Lenoir's Musée des Monuments Français (see entry 489). The cemetery is now a veritable museum of Parisian funerary art of the 19th and 20th centuries.

The famous individuals buried here include Colette, Alfred de Musset, Chopin, Champollion, Alphonse Daudet, Beaumarchais, Marcel Proust, Eugène Delacroix, Honoré de Balzac, Georges Bizet, Édith Piaf, Jim Morrison, and many others.

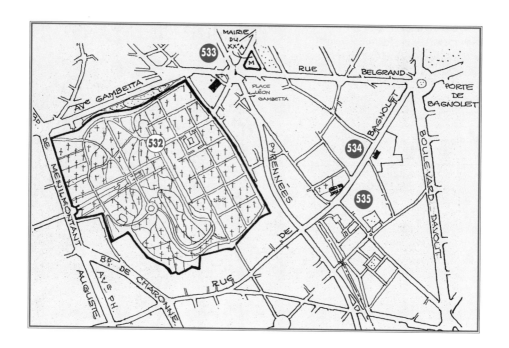

533 Théâtre de la Colline

LOCATION: 15–17, rue Malte-Brun
MÉTRO STATION: Gambetta
PATRON: French Ministry of Culture
ARCHITECTS: Valentin Fabre, Jean Perrotet,
and Alberto Cattant (1987)

*This building was originally intended for
the Théâtre de l'Est Parisien, which in the
end found another home. It contains a
main theater seating 800 and a smaller
one seating 200. The ample windows of its
façade make the reception areas seem
larger than they are.*

Pavillon de l'Hermitage

LOCATION: 148, rue de Bagnolet
MÉTRO STATION: Porte-de-Bagnolet
PATRON: The duchesse d'Orléans
ARCHITECT: Serin (1734)

This pavilion, originally a dependency of the Château de Bagnolet (destroyed), was long situated within the Debrousse Hospice enclosure but is now in a public garden. The original design has been altered somewhat: its roof terrace with balustrade has given way to a Mansard roof treatment, and two windows now flank the door in the convex central element.

Saint-Germain-de-Charonne

LOCATION: 4, Place Saint-Blaise (rue de Bagnolet)
MÉTRO STATION: Porte-de-Bagnolet
PATRON: Charonne township
ARCHITECT: Unidentified

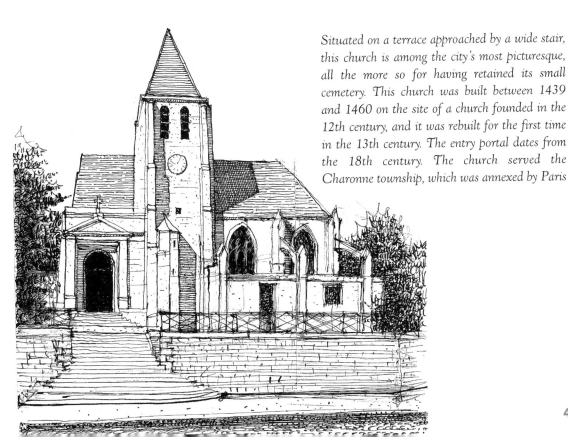

Situated on a terrace approached by a wide stair, this church is among the city's most picturesque, all the more so for having retained its small cemetery. This church was built between 1439 and 1460 on the site of a church founded in the 12th century, and it was rebuilt for the first time in the 13th century. The entry portal dates from the 18th century. The church served the Charonne township, which was annexed by Paris

Illustrated Index of Architects

Michel Andrault
(1926–)
Pierre Parat
(1928–.)
(419) Palais Omnisports
(465) Tour Totem

Jacques-Denis Antoine
(1733–1801)
(6) Palais de Justice
(268) Hôtel des Monnaies
(294) Hôtel de Fleury
(447) Hôpital La Rochefoucauld

Théodore Ballu
(1817–1885)
(11) Mairie of the 1st Arr. (tower)
(137) Hôtel de Ville
(reconstruction)
(363) Church of the Trinity
(400) Saint-Ambroise

Jacques Androuet Du Cerceau II
(1550–1614)
(113) Hôtel de Mayenne

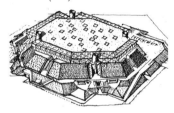

Jean Aubert
(v1680–1741)
(285) Palais Bourbon
(286) Hôtel de Lassay
(302) Musée Rodin

Victor Baltard
(1805–1874)
(32) Halles Centrales (destroyed)
(360) Saint-Augustin

Jean Androuet Du Cerceau
(1585–1649)
(114) Hôtel de Sully
(165) Hôtel de Bretonvilliers

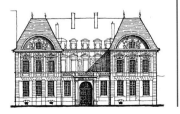

Jean-François Blondel
(1618–1686)
(382) Porte Saint-Denis

Salomon de Brosse
(c. 1565–1626)
(139) Saint-Gervais–Saint-Protais
(façade)
(243) Palais du Luxembourg

Jean-François Chalgrin
(1739–1811)
(18) Hôtel de Saint-Florentin
(192) Collège de France
(232) Saint-Sulpice (north tower)
(346) Arc de Triomphe
(352) Saint-Philippe-du-Roule
(373) Notre-Dame-de-Lorette

Germain Boffrand
(1667–1754)
(155) Bibliothèque de l'Arsenal
(207) Hôtel Le Brun
(244) Petit Luxembourg
(282) Hôtel de Beauharnais
(283) Hôtel de Seignelay
(291) Hôtel Amelot de Gournay

Libéral Bruant
(1637–1697)
(100) Hôtel Libéral-Bruant
(310) Hôtel des Invalides
(426) Chapelle de la Salpétrière

Paul Chemetov
(1928–)
(32) Forum des Halles (Place
Carrée)
(174) Galerie de Zoologie
(interior remodeling)
(420) Ministry of Finance
(in collaboration with
B. Huidobro and D. Harosteguy)
(525) Headquarters of the FCP

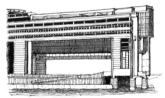

Pierre Bullet
(1639–1716)
(83) Hôtel de Tallard
(97) Hôtel Le Pelletier
de Saint-Fargeau
(237) Hôtel de Brancas
(292) Saint-Thomas-d'Aquin
(design)
383 Porte Saint-Martin

Pierre Contant d'Ivry
(1698–1777)
(28) Palais-Royal (participation)
(297) Protestant Church of Pentemont
(333) La Madeleine (original
church)

Alexandre Brongniart
(1739–1813)
(63) Palais de la Bourse
(361) Saint-Louis-d'Antin
(532) Père-Lachaise Cemetery

Robert de Cotte
(1656–1735)
(24) Saint-Roch (façade)
(51) Bibliothèque Nationale
(forecourt)
(408) Hôpital des Quinze-Vingts

Jean-Baptiste Courtonne
(1671–1739)
(300) Hôtel de Noirmoutiers
(303) Hôtel de Matignon

Gabriel Davioud
(1823–1881)
(26) Place André-Malraux
(fountains)
(135) Théâtres du Châtelet
et de la Ville
(253) Fontaine Saint-Michel
Parks, gardens, and various squares
with A. Alphand

François-Debias Aubry
(30) Caisse d'Épargne de Paris
(256) Maison Cotelle
(272) Hôtel de Chimay
(288) Hôtel de Brienne

Pierre-Alexis Delamair
(1676–1745)
(89) Hôtel de Soubise
(92) Hôtel de Rohan

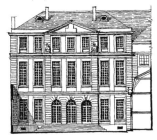

Philibert de l'Orme
(1512–1570)
(16) Château des Tuileries (destroyed)
(34) Hôtel de Soissons
(astronomical tower)
(270) Château d'Anet
(portal in l'École des
Beaux-Arts)

Pierre Fontaine
(1762–1853)
Charles Percier
(1764–1838)
(14) Wing of the Louvre
(15) Arc de Triomphe du Carrousel
(25) Rue de Rivoli (façades)

Jacques-Ange Gabriel
(1698–1782)
(313) École Militaire
(327) Place de la Concorde
(327) Colonnaded Buildings

Charles Garnier
(1825–1898)
(344) Théâtre Marigny
(reconstruction)
(362) Théâtre National
de l'Opéra

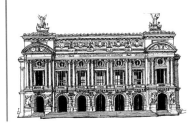

Daniel Gittard
(1625 –1686)
(54) Hôtel de Lulli
(217) Saint-Jacques-du-Haut-Pas
(232) Saint-Sulpice (2nd phase)

Étienne-Hippolyte Godde
(1781–1869)
(64) Notre-Dame de-Bonne-
Nouvelle
(104) Saint-Denis-
du-Saint-Sacrement
(235) Former Seminary of Saint-
Sulpice
(315) Saint-Pierre-
du-Gros-Caillou
(532) Père-Lachaise Cemetery
(main entrance)

Hector Guimard
(1867–1942)
(119) Synagogue, rue Pavée
(472–484) Buildings in the 16th
arr., including
(477) Castel Béranger
(479) Jassédé Apartment Building
(481) Hôtel Mezzara
(482) Hôtel Guimard

Jules Hardouin-Mansart
(1646–1708)
(21) Place Vendôme
(24) Saint-Roch (Lady Chapel)
(39) Place des Victoires
(110) Hôtel Mansart de Sagonne
(153) Hôtel Fieubet
(185) Saint-Severin (Communion
Chapel)
(311) Dome Church of the
Invalides

Jacques-Ignace Hittorff
(1792–867)
(327) Place de la Concorde
(alterations)
(344) Gardens of the Champs-
Elysées
(389) Saint-Vincent-de-Paul
(390) Gare du Nord
(399) Cirque d'Hiver

Henri Labrouste
(1801–1875)
(51) Bibliothèque Nationale
(lecture hall)
(196) Bibliothèque
Sainte-Geneviève

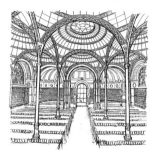

Jules Lavirotte
(1864–1924)
(317) Lycée Italien
(318) Square Rapp, no. 3
(319) Avenue Rapp, no. 29
(347) Céramic Hôtel

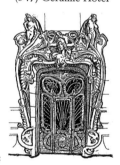

Le Corbusier
(Édouard Jeanneret)
(1887–1965)
(430) Salvation Army Hostel
(431) Villa Planeix
(442) Pavillon Suisse
and Pavillon du Brésil
(Cité Universitaire)
(445) Ozenfant House and Atelier
(468) Fondation Le Corbusier

Claude-Nicolas Ledoux
(1736–1806)
(85) Hôtel d'Hallwyll
(356) Rotonde de Chartres
(412) Barrière du Trône
(448) Barrière d'Enfer
(518) Rotonde de La Villette

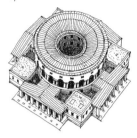

Jacques Lemercier
(1585–1654)
(14)) Louvre, Pavillon de l'Horloge
(24) Saint-Roch (design)
(28) Palais Cardinal (destroyed)
(191) Chapel of the Sorbonne
(219) Val-de-Grâce
(after François Mansart)

Pierre Le Muet
(1591–1669)
(43) Notre-Dame-des-Victoires
(design)
(87) Hôtel d'Avaux
(219) Val-de-Grâce (construction)

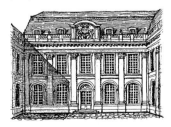

André Le Nôtre
(1613–1700)
(16) Tuileries Gardens
Gardens at Versailles,
Saint Germain en Laye, Vaux le
Vicomte, etc.

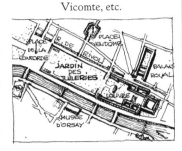

Antoine Le Pautre
(1621–1691?)
(141) Hôtel de Beauvais
(395) Saint-Laurent (1st façade)
(438) Abbey of Port-Royal

Louis Le Vau
(1612–1670)
(14) Louvre (Louis XIV)
(158) Hôtel Lambert
(159) Hôtel de Lauzun
(164) Saint-Louis-en-l'Île (design)
(269) Institut de France
(426) Hôpital de la Salpétrière,
(design)

Victor Louis
(1731–c. 1800)
(26) Théâtre Français
(28) Palais-Royal

François Mansart
(1598–1666)
(39) Place des Victoires
(51) Hôtel Tubeuf
(91) Hôtel de Guénégaud
(96) Hôtel Carnavalet
(112) Visitation Sainte-Marie
(115) Hôtel Bouthillier de Chavigny
(146) Hôtel d'Aumont (façade)
(219) Val-de-Grâce

Louis Métezeau
(1559–1615)
(10) Place Dauphine (?)
(14) Louvre (Grande Galerie)
(94) Hôtel d'Alméras
(108) Place des Vosges

Pierre de Montreuil
(c. 1200–1267)
(1) Notre-Dame de Paris
(south transept)
(7) Sainte Chapelle
(71) Refectory, Saint-Martin-des-
Champs
(265) Saint-Germain-des-Prés, Lady
Chapel (destroyed)

Jean Nouvel
(1945–
(178) Institut du Monde Arabe
(449) Fondation Cartier

I. M. Pei
(1917–)
(14) Louvre Pyramid

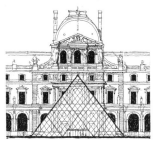

Charles Percier
see Pierre Fontaine

Claude Perrault
(1613–1688)
(14) Louvre Colonnade
(436) Observatoire de Paris

Dominique Perrault
(1953–)
(425) Bibliothèque Nationale de
France

Auguste Perret
(1874–1954)
(320) Théâtre des Champs-
Élysées
(429) Mobilier National
(487) Rue Raynouard, nos. 51-55
(488) Rue Benjamin Franklin,
no. 25 bis

(490) Conseil Économique et Social

Renzo Piano
(1937–)
Richard Rogers
(1933–)
(129) Centre Georges-Pompidou

Christian de Portzamparc
(1944–)
(432) Rue des Hautes-Formes
(459) Musée Bourdelle (addition)
(523) Cité de la Musique

Richard Rogers
see Renzo Piano

Henri Sauvage
(1873–1932)
(12) Samaritaine Dept. Store
(with Frantz Jourdain)
(222) Rue Vavin, no. 26
(471) Studio Building
(517) Rue des Amiraux, no. 134

Jean-Nicolas Servandoni
(1695–1766)
(232) Saint-Sulpice (façade)
and apartment building at no. 6,
Place Saint-Sulpice

Jacques-Germain Soufflot
(1713–1780)
(35) Fontaine de la
Croix-du-Trahoir
(197) Panthéon
(200) Former Law School

Otto von Spreckelsen
(501) Arch of the Défense

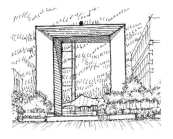

Ludovico Visconti
(1791–1853)
(14) Louvre (Napoléon III)
(57) Fontaine Gaillon
(234) Fontaine des Quatres-
Évêques
(311) Tomb of Napoléon I
(389) Rue du Faubourg-Saint-
Honoré, no. 41
(368) Hôtel de Mlle Mars

Index
(Architects and Artists)

Index

(Buildings and Monuments)